FROM SAIL TO STEAM

FROM SAIL TO STEAM

FOUR CENTURIES OF
TEXAS MARITIME HISTORY
1500–1900

RICHARD V. FRANCAVIGLIA

University of Texas Press
AUSTIN

Requests for permission to reproduce material from this work should
be sent to Permissions, University of Texas Press, P.O. Box 7819,
Austin, TX 78713-7819.

∞ The paper used in this publication meets the minimum require-
ments of American National Standard for Information Sciences—
Permanence of Paper for Printed Library Materials, ANSI Z39.48-1984.

LIBRARY OF CONGRESS CATALOGING-IN-PUBLICATION DATA

Francaviglia, Richard V.
From sail to steam : four centuries of Texas maritime history,
1500–1900 / by Richard V. Francaviglia. — 1st ed.
p.   cm.
Includes bibliographical references and index.
ISBN 0-292-72503-5 (cloth : alk. paper)
1. Texas—History, Naval.   I. Title.
F386.F68   1997
387.5'09764—dc21   97-9578

*Dedicated to the memory of Ben C. Stuart (1847?–1929)
Galveston journalist and historian who, early in the twentieth
century, began writing a similar Texas maritime history but
never lived to see its completion*

CONTENTS

ACKNOWLEDGMENTS

Many people deserve thanks for helping in the compilation of this book by providing information and illustrations, including the following:

Casey Greene, Head of Special Collections, and Anna Peebler, Galveston and Texas History Center, Rosenberg Library, Galveston; Clell Bond, Vice President and Manager of Cultural Resources/Archaeology of Espey, Huston & Associates, Inc. of Austin, Texas; Donald Hunter, Associate Archaeologist, and Charles Pearson, Senior Archaeologist, Coastal Environments, Inc. of Baton Rouge, Louisiana; Bruce Taylor-Hille, formerly Curator of the Texas Maritime Museum, Rockport, Texas and now with Southwest Museum Services; Mindy Durham, Director, and Robin Rae Moran, Curator, of the Texas Maritime Museum, Rockport, Texas; Kandy Taylor-Hille, Exhibit Technician at the Fulton Mansion in Fulton, Texas, which is operated by the Texas Parks and Wildlife Department; Don Zuris, Curator of Education, Corpus Christi Museum; Toni Carrell, Archaeologist, Ships of Discovery (Corpus Christi Museum); Thomas H. Kreneck, Texas A&M University, Corpus Christi; T. Lindsay Baker of Baylor University; Toni Lee, National Register Program of the National Park Service in Washington D.C.; Louis Marchiafava of the City of Houston Public Library; and Kurt Voss, Director of the Texas Seaport Museum in Galveston.

Two Texas historians provided photographs from their personal collections: local historian Dr. Howard C. Williams of Orange generously shared photographs of vessels in the vicinity of Orange and the Sabine River, and Eric Steinfeldt, maritime historian and collector of maritime history in San Antonio graciously provided photographs of vessels in the vicinity of Galveston. Many other people deserve thanks, including Cecilia Steinfeldt, retired Curator of Art at the Witte Museum, San Antonio; Robert Weddle of rural Bonham, Texas; Lewis Buttery of Lampasas; Rebecca Littman of East Carolina University; Tom Crew and Lois Ogelsby, Mariners' Museum, Newport News, Virginia; Lawrence Taylor, El Colegio de la Frontera Norte,

Tijuana, México; Ralph Elder, Linda Peterson, and Trudy Cruz of the Center for American History at The University of Texas at Austin; Jackie McElhaney of Dallas; Danny Sessums, Director, and Terez McKee, Curator, of the Museum of the Gulf Coast, Port Arthur, Texas; Carolyn Rose, Director of the Heritage House Museum of Orange, Texas; Tom Fort of the Hidalgo County History Museum in Edinburgh, Texas; and Gaylon Polatti, Curator of Library and Archive Collections, The Dallas Historical Society in Dallas.

Donald Frazier of Abilene, Andrew W. Hall of Galveston, and J. Barto Arnold of the Texas Historical Commission in Austin suggested many helpful changes that improved the original draft manuscript. Other staff members at the Texas Historical Commission, including Roni Morales and Philip Parisi of *The Medallion,* and Peggy Claiborne, secretary in the Department of Antiquities Protection, kindly provided graphic materials. Jenkins Garrett of Fort Worth provided some very valuable leads to Texas maritime history literature, and Mrs. Virginia Garrett provided historic maps that beautifully depict Texas maritime history. Caro Ivy Walker of Houston kindly provided a photograph of the *Belle* shipwreck excavation.

Many of my colleagues and associates at The University of Texas at Arlington were especially helpful, including Ken Philp, Chair, and Stanley Palmer, Acting Chair, of the History Department in 1995–1996; José Delgado, graduate research assistant in 1993–1995; Endowed Chair David Buisseret, and Professors Sam Haynes and David Narrett of UTA's History Department; Chandler Jackson of the UTA Arts and Architecture Library; Kit Goodwin and Maritza Pichi Arrigunaga of UTA's Special Collections; UTA graduate students David Simmons, who provided volunteer help with research on the maritime aspects of the Mexican-American War, and Jill Jackson, who located a fascinating map of the Texas coast while conducting historical research; Darlene McAllister, UTA Senior Secretary in the Center for Greater Southwestern Studies and the History of Cartography deserves special thanks for typing numerous drafts of the manuscript and offering helpful suggestions and encouragement as this project developed: Her enthusiasm and support made writing this book an especially pleasant experience. Two close colleagues read the original manuscript, offered many suggestions, and also deserve special recognition: To Gerald Saxon, avid Texas historian and Director of UTA's Special Collections, and to History professor Dennis Reinhartz—who has a special love of the Texas coast and who provided encouragement as this book took shape—I am especially grateful.

*The early history of all maritime nations is largely the story of
how the peoples of those countries conquered the sea,
and of the ships they built and sailed.*
HERBERT L. STONE, 1936,
QUOTED IN CHAPELLE'S FOREWORD TO *American Sailing Craft*

*I*NTRODUCTION

The seacoast is the threshold of American prehistory and history,
of American culture, and like most well-passed thresholds, it is
hollowed and worn. And historians routinely ignore it.
JOHN STILGOE *Alongshore*, IX

While well into the research and writing of this book, I came across a series of fascinating files in Galveston's Rosenberg Library. There, in a dusty scrapbook, lay the outline of a handwritten manuscript by Ben C. Stuart, a journalist. Stuart's many newspaper columns written in the early 1910s thrilled readers with stories of the Texas coast and the vessels that helped transform it from terra incognita to one of the world's more important coasts at the time of his writing. In his writings, Stuart recognized a peculiar fact about Texas history, namely, its general neglect of the coast. Stuart set out to change that by writing what was envisioned to be a comprehensive history of Texas as a maritime power but, alas, he died before he could complete the manuscript.

Today, nearly eighty years since Stuart began his manuscript, little has changed: The Texas coast remains, in a word, neglected. The reason for this neglect is a simple bias that has characterized Texans—and Texas historians—for more than a century. Although a tremendous amount of research and publication by academic and independent scholars has left the Lone Star State with a most impressive record of its fascinating and turbulent history, most Texas history has focused on events and themes that took place within the *interior* of the state: the battle of the Alamo, the development of the cattle drives, and the boom and bust of Texas oil fields have generally ensured that Texas historians would turn their eyes away from the coast, to the detriment of our state's rich maritime history. In a way, the coast of Texas still appears to be terra incognita—at least in the perceptions of historians, for relatively little has been written on the subject since Stuart began his monumental work.

In searching for a cause for the neglect of Texas maritime history, one must conclude that there has been a certain disenchantment with the waters of Texas by twentieth-century scholars. In 1940, for example, the geologist Ellis W. Shuler noted that the waters of Texas posed a barrier rather than an invitation to settlement. He stated that the "barrier coast line" of Texas offered a "low, uninviting shore" and "inadequate harbors." Shuler added that Texas rivers were also barriers in that they were dangerous to ford; some, like the Rio Grande, were noted for their "mud bottoms and menacing floods, or rocky, steep-walled canyons." Something of Shuler's opinion of Texas waters can be gained by his damning summary that "the low, flat, uninteresting coastline was passed by for more than a century; ugly, treacherous rivers, mud-bottomed and steep-walled, were moats of most difficult passage."[1] It is this virtual disdain for the waters of Texas that has led many to discount their importance in Texas history; and yet, as will be shown, despite their dangers the waters of Texas did provide access to the alluring interior for those who developed technologies to meet the challenge. A look at the map of Texas reveals that most communities are located on, or very near, either the coast or the state's extensive river system.

Even a casual reading of historical accounts reveals the importance of the waters of Texas; yet, when I first arrived in Texas in the early 1990s with a strong interest in the history of transportation, I inquired about a book that could provide me a comprehensive overview of our state's maritime history. None existed. There are, of course, a few important works on selected aspects of Texas maritime history, including an early (1936) popular history of the Texas Navy by Dan Hill, and the more recent and highly informative trilogy of books by Robert Weddle that cover the Texas coast in the early Spanish and French periods to the arrival of the British. Likewise, James Baughman's two classic volumes on nineteenth-century Texas shipping, as viewed through the life of shipping magnate Charles Morgan and the Mallorys of Mystic, are important works dealing with the Texas coast, as is the singularly focused and comprehensive history of Texas lighthouses by the historian T. Lindsay Baker. These are referred to frequently in this book, but to them I hope *From Sail to Steam* now adds a general, comprehensive overview of this neglected subject, hopefully of the type envisioned by Ben Stuart so many years ago.

By way of overview, the Texas coast is an inescapable aspect of our state's geography. For a long period of Texas history, in fact, the coastline was literally a sweeping zone of contact—almost four hundred miles long—between Native American, Spanish, Mexican, French, European American, and African American peoples. Throughout the centuries the Texas coast has been perceived as both an area to be avoided—partly owing to fear of diseases—as well as a zone of opportunity. The coast has remained an extremely important part of Texas history, though the interior—with its promises of untold mineral and agricultural wealth—naturally drew settlers much as it has enchanted generations of historians. To the list of introductions, inventions, and technologies that have transformed Texas—such as the horse, rifle, and barbed wire—I recommend we now add the schooner, steamboat, and other vessels that were involved in the transport of goods and people to and from Texas.

Despite the hazards encountered there, the Texas coast was often the first glimpse that new arrivals got of this new land in the early 1800s. Its maritime shipping was responsible for bringing people, goods, and ideas to Texas from far away ports of America and Europe. Because the shipping along Texas rivers has been documented to a limited degree, it will not be covered in as much detail in *From Sail to Steam* as some aficionados of the western rivers would have preferred. Nevertheless, I have emphasized the importance of river craft in several places, notably the earlier to middle nineteenth century because narratives and photographs reveal Texas harbors teeming with *both* oceangoing and river-bound vessels. Although *From Sail to Steam* is primarily what maritime historians call blue-water, or better yet, saltwater, history, it is indeed difficult, actually impossible, in Texas to separate riverine history from other aspects of maritime history. This volume, then, focuses on the vessels and shipping—the maritime history—of the Texas coast, but in so doing it also makes frequent reference to the river-going craft, especially keel boats and steamboats that were indispensable in connecting traffic of the interior with coastal maritime traffic at Texas ports in the 1800s.

Although much of the information in this book was obtained from diverse and scattered secondary sources, such as published articles and the books mentioned earlier, I have been impressed—actually nearly overwhelmed—by the bounty of primary sources. These include original newspapers, journals, and diary entries. Because there is no single depository of maritime history in Texas, writing this book took me to many locations, including university libraries, such as The University of Texas at Arlington Special Collections, and the Center for American History at the University of Texas–Austin. I have also consulted the collections at various historical agencies, including the Fort Worth Records Center of the National Archives, and the Rosenberg Library in Galveston. Being an avowed public historian, I made special use of the wonderful staff and facilities at Texas museums, including the Corpus Christi Museum of Science and History, the Port of Galveston, the Texas Maritime Museum at Rockport, and the new Museum of the Gulf Coast in Port Arthur. Additionally, several maritime museums outside of Texas were also consulted, most notably the Peabody Essex Museum in Salem, Massachusetts, and the Mariners' Museum in Newport News, Virginia. Where possible, I have tried to portray developments in shipping on the Texas coast in the context of history, geography, and the history of technology, for they are inseparable. In retrospect, it has been the effort of the archaeologists, some in private corporations, others at state agencies, that has shed considerable light on the actual vessels that traversed Texas's coast and rivers. Their work, which integrates the written records with the material found on site, helps to bring the state's maritime history back to life.

During more than five hundred years of Texas history, vessels of widely varying descriptions under many flags have plied the coast and coastal waters. These included Spanish carracks and galleons, French brigs, British frigates, U.S. schooners and steamships, and even the varied steam and sailing vessels of the short-lived Texas Navy.

By definition, maritime history also involves ports as well as the high seas, and where possible I have shown that Texas ports developed along with other aspects of the state's maritime history. The names of the larger ports—Corpus Christi and Galveston—resound in the annals of saltwater navigation. The smaller ports, such as Port Aransas, Rockport, and Velasco are also briefly discussed. Where appropriate, I also mention the vanished ports, like Indianola, Copano, or Brazos Port—that were important in the last century, and in some cases earlier, but are now more or less ghost towns and the picturesque subject of fascinating popular histories such as *Texas Forgotten Ports*. However, I should note at the outset that *From Sail to Steam* is mostly about the watercraft that plied the waters of Texas.

Although maritime mercantile cargo and passenger trade are the subjects of this book, I have not neglected the military aspects of our maritime history. Because confrontations have a way of drawing our attention, it is in the area of Texas military history that our greatest knowledge about Texas ships and shipping has occurred. For example, the Texas Navy has been carefully documented in several works, for it formed a crucial part of the history of the Texas Republic. During the Civil War, too, the Texas coast was again the center of maritime warfare and drew reporters and illustrators; a recent exhibit at the Texas Museum of Maritime History in Rockport tells the story of the Civil War along the Texas coast. Generally, however, *From Sail to Steam* provides only overviews of our maritime military history, because books can, and have, been written about naval engagements on the Texas coast. The main reason I have emphasized military history in several parts of this book, however, is that advancements in military technology and reconnaissance often led to improvements in merchant shipping.

Because a picture is indeed worth thousands of words, I have attempted to illustrate this book with examples of the important classes of vessels that have plied the coast, as well as port scenes and images of important artifacts associated with Texas maritime history. I have attempted to describe, interpret, and illustrate the more mundane "everyday" aspects of maritime transportation in this book: Cargo and passenger vessels under sail and steam, even the lowly tugboat, all have an important place in Texas history. In my search for illustrations, it became apparent that the maritime history of Texas cannot be told without maps, and thus I have included about a dozen of the more important maps and charts; when viewed through time, these maps beautifully reveal the increasing knowledge of the waters of Texas—knowledge that helped mariners, entrepreneurs, and government officials further develop these waters.

I invite the reader to join me in the search for the diverse vessels that have made contact with the Texas coast, either by accident (in the form of shipwrecks) or on a deliberate course to new points of entry and development, and the ports and rivers utilized by these vessels through time, namely, the four centuries following the arrival of the Spanish on the Gulf of Mexico, or Spanish Sea as it was once called. This story thus begins in a rather narrow, tightly defined strip of Texas geography that is only perhaps a dozen miles in width, but nearly four hundred miles long, where the rivers meet the desolate and beautiful Gulf Coast of the Lone Star State.

FROM SAIL TO STEAM

Four Hundred Miles of Desolation and Beauty

AN INTRODUCTION TO THE TEXAS GULF COAST
AND ITS NATIVE AMERICAN PEOPLES

Each time we cast off we narrow the margins
between ourselves and the environment.
A. P. BALDER, *Mariner's Atlas of Texas* (1992)

A person looking at a map of the world would be hard put to find a more distinctive or peculiar coastline than the roughly circular rim of the Gulf of Mexico. If one pretended that the roughly rounded shape of the Gulf of Mexico were the face of a clock, only the portion where the hands of the clock would sweep from about nine to eleven o'clock would include the littoral of Texas. Yet that northwestern corner of the Gulf is remarkable for many reasons. It has a distinctively shaped coastline that would seem quite simple when viewed from the Gulf but is in fact a complex mosaic of islands and estuaries. As seen in a satellite photo or detailed map (Fig. 1-1), the Texas coast consists of four hundred miles of sandspits, barrier islands, estuaries, and lagoons that follow the shore of the Gulf as it gently curves almost ninety degrees from north–south to east–west in its orientation.

In terms of current political boundaries, the Texas coast extends from the Louisiana border near the Sabine River to the international border at the Rio Grande, or Rio Bravo as it is called in the Mexican state of Tamaulipas. Interestingly, a modern (that is, post–1850) map of Texas shows how important water has been in the design if not identity of the state, for fully 70 percent of the Texas boundary is water—either the Gulf coast or rivers: sinuous or natural borders that contrast with the rigid rectangularity of the Texas panhandle.

The Shape of the Coast

The crescent-shaped land that defines the Texas coast is part of the relatively flat Gulf coastal plain. It is geologically rather stable but has seen

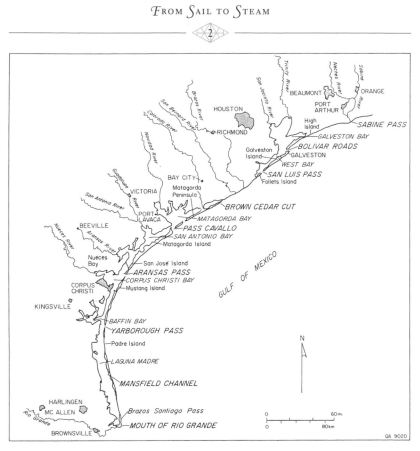

FIGURE 1-1

*As shown on a modern map, the Texas coast is a long, curving crescent of sandspits,
barrier islands, estuaries, and lagoons. The rivers that flow into the coast are also
important in the state's maritime history. Reproduced from Jeffrey G. Paine and
Robert A. Morton,* Shoreline and Vegetation-Line Movement:
Texas Gulf Coast, 1974–1982.

considerable change. There is evidence that earlier shorelines were once
lower, that is, are now under water because the level of the seas has risen
since the ice ages (ca. 1.5 million to ten thousand years ago). Thus, the
undersea topography offshore continues as part of the gently sloping coastal
plain. This means that the waves begin to form and break at some distance
from the shoreline, which is nearly everywhere lined by sandy beaches.
Unlike the rugged coast of Maine, or much of the Pacific coast in California, there are no rocky promontories or submerged canyons off the Texas
coast; this is what the Texas writer/naturalist John Tveten called "a coastline
of gently shelving sand,"[1] for here, sandy shoals that seem deceptively safe

can form a hazard to navigation, since ships sailing some distance from the coast can become stuck fast in the sand and be wrecked by the relentless waves.

The first thing that strikes the sea traveler about the Texas coast is its monotony. Viewed from the water, much of the coast appears as a thin, often dazzling, white line of sand parallel to the breakers that pound the sandy shore (Fig. 1-2). Sometimes just behind this thin white line the shore is covered with scrub vegetation. This shoreline may thus appear to be swelling green mounds from some distance, but nowhere does the topography along the Texas coast exceed fifty feet in elevation and in most places even the tallest dunes are only about ten to fifteen feet high.

Viewed from the sea, the Texas coast is in reality a banding of barrier islands, such as Padre Island, Matagorda Island, and Galveston Island, that protect the Texas coast proper. These barrier islands are a narrow band of sand that has been thrown up by innumerable storms and is constantly re-worked by the breaking waves and redistributed by the wind. Over the last

FIGURE 1-2
*The coast of Texas generally consists of low-lying sandy barrier islands that are pounded by the breakers of the Gulf, as seen at Padre Island.
Photo by the author, 1996.*

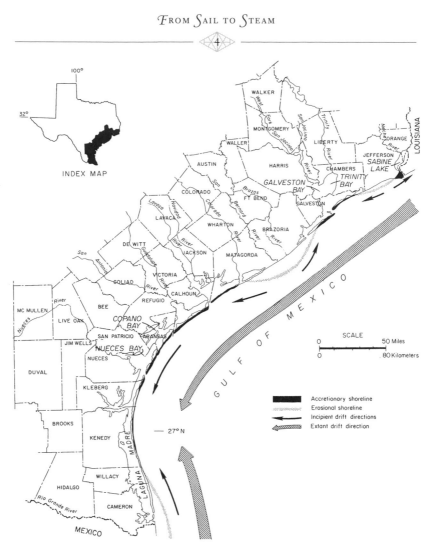

FIGURE 1-3

The Texas coastline is constantly changing, its beaches either growing by accretion or being diminished by erosion. From Robert A. Morton, Historical Shoreline Changes and Their Causes: Texas Gulf Coast, *p. 357; reproduced with permission of the Gulf Coast Association of Geological Societies.*

150 years, careful observation has shown some of these shorelines to be *accretionary* (that is, growing larger by building toward the shore), while other shorelines are more clearly *erosional* (diminishing in size through attrition) (Fig. 1-3).[2] This means that no feature on the coast is permanent and that an island may change shape after a storm. The waves and wind are constantly reshaping the Texas coast, and the barrier islands bear the brunt of this change.

Typically, the surf breaks against these barrier islands with powerful waves about two to four feet in height, but much larger waves have been recorded. Among the earliest written records of the Texas coast is the *Relación* of Alvar Núñez Cabeza de Vaca, which relates the power of the surf in the vicinity of Galveston Island:

> Near dawn I thought I heard the roar of the breakers near shore, which was very loud because the coast was low. Surprised by this, I roused the sailing master, who said he thought we were near land. We took a sounding and found that the water was seven fathoms deep. He thought that we should stay out until dawn. So I took an oar and rowed along the coast, which was a league distant. Then we set our stern to sea. Near land a great wave took us and cast the boat out of the water as far as a horseshoe can be tossed.[3]

After receiving fish and roots from the Native Americans who inhabited this otherwise desolate coast, Cabeza de Vaca and the others in his party hoped to resume their voyage, but tragedy struck as they attempted to launch their boat back into the surf. A wave soaked them, and then:

> Another strong wave caused the boat to capsize. The Inspector and two other men held on to it to survive, but quite the opposite occurred because the boat pulled them under and they drowned. Since the surf was very rough, the sea wrapped all the men in its waves, except the three that had been pulled under by the boat, and cast them on the shore of the same island.[4]

Thus began Cabeza de Vaca's odyssey on the Texas coast, which he called *Malhado* or the "Isle of Misfortune," in a desolate corner of the Spanish Sea. At this early date—1528—the Texas coast was part of a huge area called "Florida," a term used for all of the land facing the entire northern shore of the Seno Mexicano, or Gulf of Mexico. Cabeza de Vaca's descriptions reveal the power of the breakers on the coastal shores of the barrier islands and serve as a reminder that the size of a wave is usually proportional to the force of the wind that has driven that wave to shore after its long sweep, or "fetch," over the sea.

The Texas coast is thus shaped by two major forces:

• The power of the sea, which, through a prevailing southeasterly to easterly wind, creates currents that move sediment to the north on the southern Texas coast and to the west on the upper Texas coast.[5] The prevailing winds tend to reach shore perpendicularly in the vicinity of Corpus Christi, an area that locals refer to as "the coastal bend."

• The power of erosion inland, which carries sediments from the interior of Texas by way of its major rivers, such as the Brazos, the Colorado, and, to a lesser extent, the Rio Grande. Ironically, it is these rivers that supply most of the buff or nearly white-colored sand that makes up Texas beaches,[6] including the stunning barrier islands.

Behind the barrier islands are found lagoons, such as San Antonio Bay, Matagorda Bay, and Laguna Madre, that are relatively shallow and are about two to four miles wide and protected from the breaking waves along the coast (Fig. 1-4). These lagoons are reached by narrow inlets called "passes" that breach the barrier islands. The lagoons may also be joined by smaller bays that are often circular or triangular and provide further refuge from the forces of the coast. Inland from these lagoons, the Texas coast rises in a gently tilting plain. A traveler in 1834 commented on the uniformity of the coast when, on his sailing trip from New Orleans to Brazoria, he entered an inlet at the mouth of the Brazos:

This, I was informed, is a fair specimen of the entire coast of Texas. From one extremity to the other there is not an elevation, or any variety of aspect. The surface is low and flat, but destitute of marshes, so that a cart might almost anywhere come down to the edge of the water.[7]

This traveler continued his description by noting that the views of the coastal waters themselves were affected by the flatness of the topography, adding that "the low and uniform appearance of the whole coast, including that of Galveston Island, renders it almost impossible to ascertain the position of a vessel at any considerable distance from the land."[8]

Travelers were often impressed by the desolation and monotony of the

FIGURE 1-4
Behind the barrier islands are found relatively shallow lagoons or embayments
protected from the breaking waves of the gulf, as seen in this view of Laguna Madre.
Photo by the author, 1996.

Texas coast, but few were as satirical in their remarks as the Irishman Francis
C. Sheridan of the British diplomatic service, who wrote that the appearance of Galveston Island

> is singularly dreary. It is a low flat sandy Island about 30 miles in length &
> ranging in breadth from 1 to 2. There is hardly a shrub visible, & in short
> it looks like a piece of praiarie [sic] that had quarrelled with the main
> land & dissolved partnership.[9]

Another traveler two years earlier had similarly characterized Galveston
Island, and much of the Texas coast, when he wrote that "the whole island
presents rather a dreary and forbidding aspect, with nothing to relieve the
eye or diversify the prospect except three lone trees upon its southeastern
side, about midway, and which stand as the only beacon to the mariner
along this solitary and monotonous portion of the Gulf of Mexico."[10]

Later exploration and scientific observation would reveal that the Texas coast actually varies considerably in its topography and vegetation. The flattest part of the barrier islands is found near Galveston, where hurricane surges and a moister climate keep the islands flat by wave washing and grasses that stabilize the sand and keep it from forming dunes. In the dryer area along the coast near Padre Island, vegetation is more sparse and hurricanes somewhat less frequent — factors that permit the prevailing southerly winds to blow the sand into impressive dunes.[11]

Vegetation and Climate of the Texas Coast

The Texas coastline sweeps from the humid lower midsection of the United States to the semiarid scrub country of northeastern Mexico. Although many observers have commented on the sparse vegetation, trees can be found in the zone behind the sandy Texas coast, which is otherwise virtually devoid of timber. The vegetation along its southern shores is scrub/desert brush, and cactus is found along the entire Texas coast. The vegetation along the coast is a result of many factors, including the soil, but it is largely a response to the rainfall. More than 50 in. of rain are received annually in the northeastern part of the Texas coast beyond Galveston, while the southernmost reaches of the coast near Boca Chica, in the vicinity of Brownsville, receive half that amount. The south Texas coast is, in a word, semiarid, while the eastern portion is humid, perhaps subhumid. Early observers reported cypress trees growing in the freshwater marshes behind the coast at least as far south as southern Texas, though they appear to have vanished with increasing settlement and development of the coast in the 1800s. To nature we must always add humankind as an agent in changing coastal landscapes.

The vegetation along the Gulf shore of Texas is exceedingly complicated, but general patterns can be deduced. Behind the sandy coastal tidal strip, which is essentially devoid of vegetation, are low-lying sandy areas which have a profusion of viney plants and grasses. Oak motts, or clumps of oak trees, many of which are twisted into odd shapes by the wind, are common on the slightly elevated points of land. The French explorer Béranger described the shore of Bienville Island (today's Harbor Island, or Mud Island) in Aransas Bay as "completely covered with small oaks the height of a man that are full of acorns. Our men started gathering some, and a few savages who had followed us helped them; they gathered about six casks full."[12] Béranger noted that he "saw no pines in this region"[13] — an apparent reference to the fact that they were found farther north and east in what is today southeastern coastal Texas and Louisiana. Béranger also mentions mulberry trees; these can be added to a long list of trees that grow in the coastal zone. Where rivers reach the coast, their fluvial valleys are often forested with elm, cottonwood, and pecan, but most trees visible on the headlands of the Texas coast are small and gnarled—a testimony to the difficult conditions of storm, wind, and salt.

The climate of the coast is subtropical, but winter may bring cold, raw weather to its northern reaches near Galveston. At its southernmost point, the Texas coast is nearly tropical, as verified by the protrusion of nonnative tropical plants, such as citrus and palms, which were imported after the arrival of Europeans, and changed the scrubby character of the south coast to one decidedly more Edenic and overtly tropical in appearance.

Regarding weather and climate, one thing that impresses the traveler along the Texas coast is the wind. Even though tidal variation is not great along the Gulf (only about 1 1/2 feet), the wind-driven waves can often raise water levels by, in effect, piling up water against the shore.[14] Depending on the direction from which these winds blow, the level of the waters along the coast can increase, or be reduced, by several feet. For much of the year (that is, from spring all the way through November) a sustained southeastern wind usually blows from the Gulf across the coast on its way inland. This usually ensures that the area along the coast has a rather mild or moderate, and somewhat muggy, climate. The strong onshore winds also ensure that mist and salt from the waves will be blown on shore nearly constantly, stunting vegetation. Although the winds have a significant effect on the coast proper, one should not underestimate the effect of the Gulf on Texas weather far inland. Observers as early as the 1840s noted that the air from the Gulf can be felt as far north as the Red River, almost three hundred miles inland, as a persistent breeze that helps keep temperatures rather lower, but humidity higher, than might otherwise be expected. Even today, one of the most striking aspects of Texas summer weather is the warm, prevailing southerly wind of the summer that blows from the Gulf of Mexico.

NORTHERS, HURRICANES, AND OTHER WINDS

Exceptions to these prevailing onshore winds occur during the relatively brief winter period (generally late November through February), when as many as a dozen "northers" may bring colder air down across the coast accompanied by a strong north wind that may reach thirty to forty knots. Mariners have learned a great respect for the northers that blow furiously and can wreck all but the stoutest of water craft. The cold winds and rain that accompany the northers add to the discomfort of coastal dwellers but pose actual danger to mariners.

Northers—sometimes called blue northers, perhaps because they bring deep blue skies in their wake—have been known to hamper navigation for days at a time. With the arrival of a norther, skies often turn gray, and the cold feels particularly raw because of the high humidity that seems to compound the effect of near-freezing temperatures. Northers can generate waves and increase the level of the sea on the interior sides of the barrier islands that, for the remainder of the year, are normally spared. We often hear accounts of the effects of northers on the mainland, or perhaps on the coastal communities and barrier islands, but observers on vessels far out on the Gulf have left harrowing accounts. In fact, the first account of a norther on the Texas coast is provided by Cabeza de Vaca, who relates the misfortune of one member of his party, whose boat was inadequately anchored near an inlet: "At midnight the north wind blew so strongly that it carried the boat out to sea, since it had only a stone anchor, without anyone seeing it. That was the last they heard of him."[15]

For centuries, northers have savaged coastal transport, and many stories relate their fury. In 1843, Albert M. Gilliam, en route from New Orleans to Veracruz in the fairly small (ca. 90 tons) schooner *Amazon*, related a storm's arrival, which was made apparent by

> the increased violence of the wind, accompanied by that whizzing, whistling sound in its passage through the rigging of the vessel, which to a landsman is not only startling, but really makes his hair stand on end. The mate having given the alarm, by shouting out "a Norther," a storm much more destructive than any other wind that sweeps the Mexican Gulf, and which is always periodical in the months of October and November. My attention having been thus diverted, and feeling filled with apprehensions, I at once determined to go below, discovering as I did that I was in much danger, it then being night, by the swinging of the boom, as well as by the sweeping of the tackling of the vessel over the deck; and that intention was also hastened by the sudden heavy fall of rain.[16]

From "the violence with which the angry waves would beat against the side of the vessel," Gilliam could tell that "a storm of no ordinary character was raging," and an unfortunate crew member was washed overboard and lost in the raging sea.[17]

These storms on the Gulf are often followed by clear, calm weather, and the storm that brought Gilliam's schooner close to the brink of destruction was followed the next morning by relative calm. This situation presented yet another problem, because,

> however, agreeable to the old nautical adage, that "a calm always suc-
> ceeds a storm," the day succeeding the night of the gale, we were in a
> state of perfect calm; nor did we make more than twelve miles progress
> during the period of twenty-four hours.[18]

From the description above, it is possible that Gilliam's schooner encountered not an actual norther, but an equinoctial storm of considerable fury. In 1837, a traveler described the force of such a storm off the coast of Texas in the flowery prose typical of the period:

> When the storm commenced, our vessel [the *Phoenix*] was secured by
> two large anchors, which grappled with a death grasp the foundations of
> the deep. But they gave to the tempest like a reed, and notwithstanding
> two large cannon were fastened to the hawsers and thrown overboard, the
> vessel could not be kept to her moorings, and when the storm abated she
> had drifted seven or eight miles and was within a few yards of the beach.
> It appeared to me all the while as if the heavens were making battle with
> the earth, and the scene was no less terrific than we imagine the struggle
> between the spirits of light and darkness as we find it described in the
> pages of Milton. For three days and nights the very bottom of the seas
> appeared to be stirred up by the violence of the winds, and during all this
> time darkness brooded over the deep. Day and night seemed to be con-
> founded, and . . . our vessel flew before its anchors, plowing up the deep,
> and reeled and tossed like a drunken man amidst the tempest.[19]

On the Texas coast, spring and autumn are often rather placid but deceptively dangerous, for they can bring equinoctial storms packing high winds and rain. These "seasonal" storms have wrecked many vessels.

The persistent summer winds and breezes help make the Texas coast livable during the hottest time of the year, but summer, especially late summer, is a time when coastal Texans keep an especially close eye on what may otherwise seem the deceptively routine weather. Nothing along the Texas coast exceeds the fury and danger of the most intense of the tropical

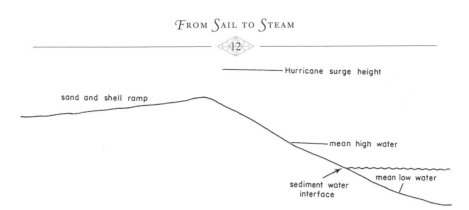

FIGURE 1-5

A generalized cross section of the barrier islands on the Texas coast reveals that the sand and shell beach ramps are above the mean high water line, but that hurricane surge heights can easily inundate this normally dry land. Reproduced from Robert Morton and Mary Pieper, Shoreline Changes in the Vicinity of the Brazos River Delta, *p. 9.*

storms: the hurricane. Heated by a nearly vertical tropical sun, the surface of the Gulf is ripe to spawn storms of intense low pressure by summer or early fall. These storms, named after the Caribbean God of the Wind (Huricán), can bring devastation to the coast and to any vessel that happens to be passing along it. During hurricanes, winds of more than 150 mph can fell trees, rip apart buildings, and generate huge waves. Surges of storm-driven waters can devastate and flood coastal ports. The power of these hurricanes is underscored by the fact that several Texas ports, including Indianola, have been virtually obliterated by them. The geologists J. H. Bowen et al. noted that "barrier islands which lie several miles seaward of the mainland bear the brunt of storm-surge floods during most hurricanes"[20] (Fig. 1-5).

Careful recording of hurricanes during the last 150 years reveals that they are more likely to hit the Texas coast earlier in the hurricane season (June-July) than Atlantic hurricanes, and that the northern Gulf coast near Galveston experiences hurricanes somewhat more frequently than the south part of the Texas coast. No part of the Texas coast, however, is free from their destruction. In describing the fury of a tropical storm at South Padre Island, Bob St. John noted that "the usually deafening sound of thunder was greatly muffled because of the locomotive-like roar of wind and rain and ocean."[21]

In addition to severe wind conditions and tricky undersea currents near the passes, mariners on the Texas coast need to be aware of the tides. Although, as noted above, the tides along the Texas coast are usually rather low in range, only up to about 1 1/2 feet, somewhat higher tides are produced when the moon is in either the full or new moon phases; these are called "spring tides." At the other extreme, when the moon is in either the first or third quarter, low tides (called neap tides) also occur. The height of the tide can be of concern to mariners because it can affect the depth of the sea in the vicinity of a ship, and to those on land because high tides, when accompanied by wind-driven waves, can inundate normally dry land. Because of the rather shallow waters in the vicinity of the Texas coast, those early sailors who reached it intact soon found they needed shallow-draft craft to explore the expansive embayments behind the barrier islands. In some cases, even the passes themselves were so shallow that small boats (variously called launches or lighters) were needed, though some of the larger passes, such as Aransas Pass, could permit the entry of ships drawing about two fathoms (twelve feet) of water.

CHARACTER OF THE COAST AND ITS MARINE LIFE

It was soon recognized, then, that there are actually two Texas coasts: (1) the beaches of the barrier islands that are pounded by surf and wind, and (2) the somewhat protected coastal lands that lie along the lagoons. Owing to the relatively simple shoreline of the barrier islands and the complex, invaginated shoreline of the bays and estuaries, Texas has about four hundred miles of the former and nearly fifteen hundred miles of the latter. The barrier islands form the outermost aspect of coast, in effect protecting the embayments and coast of the mainland from all but the most savage of hurricanes.

A closer look at the coast and its natural embayments is provided by a map prepared by Captain Monroe of Aransas Bay in 1833 and published in William Kennedy's popular 1841 book, *Texas: The Rise, Progress, and Prospects of the Republic of Texas* (Fig. 1-6). This map is actually a nautical chart that helped guide vessels like Captain Monroe's schooner, *Amos Wright*, into port by showing the depth of the water where it had been "sounded," that is, checked with a weight on a line to determine the actual depth to bottom. In taking such soundings, the lead or metal weights may be greased to gather sediments at the bottom. When brought back aboard, these greased weights help sailors determine more about the bottom: Is it sandy? Does it consist of shells? or rock? This, in turn, can help reveal much about both currents and their strength and the possible configuration of the bottom areas nearby. Note that the depths are charted on Monroe's 1833 map to a point of land, Copano Point, which is located on the tip of a

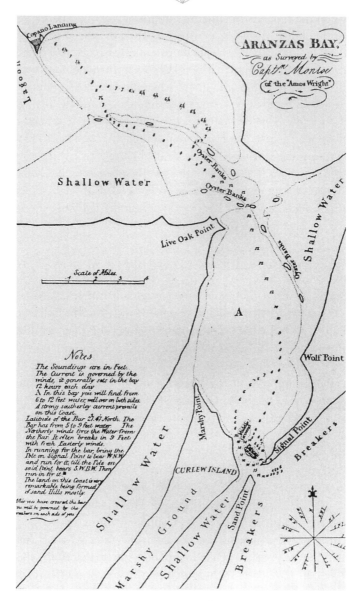

FIGURE 1-6

As seen in this map—actually an early nautical chart—prepared by Captain Monroe in 1833, Aranzas (Aransas) Bay is revealed to be relatively shallow. Note that a part of the bay has been sounded—that is, checked for depth. This map was originally published in Kennedy's 1841 Texas history. Courtesy Special Collections Division, The University of Texas at Arlington Libraries, Arlington.

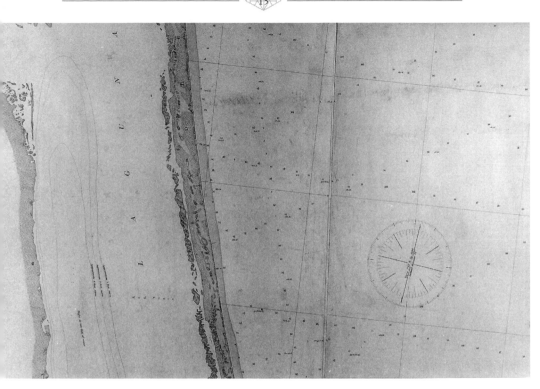

FIGURE 1-7

An 1890 U.S. Coast and Geodetic Survey chart of Padre Island and Laguna Madre reveals the gentle slope of the shoreline below the waters of the Gulf, and the large, and generally very shallow, Laguna Madre. Courtesy Special Collections Division, The University of Texas at Arlington Libraries, Arlington.

peninsula. Copano Point and many similar places on lagoons and bays provided refuge from the coastal storms that pounded the Gulf shore of the barrier islands.

As revealed in a more detailed map of Padre Island and Laguna Madre by the U.S. Coast and Geodetic Survey in 1890, the Gulf shore of Padre Island is remarkably free from obstructions and gently sloping offshore, while the Laguna Madre itself is a shallow depression varying in depth from but one foot to about eight to ten feet at its deepest closer to the mainland (Fig. 1-7).

While explorers traversed the coast in search of landfalls, many noted the wonderful abundance of marine life along the Texas coast. As one anonymous traveler in 1837 remarked,

I know of no country that I could so safely commend to the attention of the conchologist as the shores of Galveston [island] immediately upon the gulf, where the most beautiful specimens of the science may be found in the greatest profusion. For hours a large part of our crew amused themselves along the silver shore in collecting a vast number of beautiful shells.[22]

Two years later, the young Irishman Francis C. Sheridan commented upon the shellfish of the lagoons on the Texas coast in the vicinity of Galveston Island and Velasco, noting that

there were oysters also—not the melting Milton of England or the thundering Powldoody of Ireland, but a huge, long, ill-shaped shellfish—a gigantic species of the Mangrove oysters of the W. Indies, & "bearded like the Pard"—[that] . . . probably would not be bad if eaten immediately after being opened.[23]

These descriptions of Galveston and vicinity are similar to those of other locations, including the shores and lagoons of Padre and Mustang Islands on the south Texas coast, which abound in marine life. The edibility and profusion of oysters led to their frequent mention by travelers, and in some places the oyster population was so prolific that actual reefs of oysters were formed to create yet another hazard to navigation. Early observers noted that the waters of the coast teemed with fish, such as redfish or channel bass, sea trout, amberjack, and flounder. Sea turtles, too, found along the Texas coast often caught the attention of mariners and other travelers. Because they could be kept alive for up to a year with little care, these sea turtles were prized by mariners as a fresh food supply that could be kept in the holds of vessels until needed. Brown shrimp (*Penaeus aztecus*) and white shrimp (*Penaeus setiferus*) spawn in the Gulf and migrate seasonally into the estuaries and bays by way of the passes. These crustaceans are bottom feeders that form an important part of the coastal ecology in an environment that often teems with nutrients suspended in the waters of the marshes, estuaries, and bays. The younger or juvenile shrimp feed closer to shore until they grow larger and move to deeper waters, but the migration of shrimp still remains something of a mystery.[24]

The Texas coast is a highly varied environment that sustains large populations of fish, shellfish, and crustaceans. Yet, as any fisherman knows, some parts are richer than others. Although the lagoons are generally rich in fish life, for example, the very high salinity in parts of the Laguna Madre, due to

FIGURE 1-8

The common sand dollar was originally thought to be "peculiar to Texas" and was even called the "Texian Star" by Francis Sheridan in the 1840s owing to its similarity to the seal of the Republic of Texas. Illustration at left by the author; Texas seal courtesy Special Collections Division, The University of Texas at Arlington Libraries, Arlington.

the high evaporation in that area of the south Texas coast, made that large embayment rather barren. Those same conditions led to formation of deposits of salt, or *salinas*, on the shore behind the lagoons of south Texas and northern Mexico.

Among the interesting fauna along the coast is the dangerous Portuguese man-of-war, a jellyfish whose dangling tentacles contain a potent, numbing poison that entraps stunned fish. Having a finlike sail, these jellyfish are often blown into the shallows along the Gulf coast shore by the strong winds of summer, whereupon they die while turning, for a brief period, a deep purple color much like old bottle glass that has been left in the sun for years. Beachcombing the Texas coast[25] has long been an interesting pastime, especially for nineteenth-century travelers who delighted in finding natural treasures. In addition to a tremendous amount of seaweed and other flotsam washed up on shore during certain times of the year, especially after storms, the Texas coast also yields a wide variety of shells. In 1839–1840, Francis Sheridan described a beach near Galveston with "the whitest, firmest, & most beautiful sand I ever saw,"[26] where, "being no conchologist," he encountered an unusual shell, which he described as "perfectly flat, & about 3 or 4 inches in circumference, having a distinct Star of five points very accurately traced in the centre" (Fig. 1-8). This, of course, we know as the "sand dollar" (*Eichinarachnius parma*), but Sheridan "was told [it] was peculiar to Texas," and called "The Texian Star."[27] Although we now know that the sand dollar has a much wider range than the Gulf coast of Texas, Sheridan's enthusiasm recalls the relatively limited state of scientific knowledge at the time, when natural history was still in its infancy, and the fascination that many travelers had with things peculiarly "Texian."

More than a century before Captain Monroe charted the Aransas Bay and travelers of the same early Victorian era described the Texas coast, the French explorer Béranger had described in considerable detail the navigational hazards and vexing abundance of marine life in Copano Bay, noting, "I went 5 leagues into the bay to reconnoiter the lay [of the land] of this island. The mainland was still 3 or 4 leagues distant from me, and an oyster reef was keeping me from going there even with my launch."[28] The marine life of the lagoons along the Texas coast is so rich that the shellfish beds can form topographic features, such as the beds of clams and oysters noted by explorers since Cabeza de Vaca. For explorers trying to make landfall, the Texas coast can be frustrating: One might have to wade a considerable distance to shore, so shallow are the waters. The Texas coast is, in a word, rather treacherous, and for this reason good maps and nautical charts could enhance one's chances of survival. As we interpret the four centuries of maritime history on the coast, several obstacles to settlement and shipbuilding become apparent. The first is water, or rather the lack of it. Although freshwater streams and rivers flow into the coast behind the barrier islands, fresh water is generally scarce. So, too, is large timber. Even though wood can be found along the coast in many places, only a portion of it, the eastern part near Louisiana, possesses the variety of trees—tall pines and straight oaks—that can be used for hulls and masts of sailing ships. Along virtually all of the coast visible landmarks are few, and those that do exist, such as sand bars and ridges, can be transformed with the passage of storms. The generally inhospitable nature of the coast is exacerbated by the fact that, like all coasts, it is constantly changing through the inexorable forces of nature.

In order to make sense of this seemingly chaotic world of sun, sand, and water, a rich cartographic tradition developed. Although we know nothing about how, or even if, the native peoples mapped the Texas coast, it has been well mapped by the Europeans and others who landed here. Its rich history of maps and nautical charts can tell us much about the people who drafted them.[29] Captain Monroe pointed out the hazards of the Texas coast, and another look at this chart shows it to be a road map for mariners, helping them steer clear of dangers, including shoals. Like all maps, however, this one took some time to draft, and may be the result of several voyages into this particular bay.

FIGURE 1-9

The rivers of Texas form natural corridors to the interior for shallow-draft vessels, but most were navigable less than a third of their length even under the best of conditions. Seen here, the fabled Rio Grande near Roma, Texas is rather typical of the lower, wider reaches of Texas rivers within about sixty miles of the Gulf of Mexico. Photo courtesy Mario Sánchez, Texas Historical Commission.

Texas Rivers and the Gulf Coast

Once travelers reached the embayments of the coast, they often found freshwater streams entering them from the west or north. These rivers and streams constitute the third major type of water available to vessels in Texas. The Texas coast, like Texas itself, is in fact defined by rivers whose names resonate with history. No fewer than sixteen rivers enter the coast after draining large areas that vary in climate and landscape from desert to forests (Fig. 1-9). Some, like the Sabine and Rio Grande, which form the state's boundaries, are almost entirely different in character. Whereas the Sabine River traverses humid or well-watered lands throughout its length, the Rio Grande is what geographers call an "exotic" stream. Along most of its course, the Rio Grande seems deceptive, a substantial river flowing through decidedly arid country that could not sustain a river. This river, however, is largely nurtured by rain and snowmelt at its distant source in the mountains of southern Colorado and northern New Mexico. Variable in flow and traversing an arid countryside through much of its nearly fifteen hundred miles, the Rio Grande is the lifeline that nurtures Texas's westernmost city, El Paso, and a group of towns like Presidio, Laredo, and Brownsville that are spaced along the river like beads on a string.

Because they are so important to the state's maritime history, the rivers of Texas deserve closer examination. Beginning in the south of Texas at the mouth of the Rio Grande on the Texas coast, one first encounters a desolate, arid plain drained only by small, usually dry, creeks that run only after heavy rains. About eighty miles north of the Rio Grande, one next encounters the first river of sorts, Los Olmos Creek, which enters at Baffin Bay. The next large bay to the north, Corpus Christi Bay, is located at the mouth of the fabled Nueces River, which once served as the border between Mexico and Texas. Numerous creeks and rivers, including the Aransas River, enter Copano Bay, and farther northward, beyond what locals now call the "Coastal Bend," the San Antonio and Guadalupe rivers enter San Antonio Bay. Still farther north, at Matagorda and Lavaca bays, are found the mouths of Arenosa Creek and two rivers, the Lavaca and Navidad, that drain a portion of south central Texas. At the Matagorda Peninsula, the Colorado River (named for its reddish color) forms a small delta that, in effect, divides the eastern arm of Matagorda Bay.[30] Between here and the next large bay (Galveston Bay), Linville Bayou (Caney Creek) and the Brazos River enter the coast directly rather than draining into bays. The Brazos, a remarkable river, may be said to represent a typical Texas river inasmuch as it has several different personalities or moods. Beginning as a series of arroyos near the Texas/New Mexico border, it flows in a serpentine course through the reddish colored, escarpment-like hills of semiarid north central Texas before becoming a full-fledged river as it traverses the humid coastal lowlands of southeast Texas.

Although the east Texas rivers are fairly dependable in flow, like all Texas rivers they are deceptive: In periods of low water they might be full of snags, such as brush and trees, and be very shallow, while at other times they may run bank full or even jump their banks and flood low-lying areas. Two east Texas rivers, the San Jacinto and Trinity, enter the Galveston Bay. At the extreme eastern border of Texas, the Neches and Sabine rivers enter Sabine Lake. In this part of Texas, many small rivers, locally called bayous, also drain into the larger rivers or the Gulf of Mexico. These bayous are home to alligators and a wealth of bird life.

Far to the north of the Texas coast, the Red River forms the northern border of Texas and southern border of Oklahoma, but then flows into Louisiana, where it joins the Mississippi before its waters finally reach the Gulf near New Orleans. Like many Texas rivers, the Red begins as a small stream, or streams, that drain a rather semiarid region far from the Gulf, in this case the panhandle of west Texas.

Whatever their source, as the rivers of Texas flow eastward or southward toward the Gulf, their flow increases as they drain increasingly larger areas and traverse progressively wetter areas when they reach the lowlands adjacent to the coast. During their more moderate serene moods, these rivers would seem to beckon as "natural corridors" by which one could penetrate far into the interior. But as we shall see, Texas rivers could be both enchanting and treacherous in a single season.

Native Peoples of the Texas Coast

In the early years of the exploration of Texas, the Native American population was sparse in the coastal area. However, several tribes lived along the coast and environs, and it is with them that both coastal folklore and Texas maritime history must begin. To the Native Americans living along the Texas coast, the powerful waves and immensity of the Gulf must have been awe-inspiring. That may account for tribes apparently treating the coast with a respect and fear that bordered on reverence. In 1802 Martin Duralde recognized this when he wrote that "the Atacapas pretend that they are come out of the sea, that a prophet or man inspired by God laid down the rules of conduct of their first ancestors."[31] To the Native Americans of the Texas coast, the Gulf and its immediate shoreline must have seemed—and was indeed—the edge of the world.

In pre-Columbian times, the shores and islands of the Gulf of Mexico were home to a diverse population of native peoples; some, like the Maya of Yucatán, had a rather sedentary culture based on agriculture and had constructed cities and religious centers; others, like the Karankawa and other Texas coastal peoples, including the Atacapa, Cujane, Guapite (Coapite), Coco, and Copane, subsisted by hunting, gathering, and fishing for food. At the dawn of Spanish contact, the population of the Texas coast was relatively small: perhaps 1,500 to 2,000 Coahuiltecan peoples who tended to aggregate in late fall and early winter in villages of, say, 100 to 400 individuals, and disperse in warm seasons into bands consisting of 25 or fewer people.[32] Typically, these peoples roamed the coast and the embayments behind it in

FIGURE 1-10

The dugout canoe, also called a pirogue *or* piragua, *was widely used by the
Karankawa and other tribes of coastal Texas. Reproduced from W. W. Newcomb,*
The Indians of Texas, *with permission of the University of Texas Press.*

search of food. Their housing was temporary and well suited to their mobile
life-style. The anthropologist Lawrence Aten has noted that "a true maritime adaptation (open sea fishing, hunting, and transport) was never employed on the Texas coast, so far as is known, by late pre-historic woodland
cultures," nor in earlier periods,[33] as the Texas coastal Indians were probably subsisting through the collection of plant and animal resources of the
coast and estuary margins—a practice called "strandlooping."

Because much of the Gulf shore coast itself is a rather hostile place devoid of fresh water and is relatively poor in terms of land animal resources,
most Texas coastal Indians lived along the lagoons, whose brackish water
yielded large populations of fish and shellfish, including clams and oysters.
They would occasionally catch or spear fish in the shallower waters. By
rubbing fish or shark oil on their skin, the Karankawa found a way of escap-

ing the mosquitoes that bedevil the population along the Texas coast—a trait the Spanish found offensive because of the strong odor of the oils.

Like most Native American peoples who lived along the coast, the Karankawa and other Texas coastal tribes made small water craft in order to cross estuaries and lagoons, and to reach better areas for hunting and fishing. The dugout canoe, also variously called a *pirogue* or *piragua* (Fig. 1-10), was known and used by the Karankawa and other tribes in coastal Texas. Among the earliest detailed descriptions of canoes or dugouts of the Karankawa is that of Jean Béranger, who noted that

> they have very fine pirogues that can carry at least a dozen casks end to end. Apparently it takes them a great deal of time to construct one. They put fire all along the tree, and as it burns they scrape out the charcoal with dried bones that they adapt expressly to that purpose.[34]

The pirogues served to transport the coastal Native Americans from one location to another, usually if not always on lagoons. Although they possessed watercraft, these tribes of the Texas coast should not be thought of as seafarers: Most of their mobility was achieved by walking or wading, not sailing, though they did use dugouts for short voyages across lagoons and to move along the lower reaches of rivers and streams. A mural at the Museum of the Gulf Coast in Port Arthur depicts life in an Atacapa village in southeast Texas, not far from Sabine Pass, and pirogues at the shoreline are conspicuous (Fig. 1-11).

It is also reported that the Native Americans of the Texas coast created rafts consisting of logs lashed together. However, we know this not from the archaeological record—for no watercraft made by Karankawa, or for that matter other tribes of the Texas coast, have survived—but only from verbal or written descriptions of European peoples who encountered the coastal tribes in the 1500s and 1600s. Archaeologists have documented the coastal peoples' material culture, especially pottery, weapons, and housing, but their watercraft remains something of a mystery and our knowledge of it somewhat conjectural. Among the most obvious reasons for the paucity of material evidence among the natives of the Texas coast is that their boats were made entirely of wood, a substance that does not usually last very long on the coast in this climate.

And yet, archaeologists have long speculated about the watercraft of the early coastal peoples. In his popular work, *The Indians of Texas* (1961), W. W. Newcomb Jr. wrote a description of the Karankawa that was based, in

FIGURE 1-11
As seen in this conjectural view of an Indian village on the Texas coast near Sabine Pass, the Native American populations lived in small groups close to the water and made extensive use of their dugout canoes or pirogues. Photo by the author, courtesy of the Museum of the Gulf Coast, Port Arthur, Texas.

part, on the earlier work of Charles A. Hammond and others. Newcomb noted that "the Karankawa's nomadic maritime existence was made possible by the use of dugout canoes [which] . . . they fashioned from tree trunks without bothering to remove the bark." He further described these craft, noting that "one side of a log was trimmed flat, its ends blunted, and then it was hollowed out, probably with the aid of fire and much scraping." The solid section that remained formed a triangular deck at either end of the canoe. According to Newcomb, the size of these canoes "is but vaguely known, though they were large enough to hold a man, his wife, children, and household goods." These dugout canoes were propelled by means of poles, but they were not sufficiently sturdy or trustworthy to allow their use in heavy weather or very far from the protection of the shore or the coastal islands. Newcomb concluded that these vessels "were fit only for short voyages across the shallow, placid waters of lagoons and inlets."[35]

Several things can be deduced about the dugouts made by the coastal peoples: Because these dugouts were dependent to a large degree on the size of logs, they in turn varied in size. Although logs may have been washed down streams to the Gulf from the pine forests of eastern Texas, most of the trees in the area of the Gulf coast are either small oaks, larger and taller trees such as cottonwood or sycamores that are found on the mainland side of the lagoons in the freshwater fluvial lowlands, or the cypress trees of the marshlands. In any case, these logs would normally be at best medium in height and girth, not more than three feet in width. The length of dugout canoes would be determined by their function: For maneuverability and portability, the Karankawas probably restricted their length to not much longer than twenty feet; given their proportions, we can conclude that these dugouts, with a beam of 2 1/2 feet, were relatively narrow, rather heavy craft somewhat inclined to be fairly "tippy" in the absence of a keel or skeg, which was apparently unknown to these coastal tribes.

For propulsion, it is certain that the Native Americans of the Texas coast relied not on sails, but rather on paddling to propel these dugouts in shallow waters; poles might have been used to coax them across shoals and bars. Dugouts were well suited to the protected, shallow waters of lagoons — so much so that they continued to be employed by the Europeans who would later arrive on the Texas coast and would seek to explore its lagoons and embayments.

As noted above, Newcomb was not the first anthropologist to describe the Karankawa watercraft, and in fact he based his accounts on early reports. Among the most fascinating nineteenth-century descriptions of Karankawa watercraft are those by Alice W. Oliver, who as a child in the 1830s is reported to have lived close to, and interacted with, a dwindling band of the tribe. The pioneer ethnographer Charles A. Hammond records that Mrs. Oliver was the daughter of Captain Thomas Bridges, who was engaged in running the Mexican coastal blockades in the "Texas revolt against Mexico" in 1836, and that the ten-year-old girl developed an unusual relationship with the Karankawa. In the 1870s she described their mobility to Hammond, noting that "their parties usually voyaged from place to place along the coast in their *canoes*, or 'dug-outs,' which were made from large trees, the bark left on." According to Mrs. Oliver, "One side of the log was hewed flat and the log was then dug out, the ends bluntly pointed, leaving a triangular place or deck at each end." She added that "the women and children and household goods occupied the 'hold,' while the father of the family stood on the stern and poled the boat along, keeping not far away from the shore [and that] on arriving at a landing place, the men hauled the canoe up on the beach and then left the women to set up the wigwams."[36]

In a report written some fifty years after her exposure to the Karankawa as a child, Mrs. Oliver noted that, despite contact with the Spanish, Mexicans, and newly arrived Texians, their life remained virtually unchanged. She added somewhat wistfully that "the chase and fishing had always been their chief dependence and so it continued to a great extent; their habits were primitive in the extreme, but here, as always, the blighting touch of civilization left its baneful trace and hastened the doom of the fast diminishing tribe." According to Mrs. Oliver, the Karankawa "had always lived an itinerant life, passing in their 'dug-outs,' which were long and very narrow, yet capacious, from spot to spot, stopping generally where some settler had made his home, always where fresh water and brushwood for their fire were easily attainable."[37]

In 1891, the anthropologist Albert S. Gatschet summarized the Karankawas' canoes as follows:

> Their canoes were of two kinds, both being called awa'n by them: (1) the aboriginal *dugout*, about twenty feet long, narrow, yet capacious; (2) *old skiffs* obtained from the whites, much broader than the dugouts and flat-bottomed. A mast with a little sail was occasionally set up, but for want of space they were never seen paddling or rowing them. Mrs. Oliver states that neither of the two was used for fishing, but served for transportation only; and these embarkations were so frail and untrustworthy that they would never have ventured to go out upon the open waters of the gulf. The dugouts were not made smooth upon the outside, but had the bark still on.[38]

This description is interesting, for the mention of a wide-bottom skiff reveals that the Karankawas *adopted* the vessel, with its sail, wider beam, and flat bottom, from the European peoples. Thus, at the end of their existence, the Karankawa had two types of watercraft, hand- or pole-powered canoes/dugouts, which can be said to be indigenous to the Texas coast, and the small sailboat, which was imported. Their adoption of the sail-powered skiff is a reminder that maritime technology, like all ideas, spreads from a point of invention by diffusion. A good idea often finds its way, by cultural contact, to even the most remote corners of the globe, which is just how the Texas coast may be viewed at the dawn of the age of exploration. Exactly how, or when, the Karankawa adopted the technological improvements of the sailboat will probably never be known. We do know, however, that this new technology first arrived on the wind with the Spanish. Their arrival, and their impact on the maritime history of Texas, is the subject of the next chapter.

THE POWER OF THE WIND
1500–1685

They who go down to the sea in ships, they see the wonders of the Lord.
PSALMS

The Native Americans of the Texas coast had developed with no apparent concept of dominating or mastering the environment. They traveled along the coast in search of food, moving their homes periodically, but the Gulf coast was the margin of their world. Some observers considered the coastal Indians a marginalized people, hemmed in by the coast on the one hand and by even more aggressive tribes farther inland on the other. Like all Native Americans, these coastal Texas Indians were about to come in contact with peoples from half a world away who had developed a method for crossing the ocean that had separated them, with few exceptions, since the Native Americans had arrived in the New World more than fifteen thousand years previously.[1]

The Texas (and, for that matter, all other) Native Americans' paddling or poling of watercraft for mobility contrasted sharply with developments that were taking place in western Europe. There, sponsors such as Henry the Navigator had by the 1460s encouraged the exploration of the African coast by use of the most readily available source of propulsion—the wind—to power their vessels. Although sail power of ships dates back several thousand years to China and southwestern Asia, sailors in the Old World came in contact with each other and adopted techniques of sail-rigging and hull design that could enable them to take better advantage of the wind. The alternative—rowing or paddling ships—was labor-intensive, but was still necessary as ships might find themselves becalmed, and thus otherwise unable to move, in some waters for days at a time.

The sailing vessels that carried the Spanish to the New World used a system of propulsion unknown to the Indians on the Texas coast or elsewhere in the Americas. The most fundamental element of the sailing vessel is a mast (or *palo* in Spanish) that rises from the hull. Through a system of spars (*árboles*), rigging (*xarcia*), sails (*velas*), and tackles (*aparejos*), the Spanish sailing vessel captured or harnessed the power of the wind and transmitted its energy to moving the hull through the water. Optimally, a vessel would move forward by the force that the wind exerted on its sails from behind and to one side—a condition called a "large wind." However, because the desired location and the direction of the wind did not always correspond, ingenious sailors developed sail configurations that enabled them to sail forward despite crosswinds. With time, sailors developed methods of sailing almost into the wind (that is, moving forward against a headwind) by a process, popularly called "tacking," that mariners know as "beating."[2] The seemingly magical power of the wind to move vessels was a double-edged sword, however. Too strong a wind will drive a vessel out of control, sometimes onto the shore, where it may be totally demolished by rocks and/or waves. Thus, sailing vessels need to be able to take advantage of the wind's power but be able to undergo adjustments to their rigging, sometimes within seconds, to avoid being captured by the wind and either capsized, or drawn off course and destroyed. Through the centuries, the rigging of sails was intuitively designed to strike a balance between capturing the benign and avoiding the destructive forces of the wind.

The shape of a vessel's hull, too, helps determine how effectively it will move through the water in different conditions. The hull's shape also dictates how much payload a vessel can carry. This, too, is a compromise. A vessel with high sides above the gunwales can carry a heavier or larger load, such as cannons for defense or offense, in a high position. Those same high sides, however, can be hazardous in high winds, which can blow the vessel off course as the hull itself intercepts the wind and acts somewhat like a sail. Likewise, vessels that ride low in the water may be safer from high winds but can be swamped by taller seas, as waves may break over the gunwales. Thus it is that sailing vessels evolved, through a slow and often painful process of trial and error, to enable their crews to master the seas in the age of exploration, which began in the late Middle Ages (ca. 1150 to 1200) in Europe. One of the most underappreciated aspects of European contact with the New World and the entire "Columbian Exchange," was that of differences in nautical heritage and technology between the two peoples. Although Native Americans were deft at designing small watercraft used in shallow waters, they were no match for the nautical prowess of the Europeans, who had been developing vessels of trade and war for centuries before they reached the New World.

FIGURE 2-1

Used by the Spanish after extensive development in Europe, the sailing vessel often featured two or three masts with lateen rather than square rigging. The vessel illustrated here is a true galleon in that oars could be used to power it in areas or periods of calm. From Henry Culver, The Book of Old Ships; *drawing by Gordon Grant, reproduced with permission of Doubleday, a division of Bantam Doubleday Dell Publishing Group, Inc.*

The European sailing vessel of the late Middle Ages had evolved as developments occurred in many areas, including the Baltic, North, and Mediterranean Seas. By the late Middle Ages, sailing vessels in the Mediterranean featured a familiar profile, with raised forecastle and aftercastle and a low waist at center. A sternpost rudder, originally developed in northern Europe, was used to steer the vessel, which often featured two or three masts, with lateen (rather than square) rigging (Fig. 2-1). Many such vessels were true galleys, that is, had a bank (or banks) of oars that could be used to row

FIGURE 2-2

The caravel represented the type of vessel used by Spain in exploring the Atlantic and Gulf waters of America in the 1500s. From Henry Culver, The Book of Old Ships; *drawing by Gordon Grant, reproduced with permission of Doubleday, a division of Bantam Doubleday Dell Publishing Group, Inc.*

the ship in calm weather. By the 1350s, the term *carrack* was in use for large trading vessels of Spanish or Genoan origin,[3] and square rigging began to replace full lateen rigging; this, and sturdier hulls with deeper drafts, enabled Mediterranean vessels to better meet the challenges of sailing into the North Atlantic Ocean as a lively trade developed. By the mid-fifteenth century, two-masted carracks were common, and ships were increasing in size, requiring three masts, which meant that the mizzen could be rigged as a lateen to provide better balance for steering the vessel on a wind.[4]

The term *caravel*, once generically used to describe fishing vessels, reappears at this time and is applied to relatively small, sturdily built, three-masted vessels drawing a maximum of six or seven feet of water (Fig. 2-2). Lateen-rigged, caravels were fast and made good headway into the wind. Yet they were labor-intensive to operate because their complex sails required a considerable crew, and were difficult to handle in rough seas; to correct this, the fore and main masts were square-rigged, and the resulting vessel was called a *caravela redonda*. The nautical archaeologist and maritime historian Roger Smith reminds us that these vessels were a product of the "nautical revolution" that took place in less than one hundred years and "came at a time when maritime commerce between northern and southern Europe had fused elements of capitalistic enterprise, nautical skills and experiences, and the realization that distant peoples and their products could be reached by sailing into the Atlantic Ocean."[5]

Thus was the scene set for vessels of the *caravela redonda* configuration to hoist sail and set out for the New World. Three replicas of the vessels that carried Christopher Columbus from Spain to Hispaniola in 1492 are now permanently based in Corpus Christi. These vessels, like all other replicas of Columbus's *Niña*, *Pinta*, and *Santa Maria*, are conjectural, for no plans— only vague verbal or written descriptions—exist. Nevertheless, the three vessels in Corpus Christi provide a rather good idea of the size and design of the first sailing ships that touched the waters of the eastern Gulf. Following an accident with a barge that incapacitated two of the vessels (the *Pinta* and *Santa Maria*) in 1993, only the *Niña*, the most seaworthy of the replicas, and the vessel whose prototype was reportedly Columbus's favorite, sails in the Gulf on weekends. With its lateen and square sails, and small but swift hull, the *Niña* presents an intriguing sight in the Corpus Christi Harbor (Fig. 2-3).

Columbus's vessels were adequately rigged to make the long voyage. The *Niña* and *Pinta* were of the *caravela redonda* type, the former having been rerigged from a *caravela latina* because that lateen rigging was unsuitable for the Atlantic voyage. In his log, Columbus used the term *nao* to refer to his third vessel, the *Santa Maria*, in order to distinguish it from the two smaller companion vessels. The *Santa Maria* was about eighty to ninety tons, as indicated by Bartolomé de las Casas in his *Historia de las Indias*. It is estimated that the *Santa Maria* was about eighty feet long, and that she drew about six and a half feet of water. It, too, was rigged like a *caravela redonda*, but it had a more extensive sail plan—two additional sails, one topsail above the main course and a sprit sail.

Replicas of the Columbus vessels in Corpus Christi serve as a reminder that much of what is known about vessels from the age of exploration is conjectural. Vessels at the time were usually built without plans, and thus we rely on the writings of those who experienced, or sailed, them. Nevertheless, these writings reveal that there was little or no difference at that time between merchant vessels and those used for military purposes. With the increasingly aggressive territorial claims and the introduction of gunpowder to Italy in the fourteenth century, vessels soon became more heavily armed. As they increased in size, so did their armament. Heavy cannons

FIGURE 2-3
As seen in a marina at Corpus Christi, a replica of the Niña *is shown to possess both lateen and square rigging, which enabled it to sail on the oceans. Photo by the author, 1995.*

FIGURE 2-4

The astrolabe is a portable instrument constructed of metal that permits determination of the position of the sun (or other celestial bodies, such as the stars) in relation to the horizon, thus enabling a determination of one's distance from the equator and, hence, one's latitude. The three astrolabes shown here were recovered from the 1554 Padre Island shipwrecks. Those at left and right are dated 1550, while the one in the center dates from 1545—the oldest astrolabe found in the western hemisphere. From the Platoro/Kenon/Purvis Collection of the Texas Historical Commission, Austin; photo courtesy Don Zuris, Corpus Christi Museum.

were soon part of the load and became part of the design of vessels. However, they affected the weight of vessels; because too high a placement could cause the vessel to be top-heavy, cannons were soon mounted in ports along the side.

As these European vessels sailed greater and greater distances, navigational devices were required to ensure that they reached their destinations. The astrolabe (Fig. 2-4) was among the earliest to help provide mariners with an accurate reading of their positions by helping them determine latitude. An astrolabe is a portable instrument, usually constructed of metal, that permits one to determine the position of the sun (or other celestial bodies, such as stars) in relation to the horizon, thus enabling one to determine one's distance from, say, the equator. Until the development of the more sophisticated sextant in 1628, the astrolabe was indispensable to mariners.

It has been noted that "caravels and naos were Renaissance expressions of nautical design and technology; their sleek hull shapes and innovative propulsion systems allowed transoceanic voyages to become routine and the globe to be circumnavigated for the first time."[6] The arrival of Columbus in the New World was based on this nautical technology, setting off a chain reaction of aggressive exploration of the Americas, which soon resulted in Spanish vessels' sailing the waters of the Gulf of Mexico. It is likely that most Spanish sailing vessels plying the Gulf waters in the 1500s were caravels and naos not unlike the vessels that had brought Columbus to the New World.

A remarkable world map by Martin Waldseemüller in 1507 is reportedly the first to show what appears to be the entire Gulf of Mexico, including the Texas coast (Fig. 2-5). On it we can seem to recognize Florida, the familiar bowl-shaped curve of the Gulf, and the Yucatán peninsula. And yet, this map is quite enigmatic, for there were no known voyages into the Gulf at this early date. Because Waldseemüller's map is considered by many to be the first to clearly show the Texas coast, however, it demands more interpretation. How, one may ask, can it, and other maps of the period, such as the Cantino maps, show the Texas Gulf coast when no mariners are known to have experienced it at this early date?

The search for an answer to this question places us at the center of a debate in the history of cartography. Some scholars contend that the coast was indeed known at this time, actually long before Columbus's voyage, by the Portuguese, who were in possession of an ancient map prepared by the sea-faring Phoenicians.[7] Others feel that early maps showing what amounts to too much information may indeed represent pre-Columbian knowledge, but in the form of information conveyed to the early Spanish by Native Americans—perhaps the advanced peoples of Mesoamerica—who assisted the Spanish in gaining greater knowledge about the Americas than their voyages alone could yield.[8]

Others offer the possibility that Spain had opportunity to explore the Texas coast from its developing foothold in the Caribbean, and that such voyages were either kept secret or lost to the record—except for the tantalizing remnant on maps of the period.[9] Still other researchers note that geographic information (including toponymy and topography) was provided by mariners such as Amerigo Vespucci, who, they claim, delineated at least the eastern Gulf, Florida, and a substantial portion of the southeast Atlantic coast by the early 1500s.[10]

Still others, however, contend that the Waldseemüller map and other

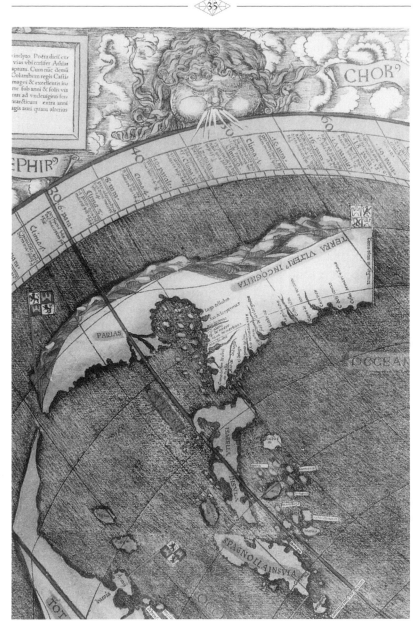

FIGURE 2-5.
*The world map by Martin Waldseemüller in 1507 is considered by some to show the
entire Gulf of Mexico, including the Texas coast, but is enigmatic because no known
exploration occurred on the Gulf that early. Courtesy Special Collections Division,
The University of Texas at Arlington Libraries, Arlington, Texas.*

early maps are quite inaccurate but that we, who have a knowledge of the Gulf today, read more into the maps than what is actually there. These map historians contend that these early maps were based on persistent but fragmentary knowledge of *Asia*, and that what *appear* to be the Gulf, Florida, and Yucatán are nothing more than primitive attempts to depict what we know today to be the Gulf of Tonkin (or South China Sea) and the land masses of China and Indochina: Their reasoning is based on the concept that cartography is largely imitative, incomplete, conjectural, and sometimes even retrogressive.[11] The latter argument, however sobering or deflating, has some merit because maps of the Gulf soon lost their beautiful simplicity and became quite convoluted as mariners more aggressively explored and charted the area after about 1520 on voyages that are documented in the Spanish archives. Like all voyages, these yielded fragmentary, but often topographically more accurate, information—for certain portions of the Texas coast at least.

Certainly, by the very early 1510s, Spanish vessels had ventured into the Gulf, and its general outline was taking rough shape on maps. Now that the Spanish realized they had not reached Asia and were confronted by a new, unexplored land mass, they began to focus their efforts on two approaches. The first involved exploiting the resources of the new lands through aggressive searches for riches and colonization. The 1519 voyage of Cortés would forever destine central Mexico to be a major focus of Spain. The coast that would later be recognized as Texas, however, was peripheral, as it was farthest from two points of intensely exploitative Spanish activity: the Indies (especially Cuba), and the southwestern Gulf closest to Mexico City. The second focus of the Spanish, however, would ensure that Texas received some attention, for it involved the search for a passageway *through* the new continent that could ensure that Spain would meet its destiny of exploiting the orient. The early 1500s thus marked a search for the legendary Straits of Anian or *passo del noroeste* (passage to the Northwest) that would consume the efforts of Spain, France, and England for generations. As it turned out, the aggressive search for the mythical strait would show explorers by the mid-sixteenth century that Texas offered no such connection; the journey of Lewis and Clark of 1803–1806, for example, still embodied a search for an easy riverine passage through the continent—a passage that would never be found.

Despite the major advances in shipbuilding technology that enabled Spain to reach the New World and expand into the Gulf, detailed geographic knowledge lagged. The area that bore the name "Florida," but which includes most or all of what we today call Texas, only slowly took form on maps. With voyages deeper into the Gulf, however, geographic knowledge began to increase as the coast was soon recognized to be rather complex — a curving embayment crammed full of river deltas and interfluves. Moreover, it should be remembered that the Spanish were not the only Europeans interested in this area. Sebastian Cabot's 1544 map reveals a crenulated coastline with names of locations on the coast placed much like the drafters of the portolan charts so common to navigators since about 1300.[12] It took several decades into the sixteenth century for the coast of Texas to take form in the minds of the Spanish, whose master map (or, more properly, mother map) in Seville was becoming more accurate with each voyage.

Who were the first Europeans to reconnoiter the Texas coast? The various arguments outlined above notwithstanding, the written record reveals that Captain Alonso Alvarez de Pineda and his sailors are generally believed among the first to explore the coast of Texas. In 1519, as part of a group sent to establish a colony at the Rio de las Palmas, near what some scholars believe to be today's Brownsville on the lower Rio Grande, Pineda is thought to have sailed into Corpus Christi Bay. His descriptions certainly portray an embayment sheltered from the coast, but that can describe many places along the Texas coast. As noted earlier, these embayments and inlets were particularly enticing to Europeans searching for a strait that could take them directly to the orient, for by now they realized that they were exploring a huge and lightly populated continent, not Asia. No indisputable evidence exists that Pineda actually landed at Corpus Christi, though the so-called Piñeda tablet, with his name and an inscribed date of 1519, claims he did. In proximity to the tablet were found pieces of an old vessel described as lapstrake held together with wooden dowels.[13] From this description, one can only deduce that the vessel featured a technique of construction common to the sixteenth-century Spanish vessels. Nevertheless, Corpus Christi bears the name recorded in Pineda's diary in commemoration of the religious holiday on which his landing on the Texas coast occurred. Despite its being named and located on an early map, no Spanish settlement would occur in Corpus Christi — or anywhere else on the Texas coast during the sixteenth century. The map attributed to Pineda (Fig. 2-6), however, is widely recognized as the first cartographic representation of the Texas coast.

The 1520s marked a time of continued Spanish exploration of the Gulf coast, often with tragic results. The first Spanish written record of Indians on the Texas coast is from their encounter with the famed Alvar Nuñez Cabeza de Vaca. In this incident, the Indians and Spanish were, nautically

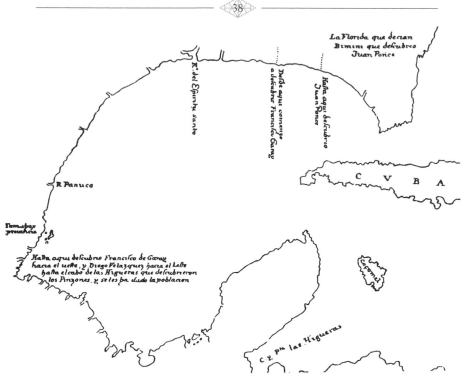

FIGURE 2-6

The so-called Piñeda chart of 1519 is from the expedition of Captain Alonso Alvarez de Pineda and is widely considered the first map to show the Texas coast. Courtesy Special Collections Division, The University of Texas at Arlington Libraries, Arlington, Texas.

speaking, more or less on the same terms. The arrival of the first Europeans to make actual documented landfall in Texas occurred, by all accounts, as a result of the disastrous Narváez expedition, which first landed on the Florida shore and then made its way westward into the Gulf on a series of improvised rafts or barges. Caught by a storm, the barges became separated and two of the battered craft were beached on an island (probably San Luis or today's Follet's Island) off the Texas coast. It was this mishap along the Texas coastline in November 1528 that would become legendary in the annals of shipwrecks along the hazardous northern shore of the Gulf. It is from this shipwreck that the *Relación* of Cabeza de Vaca was written, a story that has become among the most oft-told in Texas history but is still controversial, as scholars continue to debate exactly where the shipwrecked group of eighty survivors landed. Most accounts place the landing near today's Galveston.[14]

Cabeza de Vaca's careful recording of his group's trials and tribulations and his astute observations of the landscape and peoples have shaped perceptions of the Texas coast since they were first published in 1539. In his masterful writings, Cabeza de Vaca describes in detail his being shipwrecked with companions, most of whom died in the wreck or in subsequent altercations with the Indians. Only Cabeza de Vaca and three other survivors reached Mexico on foot after a grueling trek along the coast and inland that took six years. Cabeza de Vaca documented the Indians and their watercraft, and revealed how vulnerable the Spanish were when cast in the wilderness separate from the maritime equipment and technology that brought them to those distant shores. That Cabeza de Vaca's story continues to capture the public's imagination in Texas and Mexico is borne out by the fact that it was made into a popular Mexican feature film in 1993.[15]

The story of the Texas coast during the 1500s and into the 1600s is one of recurring tragedy, and it reveals the extent to which shipping depends on both superior skill in handling a vessel in the face of hazardous conditions and good navigational skills. Although early mariners used a process known as "dead reckoning" (that is, determining their *location* by estimating the *distance* sailed in a particular *direction*), seafarers of the period needed a more accurate method when the distances that they sailed increased: Dead reckoning is of limited utility because any miscalculation in either the distance sailed (which was measured by timing the ship's passage compared with that of a chip or log that, tied to a string, was tossed overboard) or the direction (which could be approximated using fixed landmarks or heavenly bodies such as the sun or stars) would be compounded daily. An error in either or both could result in huge discrepancies, great inconvenience, and even tragedy. Although the magnetic compass had been introduced as early as the twelfth century in the Mediterranean, and it helped sailors determine direction, a way was needed to locate the ship's actual *position* at any one time. By knowing the vessel's latitude (that is, distance north or south of the equator), navigators could come closer to determining their position. Doing so required the ability to use the sun, whose position varied according to date, and was easy to calculate. As long as sailors knew the date of the year, they could extrapolate their latitude by comparing their positions at noon with that of the sun.

Even though latitude was relatively easy to calculate, the issue of determining longitude would remain unresolved for a considerably longer time, leaving mariners with only one option—namely, making calculated guesses as to the actual location of a vessel east or west of a particular point. As early as 1498, Jamie Farrar experimented with methods of determining longitude by using lunar eclipses or positions of the rising moon in reference to the horizon, but the determination of longitude would remain elusive for at least two centuries. Thus, mariners along the Texas coast generally had a good idea of how far north of the equator—but not how far west of Seville—they were.

We have a fairly good idea how sailors and vessels of the period navigated and maneuvered, or attempted to do so, but one needs to ask several questions about the vessels themselves. How did the typical Spanish vessels of the period that conveyed sailors along the Texas coast actually look? How were their hulls designed? What type of rigging did they possess? Because vessels of the period were made using full-scale templates at the shipyard, and these templates were not saved, we have no plans in the traditional sense (miniaturized, measured drawings) for these vessels. Although the evidence is thus largely conjectural, early drawings and engravings of similar vessels reveal the characteristic curving hull, with high fore and aft castles and a low waist; some were probably naos—the generic term for any rather large cargo vessel—much like the *Santa Maria*. Their rigging consisted of square-rigged main and mizzen masts with sprit sails. Others were more properly classed as carracks, which featured three masts and multiple layered decks. Because they could expect to encounter unfriendly Portuguese or English vessels, the Spanish vessels sailing the Gulf were often armed with upwards of a dozen cannons pointing outwards through ports in the bulky hull. They often traveled in small groups of three or more, as each vessel could assist the other(s) in the event of a problem at sea (Fig. 2-7).

Although most European vessels of exploration were of this bulky appearance, it is said that the Spaniards' capture of Sir John Hawkins's *Jesus of Lubeck* at San Juan de Ulloa off the Spanish coast so incensed the Englishman in 1567 that he designed a much fleeter vessel of war that would become the prototype for the "man of war" fighting ships of the seventeenth and eighteenth centuries. Rather than building new vessels to test his ideas, Hawkins reportedly modified older vessels to lie lower in the water by cutting down their high sides, and removing the high forecastle and replacing it with a low structure set further aft on the foredeck; he increased the length-to-beam ratio of the hull from 2 1/2 to 1, to 3 to 1, resulting in a much leaner or fleeter vessel. Hawkins also squared off the rounded stern. As a result of these treatments, English galleons came to be called "low-charged."[16] These military changes so increased the performance of vessels that they spread to English merchant sailing vessels as well; the adoption of successful military

FIGURE 2-7

Spanish vessels in the 1500s often sailed in groups of three or more, as depicted in this mural at the Corpus Christi Museum. Photo by the author, 1995.

technology to other aspects of life is a common trend in maritime as well as other aspects of society. However, the Spanish reportedly did not adopt these changes until well into the seventeenth century, and thus most of the vessels sailing the Gulf coast off Texas were still high-charged and somewhat clumsy.

That may have accounted for some of the spectacular and disastrous wrecks in Spanish shipping along the Texas coast—the most spectacular of which occurred in 1554. Once again a shipwreck would bring the Spanish in contact with the native peoples and tribulations of the Texas coast, and once again it was a storm that drove vessels from farther east in the Gulf to their grief on the Texas shore. On April 9, 1554, four vessels—the *Santa Maria de Yciar*, the *San Estéban*, the *Espíritu Santo*, and the *San Andrés*— left San Juan de Ulua, Mexico, to return to Spain by way of Havana, Cuba. They had no intention of nearing Texas, which was a marginal corner of the Gulf with little prospects or promise. On April 29, however, fate intervened and three of the vessels (*Santa Maria de Yciar*; *San Estéban*; and *Espíritu Santo*) either were blown out of control, or tried to beat a storm, westward, in hopes of outrunning it, when they ran aground off Padre Island. Only the *San Andrés* arrived in Havana, and word filtered back that the other three

FIGURE 2-8

Illustration from Pedro de Ledesma's account of vessel salvage techniques, circa 1623, reveals that the Spanish were ingenious and enterprising in salvaging vessels and their contents. From David McDonald and J. Barto Arnold III, Documentary Sources for the Wreck of the Spain Fleet of 1554. *Reproduced with permission.*

vessels had come to grief on the Texas coast, which at that time was called the Costa de Magdalena or Medanos (sand bank) part of La Florida.[17] In one of the more tragic of Spain's misfortunes in the New World, virtually all of those driven ashore either were first drowned upon leaving the ships, or died of exposure, or fell under the stinging arrows of the coastal Indians. To add drama to the tragedy, a priest in Mexico reportedly had forewarned the group of the disaster but, according to oral tradition, they ignored his warning and set sail.

Written records left a fair account of the tragedy, for salvage ships soon scoured the area and retrieved what was possible to salvage (about 41 percent of the cargo) using state-of-the-art techniques. This operation included dragged chains and, possibly, divers assisted by large, heavy, metal diving bells that trapped and retained air for their use under water. An illustration from the sixteenth century (Fig. 2-8) shows some of the remarkably ingenious and enterprising techniques that the Spanish used to salvage vessels and/or their contents.[18] Under the direction of García Escalante Alvarado, six salvage vessels (four barks or *chalupas* and two large vessels—the *Mendoza* and the *Santo Espíritus*) with a crew of over one hundred, including eleven divers,[19] salvaged what they could of the vessels, which lay in about eighteen feet of water. Only a portion of the silver was recovered, and the loss of these vessels on the Texas coast represented a serious setback to Spain. It also added to the reputation of the Texas coast as a place of desolation and misfortune.

The fate of these Spanish vessels would have been relegated to archival records had it not been for hurricane Carla, which struck the Texas coast in 1961, exposing the wrecked vessels, which had lain less than two miles apart for more than four centuries. Treasure hunters flocked to the site, followed by the commercial enterprise Platoro of Indiana, which stripped much of the wreckage until a court order required that all the material taken from the wreck be returned to Texas. Today the remains of these Spanish vessels are on exhibit at the Corpus Christi Museum. The museum's exhibit features a partial conjectural reconstruction of one of them, consisting of its raised fore and aft decks, which conveys a general sense of the size and shape of a Spanish sailing vessel of the era. The artifacts from the vessel, which is assumed to be the *San Estéban*, include silver bars and coins, a gold cross, and several astrolabes. Of the vessel itself, only a few keel timbers (Fig. 2-9), iron nails, and anchors (Fig. 2-10) remain—a reminder of how fragile and ephemeral wooden vessels are in a marine coastal environment.

Using the evidence from the shipwreck and a careful consultation of the records, J. Barto Arnold III and Robert Weddle provided a detailed discussion of the technology of vessels, much like those unfortunate three that went aground off the Texas coast at Padre Island in 1554.[20] They noted that the Spanish crown had begun to encourage private mercantile shipping but had no specialized navy vessels at the time, so that "all ships were adaptable to a degree to both purposes."[21] Accordingly, these vessels were equipped with cannons, some weighing more than 750 pounds. Arnold and Weddle also noted that Alvaro de Bazán and his son of the same name had pioneered the application of a number of technological advancements in the early 1500s, including copper bilge pumps, lead sheathing to protect hulls from worms that bored into hulls (teredoes), the mixing of wood preservative into wax used to treat hulls, and the development of large (three-hundred-ton) galleons, which were faster despite being able to hold larger cargoes and a greater number of passengers.[22] Thus, although Spain soon had to limit the size of vessels in the American trade to four hundred tons, it

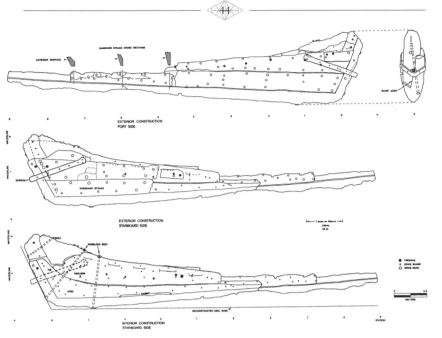

FIGURE 2-9

The Spanish shipwrecks that occurred off the Texas coast in 1554 have yielded much information about both the vessels and their cargoes. This illustration of the keel of Spanish vessels permitted a conjectural reconstruction of the vessel. Courtesy J. Barto Arnold, Texas Historical Commission, Austin.

FIGURE 2-10

Among the longest-lasting of marine artifacts are wrought iron anchors, such as these from the 1554 shipwrecks off the Texas coast at Padre Island. Courtesy J. Barto Arnold, Texas Historical Commission, Austin.

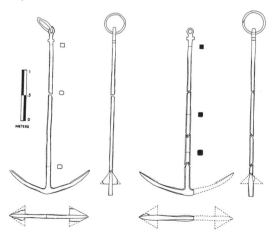

can be said that those in the sixteenth century had begun evolving from tub-like vessels to somewhat fleeter vessels with a shallower draft, less free board, and finer lines at bow and stern.[23]

Typically, vessels of the early to middle sixteenth century were steered by cumbersome tillers connected to the rudder; this tiller required great strength to control. Navigation was achieved with the astrolabe and the quadrant, a device a quarter circle in shape, calibrated in degrees from 0 to 90. By keeping the quadrant level with a plumb line and the quadrant pointed toward a pole star at night, latitude could be determined; however, such determinations were made all the more difficult by the motion of the vessel.

From the logs of the *Santa Maria de Yciar* and *Nuestra Señora de la Concepción*, we can deduce that the vessels were well supplied for the return trip. The cargo included sardines, anchovies, tuna fish, sugar, flour, raisins, and eggs packed in barrels; garlic, beans and peas, flour, and barrels of wine; rice, cheeses, hardtack, bacon/ham slabs, and olives; and barreled and dried fish, and butchered hogs. Drinking water was carried in casks. The load also included supplies to repair the vessels if needed, including grease, wax, caulking, bolts, chains, and hinges.

Because Spain was, in effect, provisioning the New World in hopes of developing producing colonies, animals were often carried on board. Larger animals such as horses, oxen, and cattle were common, and they required feed and water. So, too, did smaller animals, such as dogs, hogs, and chickens. The typical Spanish vessel, then, could be thought of as a floating supplier of colonies on its trip to the New World; hopefully, it would return to Spain with riches of various kinds, including precious metals. Records reveal a lively flow of colonists to the New World (many of whom replaced dwindling numbers of Indian slaves) and wealthy individuals returning to Spain. It should be remembered, however, that it would be another century and a half before Spain would colonize Texas. The wrecks of the vessels from 1554 merely occurred in Texas as a coincidence, or rather tragedy, occasioned by the power of the wind to upset the plans of the Spanish crown.

Many recorders have noted that daily life on board vessels of the period was monotonous and, by today's standards, inconvenient if not arduous. Cooking on board ship was done over a bin of sand to reduce the ever-present danger of fire, though some vessels possessed a *fogón*, or metal firebox that served as a galley. Drinking water was kept in casks, but wine, which was less likely to spoil and often preferred, was also stored in barrels or casks. Diseases were common, and the medical needs of the crew and passengers were met by a supply of medicine, including turpentine made from the

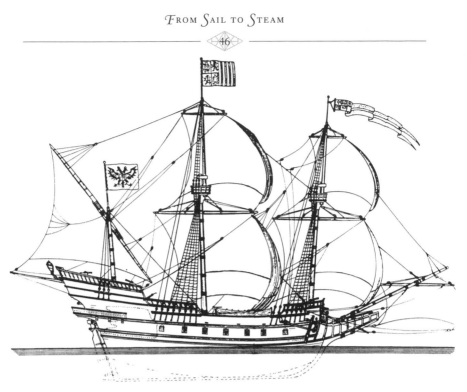

FIGURE 2-11

This starboard side plan of the Nuestra Señora de Atocha, *drawn by the shipwreck historian Bill Muir, is typical of the Spanish galleons that sailed the waters off Texas in the 1600s. From* Treasure of the Atocha, *by R. Duncan Mathewson III. Copyright © 1986 by R. Duncan Mathewson III. Published by Gulf Publishing Company, Houston, Texas. Used with permission. All rights reserved.*

trunks of pine trees, salves, and liquid and powdered medicines. Sanitary facilities were either nonexistent or very limited: human (and animal) wastes were directed over the side of the vessel or into the bilge—the latter necessitating a periodic cleaning of the ballast in the hull; on later vessels a seat, nicknamed *el jardín* (the garden) by crews, was installed at the bow; as more women began to travel, the *jardín* might be covered, helping to relieve the indignity voiced by more than one female traveler surrounded by a crew of male sailors. Sleeping locations were stratified. Many sailors slept on the decks in fair weather, and paying passengers often slept below decks in quarters that were cramped, filthy, and damp.

Although it apparently did not sail the Texas Gulf coast, *Nuestra Señora de Atocha* (Fig. 2-11) was representative of the larger vessels that were the mainstay of Spanish trade and exploration in the late sixteenth and early seventeenth centuries. *Nuestra Señora de Atocha* was built in Havana in

1620, about a century after the first recorded Spanish landfall in Texas. Most vessels of this type were bulky and, despite some armament, not particularly good in battle. Because of their high sides, these "high-charged" vessels were hard to sail into cross winds and, worse, were especially vulnerable to being blown out of control by strong winds that could catch them athwart and push them to their doom against rocky coasts and offshore shoals. Such a fate befell the *Nuestra Señora de Atocha*, which foundered off the Florida coast.

Both the written record and shipwrecks have helped us understand the design of vessels of the period, but other sources may also be consulted. Interestingly, we have learned much about such vessels not from scale drawings or plans, which did not exist at the time, but from maps, which often feature drawings of vessels (Fig. 2-12). Some of these are depicted with

FIGURE 2-12

The state of knowledge of the Gulf by the Spanish in the late sixteenth century is revealed by the beautiful Nueva Hispania Tabula Nova *(1569 and reprinted in 1599), which features a drawing of a two-masted, high-charged sailing vessel in the Pacific and a map displaying the rivers and Gulf coast of Texas in considerably greater detail than earlier maps. Courtesy of the Cartographic Collections of Mrs. Jenkins Garrett, Fort Worth, housed in the Cartographic History Library at The University of Texas at Arlington Libraries, Arlington.*

remarkable accuracy, and in some cases they are our only source of visual information about the vessels of a particular era. According to David Buisseret, a historian of cartography, "Maps and ships have now gone together for a long time, not only in the sense that Western mariners have used some form of chart for at least eight hundred years, but also in the way that historians of shipbuilding have for many years now used the visual evidence present on so many early maps."[24]

Because both maps and ships were the tools of empire, their juxtaposition is understandable. Mariners needed maps, and maps were an excellent format upon which to illustrate the vessels of the period of exploration. We can also learn about vessels of the era from models, that is, miniaturizations of the original ships. As Roger Smith noted, the first three-dimensional evidence of a fifteenth-century Iberian (Spanish) vessel occurred in the form of a votive model that once graced a church, the model builder using the maritime techniques of the day to construct the model.[25] A votive model of a vessel was often provided by a sailor who escaped shipwreck or drowning, and as such it symbolized the deep respect, even fear, that mariners had of the sea during that period.

As noted above, we also learn from the shipwrecks that are occasionally found after having been abandoned for centuries, sometimes after partial salvage operations. Thus, although only the stern part of the keel remained from one of the 1554 shipwrecks off Padre Island, it enabled nautical archaeologists and historians to deduce the vessel's length (the range being 20 meters, or 66 feet, to 30 meters, or 97 feet) and weight or capacity/displacement (which ranged from 164 tons to 286 tons).[26] From these 1554 shipwrecks much has been learned, through careful speculation and scientific observation, about the actual type of vessels that met their demise on the Texas coast that fateful spring of 1554.

Other shipwrecks plagued Spain in other parts of the Gulf during the late sixteenth and early seventeenth centuries, but for the most part the Texas coast remained a remote corner of Spain's empire. Spain claimed the area, but did little to colonize it, for she was busy defending interests elsewhere. In addition to shipwrecks and piracy in the Gulf, another event also signaled the beginning of Spain's demise as a maritime power. Half a world away, the Spanish Armada was decimated by English warships in the North Sea in 1588. The maritime historian Peter Kemp noted that Spain's losses were due, in part, to the superior design, rather than size, of English vessels. The high-charged Spanish vessels were easy targets for the lower-profile English counterparts, which, when close-hauled into the facing wind, could also outmaneuver the Spanish vessels. The defeat of the Armada proved that Spain could not protect her trade by sea power. Moreover, the fact that Spain maintained oppressive control over trade, rather than encouraging maritime enterprise as the English (and Dutch) had with the creation of the East India companies, did not bode well for the future of Spain's American empire.

Throughout the late 1500s to the middle 1600s, Spanish vessels of fairly traditional and increasingly obsolete design plied the Gulf, for the most part carrying silver back to treasuries and coffers of Spain, but precipitating an inflationary crisis in Europe in the process. Readers interested in Spanish vessels of the seventeenth century should read the most definitive work on the subject, *Six Galleons for the King of Spain*, by Carla Rahn Phillips.[27] Several voyages featuring vessels of reconnaissance had charted the coast in greater detail by the middle seventeenth century, so that the Spanish had developed a fair idea of the Texas shoreline, which seemed daunting and inhospitable—and perhaps best explored by land rather than sea.

The first century and a half of Spanish maritime history in Texas must be viewed as exploratory, but it may seem somewhat perplexing that during that period Spain made no significant attempt to actually colonize the coast. Within 150 years of Spain's first contact with the Texas coast, however, the region's geography was fairly well understood, and vessels were evolving to suit the needs of military expeditions and commercial enterprises. Increases in geographic knowledge of the Gulf, reflected in maps of the sixteenth and seventeenth centuries, were attained, as David Buisseret noted, in two stages during this period:[28]

1. 1519–1544

Beginning with the so-called Piñeda Chart after the 1519 voyage, maps correctly showed that there was no passage to the Pacific, and some marked certain features with remarkable accuracy. The Hernán Cortéz map of 1524 is in some respects less accurate than the Pineda map, but it depicts what appears to be the Rio Grande and other rivers. Maps from this period show little information of the topography inland, of course, because most expeditions were nautical.

2. 1544–1680

As a consequence of De Soto's expedition to the east and north of the Texas coast, a new style of map appeared. Significantly, these maps show the rivers of the interior; and some show a mountainous barrier to the north. Significantly, too, the maps of this period often depict Indian tribes.

The importance of rivers to exploration becomes apparent during this later period, as Texas rivers emptying into the Gulf—such as the Trinity, Sabine, Rio del Oro, Magdalena—are depicted, and the embayments of the coast are delineated in considerable detail. As French cartographers came into their own in the 1650s, maps of the Gulf featured considerably more detail and were more accurate. Spain, which had claimed much of the region since the earliest days of European exploration, became increasingly concerned about challenges to its control of its northern frontier—the northern Gulf and its marginally claimed land, including the area that would someday be known as Texas. The words *Golfe de Mexique* on French maps must have been deemed particularly galling, for they represented a threat to Spain's hegemony in the region. This threat was indeed to materialize, as France was soon to attempt the planting of a colony on the very shores of Texas claimed by Spain.

TROUBLE ON THE
SPANISH SEA
1685–1821

Texas as a Spanish province was a top priority
only when it was threatened.
ROBERT WEDDLE, *The French Thorn*

In July of 1995, Texas newspapers carried a fascinating story that was variously headlined as "17th Century Cannon Found in Texas Bay"[1] and "Artifact pulled from bay may be old cannon."[2] As reported by the Associated
Press and local papers, a three-hundred-year-old cannon weighing fifteen
hundred pounds (its weight is actually 793 1/2 pounds)[3] was recovered in
Matagorda Bay near Port Lavaca. "This achievement," according to Curtis
Tunnel, executive director of the Texas Historical Commission, "ends a
search that has been going on for 300 years, and represents a rich acquisition for the State of Texas."[4]

The epic search that Curtis Tunnel referred to has become one of the
legends in Texas maritime history—the arrival in 1685 of the French explorer La Salle, who founded the first European community, however ill-
fated, in what is today Texas. La Salle's fascinating and tragic story has been
told many times, most ably by Robert Weddle in numerous books listed in
the bibliography, including *Wilderness Manhunt* (1973), *La Salle, the Mississippi and the Gulf* (1987), and *The French Thorn* (1991). It is a story that
underscores the importance of the Texas coast to European exploration and
discovery. La Salle's story is also a reminder of how hard-pressed Spain was
to defend its northern frontier, and how poorly it did so despite having been
first to make landfall there more than a century before La Salle arrived.

The story begins with the 1684 voyage of René-Robert Cavelier, Sieur de
La Salle, who left La Rochelle, France, in four vessels on a transatlantic
voyage in search of the mouth of the Mississippi. About three hundred people
were aboard the vessels, many of them would-be settlers who hoped to
help found a French colony where the Mississippi River joined the Gulf.

La Salle sailed westward across the Atlantic and into the Caribbean, where his troubles began. One of his vessels—the unarmed cutter (*barque, caïque,* or *caiche*) *Saint François*—was captured by two Spanish vessels. Inconvenienced but not deterred from his goal, La Salle proceeded westward with three vessels—the *Belle,* the *Joly,* and the *Aimable.*[5] Disoriented, or more properly, lost, as a result of a faulty astrolabe and a debilitating mental state, La Salle found an opening on the Gulf Coast into which two vessels, the barque *Belle* and the stores ship *Aimable,* sailed. Within the shelter of Matagorda Bay, which he called "Baye St. Louis," in February of 1685, these vessels were soon joined by the *Joly* (sometimes written *Le Jolly,* or *Jolly*), which had been separated earlier on the voyage.

The record shows that La Salle thought he had found the mouth of the Mississippi, but had indeed erred. In Matagorda Bay, actually more than 250 nautical miles west of the Mississippi, La Salle attempted to establish a fort, but he met with more travails: While trying to enter a narrow channel in Matagorda Bay, the *Aimable* stuck in the mud in shallows on February 29 and sank slowly until out of sight on March 7, 1685. The group became dispirited, and experienced another major setback as the *Joly* departed for France, leaving about 180 of the despairing colonists behind[6] but taking with it other would-be colonists and considerable supplies. Obsessed with continuing the mission to settle the area, La Salle remained in charge of the colonists and, during the spring, set out with about fifty men in canoes to reconnoiter the bay. In October of that year, La Salle and fifty of his men searched fruitlessly for the mouth of the Mississippi, joined in the process by the *Belle.* Things worsened in January of 1686, when La Salle left the *Belle* to explore the land around the bay, only to return to find that his prized vessel had been driven by a norther and grounded on the sand of Matagorda Peninsula, after which she was reportedly plundered by the natives. La Salle now found himself without any seaworthy vessels and short of supplies. Created under such circumstances and experiencing such repeated setbacks, Fort Saint Louis was destined to fail. The story of this star-crossed expedition and colonization effort concludes with La Salle's murder by his own mutinous, dwindling ranks about a year later (March 20, 1687), at a location farther east in Texas (some claim near the present-day Navasota, while others place the location on the Trinity River)—as he searched for the Mississippi on foot. An ignominious death for an explorer.

Following the apparent discovery of the *Belle* shipwreck by the persistent Texas maritime archaeologist J. Barto Arnold III, researchers mounted a search of the French records in order to confirm the identity of the wreck.

In other words, although a significant amount of the vessel believed to be the *Belle* lay entombed under about two feet of silt and sand in about twelve feet of water, a comparison of what had been written about the vessel would need to be made to confirm its identity. A search of all written documentation revealed that many assumptions had been made about just what type of vessel the *Belle* actually was. The matter was made even more complex, and intriguing, because the contemporaries who reported the loss of the *Belle* did so in several languages. For example, contemporary Spanish accounts of the *Belle* reveal her to be a *fragata*. Although a modern Spanish-English dictionary would translate fragata as frigate, caution should be used in doing so: Whereas a frigate can refer to large, square-rigged war vessels intermediate between corvettes and ships of the line, an earlier definition finds it identifying a light boat originally propelled by oars but later by sail. Generically, fragata is a term often used for a tender, that is, a vessel that supplies other vessels. Most fragatas of the period were used to supply ships of war and commerce, and so the *Belle* would seem a reasonable choice to send on a colonization mission with military overtones.

Thus, although fragata may conjure certain images, the archaeologists needed to know, as accurately as possible, what the *Belle* actually looked like as an operational vessel. In *La Salle, The Mississippi, and the Gulf,* Robert Weddle used primary sources to determine that the *Belle*'s keel was 36 feet; using this dimension, original estimates of 50 to 60 feet for the entire vessel were generally considered reasonable. Initial archaeological investigations at the shipwreck site revealed that the *Belle* might be somewhat longer, approximately 80 feet in length with a beam of about 20 feet.[7] And what of her sail plan? Because French accounts of the *Belle* mention her mizzen mast and main mast, some researchers reached the logical but erroneous conclusion that she was a three-masted vessel. This conclusion was based on the fact that although the *Belle*'s foremast is never mentioned specifically, she should seemingly have one because the term *main* normally refers to a center mast, *mizzen* to the stern mast, and so, logically, the vessel should possess a foremast (that is, a mast placed in front of the main mast). Although some maritime historians were rather skeptical that a relatively small vessel like the *Belle* would have so full a sail pattern, such configurations were certainly known. However, research by Arnold has revealed that the French used the term *mizzen* for the foremast, and this revelation considerably cleared up the issue. After careful research of written French records in 1995 and 1996, Arnold concluded that the *Belle* was a two-masted, square-rigged vessel called a *barque-longue*,[8] as illustrated in

FIGURE 3-1

An artist's rendition of a barque longue, *similar in basic sail pattern to La Salle's*
Belle, *reveals a relatively small, highly versatile vessel well suited for provisioning
an expedition. Illustration courtesy J. Barto Arnold, Texas Historical
Commission, Austin.*

Figure 3-1. Excavation of the wreckage of the *Belle* beginning in the fall of
1996 was expected to confirm this conclusion. Arnold's diligent search in
the French maritime records revealed that the vessel was built in Rochefort,
France in 1683–84.[9] That would explain the Spanish references to her being
a nearly new vessel at the time of her sinking and further explain La Salle's
despair at her loss.

That the *Belle* was armed is confirmed by the written record and the
stunning discovery of the wreck in Matagorda Bay. Estimates of her armaments vary and, according to J. F. Jameson, are based on conjectural descriptions of La Salle's vessels: Some claim that the *Belle* appears to have

been armed with 48 guns, which is unlikely given her rather small size, while the *Joly*, La Salle's man-of-war and chief vessel, carried 30 guns according to the French historian Pierre Margry and 36 to 40 according to Henri Joutel, the preeminent eyewitness historian of La Salle's expedition.[10] Referring to a fragment of the log of the *Belle*, Joutel described the vessel as the smallest of the three vessels, a little frigate or barque of about a sixty-ton capacity, armed with six cannons, and commanded by two masters—Captain Morraud (or Moraud) and Pilot Elie Richaud, who commanded the vessel after the captain's death.[11] The latter description is probably reasonable: The *Belle* was probably a small, and modestly armed, vessel that was used to supply the would-be colony. A *barque-longue* of this type would normally be a rather good choice for the task, a versatile vessel in the hands of good seamen, at least in good conditions.

Although images of vessels from this period are scarce, a set of line drawings in Jean Boudriot's *Historique de la Corvette, 1650–1850* provides considerable detail regarding the type of vessels used by La Salle in the Texas exploration.[12] Maps of the period are also helpful, for many depict vessels either as part of their decoration or as a way of better illustrating the stories of expeditions they chronicle. For example, an image of "Le Jolly" is found on Minet's maps of Pass (or Paso) Cavalo entitled "Plan de l'entree du lac" (Fig. 3-2). As noted by Arnold, the map's accuracy of the shoreline is remarkable;[13] furthermore, the drawing of the *Joly*, although somewhat conjectural, generally describes French vessels of the period: Even at this small scale, one can determine the vessel's relatively low forecastle and tall afterdeck. In this drawing, the *Joly* carries what appears to be two masts, square rigging, and a prominent jib.

Among the most noteworthy of numerous illustrations depicting the vessels associated with La Salle is the beautiful sketch of the *Joly* that reportedly accompanied the letters of L'Archevêque and Grollet, the stranded compatriots of La Salle who requested that the Spanish rescue them from their plight on the Texas coast. As reproduced by the Heliotype Company of Boston (Fig. 3-3), the drawing on parchment depicts a starboard-side view of the vessel, which is three-masted and possesses the characteristic profile of French vessels of the period—a high-charged aft section with a relatively low forecastle/bow. The vessel in question also features a gracefully curved bowsprit and a prominent jib. This drawing is so detailed that the rigging and yards are shown clearly, and the sails are set on the fore and main masts, while the mizzen also features a lateen-rigged sail. An illustration of a similar but more heavily armed vessel from the period 1674 to 1730 in Léon

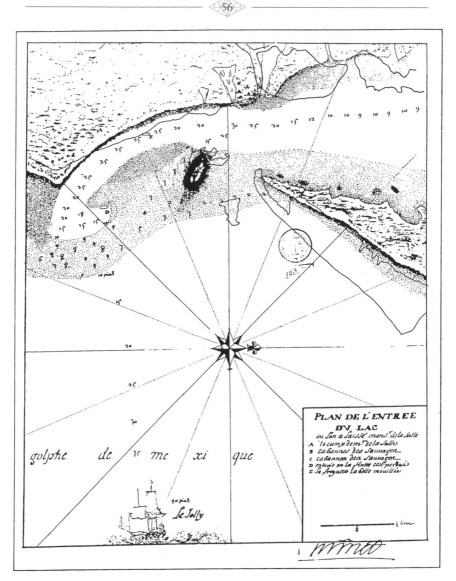

FIGURE 3-2
An image of Le Jolly *is found on Minet's maps of Pass Cavalo entitled*
"Plan de l'Entree du Lac." Courtesy J. Barto Arnold III, Texas Historical
Commission, Austin.

Guérin's classic *Histoire Maritime de France* (Fig. 3-4) confirms the basic configuration of French sailing vessels of the era that very likely traversed the Texas coast. This type of vessel represents a logical compromise: Its generous sail pattern would help make it fast, yet its lateen rigging can be set to take advantage of variable winds. Its double rows of cannons on separate decks made it a formidable adversary in military encounters, while its deep hull would enable it to haul supplies and cargo. Like all vessels of relatively deep draft, however, it was susceptible to running aground in shallow waters—a lesson learned at such a high price by La Salle in Matagorda Bay despite his using moderate-sized vessels for the expedition.

A detailed illustration of a late-seventeenth-century French warship is

FIGURE 3-3
*By far the most noteworthy illustration of La Salle's vessel Joly was reportedly found among the letters of L'Archevêque and Grollet. As reproduced by the Heliotype Company of Boston, it depicts a portside view of the vessel, which is three-masted and possesses the characteristic profile of French vessels of the period.
Courtesy the University of Texas Archives, Austin.*

found in *Le Neptune François, ou Atlas nouveau des cartes marines,* an atlas produced for the use of captains in the navy of Louis XIV.[14] This cross section or cutaway drawing (Fig. 3-5) beautifully reveals the vessel's construction and the detailed rigging. Of particular interest is the substantial construction of the hull, with its keelson. Note, too, the manner in which the masts are secured to the vessel's hull and superstructure, and the fact that virtually all parts of the rigging are identified. A hundred-gun vessel of this kind represented the epitome of naval power at the time but it is possible that such warships sailed near the Texas coast on occasion, as France maintained a strong presence in nearby Louisiana during the 1700s.

Also shown in this illustration is the essential longboat or shalop—called a *chalupe* in French or a *chalupa* in Spanish. Such longboats measured about fifteen feet in length and enabled sailors to make landfall in the many places where a large vessel drawing, say, eight feet of water could not draw

VAISSEAU DE 80 CANONS.

(DE 1674 À 1730.)

FIGURE 3-4

Illustration of a similar but more heavily armed and substantially larger vessel from the period 1674 to 1730 in Léon Guérin's classic Histoire Maritime de France *(Paris, 1854) confirms the basic configuration of French sailing vessels of the era that very likely traversed the Texas coast. Author's collection.*

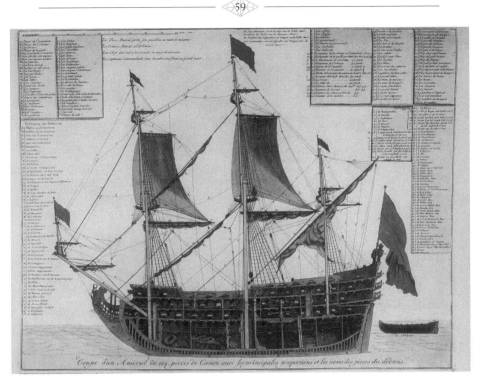

FIGURE 3-5

One of the most detailed illustrations of a late seventeenth century French warship is found in Le Neptune François, ou Atlas Nouveau des cartes marines *(Paris, 1693), an atlas produced for the use of captains in the navy of Louis XIV. This cross section, or cutaway drawing, beautifully reveals the vessel's construction and rigging.*

up alongside the shore. The Texas coast was typical of such shoal environments, and the chalupe was indispensable in getting people and supplies to shore. Thus the French sailors in La Salle's expedition noted in a journal entry of January 17, 1685, that "we were obliged to anchor, and anchored in seven fathoms, sand and mud" but then "set sail to bring ourselves near the *Aimable,* and the wind was south, light wind, and our longboat went aboard and Monsieur de La Salle got into it to go to land, but as the sea was too high he could not land and returned aboard the said ship and ordered a cannon to be fired to bring in their longboat."[15] The next day, it was reported in the journal that "Captain Aigron's longboat came aboard, and his people got into our longboat to go and search for a man who had remained on shore the evening before."[16] These journal entries show how commonly longboats were depended upon to help transfer people between vessels and land. They also served to convey people and goods from one anchored vessel to another.

La Salle's attempts to create a settlement on the Texas coast naturally prompted the Spanish to send expeditions out to reconnoiter the area with the express purpose of finding, and stopping, any French intruders. Captain Alonso de Leon pursued any information about the ill-fated French settlement, piecing together the tragic story, but he "was uncertain whether some French vessel might have come afterwards with settlers for the bay [of Espíritu Santo]." So he led a second expedition, stating: "I myself set fire to the fort, and as there was a high wind—the wood, by the way, was from the sloop brought by the Frenchmen, which had sunk on entering the bay—in half an hour the fort was in ashes."[17]

The quote reveals the Spanish concern about stopping the French at all costs, but it also helps point to the confusion that has persisted about the actual vessels used at the time. In the original Spanish, the word Urca (Vrca) was translated by Lilia Casis in 1899 as "sloop," but this should not be confused with what we would call a sloop today (that is, a boat or vessel with but one mast). A more thorough search for the meaning of the word *Urca* reveals the definition *storeship* (or what is similarly called *hooker*), especially a broad-beamed, rather large (and often hard-to-maneuver) cargo/transport vessel.[18] Interestingly, the word *Urca* appears to have come into the Spanish language through the French, its possible source being *hourque*, which was in turn derived from the German *hulke*—a flat-bottomed, slow-moving transport vessel with bulging sides.

The Casis translation of Urca as sloop is understandable, because several older dictionaries define an Urca as "a hooker, dogger; a pink built and sloop-rigged vessel, and a storeship." The meaning as well as the origin of the term *sloop*, then, is vague. According to Romola and R. C. Anderson, "At one time there was a sloop rig and a sloop rating, or class, and the two had nothing whatever to do with one another," and "to make matters worse, a book of 1750 says that sloops 'are sailed and masted as men's fancies lead them, sometimes with one mast, with two, and with three.' "[19] We should thus be careful not to confuse historic or even ancient terms with what was sometimes called a sloop in the nineteenth century and is always called a sloop today, that is, "a single masted, fore-and-aft-rigged sailing boat with a short standing bowsprit or none at all and a single headsail set from the forestay."[20] Although the term sloop derives from the Dutch *sloep* (similar to sleuth) and—being a single masted, fore-and-aft-rigged boat that is often rather "pink" (that is, narrow in the stern) and a fast sailer—seems to imply deftness and speed to us today, the term was used just as accurately in the seventeenth century for a rather ponderous, broad-beamed supply ship. To the generally complicated nomenclature of sailing vessels, then, the historian must add the pitfalls of semantics.

BRIGS AND FRIGATES

This is as good a place as any in the maritime history of Texas to look more closely at the common term *frigate*, which has come to signify an armed, speedy, seaworthy sailing vessel of medium size, usually three-masted. Some maritime historians attribute the frigate to the Englishman Peter Pelt, who in 1646 copied the design of a French vessel in building the *Constant Warwick*, but this vessel was not called a frigate at the time. It is possible that the first frigate was constructed in Dunkirk, which specialized in building fast privateers, and this might explain the French appellation.[21] The frigate of the eighteenth century was two-decked with twenty-four to thirty-two guns, but had only one or two guns per side on the lower deck, carrying oars there instead. Some maritime historians believe that these vessels underwent an evolution of sorts: The lower guns were rather useless and were replaced, while oar ports were shifted to upper decks before disappearing. The first vessels of the new pattern were mentioned in France in 1752, followed a few years later in England. Rather than serving to define a frigate, however, these suppositions more or less imply that advances in maritime technology were occurring in France and England somewhat more rapidly than in Spain. According to some, France had begun this period of rapid, aggressive maritime development nearly a century earlier, when it created a navy and built the large, heavily armed vessel *Superbe* in 1672 — that is, a dozen years *before* La Salle reached the Texas coast.

It was during this period that the brigantine, or brig, also appeared. The term originated in the Mediterranean, where it referred to a small, lateen-rigged vessel mainly intended for rowing, but by the seventeenth century it was used for a two-masted vessel with an ordinary square-rigged foremast and a taller square mainsail that was soon exchanged for a gaff sail with a boom. Eventually the term referred to a man-of-war that had a combination square and gaff and boom mainsails.[22] Importantly, vessels of this type sat fairly low in the water, were rather well armed, and were rigged to be fast, maneuverable sailers — the ideal combination needed in a vessel that would be used for either privateering or offensive military actions at sea. Again, it is significant that many of the advancements in warships were taking place among the Dutch, French, and English. Spain found itself taking an increasingly defensive position.

Maritime historians of this period must consult numerous sources of information to determine the design and appearance of vessels. By the seventeenth and eighteenth centuries, highly detailed miniature warships began to be produced under commission of European governments. Called Admiralty Models by the British, these miniature replicas of proposed warships were deemed a necessary part of the funding and production cycle. These models demonstrated to political leaders the armaments and troop-carrying capabilities of vessels, and they were frequently so highly detailed that they might be said to be exact replicas of the prototypes. Recently, a series of Admiralty Models were examined with a fiberoptic scope which probed the interiors of hulls and "a miniature seventeenth century mariner's world was revealed in fantastic detail—the copper pans and cauldrons of galleys, tools and implements of masters, bosuns, and carpenters, even the rich parquet decks of captains' cabins, all submerged in darkness for three hundred years."[23] It has been speculated that such meticulous attention to detail revealed a belief in invisible forces, such as magnetism and gravity, that were interconnected and that had the power to affect human endeavors. Thus, a model needed to be a perfect reflection of its prototype because "when preparing to build that most technical of creations and launch it into that most dangerous of environments, perhaps to decide the fate of nations in pitched battle, who was to say if the smallest deviation from perfection in the creation of a model might court disaster for the full scale ship in a world of full scale peril?"[24] Whatever the motive for these incredibly detailed Admiralty Models, they represent for the maritime historian an incredible source of three-dimensional information about vessels. These models reveal the changing design and evolution of oceangoing vessels used in an era of military expansion—an era that was manifested on the Texas coast as Spanish, French, and British vessels began to encounter each other even in the far northern corner of the Spanish Sea.

𝒱ᴀʟᴜᴇ ᴏꜰ Ѕʜɪᴘᴡʀᴇᴄᴋѕ

Shipwrecks, of course, can be especially helpful in revealing information about vessels of this era. Just as maritime historians learned much about the Spanish from the 1554 shipwrecks off Padre Island, the wreck of *Belle* is helping us to better understand French maritime history on the Texas Gulf coast. The shipwreck site of the *Belle* is atypical in that it was discovered following a concerted search that lasted nearly twenty years. More often, a shipwreck is exposed by accidents, such as dredging, or results from a re-working of the site by natural forces, such as storms. Shipwrecks once completely covered with water and sediment may become visible as advances in technology within the last several decades now enable underwater archaeologists to locate and even explore shipwrecks through the remote-sensing techniques outlined below:[25]

Magnetometer

Beginning about 1965, magnetometers were used to detect deviations (called anomalies) from the earth's normal magnetic field; these anomalies may be caused by iron and other ferrous metals often used in the construction of vessels. Naturally a larger vessel featuring more iron in its construction is normally easier to locate than, say, a smaller vessel that was constructed with a minimum of iron. Archaeologists searching for shipwrecks can normally locate or pinpoint a wreck by its "signature"—a cluster of points indicating the intersections of negatively and positively charged fields, as measured in gammas.

Side scan sonar

Sonar, the sending of sound waves that are reflected back to the source, has been used to detect objects underwater since World War II. Because dense objects are good reflectors, underwater archaeologists use side scan sonar to detect the hulls of vessels. Because side scan sonar is dependent on many factors, including the condition and configuration of the "target" (the object being searched for), it may be difficult to interpret. Side scan sonar is limited in its ability to penetrate sand and other sediments, and thus an underwater target must be relatively exposed before it can be detected. Nevertheless, side scan sonar has helped archaeologists locate vessels that would otherwise be very difficult to locate visually in the often turbid, silt-laden waters of the lagoons of the Texas coast.

Fathometer

This instrument accurately determines depth using acoustic energy (another type of sonar), and thus permits the detailed mapping of the bottom of a given site. This serves two purposes: First, it reveals much about the bottom conditions of the site and, secondly, it can detect objects, such as a shipwreck or portions thereof, that protrude from the bottom.

Many factors affect the location and conditions of a shipwreck, including events at the time of the sinking: Was it caused by the weather? By acts of piracy or warfare? By sabotage? By negligence? Conditions and causes will determine whether the wreck is largely intact or broken up when it arrives at the bottom, but currents can alter the condition and location of a shipwreck, sometimes effectively redistributing the wreck, as can waves or current action from abnormal events such as powerful storms. Just as sedimentation can cover a wreck, natural scouring by currents and human activity, such as dredging, can expose and further erode a wreck and its site. It should be emphasized that archaeologists look for more than the shipwreck itself, for they are interested in the *story* told by the wreck. Thus, it is essential to understand the entire site, including slope, condition, and type of sediments, in order to determine the history of the wreck. In fact, the site and the wreck must be considered a unitary environment—much as a crime cannot be separated from the crime scene. The site contains the evidence enabling researchers to understand a historic event. The physical evidence at the wreck site must be compared with other evidence, such as written and verbal accounts, before a complete understanding of what occurred is possible.

In the case of La Salle's vessels, the written records are being carefully compared with the wreck site of the *Belle* (Fig. 3-6), which has yielded a nearly complete skeleton, presumably that of one of the hapless expedition members who perished either from privation or violence. The wreck site has also yielded a remarkable amount of material, including the bronze cannon with its beautifully depicted crossed anchors, ceramic jars (some in virtually perfect condition and sealed, actually containing the residue of original contents), casks, hawk bells, rings, and other metal objects. Surprisingly, even wooden portions of the vessel were well preserved (Fig. 3-7). Initial archaeological investigations revealed these to be the frame and ceiling planks of the hull, exceedingly rare evidence in a marine environment, like that of the Texas Gulf coast, that is normally so destructive of wood. Among the more fascinating pieces of evidence confirming that the shipwreck being excavated is indeed the *Belle* are several pewter plates stamped LG, which apparently once belonged to the expedition's commissary, Sieur Le Gros. The ill-fated Le Gros died of complications suffered from a rattlesnake bite at the fort, and after his death the plates became the property of La Salle. A pewter porringer found near the aforementioned human skeleton is also inscribed with a French name, C. Berange.

The provenance of these artifacts (that is, their actual relationship to each other in *space*, which is essential for understanding their relationship in *time*) helps to corroborate the shipwreck site as that of the *Belle*. Indeed,

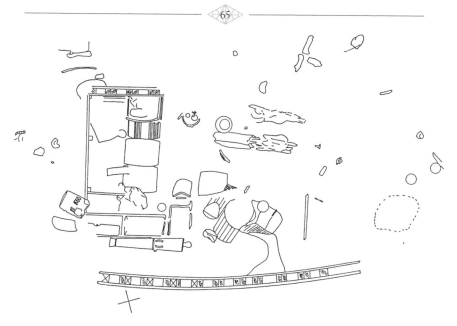

FIGURE 3-6

Preliminary site plan for test excavations of the Belle *reveals a cross section of the lower portion of the hull, including ribs (bottom), bronze cannon (lower left), and numerous casks, jars, and other artifacts strewn about the site—all being important clues in determining the configuration of the vessel and the circumstances surrounding its demise. Courtesy J. Barto Arnold, III, Texas Historical Commission, Austin.*

it was the convergence of *written* information with the *material* at the wreck site that led Arnold to the "unusually unequivocal assertion" that the *Belle* had been located.[26] Thus, provenance is determined by a painstaking comparison of the written records and a detailed mapping of the wreck site. That further explains why treasure hunters who remove artifacts from sites do such irreparable damage; they well might tamper with the evidence to such a degree that an understanding of the site is compromised, and an ability to reconstruct what happened is therefore lost.

The discovery of the *Belle* was of international significance, for the remains of *any* French ship from the seventeenth century, much less La Salle's, represents a world-class archaeological find. Although recognition by the National Register of Historic Places is often associated with buildings, vessels and shipwreck sites are also eligible. The *Belle* (site) can be listed on the National Register by describing the vessel and outlining its significance. To do so, one would need to "link the vessel to international, national, regional, or local historic contexts," and to "convey the vessel's participation

FIGURE 3-7

Since its discovery in 1995, the wreck site of the Belle *has yielded a remarkable amount of material, including three bronze cannons. Illustrated in a February 1, 1997, photograph is a substantial part of the lower portion of the hull, remarkably intact. The bow of the vessel (foreground) contained the skeleton of one of the expedition members and just beyond the first bulkhead two bronze cannons can be seen on the starboard side of the vessel. (Photo courtesy of Caro Ivy Walker of Houston, Texas.)*

in specific historical events."[27] The *Belle* shipwreck's listing in the National Register is based on the four major criteria, namely: (1) its association with *events* that have made a contribution to the broad patterns of our history (in this case the French exploration of the Texas coast); (2) its association with the lives of *persons* significant in our past; (3) its embodiment of the distinctive *characteristics* of a type, period, or *method* of construction (indeed the wreck of the *Belle* represents characteristics of French naval architecture); and (4) its ability to yield *information* important in Texas *prehistory* or *history*—and certainly the *Belle* is yielding information about early European culture's contact with the New World and, perhaps, its Native American population.

The wreckage of the *Belle*, including its cargo and spectacular bronze cannon, as well as the entire outline of the vessel's hull, has already yielded important information about both *maritime architecture* and the *events* of the time. Given the generally destructive nature of the maritime environment, locating a significant portion of the *Belle* after it had rested in its nautical grave for more than three hundred years was indeed a phenomenal achievement. So, too, was stopping or stabilizing the deterioration of the wreckage even after it was excavated—a task made possible by immersion in a chemical bath that removed encrustations and stopped destructive chemical processes. The fabric (as preservationists call historically preserved materials) of the *Belle* will continue to yield important information about the French effort to colonize the Texas coast in the 1680s. The large amount of provisions, and the care with which they were stored, reveals that the French were prepared to persevere on the hostile Texas coast. As historic events would prove, however, the *Belle* figured in one of the great tragedies or debacles of the age of exploration and colonization. Ultimately, of course, the National Register is not only about artifacts, but rather about *information* from the past that they reveal, which is to say the *story* they tell.

Eligible for the National Register of Historic Places, the wreck of the *Belle* is ensured some measure of protection from federally funded construction projects such as waterway dredging or harbor construction. The *Belle* is also ensured recognition, since the expertise of the state underwater archaeologist J. Barto Arnold and the "Ships of Discovery" archaeologist Toni Carrell and others will help both the public and scholars to better understand one crucial chapter in Texas maritime history. A project of such importance and magnitude has involved close public- and private-sector cooperation, with the Southwest Underwater Archaeological Society (SUAS), and the U.S. Navy Reserve mine-sweeping unit from Galveston assisting

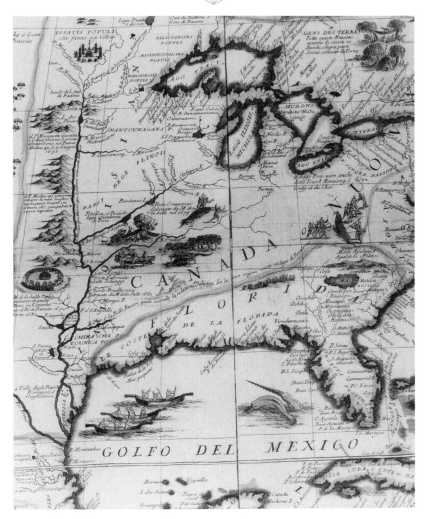

FIGURE 3-8

La Salle's experiences resulted in maps of the Gulf that compounded geographic errors while providing more detail in others. Here, a portion or detail of Vincenzo Coronelli's 1688 map of North America places the mouth of the Mississippi near La Salle's Fort St. Louis in Texas. Courtesy Special Collections Division, The University of Texas at Arlington Libraries, Arlington.

the Texas Historical Commission crew in the mapping of the wreck site. The public's response was instantaneous and positive: More than 1.7 million dollars was appropriated by the Texas legislature in November 1995 to ensure the proper excavation and protection of the *Belle*; and considerably more than that sum, about 4 million dollars, was solicited from private sources to assist with the excavation.

A portion of this project's expense was applied toward the construction of a cofferdam similar to those that have been used in the successful excavation of historic submerged vessels in Europe. The cofferdam is a watertight structure consisting of metal plates driven into the surrounding sand and mud bottom, creating an enclosure out of which all the water is pumped. The outer dimension of the cofferdam around the *Belle* site is 148 feet by 118 feet, and it extends five feet above the water's surface. The cofferdam is covered by a steel roof to further protect the archaeologists from the elements. A mobile crane inside the cofferdam was used to lift larger artifacts. The construction of the cofferdam presents something of an irony: the excavation of a once-submerged shipwreck site that becomes, in effect, a terrestrial site. As noted in the media, the *Belle* shipwreck site on Matagorda Bay "will be the first in this hemisphere designed to allow excavation of a submerged shipwreck on dry land."[28] After a careful analysis of all materials, portions of the wreck will be exhibited in museums in Texas; the first such exhibit of the original artifacts taken from the site in 1995 opened at the Corpus Christi Museum of Science and History in August of 1996.

NAVIGATION, EXPLORATION, AND MAPPING

The historical record and archaeological excavations of the *Belle* shipwreck help paint a picture of an initially well-outfitted but poorly administered colonization effort. Despite having fine vessels, La Salle's navigational blunder doomed the expedition from the outset. La Salle went to his grave believing he was close to locating the mouth of the Mississippi in Texas, and his misadventures were immortalized cartographically. For example, Vincenzo Coronelli's 1688 map of North America (Fig. 3-8) places the mouth of the Mississippi near La Salle's Fort St. Louis. And yet, this map also includes much accurate detail, for like all cartographic efforts it is based on erroneous as well as accurate information. While it is easy for us today to criticize such maps for their seemingly gross errors in locating geographic features, it should be remembered that two factors kept most explorers of the Texas Gulf coast in a state of confusion. These were:

Geographical

the deceptively monotonous quality of the Texas coast, with its convoluted embayments and intricate lagoons and bays behind an otherwise simple line of barrier islands, and

Navigational

the inability of explorers to determine their longitude, which kept them from understanding how far west they were from fixed meridional points such as France or Seville.

The issue of determining actual location at sea (and, for that matter, on land) continued to vex mariners and cartographers, for it also required the determination of longitude, which in turn requires knowing the position of the vessel at noon in relation to the exact time at a distant fixed point. Doing so requires a timepiece, called a chronometer, that must be carried on board. As early as 1714, in response to numerous maritime disasters, the English Parliament established a Board of Longitude and offered a reward of twenty thousand pounds to the person who could determine longitude within thirty miles after a voyage of six weeks. The fact that an accurate marine chronometer was invented, by John Harrison, only in the mid-eighteenth century (1753) helps explain why most maps until about 1750 (and often years after, actually) were inaccurate as regards their east–west placement of features.[29] It also explains why mariners were easily confused as to how far west (or east) they really were at any moment. Thus, it is easy to understand, at least in part, why La Salle may have thought he was several hundred miles farther east (that is, near the mouth of the Mississippi), when in fact he landed well within present-day Texas. In truth, longitude remained difficult to determine well into the nineteenth century, as many vessels did not possess dependable marine chronometers until that time.

Just as the correct determination of longitude would await the widespread use of chronometers in the eighteenth century, the proper depiction of the geography of the coast would occur only after numerous voyages of discovery had slowly yielded its correct shape on navigational maps. On the Texas coast, as on all coasts, accurate mapping occurred only as nautical and terrestrial exploration coincided. Thus, knowledge of the Texas coast accrued as a result of both maritime and overland journeys of exploration. This semiarid, lightly settled, and fairly inhospitable northern fringe of New Spain was explored periodically by other French expeditions, causing renewed consternation on the part of Spain.

It should be remembered that Spain had responded to La Salle's 1685

FIGURE 3-9
*The Gulf historian Robert Weddle calls the presidio and mission at Goliad the
"Guardian of the Coast," for it was intended to protect the Texas coast against
foreign intruders. Photo by the author, 1993.*

incursion into what was claimed to be Spanish territory by sending Alonso
de León on expeditions in 1686–1687. Half a century later, Spain also responded militarily to Jean Béranger's expedition: Whereas Béranger's descriptions of Mustang and St. Joseph Islands and Live Oak Point may be
viewed as classics in the literature of Texas coastal exploration today, to Spain
they were clearly disarming and alarming, for they helped increase knowledge about, and hence access to, the coast by foreign powers. Spain reacted
predictably. In 1722, the Marques of San Miguel de Aguayo was sent to drive
the French out of east Texas. A secondary force reoccupied the area around
Matagorda Bay, which was then known as La Bahía del Espíritu Santo. It
was the presidio and mission at La Bahía that relocated in steps to near
present-day Goliad by 1749. The Gulf historian Robert Weddle calls the
presidio and mission at Goliad (Fig. 3-9) the "Guardian of the Coast," for it
was intended to protect the Texas coast against foreign intruders.[30]

By the mid-eighteenth century, the Spanish carried out explorations of
the coast by both sea and land, the latter taking the form of well-provisioned

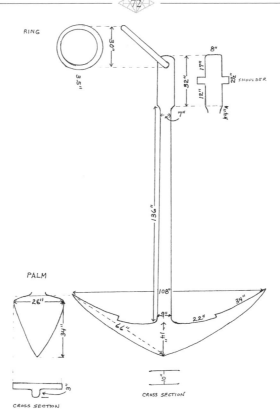

FIGURE 3-10

Some maritime historians believe an anchor measuring 17 feet 9 inches that was found by a shrimping boat crew in the 1960s was from the Corazon de Jesús y Santa Barbara, *an English-built ship that was sold to Spain. Drawing courtesy Danny Sessums, Director, Museum of the Gulf Coast, Port Arthur, Texas.*

expeditions by troops: Such was the journey of Joaquín Orobio y Basterra, commandant at La Bahía, who marched overland in 1747 to explore Corpus Christi Bay (which was called San Miguel Arcangel) and Baffin Bay (which was called Lago de la Santísma Trinidad).[31] By mid-1765, Spain had become concerned about reports by the Malaguitas Indians of the coast at the lower Rio Grande that white invaders, "certainly meaning Englishmen," were forming a settlement on the "Islas Blancas" (white islands) between the Nueces and the Rio Grande—what we today call Padre Island.[32] In 1766, Ortíz Parilla traveled overland to explore the Guadalupe River, Matagorda Bay, and perhaps the area that would later become Indianola. As these expeditions increased Spain's knowledge of the coast, however,

Spain continued to face weather-related problems on the Gulf: In 1766, a hurricane wrecked a convoy of Spanish vessels off the northern Gulf coast. Although the merchantman *El Nuevo Constante* was lost off Louisiana, another vessel in the convoy lost in the same storm—the *Corazón de Jesús y Santa Barbara*, appears to have blown aground on the Texas coast, probably between the Sabine River and High Island.[33] The *Corazón de Jesús y Santa Barbara* was an English-built vessel that was sold to Spain, and some maritime historians believe that an anchor measuring 17 feet 9 inches that was found by a shrimping boat crew in the 1960s was from this vessel.[34] This impressive 3,400-pound anchor (Fig. 3-10) is currently on exhibit at the Museum of the Gulf Coast in Port Arthur.

THE BRITISH THREAT

Although Spain had originally jealously guarded the coast from the French, the British turned out to be a major threat by the latter 1700s. Presumably the first British vessel officially to land in Texas—the appropriately named schooner *Britain*—caused a major incident when she blundered into La Bahía in early April 1769. The schooner's hapless passengers (which consisted of thirty-four Arcadians and forty Roman Catholic Germans) had planned on arriving in New Orleans, but their drunken, arrogant skipper accidentally sailed on to Texas, where, running short of provisions, the passengers commanded him to land. This he did, but only after grounding the vessel on a sandbar three times, according to depositions.[35]

Tensions mounted as the Spanish authorities, who were under strict orders to prevent any English incursion into their territory, detained the *Britain* and its crew and passengers. While the situation was being resolved, which took several months, the Arcadians and Germans were allowed to work on nearby ranches—provided they returned nightly. The British crew, however, were more or less prisoners. When the situation was finally resolved months later, the settlers had to trek back to Louisiana by land because the sails on the *Britain* had become so deteriorated that the vessel was no longer seaworthy.

Spain's paranoia about the British was justified; the British government protested the seizure of the *Britain*, and ordered the HMS *Druid* (a frigate) and the *Florida* (a privately owned sloop) to sail for Veracruz, ostensibly to impress the Spanish viceregal authorities. These vessels were predictably refused admission to the Veracruz harbor by the Spanish, who had two warships waiting to repel any intruders, but the British were able to accomplish the real purpose of their ruse—an espionage mission to chart the harbor at Veracruz. Thus, an incident on the Texas coast had repercussions for two world powers locked, as it were, in a power struggle on the Gulf. These tensions forced Spain to focus on guarding and developing the Texas coast.

Continued rumors of English intrusion into the Texas coast in 1772 prompted the Texas governor, Barón de Ripperdá, to order Capt. Luis Cazorla to contact any intruders and determine their purpose.[36] Cazorla marched with forty-three soldiers and five coastal natives, and was joined by other troops; their mission took them along the coast beyond the Brazos River, where Indians revealed that Frenchmen had operated in the area for years as agents, buying from the English and selling to the Indians. Further tortuous travel along the coast, including an attempt to reach the Trinity River, revealed little. However, a second group came across the signs of an earlier disaster suffered by either a French or Spanish vessel: a ship's boat and rotted sea chest embedded in the sand.[37] In the late spring of 1776 Cazorla investigated Indian reports of a shipwreck and massacre of the crew by Karankawa Indians, and he encountered the wreck of what some writers describe as a deep-draft English commercial frigate,[38] which had been broken open by the waves, its cargo having been taken by the Karankawa. To add to the grimness of the scene, the decomposed body of an English sailor was found amid the broken masts and spars of the vessel.[39] This and other incidents further convinced the Spanish that the Texas coast was both vulnerable and treacherous. Yet they knew that it must be opened for trade in order for the province to develop.

SPAIN'S DILEMMA:
COASTAL DEVELOPMENT OR NEGLECT

The Texas coast was difficult to master, however. Attempts to found missions met with limited success owing to predations by hostile Karankawa-Copano Indians that posed a major threat to navigation as they attacked sailors landing on the shore with deadly arrows. Despite these setbacks, numerous Spanish expeditions continued to explore the Texas coast in the 1770s and 1780s. El Copano was at first used to resupply missions near Goliad: By 1785, the port of El Copano was opened for trade by Viceroy Don José de Gálvez, but it reportedly developed into a haven for smugglers and pirates. Some progress, however, was made: Conducted at the request of Governor Bernardo de Gálvez, an expedition by the pilot José de Evía resulted in a careful study of the Texas coast between 1783 and 1786. Maps of this period show the coast in considerable detail, for the convergence of maritime and terrestrial expeditions by that time enabled a comprehensive understanding of the major features, including mouths of rivers, embayments, lagoons, and barrier islands. One of these barrier islands—Galveston—would be named in honor of the Spanish governor. Another, Padre Island, was named as a reference to Father Nicolas Balli, who was granted the land in 1800. By the early 1800s, the Texas coast was lightly settled—mostly in the form of ranchos. The few nominal ports were little more than landing places that served a vast, marginally developed interior.

Despite its being better mapped by the seventeenth and eighteenth centuries, the Texas coast still remained a navigational terra incognita during the period. Navigational mishaps brought more than one vessel to the Texas coast: A navigational error by Gerrais de La Gaudelle of the *Maréchal d' Estrées* resulted in Simars de Bellisle's being cast away on the Texas coast in 1719, and the *Superbe* was wrecked at Matagorda Bay by a miscalculation of Chevalier Grenier in 1745.[40] In addition to an inability of mariners to determine their locations by celestial navigation, the Texas coast's generally similar appearance over large distances has led to errors in the other major navigational form available: terrestrial navigation. Evidence suggests that numerous vessels have blundered along the Texas coast in a search for some particular landmark—a search that could prove futile, given the similarly monotonous, uniform appearance of the coast over long distances and, in addition, the similarities of some of its major embayments. When one considers the challenge, in the seventeenth or eighteenth centuries, of identifying a particular location on the Texas coast in the absence of today's navigational landmarks—communities, towers, lighthouses, and the like—these sometimes fatal mistakes in navigation become more understandable.

By 1776 Spain had created political and military subdivisions out of its huge area called the Eastern Internal Provinces, in an attempt to administer and govern the area more effectively. One of these, Texas, included the area north of the Nueces River to the Sabine River, while the area south of the Nueces was included in the new state of Tamaulipas.[41] Spanish administrators and political officials in Texas remained perplexed about how to interpret the coast: Hugo O'Conor summarized the persistent problems when he noted, almost a century after La Salle's ill-fated expedition, that "Texas, which is also found more than a degree beyond our line, has been of the overseas possessions of Spain the most costly, although of very little utility; the largest, although unknown, and the one that has produced the most hostilities; but the one of greatest importance on many counts, since none of the others can match it."[42] In his exhaustive report to Teodoro de Croix in 1777, O'Conor addressed the Texas coast in considerable detail: "To the south or better said on the Gulf of Mexico coast, next to the Presidio de la Bahía del Espíritu Santo, lives grouped together the Karankawa nation, who, if up until now they have caused little trouble, have lately shown the detriment that their being nearby is for those who are cast ashore on [this coast], against whom they have committed many inhumanities."[43] O'Conor recommended that these Indians be persuaded to be missionized or removed forcibly from the area, "because not being able to be useful in the wrecks of vessels that frequently run ashore on that coast, it is better that those who save themselves find it uninhabited than be left to fall into their hands to become a sacrifice—thereby avoiding the erection of a fort recently considered."[44] O'Conor had good reason to be cognizant of the frequent shipwrecks, for a complete total of vessels that came to grief on the Texas coast has yet to be determined.

In addition to shipwrecks, O'Conor was concerned about the Indians, who were either indifferent, or hostile, and about the other European powers that were gathering to the east. His report mentions that a fort could become, in effect, a double-edged sword. O'Conor candidly noted that such a fort "would certainly be useful to the mariners amidst the dangers that abound on that coast, but perhaps with it the way would be open for illegal trade which the province of Texas does not much need in view of their having it on many sides due to the nearness of the English and French."[45] History would prove O'Conor's statement partly correct, for at the time he wrote his report the British vessels were becoming a more common sight on the Spanish Gulf, as revealed in correspondence and a map from the late eighteenth century (Figs. 3-11 and 3-12). And yet, even Britain's claim to this part of the Gulf would be tenuous, as they themselves would ultimately be driven from it by a new power that was created at the time O'Conor wrote his report. This new nation on the eastern seaboard, the United States of America, would prove a far greater threat in the next generation than either the English or the French.

No discussion of Texas maritime history during the eighteenth and early nineteenth centuries would be complete without brief reference to the creation of New Orleans (or Nouvelle Orleans as it was called by the French, who established it in 1719). Although the creation of this city troubled the Spanish crown, it was in no position to resist. Located in Louisiana, New Orleans became the major city on the Gulf coast in the early 1800s, and much of Texas maritime traffic was directed toward the Crescent City as an

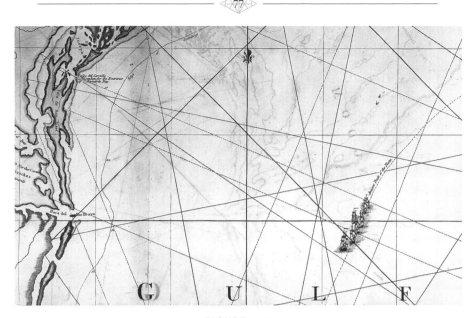

FIGURE 3-11
British map by Thomas Jeffrys of the Gulf from 1775 reveals the coast of Texas in considerable detail, and depicts several sailing vessels in the Gulf—an ominous sign for Spain and a great concern to Spanish Texas. Courtesy Special Collections & Archives Department, Texas A&M University–Corpus Christi, Bell Library.

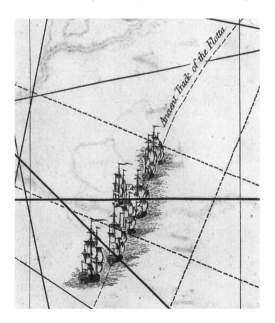

FIGURE 3-12
A detail of Jeffry's 1775 map reveals eight vessels, including three-masted warships, on the track of the flotta. Courtesy Special Collections & Archives Department, Texas A&M University–Corpus Christi, Bell Library.

entrepôt. New Orleans is situated on the Mississippi River, distant enough from the Gulf to shelter it from its storms and waves, but still close enough to provide access to the open sea. The location of New Orleans was indeed strategic, for it is at the junction of what were evolving into two major routes of exploration and commerce into what would come to be termed the Southwest of the United States—the Mississippi and the Gulf. Interestingly, the very site of New Orleans was debated, for François Broutin, the engineer-in-chief responsible for laying out the community, noted that if the actual site had been left to him to decide, he would have selected Biloxi instead![46] France ceded Louisiana to the rather young United States in 1803, a move resisted by the British, who were intent on reasserting their presence to the west of North America—which included Louisiana. The successful U.S. defense of New Orleans in the War of 1812 marked a major setback for the British. It also had consequences for Spain, for it should be remembered that New Orleans was a nominally Spanish city from 1763 to the early 1800s, when it began to experience the arrival of European Americans intent on making it part of the United States.

Like New Orleans, virtually every Texas port that developed would lie at the mouth of a river, such as the Brazos, Colorado, Trinity, or Nueces. Such a location ensured that the hinterland could be served and tapped. Also, a community's location close to the Gulf, yet sheltered from its storms, ensured its proximity to open waters and hence its proximity to developed or developing markets. It was this aspect of geographic location of ports that so vexed the Spanish, for they exhibited a decided fear of creating ports not so much to discourage trade or enterprise, but rather because they recognized that an enemy could conquer that port and thus gain access to, and hence control of, not only the port (and coast adjacent to it) but also the entire hinterland.

The crown considered opening up this part of the Gulf coast to trade when, in 1791, New Spain's Count of Revilla Gigedo issued an elaborate set of instructions for the extensive reconnaissance and exploration from the Rio Grande to the Red River; included in the proposed jaunt was the search for a suitable port on the Texas coast to serve as an entrepôt for reciprocal trade between Texas and Louisiana on the northern Gulf coast as well as the distant ports of Havana, Veracruz, and Campeche.[47] This proposed exploration also was intended to better secure Texas from marauding Indians and invaders from the United States and to better define the eastern boundary of Texas, but it was never undertaken. As a consequence, the Texas coast remained in a state of administrative neglect and political confusion. Robert Weddle has noted that Spain's involvement in the Napoleonic wars of the early nineteenth century witnessed the loss of Louisiana to the French. Thus, as the Age of Enlightenment drew to a close, Spain had yet to fully understand the Texas coast, much less open it for development. In *The Spanish Frontier in North America*, historian David Weber noted that some contemporaries found Spain's failure to build Texas ports and hence stimulate trade deplorable, as when Anthanase de Mézières chided Teodoro de Croix in 1779: "What an abuse! Do you not have the sea so nearby?"

PRIVATEERS AND PIRATES

By the late 1700s, the Gulf had become the scene of increasing activity as Britain, France, and Spain vied for control of vast sections of North America, including Texas. Because standing navies were not large enough to counter threats in far-flung areas that were being defended, governments often relied on privateers to assist. According to the maritime historian Howard Chapelle, a "privateer is a privately-owned vessel, armed and manned at her owner's expense for the purpose of capturing enemy merchant craft in times of war," and "the great American deity 'Speed', had no more devout worshippers than the designers and builders of privateers."[48]

Although privateers might use any kind of watercraft, certain speedier vessels were better suited to the activity, as they were more likely to seize other, slower vessels and less likely themselves to fall prey to military vessels. Privateers needed to be lighter, carrying only enough guns to overpower lightly armed merchant ships. Chapelle further notes that lighter construction was achieved by keeping weight out of the ends of the vessel. Also, because privateers were interested in taking only valuable goods, not bulky cargoes, privateers could have rather small hulls. Privateers thus had to be small but good sailers—carrying as much canvas as could be spread as quickly as possible.

Beginning in the 1770s, many U.S. vessels began to be built along these lines, for they had to be used in resisting the British. Approximately one hundred feet in length and often schooner-rigged, the typical sailing vessel of the east coast could also carry armament when it was required. Other rigging configurations were also seen, including brigantines. However rigged, these late-eighteenth-century vessels marked a striking contrast to earlier, more ponderous predecessors. Sloops, too, found their way into the thriving merchant trade of the early U.S. republic. As U.S. interests shifted to the Gulf by the early nineteenth century, these vessels could be found off the

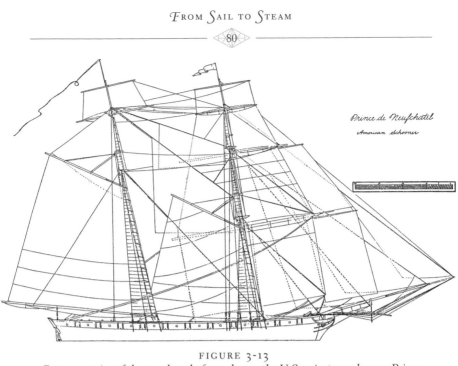

FIGURE 3-13

Representative of the new breed of vessels was the U.S. privateer schooner Prince de Neufchâtel, *which had a major role in the War of 1812. From* The History of American Sailing Ships, *by Howard I. Chapelle. Copyright 1935 by W. W. Norton & Company, Inc.; renewed © 1963 by Howard Chapelle. Reprinted by permission of W. W. Norton & Co., Inc.*

northeastern coast of Mexico, which is to say, Texas. Representative of the new breed of vessels was the U.S. privateer schooner *Prince de Neufchâtel*, which had a major role in the War of 1812 (Fig. 3-13).

Among the more vexing problems faced by the Spaniards was piracy, and few pirates were more enterprising and better organized than the legendary Laffite brothers, in particular Jean Laffite. Laffite's early life is something of a mystery. Some claim that he was born in France about 1780, the younger of the two brothers, who moved with his family to Hispañola. By the early 1800s the brothers moved to Barataria, where they engaged in active privateering. Conditions at the time were ripe for such activities, as British, Spanish, and U.S. interests intensified. The Laffite brothers pledged their services to Spain, but by 1816 they conspired to open a privateering port on the Texas coast from which they would attack Texas.[49] Organizing a rebel government at Galveston in 1817, Laffite attracted the interest of certain European Americans, including George Graham and James Long, who encouraged him to take possession of the entire Texas coast to the Rio

Grande, then surrender it to the United States in a fake battle. Laffite, however, maintained his lucrative privateering rather than becoming further involved in the intrigue. The U.S.-backed interests forced Laffite out of Galveston by 1821, when he departed for the Yucatán, where, some sources claim, he died in 1826.

By the time Francis Sheridan reached Texas in 1839–1840, Jean Laffite's reputation had reached mythic proportions, it being said that he was a Robin Hood of sorts who had "at one time no less than 12 *vessels* scouring the Gulf," and "whose sailors adored him."[50] Sheridan noted with some delight that Laffite "was fond of the Yankee & I believe seldom molested their vessels, but with Spain he declared war."[51] Like all privateers, Laffite used vessels well suited to privateering, and his schooners and brigs harassed merchant ships until he desisted by agreement. Spain, however, had little reason to rejoice, for the U.S. ability to depose Laffite was ample testimony to their growing power on the Texas coast. Laffite's exploits brought him to virtually every part of the Texas coast. Although he frequented Galveston Island and used it as a base of operations, Laffite was often active in the Port Isabel area of South Padre Island, being drawn there by the wells along Laguna Madre from which he could secure fresh water unmolested.

The name Laffite is nearly legendary in Texas maritime history, but Galveston Island is also associated with the activities of another Frenchman, the mariner Louis Michel Aury (ca. 1788–1821), some of whose original letters and maritime-related documents are in the Center for American History at the University of Texas at Austin.[52] Aury's career ran parallel to, and then actually crossed, Laffite's: After service in the French Navy and French privateers in the early 1800s, Aury became involved in running the Spanish blockades off the northern Caribbean coast of South America for the Grenadine Republic. Given the animosity toward Spain by many Frenchmen in the early 1800s, Aury's activities are understandable. In 1816 Aury entered Texas maritime history as he offered his services to a group of New Orleans associates who planned to develop a Mexican rebel port on the Texas coast as part of a revolt against Spain. In late summer of that year, Aury attempted to deliver to Galveston several prize vessels seized in the Gulf near Belize, but most of them and their cargoes were lost upon entry of the tricky pass at the mouth of the harbor. Aury was wounded by mutinous Haitian sailors, who sailed back to Haiti with considerable booty, but his wounds were not serious, and he was named resident commissioner at Galveston, where the rebel flag was raised on September 13. Aury's privateering activities were based out of Galveston, where a small community of

FIGURE 3-14
*A frigate of 1820 reveals that fighting vessels had become quite sleek by the early
nineteenth century. From Henry Culver,* The Book of Old Ships; *drawing by
Gordon Grant, reproduced with the permission of Doubleday, a division of
Bantam Doubleday Dell Publishing Group, Inc.*

shacks was developing on the sheltered side of the island. Of the numerous
vessels seized by Aury, one is said to have carried a cargo of specie and
indigo valued at about $778,000.[53]

It has been noted that the fledgling Galveston was far from a peaceful
community at this time, for it was rife with miscreants and political intrigue.
Aury's tenuous hold on the island community weakened as a filibustering
expedition aimed at seizing Texas from Spain was mounted by Francisco
Xavier Mina and arrived in Galveston on November 22. After considerable
intrigue and negotiation with New Orleans backers of the filibustering ex-

pedition, Aury sailed Mina's vessels from Galveston to the Santander River farther south on the Gulf coast, while Mina was placed in charge of the army. Aury commanded a force of eight vessels and 235 men which stopped at the Rio Grande for fresh water on their way south. However, Aury's departure on April 7, 1817, in effect left Galveston open for the Laffite brothers, who undermined the port's ersatz government during his absence and called

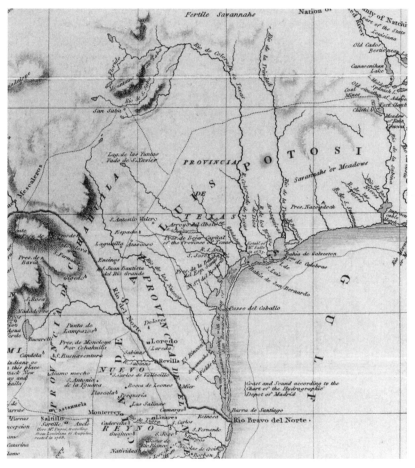

FIGURE 3-15

Zebulon Pike's 1810 map of New Spain was likely inspired by a map by the German naturalist and statesman Friedrich Wilhelm Karl Heinrich Alexander von Humboldt. Pike's map shows the Texas coast and rivers in considerable detail and helped encourage Euro-American interest in the region. Courtesy Special Collections Division, The University of Texas at Arlington Libraries, Arlington.

the rough-hewn privateer base community Campeachy (perhaps a corruption of the Mexican port Campeche). Despite an attempt to establish himself on Matagorda Bay and re-establish himself in Galveston, Aury was unable to regain his control of the Texas coast. By July of 1817, Aury formally resigned his commission as ruler of Galveston Island, and sailed away to the Florida coast, where he participated in raids on Spanish positions there. As is the case with Laffite, the exact time and place of Aury's death is uncertain.

By about 1820, then, the Texas coast was nominally in Spanish hands, but was seriously threatened from within by rebellion and encroached upon by the vessels of the British and the United States. As represented in a drawing of a frigate from 1820, vessels at this time had attained a profile that enabled them to sail swiftly and adroitly, and to train more than a dozen guns on an opponent (Fig. 3-14). This type of vessel so actively developed by the U.S. and British shipbuilders would soon be put to use along the Texas coast as the United States flexed its muscles in the Gulf. The developments of armed vessels would coincide with the rising mercantile trade to the area, so that vessels were prized for how well they could be employed both in battle *and* in transport.

Maps of this period likewise revealed a growing sophistication and knowledge of the entire coast by U.S. seafarers. In this regard, the 1810 map of New Spain by Zebulon Pike (said to have been copied in part from Alexander von Humboldt's ambitious 1809 map of New Spain) reveals considerable detail along the Texas coast (Fig. 3-15)—detail that would help make U.S. expansion into the area much easier despite great concern from Spain. By about 1820, Spain was attempting, but essentially failing, to keep the Texas coast and all of the northern frontier away from marauding powers. Spain even attempted to conceal geographic information about the coast from foreign powers by guarding maps of the area jealously. But to no avail: Those foreign powers were now frequenting the waters off Texas with alarming regularity, and gaining knowledge of its contours and potential with impunity. The early nineteenth century thus brought with it changes that would witness Spain's permanently losing the Texas coast in 1821, as revolution would soon tear México, and its province Texas, from the dwindling Spanish empire in the New World.

Smoke on the Horizon
1821–1836

Whoso commands the seas commands the trade of the world; whoso commands the trade of the world commands the riches of the world.
SIR WALTER RALEIGH

By the early 1800s, Spain still held the Texas coast but was very aware that its hold was weakening as both British and U.S. vessels sailed into the area with greater frequency. Ports had begun to spring up along the Texas coast in response to the demand for goods in the communities of the interior. There is evidence suggesting that much of this trade was illicit, that is, smuggled in direct violation of Spanish trade restrictions. Spain had been unable to suppress a burgeoning maritime trade, which began to stimulate the development of ports like the fledgling La Bahía, appropriately named for its strategic location at the southern end of Matagorda Bay. La Bahía, it will be remembered, served as a point of arrival for the missions near what would later become Goliad; this gateway helped ensure the development of the province's largest city, San Antonio de Béxar, which lay about one hundred miles inland from the Gulf. By the beginning of the nineteenth century, however, these ports seemed to develop in spite of Spanish trade restrictions that had debilitated all of New Spain, a condition that had helped precipitate the numerous revolutions that ultimately led, in 1821, to the creation of an independent Mexico.

The Mexican Navy

The new nation, Estados Unidos Mexicanos, which included Texas as its most remote northeasterly territory or province, faced intense challenges, many of which occurred on the seas. Among the first orders of business were the creation of a navy and the need to sustain, and encourage, trade with other nations. The Mexican Navy was created to deter Spain from reclaiming territory lost in 1821. Mexico's embryonic navy consisted of six gunboats, two sloops-of-war, one brig, and two launches.[1] By October 1825, a new Mexican brig, the *Guerrero* was added to the fleet. Designed by Henry Eckford, the *Guerrero* was destined to be the flower of the Mexican Navy; it was one of the elements that lured U.S. naval officer David Porter to take an official leave of absence from the U.S. Navy and assume command of the Mexican Navy in July of 1826. It was not unusual for such crossovers to occur, as highly skilled naval commanders were in demand. Porter's difficulties with the Mexican Navy are documented elsewhere—difficulties in part occasioned by his poor knowledge of the Spanish language and his "fantastic idea that Mexico should build him a steam frigate and give him an allowance of $13,000 a month."[2]

Although Mexico inherited several important coastal ports, the only port of any consequence permitted by Spain in Texas had been Espíritu Santo Bay. Thus, Mexican Texas was underdeveloped as regards its ports, despite the fact that a small naval force could help defend its northern Gulf coast frontier from possible attack. However, located along the south-central Texas coast, the port of La Bahía proved to be far from the part of Texas that began to feel the pressure of population development from European Americans seeking new opportunities in the Spanish frontier lands—the northeast coast bordering on Louisiana. It was this movement of European Americans that would ultimately prove a far greater threat to Mexico than its still angry former parent, Spain.

The Misadventures of the Schooner *Lively*

By the early 1820s, Mexican authorities were being urged to reconsider their relatively restrictive view of the Texas coast, and no person was more persuasive in this regard than Stephen F. Austin. Known as a tireless promoter of Texas in the 1820s, the Virginia-born Austin was part of a peripatetic, originally Yankee family headed by Moses Austin. Ever in search of opportunity, Moses had moved his family to frontier Missouri in continuing pursuit of lead-mining interests and commercial trade. After financial setbacks in Missouri, in 1819 the senior Austin eyed Texas, where he hoped to develop a colony with the blessings of the Spanish crown. Upon the death of his father, Moses, Stephen Austin became actively involved in the promotion, colonization, and improvement of Texas, first as a loyal Spanish, and then Mexican, citizen after 1821. Eugene Barker's detailed synthesis of the Austin papers of the 1820s and 1830s records Austin's persistence in advocating the

FIGURE 4-1
Schooners proved to be extremely important in early nineteenth-century Texas
trade and changed rather little throughout the nineteenth century. A Galveston
photographer, H. H. Morris, recorded this one about 1900.
Courtesy Rosenberg Library, Galveston.

development of ports and maritime trade. The port of La Bahía de San
Bernardo was authorized in January of 1821, and Austin landed there in
October of that year, reporting a plan to explore the coast in search of the
best location for the port.[3]

The Texas coast that Austin first encountered in the 1820s was still a wilderness but was becoming less remote as revolutionary developments swept
maritime transportation. A wide variety of small, fast schooners had reached
near perfection on the Atlantic coast from New England to the Chesapeake
Bay. The story of the arrival of the schooner *Lively* with the first contingent
of Austin's colonists in 1821 has been told and retold, but it bears repeating
here inasmuch as confusion about the vessel's fate resulted in much speculation, some of which turned into folklore. We know little about the *Lively*,
except that she was a schooner of moderate size (approximately thirty tons)[4]

that carried about twenty settlers plus a small crew of about four to five. Although the *Lively* sailed during a time when drawings or plans of vessels were rare, she was probably similar to schooners common throughout the nineteenth century, as widely photographed by century's end (Fig. 4-1).

We do know that the *Lively* left New Orleans on about November 27, 1821, for the mouth of the Colorado River, where she was awaited by Stephen Austin himself, but failed to arrive on schedule. What, Austin pondered as time dragged on, had happened to the vessel and its prospective colonists?[5] One of the vessel's passengers, a Mr. Lewis,[6] a Kentuckian native and riverboat clerk who had been invited by Austin to join the colony, provided a fascinating account of the *Lively*'s enigmatic 1821 voyage to Texas. According to Mr. Lewis, who mentions that the schooner was called the "Little Lively," and that she had been overhauled before the voyage, her crew was skippered by a "Yankee miscreant" and contained "an 'old salt,' a negro, as cook. And a good one he was, besides every inch a sailor."[7] In addition to her crew and passengers, the *Lively* carried provisions and tools for the new colony. Accounts of her voyage to Texas revealed that she carried sacks of salt, barrels of mess pork, flour, Irish potatoes, a cask of bacon, several barrels of pilot and sea bread, rice, and lard.[8] Above this freight and ballast, a "second floor" (i.e., deck) had been constructed for the immigrants.[9] Two or three days out, on the "blue gulf," as Lewis called it, the *Lively* encountered a terrible gale that blew for thirty-six hours; this gale was followed by calm that lasted "a similar length of time," only to be succeeded by "a fine east wind" that enabled them to sail past the opening of Galveston Bay.[10] In yet another navigational error of the type so common along the Texas coast, the crew of the *Lively* mistook the Brazos River for the Colorado River and landed there instead.

Hearing no word, the downcast Stephen Austin assumed that the *Lively* had been lost at sea; rumors soon developed, including one seemingly worse than shipwreck, namely that the crew and passengers had been starved by Indians. However, because some observers had reportedly witnessed the *Lively* sailing away (that is, westward) from the Brazos, some assumed that she continued on to the Rio Grande in South Texas, where, it was later rumored, she became a pirate ship. Although we may never know the ultimate fate of the *Lively*, a historian has surmised that "there is little doubt that the *Lively* succeeded in finding the Colorado . . . and returned safe to New Orleans," and that she made a return trip to "the Texas coast in May or June, 1822, [where] she was wrecked on the western end of Galveston Island," and her passengers were taken on board the schooner *John Motley* and put ashore at the proper landing place at the mouth of the Colorado.[11] This indicates that the *Lively* was involved in two misadventures on the Texas coast, the first embarrassing and the second probably disastrous. It is interesting that the reports from the *Lively*'s original 1821 voyage mention several other sailing vessels in the vicinity of the mouth of the Brazos that had witnessed her passage, an indication of the brisk trade, some of it privateering, that was occurring on the Texas coast in the early 1820s. Also of interest is Stephen F. Austin's close associate Joseph Hawkins, who, fearing that the *Lively* had been lost, "secured another vessel, a sloop called the *Only Son*, to sail to Texas to search for the lost schooner, or to carry another load of immigrants to the colony, or both."[12] From the records of the time, we are left with the picture of numerous sloops and schooners, of which the *Lively* was but one, plying the waters of the Texas coast; many, like the *Lively*, had Yankee skippers at the helm. Whatever her fate, the *Lively* was probably representative of the schooners of the period.

The eyewitness Mr. Lewis left a vivid account of the trials and tribulations faced by the first colonists who were mistakenly delivered to the wrong location by the *Lively* in 1821. Some attempted to settle in what was then the Texas wilderness along the lower Brazos near the Gulf but ultimately found their way back to the United States after their food supplies had dwindled. Doing so required making a boat to navigate the rivers: Lewis described in considerable detail the construction of a skiff, which took about two weeks. A skiff is variously defined as a small sailing craft, usually open, or simply a rowboat. Lewis's description mentions a small sail, probably a sprit sail, that would give the skiff an added advantage in a breeze but, like all sails, could become a hazard in windy weather by capsizing the vessel. In just such a high wind, the sail on Lewis's skiff luckily wrapped around the mast, probably saving those on board. Although rather rarely mentioned, the skiff was important in helping colonists gain access into the interior lagoons and lower reaches of Texas rivers, a reminder that lowly or mundane boats made exploration and colonization, and sometimes the return to civilization, possible.

It was the schooner, however, that enabled colonists to travel great distances in the early 1800s. Although little is known about the schooner *Lively*, we do know that similar schooners usually carried two masts, were about sixty feet long, and displaced about fifty tons. Possessing two or more masts rigged fore and aft, schooners like the *Lively* were usually fairly fast and very versatile. Although schooners like the *Lively* carried passengers and cargo officially sanctioned by Spain, enterprising mariners also used the schooner for illicit purposes, especially privateering. Spanish, and later Mexican, tariffs had positioned the coast for a lively trade in smuggled goods. It was on the Texas coast that schooners soon found themselves in a thriving smuggling trade. This was natural because "smuggled goods are commonly handled in comparatively small cargoes, and small vessels are more easily handled in the small smuggling ports and the schooner, being a narrow fleet vessel with a small crew, made the ideal smuggler."[13]

STEPHEN F. AUSTIN AND THE OPENING OF THE TEXAS COAST

Despite problems with the arrival of colonists on the *Lively*, water access to Texas would prove feasible and popular. Austin had anticipated the importance of the waters of Texas for colonization, having obtained, on August 17, 1821, permission to explore the country along the Brazos River and to sound the entrances and harbors lying adjacent to the river.[14] Recognizing the importance of maritime connections, Austin also was an advocate of opening ports as early as the fall of 1821. Being very perceptive, Austin noted at this early date the governor's reluctance to allow a new colony at Galveston, which was too near the United States. Perhaps in deference to these official concerns about Galveston, Austin instead worked to first open up the more-distant Colorado River to trade. He also began to develop trade by shipping goods to the far-southerly port of Copano Bay, which was often called Capano Bay in early correspondence. By 1822, only two major settlements—Bahía and Béxar—existed among the numerous Indian tribes of south-central Texas. A letter from Governor Antonio Martínez to Gaspar López outlined the conditions of maritime trade, noting that La Bahía should be declared a major port, and adding that two gunboats were necessary to control pirates and smugglers.[15]

Meanwhile, Stephen Austin's associates who kept up with news from the United States were becoming ever more aware of developments in maritime transportation. The Mexican government hoped to encourage more effective navigation of the rivers of the Mexican Republic, and it recognized at this early date the potential of steam power. The government offered incentives to the parties who would introduce successful steam navigation, including a virtual two-year monopoly on all such trade. Aware of developments in technology, as early as April 1824 George Robb informed Austin that the ports on the Brazos, and the Brazos River itself, appeared to be excellent prospects for a *steam boat*, and after this date increasing mention is made of steam propulsion on the waters of Texas.[16] By this time, Austin was actively involved in maritime trade, which was centered on New Orleans, and the ports of Texas began to develop slowly in response to his efforts. Austin continued to operate on the premise that the key to opening Texas lay in its waterways, and technological developments in maritime transportation would soon coincide with his vision of land development in the form of large *empresarios*.

Privy to an incredible wealth of geographic information about the coast, the enterprising Austin asked for authorization to extend his colony to the mouth of the San Jacinto and in the Galveston area by August 1824, noting that failure to do so would result in its reverting to a state of "lawlessness and piracy" that had formerly characterized it.[17] Also cognizant of the importance of access to Texas by water, Austin's associate and backer Joseph H. Hawkins made frequent reference to maritime developments, as when he commented on the prospects of the small settlement ("a house or two") at the mouth of the Colorado River, noted that he was taking three vessels to the mouth of the Guadalupe River, and added that there was an encampment at the mouth of the Brazos River that could help facilitate colonization.

But it was Galveston that continued to lure most empresarios and entrepreneurs who sought to develop Texas. In November of 1824, Austin asked the president of Mexico to authorize a settlement on Galveston Island so that cotton could be shipped to England as soon as a cotton gin became operational. Austin wrote a letter to the Mexican congress requesting the establishment of a major seaport there. This was followed by Baron de Bastrop's proposal, which would authorize Galveston as a major seaport due to its having a reported eighteen-foot depth at the bar; Bastrop's report continued by noting that ports at Brazos and Matagorda offered depths of [only] 8 and 4 feet, respectively. Bastrop summarized conditions by stating that the interior settlements of Béxar, Bahía, and San Felipe needed the port at Matagorda, further stating that Galveston and Brazos were "vital" to the future of the Mexican Republic.[18] Bastrop urged pushing for full enforcement of a royal order opening Matagorda and Bahía, at the same time pressing for Brazos, Colorado, La Baca, and Galveston as "intercoastal" ports.[19] The opening of a major port at Galveston, exact location to be determined, passed by unanimous vote on May 25, 1825.[20] Mexico, it seemed, would do what Spain had been reluctant to do, open the Texas coast to development.

Cartographic knowledge kept pace with Austin's aggressive development plans, and probably aided them. By the mid 1820s, Austin recognized the need for mapping of the coast as well as the entire province, both as a tool for actual development and as a catalyst for generating more interest in the area (Fig. 4-2). Austin used existing maps, inspiring the first separately printed map of Texas in 1826 by Fiorenzo Galli, which makes note of "the small submerged islands" off the coast, and remarks that "there is a lagoon from the Santiago Bar in the State of Tamaulipas all the way to the vicinity of the mouth of the Brazos River."[21] While we recognize this "lagoon" as several lagoons, including Laguna Madre and Matagorda Bay, the map continues with an ominous note about the bar at the Brazos, to the effect that it "is bad because it is only 6 feet deep and the current is very strong," and "consequently the landing place most frequently used is Trinity Bay or Galvestown [sic] to take the Cíbola Creek [Buffalo Bayou] by which ships up to 100 tons burden can come up within 22 leagues of the *Villa* of Austin."[22] The map also references the magnificent Matagorda Bay as having "4 rivers which make it easy to land: 1. The Colorado River to the north; 2. The Lavaca (a river or creek) where ships enter; 3. The Garcitas [Little Herons]; and 4. The San Antonio River."[23] Thus, by the 1820s, Austin had a blueprint for the development of maritime trade, which would naturally focus on the passes or openings through which the great rivers of Texas—and hence the interior—could be reached.

By the spring of 1826, Austin's papers documented a vigorous maritime trade beset by problems: The Mexican Senate's approval of Galveston Port was stalled in the lower house and Indians attacked European Americans arriving in a small boat, wounding two and killing two of the new arrivals—an action that prompted calls for the removal of Indians from the area around Matagorda.[24] As trade from the United States increased to the Austin colony, it was noted that U.S. law would require a vessel of over thirty tons, which was bigger than the sloop, the *Roberts*, that currently was serving the route from New Orleans. Austin also implored to authorities: "Get me several row and sail boats, of 10 men capacity each, deliver(ed) at Matagorda soon" in order to be able to "conduct a complete coastal survey."[25] In response, Austin was informed that a schooner of three-foot draft that would "be perfect for the survey project" had been purchased, and that a "master and good crew" could be obtained for $135 per month with provisions and everything included, while the smaller boats were being sought.[26]

Austin received disconcerting reports from the San Jacinto area that only one boat would meet his needs, but that it might be worm-eaten. The report added that there might be another on the Trinity, but that people had been seen illegally raiding the *Mary* for ropes, blocks, tackles, and so forth. Un-

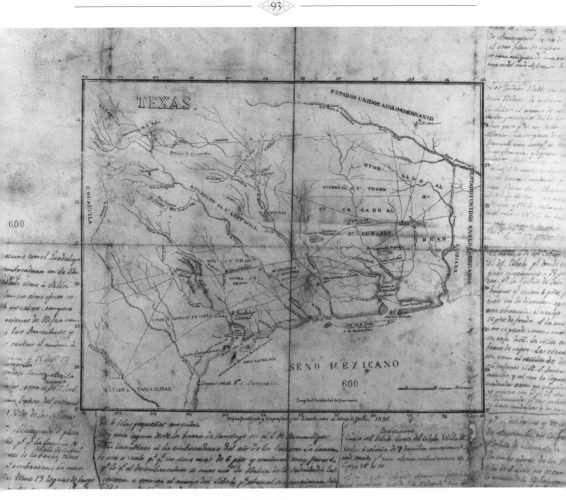

FIGURE 4-2

*Recognizing the need for mapping of the coast as well as the entire province as a
catalyst for generating more interest in the area, Stephen F. Austin inspired the
creation of maps, including the first separately printed map of Texas in 1826
by Fiorenzo Galli, shown here. Courtesy Special Collections Division,
The University of Texas at Arlington Libraries, Arlington.*

daunted, Austin reported to Erasmo Seguín that he would be conducting a survey, and drawing a chart, of Galveston Bay. Austin wrote a long letter to Seguín, noting that after surveying, he found Galveston's port to be "superb," but the area still so "wild and desolate" that a customs house should be established temporarily at the mouth of the Brazos, which was "civilized" and nearer to settlements. Austin also recommended customs houses at the mouth of the Colorado and at Matagorda.[27]

VESSELS AND PORTS OF THE MEXICAN TEXAS COAST

Stephen F. Austin's correspondence from the period offers a glimpse of the vessels of the era that sailed into this part of Mexico. In his prolific correspondence with Mexican officials, some of whom shared his vision of coastal development, Austin often mentions vessels by either type or name. For example, he wrote to R. Machada, through the agency of Col. Ahumada, stating, "I got you a sloop and small boat to be delivered at mouth of San Ant[onio] river, fully equipped & provisioned"; and in a letter to Ahumada, Austin noted that the six-ton sloop was purchased, in part, because it was a better vessel that would then serve for coast guard duty or sailing to Tampico.[28] Empresario Green C. DeWitt reported to Austin in September of 1826 that the schooner *Despatch*, of fifty tons, had been contracted to provide regular service, and that a lighter (30 × 12 feet) warehouse and other facilities were under construction at Labaca for the sake of commerce and immigrants coming to Texas.[29] A deposition by J. L. Phillip to Austin noted that the schooner *Augusta*, sailing to New Orleans from San Jacinto, stayed away from the Crescent City, transshipping its cargo to another schooner to protect it from seizure by United States authorities on account of debts.[30] Austin's correspondence reveals that the *Augusta* returned to Texas, bringing five families to the mouth of the Trinity at Anáhuac. Contraband and illegal cargoes as defined by Mexican authorities also plagued Austin; this was exemplified when he wrote to the *ayuntamiento* at Béxar protesting seizure of a cargo at Labaca and asking for clarification of the laws granting duty-free trade rights—an issue that would become explosive by the 1830s.

In east Texas, Anáhuac had begun to develop on Galveston Bay in order to serve as a port for the now nearly moribund missions in the vicinity of Nacogdoches. An order by the Congress of Mexico established the port of Galveston as a port of customs entry on October 17, 1825, but fourteen more years would pass before a city was established there.[31] Scattered along the Texas coast, these ports were primitive, often no more than a customs house or at most a cluster of houses huddled behind makeshift piers or landings that enabled vessels to unload and load their small cargoes and the few passengers who traveled by the small sailing vessels such as schooners and sloops. Those vessels that drew deeper water stayed some distance from the shore while they were loaded and offloaded by lighters. This additional handling added to the cost of shipping and increased the likelihood of damage to cargo.

Many early travelers recorded their concern about the primitive conditions in early Texas ports, and these conditions could be attributable to generations of neglect. Under Spanish rule, the interior of Texas had developed rather more rapidly than the coast because Spain had put most of its efforts into establishing missions inland. Furthermore, Spain had retarded the growth of Texas ports by requiring all trade to enter Mexico by way of Veracruz. The ports were thus undeveloped because Spain had encouraged the use of roads rather than its waters. Of these roads, the *camino real* served as the major thoroughfare connecting the communities on the Texas frontier (e.g., San Antonio and Nacogdoches) with the major communities of Mexico, including Monterrey, Saltillo, and Mexico City. It was this primitive pattern that the European Americans arriving under Mexican rule inherited, and began to rectify by the mid 1820s. Texas maritime historian Jim Dan Hill claimed that "by 1825, Galveston, Brazoria and Matagorda were *de facto* ports of entry [but] Espíritu Santo Bay was still deserted."[32]

This development of ports along the northern Mexican (that is, Texas) coast was accompanied by rapid developments in maritime technology and naval architecture. By the early 1820s, larger square-rigged vessels of the clipper design had been developed; many of these had the sleek low-hull profiles inspired in part by British and U.S. warships, such as frigates. These vessels rarely ventured far into the Texas corner of the Gulf, however, as they generally sailed between established ports. For the Texas trade, schooners, which were both maneuverable and solid vessels able to carry substantial cargoes, became the vessel of choice (Fig. 4-3). By the early nineteenth century, then, sailing vessels were becoming specialized: clippers or larger square-rigged vessels for transoceanic shipping and schooners for coastwise shipping. All of these developments in sailing technology symbolized the coming of age of U.S. merchant shipping in the brief half century since independence had been won from Britain. The changes did not bode well for Mexico, for an increasing number of freewheeling enterprising European American sea captains used the sailing technology to defy Mexican control of shipping as they found their way to the Texas coast.

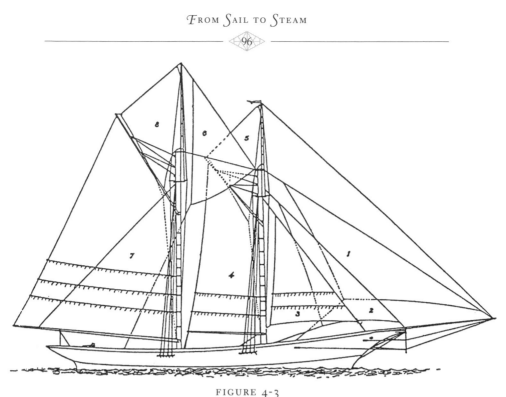

FIGURE 4-3
*Schooners similar to the craft illustrated here became the mainstay of the Texas
maritime trade by the 1830s. Source: Robert Taggart, "Evolution of Vessels Engaged
in the Waterborne Commerce of the United States," 1983; and Charles E. Pearson*
et al., Underwater Archaeology Along the Lower Navidad and Lavaca Rivers,
1993. *Reproduced with permission.*

Stephen F. Austin recognized that Texas was provided a natural access
by water. To Austin, the rivers of Texas beckoned as natural entryways to the
province's interior. Many travelers and settlers, including Ohioan Joseph
Chambers Clopper, shared Austin's views. Clopper helped develop a parcel
of land that his father had purchased on speculation in the late 1820s. His
journal describes a journey to Texas from New Orleans on the schooner
Little Zoe in late 1827. After a sometimes harrowing trip on this small schooner (burden twenty tons), "a Gondola that scarcely wakes the tide," the company finally found their way into Galveston after being blown off course
and spending the better part of a day finding the entrance. Once inside the
harbor, which they entered only after "striking on the bar," they found their
way into "a deep and commodious harbor" that connected with the rivers to
the interior. Clopper described the "meandering San Jacinto" and the mouth
of Buffalo Bayou as

the most remarkable stream I have ever seen—[which] at its junction with the San Jacinto is about 150 yds in breadth having about three fathoms water with little variation in depth as high up as Harrisburg—20 miles—the ebbing and flowing of the tide is observable about 12 miles higher the water being navigable depth close up to each bank giving to this most enchanting little stream the appearance of an artificial canal in the design and course of which nature has lent her masterly hand.[33]

Even at this early date, Harrisburg's advantages were well appreciated; despite its being but "6 or 8 houses scatteringly situated," Clopper realized that "being situated at the head of navigation," Harrisburg "only wanted a population a little more dense and a few capitalists of enterprise and energy to render it one of the most important towns in the colony."[34] Clopper likewise recognized the potential of the Brazos, noting: "There is more than one individual on this *Mississippi of Texas*, as the Brazos may well be termed if small things may be compared with great, who will turn out more than 100 bales of cotton and sugar cane proportionally." In describing Austin's colony, Clopper noted that "vessels do not yet approach nearer than within 60 miles of Sanfelipe [*sic*]—but at a small expense [the river] can be rendered navigable for small steam vessels the whole distance up 160 miles by water and 80 by land from the seaboard."[35] If, by the mid 1820s, enterprising European Americans intuitively recognized and began to promote the potential of the rivers for steam navigation, their early writings were to prove prophetic in light of aggressive maritime-related developments that would soon open up the province of Texas to a steady flow of European Americans.

By the late 1820s, Austin's brother James and cousin John became active players in the maritime trade to Texas. James and John Austin asked for papers that would authorize a schooner they had purchased to ship Texas products from the mouth of the Brazos to Matamoros, Tampico, and other Mexican ports. The empresario himself wrote to authorities asking for help in getting a Mexican flag for his relatives' schooner, and on the recommendation of Captain General Anastacio Bustamante, the Navy department issued instructions in January of 1829 that permitted the clearing of the schooner *Eclipse* from Matamoros.[36] As if to underscore the risks of shipping along the coast at this time, however, the *Eclipse* was lost, an event that prompted Austin to write to General Mier y Terán recommending that a *steamship* would be better for the coastal trade between the Texas colonies and

Matamoros,[37] which was situated on the lower Rio Grande. With this correspondence we anticipate the actual arrival of the first steam-powered vessel
into Texas — the *Ariel*.

THE MISADVENTURES OF THE *Ariel*

European American Texans had speculated for several years about the need
for steamboats to open the interior, and in April 1828 two enterprising individuals, Col. Juan Davis Bradburn and Stephen Staples, were granted a
concession to operate a steamboat. Though their partnership efforts failed,
their visions became reality when Henry Austin, one of Stephen Austin's
nautically oriented cousins, became involved in the project and arrived with
his New York-built steam-powered vessel early in the summer of 1829.[38] The
October 24, 1829, issue of *The Texas Gazette* reported that "Capt. Henry
Austin of New York arrived at the mouth of the Rio Bravo in June last with
the STEAM-BOAT ARIEL, destined to make an experiment of steam navigation on that river"; the report added that "this is the first effort that has
been attempted to introduce this new species of navigation on any of the
rivers of the Mexican republic, and it displays a degree of bold adventurous
enterprise highly creditable to the man who has successfully undertaken
it."[39]

This "new species" of boat propelled by the power of steam is widely
attributed to the Yankee inventor Robert Fulton, who some two decades
before (1807) had successfully demonstrated the use of steam on New York's
Hudson River. Fulton capitalized on the principle, known and used by the
English, of a reciprocating steam engine that was connected to paddlewheels
which would in turn drive the vessel (Fig. 4-4). After remarking upon Fulton
and the U.S. origins of steam riverboats that were freeing river navigation
from the slow pole boats and keelboats of the era, *The Texas Gazette* noted
that even Europe was now "compelled to draw upon the genius and enterprise of the new world, and steam-boats now swarm on all her rivers and
bays." The report added that "the object of Capt. Austin is to introduce this
improvement in navigation, into the Mexican republic, and by its means, to
open a speedy and SAFE communication by water, on the Rio Bravo, from
the sea coast into the most interior and central region of the Mexican territory, comprehending Coahuila, Chihuahua, and New-Mexico."[40] These
sentiments expressed the writer's hope that Austin's steamboat *Ariel* would
be as successful as the steamboats that were inspired by Fulton's *Clermont*
and were daily revolutionizing commerce in the east.[41]

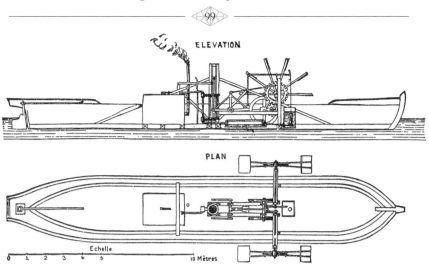

ELEVATION

PLAN

FIGURE 4-4
As depicted in this original drawing, Robert Fulton and his partner first built a successful steamboat in France in 1803, capitalizing on the principle of a reciprocating steam engine that drove the paddlewheels. Reproduced from Thomas W. Knox,
The Life of Robert Fulton, *1886.*

Although the *Clermont* revolutionized U.S. maritime transportation, maritime historian Paul Forsythe Johnston estimates that it actually took about a decade for steamboats to begin regular operation in the northeastern United States, as a result of Fulton's restrictive patents.[42] Thus, at the time that Henry Austin's steamboat *Ariel* ventured to the Mexican province of Texas in 1829, steam propulsion was indeed something of a novelty, in an age when communications still traveled at a rate no faster than the horse — or a swift sailing vessel. Placed in historical and geographical context, the steamboat freed travelers from sole dependence on river currents, and the early nineteenth century witnessed a remarkable penetration of the interior of the North American continent. Opening these same rivers as pathways of commerce became a passion with entrepreneurs in the period. According to newspaper reports, Henry Austin succeeded in getting the *Ariel* to operate as far as Revilla, about three hundred miles upriver from the Gulf on the Salado River, a tributary of the Rio Bravo (Rio Grande). Austin also reached Camargo, on the San Juan River, which also flows into the Rio Grande. Despite much investment of energy, however, Austin's efforts were not financially successful, and he decided to return to the United States with the *Ariel*. On that voyage, the *Ariel* was wracked by waves and wind when it grounded on the Brazos bar, proving first-hand the hazards of navigation on the Texas coast. The mission of the first steamboat to Texas thus ended in failure.

And yet, the failure of the *Ariel* should be placed in the context of both the rather primitive conditions in Texas in the late 1820s and early 1830s, and Austin's high expectations. Henry Austin's biographer, William R. Hogan, noted that several factors, including a sluggish economy, the conditions of the river, and Austin's personal difficulty in establishing business relations in Mexico may have overwhelmed this Yankee entrepreneur. Of the failure of the *Ariel*'s mission, Henry Austin himself intimated to his cousin Stephen on May 27, 1830, that "nothing but my pride and the censure to which I should expose myself by abandoning a project of my own choosing has induced me to continue here so long."[43] To a wearying Henry Austin, even the Brazos River presented poor prospects, "unless the river could be made more navigable and connected by canal to Galveston Bay"; of the virtual wrecking of the *Ariel* on the Brazos bar, he added dejectedly that she was "leaking badly & her chimney blown away."[44] Mary Austin Holley characterized the beating that both the *Ariel* and Henry Austin had taken when she poignantly wrote that "pretty 'Ariel' which left New York with such excited expectations of untold wealth . . . now lies a wreck and a monument of the futility of premature labors, on the Buffalo Bayou, Texas."[45]

The *Ariel*'s adventures cast a spell on later generations of historians, who could only admire Austin's pluck and the vessel's revolutionary, seemingly animate technology. The popular southwestern historian Paul Horgan wrote romantically about the *Ariel* in his epic book on the Rio Grande nearly half a century ago, noting that "she paddled along bustily like a heavy, changeling swan that could never leave the water, though giving to the sky from her tall black neck a proud and billowing banner of dense smoke shot through with huge sparks of burning wood that crackled upward when the boilers were stocked anew."[46] In a direct reference to Austin's experiences with the steamboat *Ariel* on the fickle Texas rivers, Horgan concluded somewhat wryly that "there was something absurdly valiant in taking a steamboat where there was no water."[47]

With the misadventures of *Ariel*, Henry Austin had unwittingly discovered two realities that make navigation so problematical in Texas. First, its coast is always hazardous due to the treacherous bars obstructing access over, or into, the passes—and always susceptible to the uncertainty of weather. Second, the flow of Texas rivers is highly variable because of the wide variation in the amount of rainfall received in any particular year, or any particular part of the area. The farther south and west one goes in Texas, the more

arid the climate: Thus, west Texas rivers are especially difficult to navigate
for they are usually shallow and their levels very erratic. It is ironic that
Austin chose the Rio Grande, for his perceptive cousin Stephen F. Austin
had noted that the arid countryside along the river seemed marginal. However, even the normally more predictable rivers of the more lush east Texas
vary seasonally in their flow. A river that is navigable after spring rains may
be nearly dry in the summer, especially if that summer experiences a drought.
This fluctuation would prove vexing to those who promoted river traffic.
History would show that opening the Texas rivers to trade required a good
deal of persistence, hard work, patience, and luck. Although Henry Austin
met with defeat in his venture, other European Americans would soon bring
steam-powered boats into Texas—and would have considerably better luck
with their ventures.

The *Ariel* was presumably named for the prankish sprite in Shakespeare's
Tempest. In his thesis, "Steamboating on the Lower Rio Grande River,"
Stephen A. Townsend noted that the 86-ton vessel had a 100,000-pound
(50-ton) cargo capacity and drew about five feet of water when loaded.[48]
These figures indicate that the *Ariel* was typical of the small riverboats of the
era, and should not be confused with the larger vessels that were being developed to serve the growing trade on the larger western rivers such as the
Ohio and Mississippi. An illustration of the *Ariel* has yet to be located, but
the Texas maritime historian Tom Fort, who has compiled an impressive
file on the vessel, speculates that she was probably propelled by two paddlewheels amidships (much like Fulton's pioneering vessel), and may have
been rigged for sail with a bowsprit.[49] In Spanish, steam-powered sidewheel
riverboats like the *Ariel* would be called *vapores fluviales a ruedas*. To date,
the *Ariel*'s appearance remains something of a mystery—not surprising con-
sidering she operated at a time when many vessels were made without detailed plans, and illustrations were still very rare in newspapers. Those same
early newspapers, however, occasionally used stylized images of vessels in
advertisements (Fig. 4-5). Two in particular from *The Texas Gazette* are of
interest to maritime historians. Using a stylishly rigged schooner vessel in
profile, the September 24, 1829, issue notes, under a heading "New Orleans,"
that "the substantial schooner AUGUSTA, P. Dunn, Master, will leave Harrisburg for the above port, on the 15th of October. For freight or passage, apply
to the Master, on board, or to John D. Taylor, Harrisburg."

About a month later, *The Texas Gazette* (October 24, 1829) amended the
earlier advertisement by noting that "owing to the sickness of Capt. Dunn,
the AUGUSTA will not sail until the 25th, *Instant*, on which day, she will

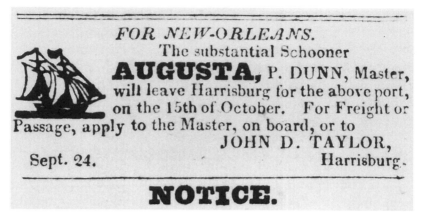

FIGURE 4-5

Early newspapers occasionally used stylized images of vessels in advertisements. This, from the Texas Gazette *of 1829, is of interest to maritime historians for it is among the earliest of visual depictions of Texas vessels used by European Americans. Courtesy of the Center for American History, University of Texas at Austin.*

positively depart."[50] The schooner *Augusta* presumably sailed, but, as fate would have it, it was again mentioned several months later in another issue of *The Texas Gazette*, this time not to announce her sailing dates or the health of her captain, but rather to proclaim the *Augusta* was for sale. The advertisement, featuring the same stylized silhouette of a vessel, announces "PUBLIC SALE. Will be sold at public sale, at the town of Harrisburg, on Saturday the 13th of February next, (if not disposed of at private sale, previous to that time) the schooner AUGUSTA, as she now lays, in Buffalo Bayou, with her Tackle, aparel & c." The advertisement further advised that "she can be sent to sea at a small expense—Terms—Payable in cows, horses, or *cash.*" Prospective buyers were instructed to apply to Captain Dunn.[51] Given the scarcity of capital in the province at the time, it is not surprising that goods instead of cash could secure the vessel, although the italicizing of the word *cash* in the advertisement surely indicated the preference for specie.

That the graphic depicting the *Augusta* was simply a stylized representation of a vessel is seen in another advertisement that appeared in *The Texas Gazette* of July 3, 1830, which used the very same illustration to advertise an opportunity to travel: "For New-York via South-West Pass. The fast sailing sloop NELSON, Brown, Master—will sail from Brazoria, in five or six days, and will land passengers at the south-west pass.—For freight or passage, apply on board at Brazoria, J. Brown." Evidently, the newspaper's publishers had no reservations about using the same illustration for numerous advertisements, whether the vessel in question was a schooner or a sloop, or possessed some other sail pattern. Even in the late 1820s and early 1830s, standardization and stylization led to the use of generic images to convey maritime travel. This should warn maritime historians that an illustration purporting to be a particular vessel may not be an accurate depiction of that vessel. Indeed, one should regard drawings or engravings from the period with suspicion, for they depend both on the artist's sometimes limited awareness of maritime technology and the credibility of sources that the artist used in making the illustration.[52]

OPPORTUNITIES AND DISILLUSIONMENT

The same period that the *Ariel* first introduced steam power to Texas and experienced such disappointing setbacks in the process (1829–1830) also witnessed a continued influx of European Americans and other immigrants. At this time the term *seaboard* came into use in reference to the Texas littoral, a usage clearly traceable to the geographical origins of many of those who used it—the eastern seaboard of the United States. Many of the newcomers were bent on one general mission: to open up the country to development, including agriculture and mining, and thereby to open up its "natural" trade routes in the process. A similar process had been used about two generations earlier as the commercial development of the U.S. eastern seaboard spread inland. In letters written to his associate Martin Van Buren in 1829, David G. Burnet, a New Jersey native and an aspiring colonizer, anticipated the development of the province of Texas into two powerful and wealthy zones or states, "the one rich, populous & maritime, the other interior, but possessing exuberant soil, indefinite [sic] mineral wealth, & a most delightful climate."[53] To link the maritime zone with the interior, riverboats were envisioned. Visionaries thus imagined the Texas hinterland, with its untold wealth, awaiting only the tools of the agriculturalist and miner, and the skills of the mariner, to open world markets. Interestingly, that interior hinterland could not, and would not, develop until the Texas ports were improved and the rivers opened to commerce. Virtually all astute observers recognized that the Texas coast had to be developed in order to make this dream a reality. As we have seen, Stephen F. Austin had been acting on that premise throughout the 1820s as he constantly beseeched the Mexican authorities to liberalize tariffs and encourage, rather than suppress, coastal trade.

The Austin correspondence of the late 1820s reveals how actively this empresario endeavored to open up maritime trade. He pushed Mexican authorities to open a port at the mouth of the Brazos, which soon bore the name *Brazoria* in Austin's correspondence. In this effort to develop the coast, Austin's skill as a diplomat became apparent. However, while Austin pushed for numerous ports, especially Galveston, the authorities vacillated and in fact were seemingly unable to decide which port, if any, should be opened. When La Bahía was threatened with closure, Austin argued that Bahía, Nacogdoches, and Galveston should *all* be active ports, as this would stimulate trade to all regions of the province.

Because Mexican law prohibited foreigners (i.e., colonizers from the United States) from settling within approximately ten leagues of the coast, much of the empresario development took place somewhat farther inland. By the late 1820s, much of Texas back of this "coastal reserve" to about three hundred miles inland was divided into several large land grants that were developed and promoted by empresarios. As early as 1824, Don Martin de León had settled Mexican families and founded a town along the lower Guadalupe River. Irish and U.S. colonists also settled here, and two Irish empresarios, James Power and James Hewetson, encouraged Irish immigrants to settle near the coast north of the Nueces River. However, many empresarios and colonists met with defeat. For example, in East Texas David Burnet, Lorenzo de Zavala, and Joseph Vehlein had obtained separate contracts but sold their lands on October 16, 1830, to the Galveston Bay and Texas Land Company, a speculative, immigration-based enterprise that had enticed settlers from Germany and Switzerland to migrate to Texas. Upon arriving by sailing vessel from New York, however, these immigrants were stranded at the mouth of the Trinity River due to the Mexican ban on immigration that was imposed in 1830. Although permitted to build huts and cultivate gardens, they were denied the ability to obtain title to the land, and thereafter slowly assimilated into the Texas population.[54] Whatever their fortunes, most immigrants of this period arrived by the sea. However, it should be noted that some empresarios, particularly Sterling C. Robertson of the Nashville Company, whose large grant (The Robertson Colony) was landlocked, evidently also encouraged immigration overland from Tennessee and other states. Nevertheless, even many of these colonists traveled to Texas, in part using river transportation, such as keel boats and early steamboats.

The Mexican authorities, of course, were anxious to keep a close eye on immigration. They attempted to monitor, and tax, all maritime trade into Texas and Coahuila. They also remained concerned about defending the ports along this part of their coast. By early 1831, Stephen F. Austin wrote to Benton, noting that when Texas grew, U.S. consuls would be needed in Galveston, Brazoria, Matagorda, and Aransas and adding that most trade in Texas was currently going through Brazoria.[55] In a letter to Minister Alamán, Austin had earlier advocated to authorities the need to open these ports to free maritime trade, citing the problem of charging multiple tonnage fees (which, as Austin cited in the letter, had been levied against the schooner *Champion*) as needing to be promptly corrected.[56]

Meanwhile, correspondence from Austin's cousin John reveals several schooners in the trade from New York to Texas, including the *Nelson* for Brazoria, the *Glide* for Anáhuac/Galveston Bay, and the packet *Boston* (which was intended to be kept in the Texas–New Orleans trade) for Matagorda.[57] By June 30, 1831, customer receipts at Galveston and Brazoria totaled 152 tons, yielding revenues of $297 for the first half of the year; no doubt, the real figure would be higher, as contraband was moving readily into the Texas coast because there were so many anchorage points that schooners could slip into and out of virtually undetected. As a loyal Mexican citizen, Austin attempted to reduce this chaotic situation and to ensure that maritime trade was properly regulated. However, the issue of unregulated maritime trade, and the strong countermeasures by the Mexican government, would prove to be seeds for the Texas revolution.

REBELLION ON THE WATERS OF TEXAS

Tensions had been building for several years. The Mexican tariff laws of 1827 created considerable discontent, for they imposed a duty of $2.12 1/2 per ton on all foreign vessels—many of which were U.S. ships—entering Mexican ports. The now highly respected Stephen F. Austin urged General Mier y Terán to ease restrictions to trade, which he did in 1830. That year marked the beginning of deteriorating conditions on the Texas coast, however, for in May of that year Terán's subordinate George Fisher began attempting to collect tonnage fees at Brazoria. Later that year, Mexican garrisons arrived at Velasco, between the mouth of the Brazos and Brazoria, and at Anáhuac.[58]

In December 1831, Fisher's insistence that all vessels entering or leaving Brazoria must have clearance papers ratified at Anáhuac led the crews of two vessels at Brazoria to defiantly overpower Mexican waterfront guards and set sail without obtaining clearance documents. In disregard of the Decree of 1830 that opened coastwise commerce, Colonel John D. Bradburn, a filibuster from Virginia, insisted that a sixty-five-ton schooner pay fees every time it entered Texas waters on a voyage from Tampico. Its owner, S. Rhoads Fisher, calculated that these fees would total $552.50, and that "no vessel can stand this and unless a change is made the trade must be abandoned."[59] Bradburn did not relent, however, and in fact urged tighter military control. Bradburn's attitude precipitated a militant reaction in numerous places along the coast, especially in the vicinity of Anáhuac, where Texans blockaded Mexican ports to seize supplies and armaments. They improvised a fleet of schooners (the *Stephen F. Austin*, *Waterwitch*, and *Red Rover*) which cruised up and down Galveston Bay. On June 5, 1832, the *Waterwitch*, under the command of Captain Kokernut, seized a vessel that was carrying provisions for the Mexican garrison at Anáhuac. Shortly thereafter, the *Stephen F. Austin*, under the command of Captain Scott, seized a boat at the mouth of Double Bayou, and Captain Spillman captured two boats off Cedar Point.

The Texans, who ostensibly had viewed favorably the Mexican Constitution of 1824 (with its support of states' rights), now found recent events intolerable. Their "Turtle Bayou Resolutions" listed grievances, a number of which pertained to maritime trade. Using the seized schooner *Brazoria*, Captain William Russell commanded forty troops who forced the surrender of Lt. Col. Ugartechea's troops at Fort Velasco in June of 1832. This marked the first in a series of battles that would ultimately nullify tariff regulations, reopen this part of Mexico to U.S. immigrants, and remove Mexican troops. Significantly, the schooner *Brazoria* served as a battlement for the Texians in this battle. Bolstered, the Texan fleet reached Galveston Island, and took possession of the customs house after capturing the deputy collector.[60] In these and other actions in 1832, Texans considered themselves to be supporting the enigmatic but revolutionary General Antonio López de Santa Anna. That, however, would soon change.

By the early 1830s, smoke appeared on the horizon as a greater number of steamboats and steamships, called *vapores* or *buques de vapor* in Spanish, ventured farther from New Orleans to capitalize on a liberalizing trade with Mexico. Some, like the small steamboat used by Benjamin Milam in 1831 to reconnoiter the Red River, anticipated the flourishing river trade that would develop in relation to cotton production a generation later. Others, better suited to maritime travel, plied the coast carrying cargoes between the primitive but developing ports such as Velasco and Matagorda; as they did, skirmishes increased on the coast. Although Texans had petitioned for separate statehood under the Mexican constitution, the reforms of 1833 eased tensions somewhat. However, by 1834 Texans began to chafe under the increasingly centrist policies of General Santa Anna, who seemed to betray them by announcing the Plan de Cuernavaca. During the spring of 1834, an inspection tour of Texas by Colonel Almonte revealed unprecedented smuggling,[61] no doubt most of it by schooners under the command of rebellious European American skippers. Santa Anna's response to this recalcitrance was the reestablishment of customs houses at Anáhuac and Galveston. To enforce this action, the Mexican Navy's schooner-of-war, *Moctezuma*, "began prowling up and down the coast in the role of a revenue cutter."[62] Tensions increased when news arrived in Galveston that the customs collector at the port of Brazoria collected only tonnage and port fees, while officials in Galveston Bay in addition demanded payment of high Mexican tariffs. European American Texans were further incensed that the fees in the Galveston Bay area could be paid in credit by some, while payment in cash was demanded of others. In actions considered revolutionary and incendiary, Texans refused to sell supplies for garrisons and burned lumber that had been collected for rebuilding the fort at Anáhuac.

Naval action along the Texas coast heated up as the schooner-of-war *Moctezuma* seized the *Martha*, a Texas-owned, U.S.-registered vessel suspected of being involved in smuggling. In her role as revenue cutter, the *Moctezuma* acted to stop the illicit trade, and escorted the *Martha* to Matamoros at the mouth of the Rio Grande. At that time Matamoros, or Matamoras as it was often spelled, was a bustling river and seaport, and had already witnessed the arrival of Henry Austin's steam boat *Ariel* five years earlier. Given the *Martha*'s U.S. registry, her seizure by the *Moctezuma* incensed not only Texans but also Captain Ezekiel Jones, who was in command of the United States Revenue Cutter *Ingham*, which was plying the waters off Texas searching for slavers, an excuse that many U.S. cutters used to patrol the waters off foreign coasts.

As the story has been told and retold, the commander of the *Moctezuma* evidently thought the *Ingham* was another smuggler, and bore down on her in the Gulf well off the mouth of the Rio Grande.[63] *Ingham* fired a broadside at the *Moctezuma*, and urged battle, but the *Moctezuma* fled to the mouth of the Rio Grande. In his haste, the skipper of the *Moctezuma* ran aground on the bar, jettisoning some cargo, and in the process damaging the vessel so severely that it was effectively out of commission for several months. To add to this insult, Captain Jones followed the *Moctezuma* into port, reprimanded the ship's skipper, and won the release of all the "American" citizens on the *Martha*.

The presence of the *Moctezuma* emphasizes the role of the Mexican Navy, which was to convey and protect military movements to Texas by bringing them to the port nearest their destination, thereby avoiding a grueling march through barren and otherwise inhospitable country. Thus it was that Hugo O'Conor's concern was becoming a reality: That is, the use of the ports for the arrival of friendly troops was actually facilitating the penetration of the interior by sea-borne enemy troops, in this case consisting of the very European Americans that Mexico had originally permitted to settle in Texas.

Meanwhile, conditions worsened on the north coast of Texas near Anáhuac. A small flotilla of several Mexican Navy vessels, including the schooner-of-war *Correo de Méjico* (under the command of Thomas Thompson), the *Josefa*, and *Ana Maria* arrived at Galveston Bay. Dismayed to learn that the customs houses were deserted, Thompson and Lt. Don Carlos Ocampo of the Mexican Army tried to restore authority. Thompson warned the citizens of Anáhuac against maintaining their militia, and threatened to burn the town when they ignored this warning. Proclaiming himself "commander of the coast from Tampico to the Sabine" (which, of course, includes the entire Texas coast), Thompson precipitated discontent throughout the north coast area. Discontent further mounted when Thompson reportedly illegally seized a small sloop belonging to A. C. Allen and converted it into a tender in order to supply and provision the *Correo de Méjico*.

VICTORY AT SEA

To underscore the importance of the sea to Texas history during these turbulent times, it should be remembered that Stephen F. Austin's increasingly vocal support of change had led to his incarceration in Mexico, which had embittered him and disposed him toward the growing belief that Texas should become part of the United States. He arrived back in Texas on the *San Felipe*, a schooner armed and under the command of Captain W. A. Hurd. Returning at a propitious moment—just after the *Tremont* had been apprehended by Thompson for failure to show a manifest when it was leaving Brazoria with a cargo of lumber for Pensacola—the *San Felipe* arrived to find that the small steamer *Laura* had managed, by an aggressive use of arms and deft maneuvering, to seize and tow the *Tremont* from the immediate vicinity of the *Correo de Méjico*, while both sailing vessels had been becalmed. Leaving the *Tremont* well out of range of the *Correo de Méjico*, the steamer *Laura* then met Austin's vessel (the *San Felipe*) and towed it into port.

As if this show of activity were not enough to prove the significance of steam power in naval maneuvers, the *Laura* entered the fray again. The next day the *San Felipe* had caught up with Thompson's *Correo de Méjico*, which had managed to flee after the prior evening's encounter after a breeze had sprung up. The *San Felipe* had inflicted heavy damage, but now, both the *San Felipe* and *Correo de Méjico* again were completely becalmed within sight of land near Velasco in what amounted to a stalemate. The versatile *Laura* arrived and helped maneuver the *San Felipe* into the correct position for the guns on Austin's vessel to rake the *Correo de Méjico*, causing Thompson to surrender. Thus, according to Jim Dan Hill, "the first fight in the successful Texan Campaign of 1835 had all of the essentials and results of a naval engagement for sea control, or naval supremacy, in which the Texans were victorious."[64] The *Laura* had arrived in Texas to open up the trade of the lower Brazos, and other steamboats, such as the *Cayuga*, were also involved as early as 1834 in what promised to be a lucrative cotton-shipping trade on that river. These small steamboats not only helped the European Americans open the commercial trade along the rivers and coast, but also showed their potential in warfare.

By the fall of 1835, the Mexican maritime forces had assumed a defensive, rather than offensive, position as Texians continued to fight the Mexican government and, surreptitiously, organize a government, which included a Naval Affairs Committee. Mexico had placed two vessels, the *Veracruzana* and *Bravo* (formerly the *Moctezuma*), in service to defend the coast, but Texians now developed an aggressive stance. Their strategy involved developing a strong offensive, including involving foreign powers in the blockade of Mexican ports. Privateering flourished, and minor confrontations occurred, encouraging the formation of a Texas fleet, or more properly, an incipient Texas Navy. It now became commonplace to arm privateering and trading vessels. Two vessels, the *William Robbins* (renamed the *Liberty*) and the *Invincible*, formed its nucleus.

In the spring of 1836, it was clear that the rebellious Texans had control of the sea. According to Dan Hill, the *Liberty*, under the command of Commodore Charles Hawkins, had captured the Mexican schooner *Pelícano*, which carried in its cargo munitions hidden in food barrels in an effort to keep these arms from being seized by the privateers. This, Hill noted, indicated that Mexico was feeling the effects of the Texans' aggressive naval policy.[65] The *Invincible* also seized the U.S.-owned brig *Pocket*, which was on a mission to supply Mexican troops. This constituted yet another serious blow to Mexican forces, which had recently prevailed at the Alamo and

Goliad but would soon be devastated at San Jacinto by Sam Houston's well-supplied and aggressive forces.

Cᴏɴᴛʀᴀʙᴀɴᴅ ᴀɴᴅ Cᴏʟᴏɴɪᴢᴀᴛɪᴏɴ ᴀᴛ ᴛʜᴇ Eɴᴅ ᴏꜰ Mᴇxɪᴄᴀɴ Rᴜʟᴇ

Events during the spring of 1836 reveal how marginal Texas was to the centers of power in both Mexico and the United States, and how illegal trade was thriving on the coast. No contraband was more forbidden by the United States than the maritime slave trade, for horror stories of human cargo treated brutally by slave traders had become legion. The slave trade was prohibited by the United States and cutters patrolled waters to ensure that the prohibition was enforced. And yet, Galveston maritime historian Ben C. Stuart speculated that several cargoes of African slaves were probably landed along the Texas coast, citing the one documented example of the illicit trade—the arrival of the schooner *Dart*, which sailed into Galveston harbor and anchored at its east end in March of 1836 with a cargo of some "seventy-five to eighty young Africans." According to Stuart, the Africans were reportedly transferred to Edwards Point and, after the Battle of San Jacinto, scattered throughout the coast country.[66] With the passage of stringent laws under the Republic of Texas that prohibited the importation of slaves from points other than the United States, this trade presumably ceased, but stories still linger of slaves imported by sea during this tumultuous period in Texas history.

By the twilight of Mexico's rule over Texas in 1834, maps were produced and widely marketed to European Americans and Europeans. The lure: Texas as a land of opportunity as represented graphically using information by Stephen F. Austin and others. As if to underscore the importance of maritime trade, one of the more popular maps of "Coahuila and Texas" in the period, which appeared in the guidebook *A Visit to Texas* (1834) (Fig. 4-6) clearly indicates the depth at the Galveston Inlet (12 to 16 feet of water) and Brazos de Dios (3 1/2 feet to 5 1/2 feet). That the passes were marked so prominently is a tribute to the efforts of the Mexican Navy, which prepared nautical charts of the important harbors. The popular maps are also a tribute to the efforts of Austin and others who sought to develop the province by stimulating maritime trade on both the saltwaters and freshwaters of the province.

A remarkable rare map of Texas from the period illustrates the grants in possession of the Colorado and Red River Land Company (Fig. 4-7). It also

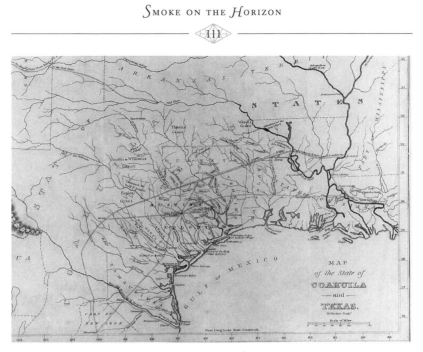

FIGURE 4-6

Map of Coahuila and Texas in 1834 shows prominently the importance of maritime access, for it gives the depths to the bar at Galveston and Brazos del Dios (Velasco). Courtesy Special Collections Division, The University of Texas at Arlington Libraries, Arlington.

shows the coast in considerable detail, indicating the depths over the bar at Galveston to be "14 to 16 feet"; at the Brazos de Dios to be "4 1/2 to 7 feet"; and at Passo de Cabello to be "12 to 17 feet." This map indicates coastal communities such as Copano and Velasco, while also showing those fledgling communities slightly farther inland, including Brasoria and Harrisburg. This map further identifies the major bays, including Galveston, West, and Matagordia [*sic*], while showing inlets and passes such as Aranzas Inlet, West Pass, and the Sabine Inlet. Characteristically, the rivers of Texas are also shown in great detail, a testimony to their potential: The Rio Grande is noted to be eighteen hundred miles long, with the well-intended but incorrect statement that "it rises in the latitude of New York."[67] Somewhat symbolically, and overenthusiastically, the Rio de San Antonio is shown leading to the smaller Rio Medina, from which a dotted trail leads to "rich silver mines" that were never actually discovered despite herculean searches throughout the nineteenth century. To promoters of the era, Mexican Texas beckoned as both Eden and El Dorado. The maps of Texas recognize that

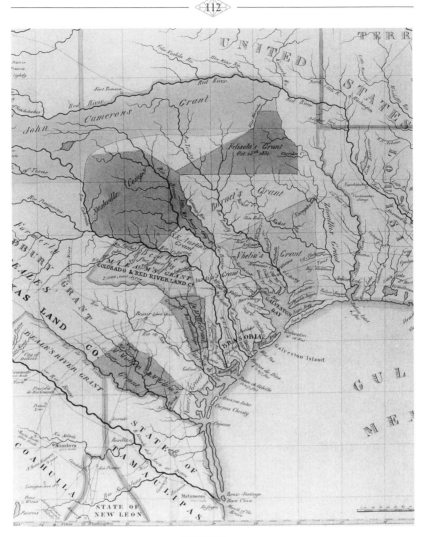

FIGURE 4-7

Detail of a rare map of Texas showing the grants in possession of the Colorado and Red River Land Company (1833) depicts the Texas coast and rivers entering it with considerable accuracy. Note the depths over the bars at Sabine Inlet, Galveston, Brazos de Dios, and Passo de Cabello—passes that were in effect gateways permitting travelers to enter the protected harbors and rivers leading to the interior of the province. Map courtesy of the Cartographic Collections of Mrs. Jenkins Garrett, Fort Worth, housed in the Cartographic History Library at The University of Texas at Arlington Libraries, Arlington.

FIGURE 4-8

The one dollar (peso) and three dollar (peso) notes of the Commercial and Agricultural Bank of Texas from 1835 indicate concessions to European Texians; they feature maritime vignettes in the form of a Native American paddling a canoe (top) and a harbor scene complete with a ketch and schooner. Courtesy Special Collections Division, The University of Texas at Arlington Libraries, Arlington.

the passes, ports, and rivers were, in effect, corridors by which the fabled interior would be developed. Such high expectations can be added to the many factors that led to revolution as European Americans challenged Mexican control of the province after arriving in large numbers. It has been estimated, for example, that twenty-five thousand settlers entered through Velasco alone from 1821 to 1835,[68] bringing with them increasingly high expectations and an increasingly belligerent attitude toward Mexico.

The importance of maritime trade, and the power wielded by European Americans under Mexican rule, are seen in the notes of the Commercial and Agricultural Bank of Texas. Printed in English and revealing that a dollar and a peso were equal in value, the one-dollar/peso and three-dollar/peso notes of this bank from 1835 are of special interest, for they depict

maritime subjects. The one-dollar note features a Native American paddling a canoe that is clearly not indigenous to Texas, for it is not a dugout.
The scene on the three-dollar note features two sailing vessels, a small ketch
and a schooner, in a harbor scene, possibly Velasco or Galveston (Fig. 4-8).
The livestock, sheep shearing, and hunter featured on these notes convey
an impression of the frontier agricultural bounty of Texas—a province whose
economy was heavily dependent on water routes to the outside world.

Like the political and military records of the time, the images on bank
notes and the content of maps confirm that European Americans had developed a tenacious claim on Texas. They utilized its waterways very effectively to gain access to granted, fertile lands a considerable distance inland
from the coast. The story had a familiar ring: At the time of the Texas revolution in the winter of 1835–1836, Mexico found its northeastern frontier
eroding as aggressive European Americans first developed a maritime trade
and then used those very vessels to gain independence from the mother
country that had encouraged their immigration. Interestingly, the same com-
plaints that had been used two generations earlier by British colonists to
create the United States of America—arbitrary tariffs and a curtailment of
maritime trade to the colonies—were now reapplied as Texas became, following the successful revolution in the spring of 1836, an independent country suspended between two powers: the United States and Mexico.

On the Waters of the
Lone Star Republic
1836–1845

The Texas Navy. . . . It is no exaggeration to say that without it there
would probably have been no Lone Star Republic and possibly the
State of Texas would still be a part of Mexico.
THEODORE ROOSEVELT, 1936

Newspaper headlines in the summer of 1995 heralded yet another major shipwreck discovery that helped make 1995 a banner year in Texas maritime archaeology: "Wreckage of Texas Navy Ship That Aided Sam Houston Believed Found" marked the lead-in to an engrossing story about a shipwreck that, according to the reporter, was "almost certainly" the *Invincible*, "a nearly 84 foot schooner that helped Gen. Houston before the battle of San Jacinto by capturing arms and other supplies from two Mexican ships and delivering them to Texas troops."[1] The story dramatically added that, from a "graveyard of shipwrecks," self-styled shipwreck hunter Clive Cussler pinpointed a sandbar off Galveston that has claimed many vessels, and felt with 99 percent certainty that the *Invincible* had been located along with the wreckage of several other vessels. Like many wrecks, the actual identity of this one must be considered conjectural until more evidence is found. Hopefully, the *Invincible*'s wreck has been found, as it would likely shed considerable light on this important vessel and her role in Texas history. The *Invincible* was briefly mentioned in the previous chapter, but her life under the Republic of Texas is revealing. The 125-ton schooner *Invincible*'s enduring fame is due in part to her having been selected to transport the captured General Santa Anna to Veracruz after the Battle of San Jacinto in April of 1836, only to be prevented from doing so by the Texas contract vessel *Ocean*, under the command of General Thomas Jefferson Green. The latter part of *Invincible*'s varied career must be placed in the context of historical events and conditions on the Texas coast during the tumultuous early years of the Texas Republic (1836–1845). This chapter offers a glimpse of the varied vessels that served Texas during the Republic, of which the *Invincible* was but one, despite the fact that its wreck on the bar near Galveston has become a part of Texas history and folklore (Fig. 5-1).

THE EARLY TEXAS NAVY

As the Texas Republic was created with considerable bloodshed in the spring of 1836, both Texas and Mexico realized the significance of the sea, or rather the Gulf, as a point of access to the new republic. Ironically, it was Mexico that recognized the potential of invading Texas by sea—a concept that Texas knew all too well, for as we have seen, it was how they had gained their foothold in the Republic in the first place. Mexico employed a number of U.S.-owned vessels to supply its troops in the spring of 1836, providing good reason for the Republic's early concern about the possibility of sea-borne invasion. That this concern was valid is seen in an interesting footnote to Texas history, namely the exploits of the "Horse Marines," a voluntary group of rangers who patrolled the coast on horseback in May and June of 1836. Learning of a suspicious-looking vessel on Copano Bay on June 2, Major Isaac Watts Burton hurried to the coast to lie in ambush for the mysterious vessel by signaling distress and waiting for a response. The vessel first hoisted both the U.S. and Texan colors, but these signals deliberately went unanswered by the rangers. Mexican colors were then hoisted by the vessel, and were immediately answered by the Texans, who feigned being Mexicans in distress. When the captain and four crew members came to aid, they were immediately seized and replaced by sixteen rangers, who managed to row back and board the vessel, which turned out to be the U.S.-owned schooner *Watchman*, and seize the vessel and her provisions. Unfavorable winds kept Burton from sailing the commandeered schooner to Velasco as a prize of war, but this delay soon paid dividends. On June 17, two more schooners, the *Comanche* and the *Fanny Butler*, were also deceived, as Burton had required the *Watchman*'s skipper to decoy their captains aboard the vessel. There they were promptly seized—along with their cargoes of supplies bound for the Mexican army. The three hapless vessels were first taken to Velasco, then Galveston, as prizes of war, but they were soon returned to their U.S. owners.[2]

Always under the threat of invasion from Mexico, which never accepted Texas's claim of sovereignty, much less its holding of the land between the Nueces and Rio Grande from the Gulf coast inland, the Republic of Texas recognized the need for both an army and a navy. Although the Texas Navy

FIGURE 5-1
"The Wreck of the Invincible*" is graphically portrayed in this sketch by E. M. Schiwetz. Courtesy Naval Historical Center and Texas Maritime Museum, Rockport.*

has been covered in a number of books and articles,[3] a look at it in the context of the state's overall maritime history is in order. In fact, an interpretation of the Texas Navy in the context of the history of the Texas Republic makes it a nearly perfect mirror of those times, for the Texas Navy, like the Republic itself, was enterprising, underfunded, and administered chaotically.

There were, in effect, two Texas navies. The first could trace its roots to the months before independence was claimed on March 2, 1836. As noted earlier, the rebellious General Council passed a bill on November 25, 1835, providing for the organization of a navy, the purchase of four schooners, and the issuance of letters of marque to privateers. The latter were viewed as temporary but, as we know, their effective action virtually paralyzed

Mexican vessels controlling the Texas coast in the fall of 1835. The four schooners purchased in January of 1836 had varied backgrounds: *Liberty* (formerly the *William Robbins*) was sixty tons and had been a privateer; *Invincible* had been built in Baltimore as an African slaver; *Independence* (formerly the U.S. Revenue cutter *Ingham*) had performed ably in the previous fall; *Brutus* was a 125-ton schooner. All served under the newly appointed commodore, Charles E. Hawkins, but this first Texas navy lasted only until the summer of 1837, when all vessels had been lost to creditors, the sea, or hostile Mexican vessels in a series of events and mishaps that read more like fiction than history.

For example, the schooner-of-war *Liberty*, which had made several captures of Mexican vessels on its first cruise from January to May of 1836, and had run in convoy with the schooner *Flora* to New Orleans, was sold there because of the Texas government's inability to pay for the repairs. The *Independence* began a brilliant career by capturing several small vessels on its first cruise between January and March of 1836, but it went to New Orleans after a brief stint out of Galveston. At New Orleans the Navy suffered a setback as the young commodore Hawkins unexpectedly died, leaving the *Independence* in command of George Wheelwright, who left New Orleans with the ship undermanned. On the voyage to Galveston, the *Independence* was seized by two Mexican vessels after a four-hour running battle on April 17. In September 1836, financial problems still plagued the Texas Navy, and the *Brutus* and *Invincible* nearly met a fate similar to that which had befallen the *Liberty*, but they were saved by Samuel Swartwout, an Englishman who paid for repairs. Within a few months, however, both these vessels would be lost: The *Invincible* and *Brutus*, taken out on a cruise by Secretary of the Navy Samuel Rhoads Fisher in defiance of Sam Houston's penurious order not to sail, was grounded on a sandbar and destroyed. The possible discovery of the wreckage of the *Invincible* on the submerged bar near Galveston once again underscores the hazardous nature of the Texas coast: *Brutus*, of shallow draft, had gone to the rescue of the *Invincible*, but was herself grounded temporarily, then freed, only to be later lost in a storm in October 1837.

This first Texas navy, then, was ill-fated, but it typified the problems of the fledgling, ambitious, and financially overextended republic. For the period of a year and a half from September 1837 to March 1839, in fact, Texas had no effective navy at all; even though the Navy had purchased the brig *Potomac* in 1838, she had only been used as a receiving ship at the Galveston navy base.

In his third address to the Senate on April 10, 1838, Mirabeau Lamar lamented the condition of the Texas Navy in relation to Mexico's, when he asked: Is Texas so without resources that she cannot put an equal force afloat?[4] It has been pointed out that Texas was indeed fortunate that Mexico had other problems and distractions at this time, including the Panic of 1837, a revolt in northern Mexico, and a crippling French blockade and seizure of the Mexican fleet, which consisted of about eight vessels, at the Gulf port of Veracruz.[5] Illustrations of vessels from this first navy—including those by Emil Bunjes, E. M. Schiwetz, and Don Davis—are largely conjectural, having been done in the twentieth century to commemorate the vessels that served so ably during the first two years of the Republic. They are nevertheless based on available information and thus provide a good general picture of these important vessels.

The Second Texas Navy

The second Texas Navy began as a result of the earlier appropriation bills of October and November of 1836 ($135,000, which was stipulated for four new vessels, none of which were ordered until the first four were lost!) and November 4, 1837 ($280,000 for the building of six vessels). Frederick Dawson, of Baltimore, was contracted to build six vessels, but the first of these did not arrive until June of 1839—more than a year after President Lamar's impassioned pleas for a stronger navy. In the meantime, the second vessel to serve the new Texas Navy was purchased in November 1838 and arrived in March of 1839: the *Zavala* (formerly the steam packet *Charleston*) had been fitted out for service as a naval vessel. Although the small *Laura* had earlier shown the virtues of steam in military operations, the *Zavala* was larger and suited for action on the high seas. It featured the distinctive walking beam mechanism that enabled the power from the steam engines to be transferred to the huge paddlewheels amidships. Interestingly, the *Zavala* was the only steamer ever employed in the Texas Navy; it was reportedly the first steam warship operating on the Gulf of Mexico.[6]

A closer look at the history of the *Zavala* is in order, for the *Charleston's* acquisition by the Texas navy reveals much about the pragmatism and hopes of the era. Built in Philadelphia in 1836, the *Charleston* was a more or less typical steamer of the period: She measured 201 9/10 feet in length, 24 1/10 in breadth, and 12 feet in depth, and weighed 569 15/95 tons; based on sketches of the period and a recent conjectural drawing by Elizabeth R. Baldwin (Fig. 5-2), she had a round stern, a flush deck, and a scroll head. That the

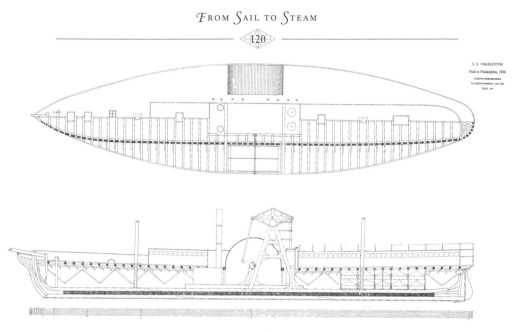

S. S. CHARLESTON
Built in Philadelphia, 1836

CONSTRUCTION DRAWING
ELIZABETH R. BALDWIN MAY 1992
SCALE 1:96

FIGURE 5-2

A conjectural drawing of the Zavala *by the maritime archaeologist Elizabeth R. Baldwin shows the distinctive walking-beam engine, covered paddlewheel housings, and the positions of two masts. Reproduced with permission of the* INA *Quarterly and Elizabeth R. Baldwin.*

Charleston was constructed of heavy timbers and had suffered damage in an October 1837 storm off Cape Hatteras made her available at a bargain; so, too, did the fact that she could be purchased with Texas bonds.[7] The *Charleston* was repaired and altered for the Texas Navy in New York City by the South Carolinian James Hamilton's consortium. Hamilton noted that "she will be completely fitted out to answer the purposes both of a marine frigate, and a mail and passenger boat," indicating that the administrative officers of the Texas Navy envisioned her serving as a government packet in service between Galveston and New Orleans in addition to keeping the Texas coast clear of unfriendly Mexican vessels.[8]

The bulk of the new Texas navy consisted of sailing vessels of several classes. In 1839, Dawson delivered three 170-ton schooners: *San Jacinto*, *San Antonio*, and *San Bernard*, which arrived in June, August, and September, respectively. In September and December of that year, two 400-ton brigs, the *Wharton* and the *Archer*, joined the fleet, the 600-ton sloop of war *Austin* having arrived in October. Thus, by the spring of 1840, the Texas Navy consisted of eight vessels. Its new commodore, Edwin Ward Moore, was appointed by President Lamar, who served as commander-in-chief.

Moore's biographer, Tom Henderson Wells, states that Moore may have first come in contact with the Texas Republic when his U.S. naval vessel *Boston* captured the Texas privateer *Terrible* in September of 1836.[9] Like many U.S. naval officers, Moore realized that opportunities for advancement were limited in his current position. The prospect of an advancement as commodore of the Texas Navy so tempted Moore that he apparently began recruiting sailors for it before he left the U.S. Navy, an action that precipitated proceedings for his court-martial in 1839. However, Moore resigned in July of that year before any action could be taken, and he arrived in Galveston on October 4 on the SS *Columbia* in time to survey the first vessels of the new navy. These included the little schooners *San Jacinto*, *San Antonio*, and *San Bernard*, the ninety-five-ton schooner *Louisville* (which was often called the *Striped Pig*), and a rigged watering vessel complete with sails and seven water casks that had been purchased for $4,000. Moore also saw the most impressive vessel in the fleet, the steamer *Zavala*, which had three boilers, reciprocating steam engines that propelled two paddlewheels amidships, and a full set of sails. Though the *Zavala* has been characterized as a "sweet-handling ship," some sources considered her a temperamental vessel that could burn, in order of preference, coal, cordwood, or even furniture (when the need required). Like the U.S. Navy, which had only one steamship that had been acquired in 1838, Texas found steamships difficult to repair for lack of experienced mechanics and machinists. To meet this need, the Texas Navy pirated engineers off the steamer *Rochester*, but soon had to send the *Zavala* to New Orleans for extensive repairs and retrofitting to a ship-of-war, including new parts in the main engines, additional guns and berths, replacement of a portion of her berth deck, a new foremast, and some new copper sheathing to the hull.[10] Recently, a maritime archaeologist/historian questioned whether the *Zavala* needed such extensive repairs so soon after its rebuilding, the implication being that the inexperienced Mr. Hinton, who was overseeing repairs, may have been misled, and hence fleeced, by the repairers in New Orleans.[11]

The bulk of the Texas Navy consisted of sailing vessels, and the Navy sought to keep its sailors in shape despite periods of inactivity caused by sporadic funding and political squabbles that reached to the Navy's headquarters in Austin. As these sailors gained experience, they were tested by the hazards of the Gulf coast. That the winds of the Texas coast could continue to play havoc with sailing ships was demonstrated by an incident that befell the *San Jacinto*, which lay at anchor on a calm morning off Velasco in 1840 while conducting a drill in handling the sails and rigging. After a rigorous morning of drills, the captain foolishly allowed all hands to eat lunch without leaving a watch. Seemingly from out of nowhere a sudden squall caught the captain and crew off guard, quickly tipping the vessel over on her side. Only the quick action of the captain, who cut loose the boom, saved the otherwise doomed vessel, which soon righted itself while the dumbfounded crew looked on in amazement and terror.[12] In truth, the sailors of the Texas Navy were a diverse lot possessing varied skill levels; many had been recruited in forays to ports as distant as New York, where Commodore Moore was actually arrested in 1840 for violating U.S. law prohibiting recruiting by foreign navies in the United States.[13]

Although Moore was operating individually during these forays, his actions called into question the ethics of the Texas Republic's government, especially President Lamar, who used the Texas Navy creatively, if not opportunistically. In fact, Lamar used the Navy to further debilitate his archenemy, Mexico. By 1840, Mexico was plagued by a revolt in the Yucatán similar in some ways to that which had ripped Texas from it four years earlier. Lamar ordered Commodore Moore to explore friendly relations with the Yucatecans, who consisted of conservative Mexican rebels and a number of U.S. filibusters who envisioned a slave-holding republic in the tropics. Lamar's effort came to fruition in September of 1840 as Yucatán agreed to pay Texas eight thousand dollars per month for the upkeep of the Texas fleet, meaning in effect that the Texas Navy was being leased as a privateering service to a rebel government—an action justified by Texans' hatred of Mexico. What seems like a questionable international political action is made more understandable by the fact that the Texas Navy was woefully underfunded, the Congress (apparently lulled by the temporary armistice with Mexico) having cut naval appropriations in 1840.

A fleet of three Texas vessels (Fig. 5-3), the *Austin, San Bernard,* and *San Antonio,* thus sailed for Yucatán on December 31, 1841, the very day that Sam Houston was inaugurated as the third president of the Republic of Texas. Houston immediately suspended the agreement with Yucatán and reordered the return of the fleet, but the orders were not received by Moore until March. Meanwhile, the *San Antonio* was being refitted in New Orleans, and with confusion and anti-Houston sentiment running high her crew mutinied, killing one officer. Although the mutineers were captured by U.S. authorities and eventually punished, the actions on the *San Antonio* symbolize the volatility and near disarray of politics in Texas at the time.

The *San Antonio* was refitted and it left for Yucatán in September of 1842 but was presumed lost in a storm, as it never reached its destination. The

FIGURE 5-3

The Texas Navy sloop of war Austin *was built for the Republic of Texas in Baltimore, Maryland, and launched in 1839 as the* Texas. *This vessel served the U.S. Navy until 1848, and this drawing was made by midshipman Edward Johns, a member of the vessel's crew under the Texas Navy. Courtesy Naval Historical Center and Texas Maritime Museum, Rockport.*

steamer *Zavala* also exemplified the Texas Navy's problems, as it had deteriorated badly for lack of funds. It was deliberately run aground at Galveston to prevent its sinking and was reported partially scrapped in 1844, though its submerged funnel remained visible alongside a pier in the Galveston harbor for another two decades.[14] President Houston's withholding of funds appropriated by Congress for the Navy caused public consternation and resulted in outright rebellion by Moore, who had raised nearly thirty-five thousand dollars in funds to repair the Navy's ships. Ordered to return to Galveston to repair the fleet there, Moore refused on the belief that Houston would seize and sell the Navy upon his return. Moore thus renewed negotiations with Yucatán in outright defiance of the commander-in-chief of the Republic of Texas. The *Austin* and the *Wharton* joined the other vessels of the Texas Navy, engaging a Mexican fleet on May 2 and 16, 1843. By now the Mexican fleet contained at least two ironclad steamers, but these battles were indecisive. Nevertheless, they were startling, for they meant that the renegade Texas Navy was fighting for a rebel government nearly a thousand miles from home on the other side, as it were, of the Gulf of Mexico!

FIGURE 5-4
In May 1840, William Bollaert sketched the Texas Navy at anchor in Galveston, depicting (left to right) the steamer Zavala, *schooner* San Bernard *(behind* Zavala), *sloop-of-war* Austin, *revenue cutter* Santana, *schooner* San Antonio, *brig* Galveston *(later* Archer), *and brig* Wharton. *Courtesy Naval Historical Center and Texas Maritime Museum, Rockport.*

In a move that symbolized how out of control the Texas political situation was at the time, Houston had proclaimed that the Texas Navy were "pirates" and urged any friendly country to execute its capture and return. This action caused Moore to return home to a hero's welcome in Galveston, and a peremptory dishonorable discharge by Houston. Houston also convinced Congress to authorize the sale of the Navy (which had dwindled to four vessels, the *Austin, Wharton, Archer,* and *San Bernard*) at auction. The citizens of Galveston were so outraged by the actions of Houston (and Congress) that they forcibly prevented bids at the auction, thereby returning the Navy to the Republic, in effect overruling their own elected government. In point of fact, however, there remained little need for a Navy by 1843, for a truce with Mexico had been signed that rendered the Navy pretty much unnecessary. This truce, coupled with the U.S. government's agreement to protect Texas until her annexation as a state two years later, ensured that the Texas Navy would remain inactive for the last two years of its, and the Republic's, existence.

Vessels of the Texas Navy were frequently commented upon by travelers, and they were occasionally sketched in the Galveston harbor in the early 1840s (Fig. 5-4). Despite its setbacks and sometimes questionable military endeavors, the navy nevertheless served to inspire travelers, for the vessels and the flag of the Texas Navy reminded all of Texas's independence. The ever-observant Mrs. Houstoun commented on the *San Jacinto* when she noted, from her schooner yacht, *Dolphin,* in 1842 that "there is a beautiful corvette lying near us, a long low hull, and raking masts; at the mainmast is flying a small flag, with one star on its brilliant white ground; it is the star of the young Republic of Texas."[15] A rousing poem in the January 7, 1842, issue of *The Daily Bulletin* (Austin) captured the sentiments of many Texans:

> Float on . . . Navy, whilst a foe
> To Texas breathes in Mexico;
> Till every tyrant on her shore
> Shall tremble at the name of Moore. . . .[16]

How should the Texas Navy be viewed in retrospect? Although a number of scholars imply that the Texas Navy was a manifestation of Texans' militancy and their desire to colonize the entire Republic in the mold of Southern U.S. (that is, slave-holding) culture, it should also be remembered that Texans felt a need to defend themselves from external threats. Mexico vocally, and sometimes militarily, disputed the very existence of an independent Texas, as evidenced in the short-lived but sobering capture of San Antonio in 1842. However many Texans thought a navy essential, their virtually bankrupt republic could in reality ill afford one.

MERCANTILE SEA TRADE OF THE REPUBLIC

Amid continuing disputes about the purpose and validity of a navy, Texans set about to open up the entire Republic to trade. Naturally, much of their effort focused on the most potentially profitable area in which to grow subtropical crops such as sugar cane and cotton: southeast Texas in the vicinity of the mouths of the Sabine, Trinity, and Brazos rivers.

During the tumultuous spring of 1836, the port of Velasco figures heavily in Texas history. Situated on an embayment at the mouth of the Brazos River, Velasco was the site of ratification of a treaty that brought to a close outright hostilities between Texians and Mexicans. It was here that Thomas Jefferson Green, "the fiery and skillful propagandist in the service of Texas," had landed on the steamer *Ocean* on June 1, 1836, to begin a blustery campaign of intrigue that found him seizing the schooner *Invincible*, which was to carry Mexican president Santa Anna back to Veracruz.[17]

The filibustering and enterprising Green was one of the many who soon invested in the ill-fated Texas Railroad, Navigation and Banking Company, a grandly conceived scheme that would have constructed an internal improvements network of canals and railroad lines linking the lower Rio Grande and the Sabine—that is, interconnect and improve the entire Texas coast. When the TRN&BC fell victim to several realities—including the panic of 1837, its own investors' ineptitude, and the actions of Sam Houston's administration—Green turned his attention to making Velasco a major port that would compete with Galveston as a trade center.[18] The rivalry between Velasco and Galveston was typical of the rivalries that would characterize communities on the entire Texas coast. Texans, flush with victory at San Jacinto, would seek to improve the coast and, in so doing, create a new empire. Green was not alone in his boosterism of Texas ports in the late 1830s. Francis Moore Jr. commented on Velasco in 1840 that "several capitalists have located here, and have given a new impulse to business," adding that, "if steamboat navigation gains the ascendancy on the Gulf, this harbour will require but little improvement to render Velasco one of the most important places on the coast of Texas."[19]

Moore's comments might have been appreciated by Thomas Jefferson Green and other Velasco boosters, until, that is, they read his description of Galveston, whose "harbour is the best in Texas, and will undoubtedly at no distant day become the center of a commerce rivalling that of many of the first commercial cities of the world."[20] These types of claims notwithstanding, developers of Texas ports during the Republic were well aware that considerable improvements would have to occur before the coast could be open to full-blown maritime trade. A typical lament was voiced by an anonymous traveler in 1837, who expounded eloquently on the nearly unlimited potential of farmlands along the Brazos River, but condemned maritime access to it in the following prose:

> The bar at the mouth of this river, which is formed by the quicksand that is constantly thrown up by the waves of the sea and arrested by the cur-

rent of the stream, never can be removed and makes the entry into the harbor at its mouth so extremely dangerous that the different insurance offices throughout the United States, as I was told, from repeated wrecks that have occurred in the attempt, have refused to grant policies upon any vessels entered for this port at any premium. This is to be regretted, as the country upon this stream is esteemed the most productive portion of Texas.[21]

This traveler points out an interesting aspect of maritime trade that is often overlooked: insurance. By the early nineteenth century, it had become increasingly common for vessels of trade to be insured, either through London or a number of insurance companies that proliferated on the east coast—especially in Connecticut—as trade flourished and investors put more and more of their financial resources into backing shipping. Port facilities, too, could be insured, but insurance companies were well aware of the hazards posed by storms to Texas ports.

The Texas population boomed during the late 1830s. It was reported by the *Telegraph and Texas Register* in May of 1837 that "crowds of enterprising emigrants are arriving in Texas on every vessel," and six thousand immigrants had crossed the Sabine River by ferry.[22] Although the area immediately behind the coast developed a reputation as an unhealthy area of miasmic swamps unfit for settlement,[23] colonists continued to flock into developing coastal communities like Velasco and Galveston, with their "salubrious" onshore breezes. Soon, communities several miles inland from the coast, such as Washington on the Brazos and the fledgling Houston, began to thrive, as both plantation owner and small farmer alike anticipated an Eden of sorts in the interior Texas wilderness. They soon discovered the coast to be an excellent vacation spot, for despite its fairly high temperatures and humidity its breezes seemed to take the edge off the long, hot Texas summers.

It was, of course, to Texans' advantage to develop the entire coast as far south as the Rio Grande if possible, as both a buffer to Mexican threats and a way of realizing the potential of what some saw as an area of promise for agriculture and stock raising. Thus, the area around Goliad (the former La Bahía) received colonists from both the United States and foreign countries as immigration, or "emigration" as it was almost universally called in Texas at the time, brought new arrivals to the Republic. By the late 1830s and early 1840s, emigrant guides became common tools for luring immigrants to Texas, but there is no question that those who developed the early Texas maritime trade were from the United States and hoped to intensify its connections with eastern or southern U.S. ports.

STEAM PACKETS TO THE REPUBLIC

Although the Republic of Texas could be identified with certain Southern traits, a considerable number of enterprising Yankees either made Texas their home or operated business enterprises there. The New Yorker Charles Morgan was among those Northerners who seized the opportunity to develop Texas, and he did so using the sea as a main artery of trade. Morgan knew that opening the huge, roughly triangular area of southeast Texas to trade required the aggressive development of maritime transportation—a type of capitalistic venture that he had employed in developing the New York–New Orleans steamship routes. As the maritime historian James Baughman noted in *Charles Morgan and the Development of Southern Transportation*, the most important book on mid-nineteenth-century Texas/Gulf commercial maritime history written to date, Morgan and his partners recognized that "a host of small ports could be linked to the great entrepôt of New Orleans on a more regular basis [and] the New Orleans–Texas trade looked especially promising."[24]

Thus it was that Morgan's *Columbia*, under the command of John T. Wright, inaugurated steam packet service to the new Texas Republic in 1837, connecting the fledgling port cities of Galveston and Velasco with New Orleans. Somewhat symbolically, *Columbia* was a Yankee vessel that began her service in 1835 in the New York–Charleston trade. Illustrations of the period (Fig. 5-5) show her to be a sidewheeler with a tall, single funnel or smokestack. As reassigned, the *Columbia* proved well suited to the treacherous, shallow waters of the passes and bays of the Texas coast because of her light draft and superior maneuverability.[25]

As numerous Texas historians have noted, Mary Austin Holley characterized the *Columbia* to Mrs. William Brand in 1837 as "the most perfect boat. . . . the best [that] I have ever seen," describing the ship's linen, silver (or what appeared to be silver) forks, ivory knives, and lady-like chambermaid.[26] That Mrs. Holley was impressed by steamers of the Morgan line is apparent from her praise for the *New York* in 1839. She described the vessel as having a main cabin that glistened with polished mahogany set off by white satin damask and dimity draperies, and featuring stained glass windows, decorated with the arms of Texas, that overlooked a dining table replete with fine porcelain embellished with "a blue device—representing

FIGURE 5-5
The sidewheeler steamship Columbia *enabled Charles Morgan to open the Texas ports of Galveston and Velasco to shipping from New Orleans in 1837. Seen here is a lithograph by J. H. Bufford from a drawing by Haswell, the steampacket* Columbia *churns along the coast. Courtesy William and Mary College, Williamsburg, Virginia; and the Mariners' Museum, Newport News, Virginia.*

the New York at Sea with the Texas eagle hovering over her." Mrs. Holley was also impressed by the *Columbia*'s engraved crystal, as well as its white chambermaid and Irish waiters, which were always at her service.[27] Morgan can be credited with bringing luxury to Texas travel, for the cabins of his steamships were opulent, at least for those who could afford the luxury of the main cabin; steerage passengers below decks had more modest accommodations, while those booked on deck passage had, needless to say, Spartan accommodations.

After 1838, Morgan's *Columbia* and other vessels, including the *New York* and the *Savannah*, faced stiff competition from the *Neptune*. As shown in a

FIGURE 5-6

After its introduction in 1838, the steamship Neptune *of the Reed-Pennoyer Line provided stiff competition to Morgan's* Columbia *on the New Orleans–Galveston run. Courtesy Mariners' Museum, Newport News, Virginia; Eldredge Collection.*

contemporary illustration (Fig. 5-6), the *Neptune* appears to have two stacks mounted in line. No doubt this was an error in perspective by the artist, who wished to draw a side view of the vessel while still depicting the two stacks, which were likely side by side. The *Neptune*'s hull was 215 feet long, 25 feet, 4 inches wide, and 14 feet deep. She is listed as having a 200-horse-power steam engine, and was clearly a competitor to Charles Morgan's *Columbia.* The *Neptune*'s owners, the Reed-Pennoyer line, made things more difficult for Morgan by accepting Texas money at the rate of fifty cents on the dollar, while competitors required specie or New Orleans banknotes.[28]

The importance of steam power to Texas maritime trade was observed by the Rev. A. B. Lawrence, who noted of Galveston in 1840 that "several steam packet ships ply regularly between it and New Orleans, and a large number of steam boats take their departure hence for Houston, the Trinity, Sabine, San Jacinto, the Brazos, etc."[29] Lawrence's use of the words *steamship* for the maritime trade and *steamboat* for river trade was quite accurate, but indeed indicated that he was, as he called himself, "a resident emigrant" to the new republic. In regard to nomenclature used for steam-powered vessels during this period, it is interesting to note that Texans along the coast at this time continued to call virtually *any* watercraft of any size a "boat." The term *ship*, in fact, does not come into common use until the twentieth century, even though the designation SS, for steamship, was officially used by the mid-nineteenth century. More properly, the term *ship* also refers to a large sailing vessel having a bowsprit and usually three masts, each composed of a lower mast, a top mast, and a top gallant mast. This accounts for the listing of "ships" along with vessels often also thought of as ships — such as schooners and barkentines — in the nineteenth century records of ports.

But it was the steamship that caught the attention of travelers at the time. With characteristic early Victorian charm and conviction, the steamship lines promised safe and convenient passage in luxurious surroundings. The *Civilian and Galveston Gazette*, November 9, 1838, contained an advertisement of McKinney and Williams, which noted that the "highly finished and fast running steam-packet, *New York*, Capt. J. T. Wright, would arrive on the 20th to ply as a regular packet between New Orleans and Galveston." The *New York* was described as "a most beautiful boat, less than one year old [which] can accommodate 200 passengers, and carry 600 barrels of freight." According to Ben C. Stuart, she was 180 feet on deck, and had a 22-foot breadth of beam and 11-foot depth of hold. The agents also noted that the boat "will please the most fastidious; and the subscribers flatter themselves by the aid and cooperation of Capt. Wright, and the other owners to so conduct the business of the boat, as to give general satisfaction; and pledge themselves so far as is within their power, to consult the great interest of the country, and particularly that of the currency, with a due regard always to our duty towards the owner of the *New York*."

Steam-powered vessels were a common sight in the waters of the Texas Republic. Although he did not visit Texas, Charles Dickens traveled to America in the late 1830s and compared vessels in England with those he found here. The ever-observant Dickens noted, after a trip on the sidewheel paddle steamer *New York*, that

> the great difference in appearance between these packets and ours is that there is so much of them out of the water, the main-deck being enclosed on all sides, and filled with casks and goods, like any second or third floor in a stack of warehouses, and the promenade or hurricane deck being atop of that again. A part of the machinery is always above this deck; where the connecting-rod, in a strong and lofty frame, is seen working away like an iron top-sawyer.[30]

Dickens could have easily been describing any of the larger steam packets traversing the waters of Texas, many of which were of this U.S. design, that is, sidewheelers of wide beam that featured two decks (one closed, the other open) and tall "black chimneys," while "the man at the helm is shut up in a little house in the fore part of the boat (the wheel being connected with the rudder by chains, working the whole length of the deck)."[31] Illustrations of the period often show passengers congregating on the open decks, presumably enjoying the fresh ocean breezes as a banner of smoke from the stack trails along to indicate the vessel's brisk progress—often about ten knots. As noted by historians of technology, illustrators of the time often took great pleasure in depicting this smoke, for it also symbolized progress of a different kind: the progress of civilization.

Steamships had a profound effect on the shipping of both passengers and goods, for they were much faster than the schooners, which remained the mainstay of Texas nautical traffic during the Republic. Whereas a schooner could take as long as a week to arrive from New Orleans as a result of adverse wind conditions, steamers regularly made the run from the Crescent City to Galveston in under two days. From descriptions of the time we are left with a vivid picture of steam-powered nautical transportation revolutionizing Texas as steamboats and steamships served the Republic. Typically the former had flatter bottoms and wider hulls to carry large amounts of bulk cargo, such as bales of cotton, on shallow rivers like the Colorado and Brazos; the latter—steamships—had deeper and narrower hulls, to enable them to move more quickly and safely through the sometimes rougher water of the high seas. Both steamboats and steamships were propelled by paddlewheels, but the oceangoing vessels featured narrower hulls that drew considerably more water than the flatter-hulled steamboats intended for river transport. Thus it was, by the 1830s and 1840s, that the evolution of steam power went in two more or less separate directions: river boats for the inland trade and steamships for the ocean trade. The bays and harbors of the Texas coast were common ports where these increasingly distinctive steam-powered watercraft were sheltered, sometimes side by side. However, in the typical Texas harbor of the time, steam-powered vessels were well outnumbered by sailing vessels of all kinds, especially schooners and sloops.

STEAMBOATS ON THE REPUBLIC'S RIVERS

The Republic of Texas relied heavily on steamboats to open up the country to settlers and the rivers to trade, and many of the Republic's most promising communities flourished along rivers or on embayments where steamboats could tie up to load goods and people. Numerous Tennesseeans traveled to Texas via the Red River, which traversed the rich prairies and the Cross Timbers of the northern part of the Republic. The papers of Mirabeau B. Lamar note that "about the middle of February 1836 the Steam-Boat, Rover, commanded by Benjamin Crooks, landed at several places along the Texian line betwen [*sic*] the white-oak shoals, and Jonesboro; having on board emigrants from the United States . . . all having left their homes in the fall of 35 for the young Republic."[32] Also in 1836, the steamboat *Yellow Stone* reached San Felipe on the Brazos River, and in January of 1837 the nearly legendary *Laura* navigated Buffalo Bayou at a time when most of the Texas rivers were being opened up to steamboat traffic at their lower reaches. The maritime historian Ben Stuart was among the earliest to write about steamboats in Texas,[33] and more recently a number of excellent works have been written on navigation on the individual rivers. The history of steam navigation on the Brazos River has been told in considerable detail by Pamela Puryear and Nath Winfield Jr.[34] The Brazos presented a more or less typical pattern in that only the lower river (closer to the Gulf) was easy to navigate; farther upstream toward the "middle reaches" of the river, navigation became more difficult owing to the narrowing channel and rocky bottom. Steam-powered vessels like the *Yellow Stone* had a pivotal place in events in the early Republic, for they were well suited to the deeper waters of rivers on the coastal plain within about fifty miles of the Gulf. *Yellow Stone* was a sidewheel steamer built in Louisville, Kentucky, in 1831. She measured 122 feet in length, was 20.5 feet in width, and drew 6 feet of water while displacing 144 tons.[35] *Yellow Stone* had worked the Missouri River before coming to the Brazos in 1835. She reportedly carried Mobile Grays to fight in the Texas Revolution, was used by Sam Houston to transport his army across the rain-swollen Brazos River on their way to San Jacinto, carried the wounded Houston and captured Santa Anna to Galveston, and fittingly carried the body of Stephen F. Austin to Peach Point Plantation for burial. Like many Texas vessels, *Yellow Stone* is thought to have come to grief by being snagged and sunk on the Buffalo Bayou in 1837,[36] but there is considerable uncertainty as to her ultimate fate. A bell exhibited at the Alamo is said to have belonged to the *Yellow Stone* and commemorates her nearly legendary reputation in Texas.

The annals of the early Texas Republic reveal that steamboats were flourishing on the rivers, many venturing as far upstream as conditions would permit. By May of 1838, it was reported that the *Branch T. Archer*, a shallow-draft steamboat, had ascended three hundred fifty miles up the Trinity River—a feat made possible, no doubt, only by high water occasioned by late spring rains. By 1840 two small steamboats, the *Mustang* and *Lady Byron*, were in operation above Brazoria on the Brazos River. The most versatile steamboats had a shallow draft, say less than three feet, and could thus travel farther upstream.

Because the Republic of Texas had a great deal of difficulty funding and coordinating improvements, companies were often chartered to clear the logjams (called "rafts") that obstructed rivers. Steamboats were beautifully suited to the lower reaches of the Texas rivers, and many steamed hundreds of miles inland, but only when conditions permitted: Dry spells usually signaled a curtailment of river trade. Typical, perhaps, of Texas steamboats was the *Kate Ward*, which was constructed and launched at Matagorda especially for the trade on the Colorado River. Built in the spring of 1845, the *Kate Ward* was 110 feet long, had a beam of 24 feet, and drew 3 feet of water. The *Kate Ward* was mainly used in the cotton trade, and could hold six hundred bales on her deck. The typical Texas steamboat of the period was in reality somewhat smaller than the largest craft seen on the wider and deeper rivers farther east, such as the Mississippi and Ohio. Texas steamboats usually had at least two decks and featured an ornate pilot house. Fittingly, the upper deck of larger steam riverboats was called a "texas deck" — a term used widely on rivers as far west as California, Oregon, and even British Columbia, in the nineteenth century.[37]

Because this was an era in which speed began to become equated with success, and because river traffic increased, stories were soon heard about steamboat races. Perhaps the most legendary race during the period of the Texas Republic occurred when an enthusiastic Sam Houston commanded a steamboat bearing his famous name in 1838, and demanded that its captain race another vessel, the mail packet *Courrier* [sic], from Galveston to Houston. To further motivate the crew, Houston promised them a basket of champagne. As related by the young adventurer Henry Woodland, who was a crewman on the victorious *Sam Houston*, "Barrels of lard, tar and fat bacon were brought to us which we threw into the furnice [sic]." After describing the race in considerable detail, Woodland concluded:

> Never shall I forget the race between the Houston and the Courier and it has ever been a mystery to me why we were not all blown to eternity, for the boilers when we stopped were so hot and so great was the pressure of steam on the machinery that the whole boat trembled like a man with a violent ague. Next morning the fireman was missing and was never heard of any more. It was supposed that he fell over board and was drowned.[38]

In steamboat races of this type, crews learned that greater boiler pressure could be obtained by tying down safety valves in an effort to generate as much steam as possible. This was, needless to say, a highly dangerous practice. In reality, steamboats were dangerous enough even with safety valves operational, as numerous catastrophic boiler explosions during the period attest.

TUGBOATS AND TOWBOATS

Although the opulent appointments and fascinating machinery of the steamboats and steamships elicited much comment from travelers, the versatility of steam power was seen in other, less spectacular craft of the period. Smaller steamboats could navigate nimbly, and their versatility in towing other boats was soon apparent. With the development of steam propulsion came a revolution in shipping. The *towboat* was especially effective in pulling sailing vessels through narrow or otherwise hazardous areas, including the entrances to ports or harbors, where obstructions and shallow areas could cause disaster. Before the advent of steam, larger ships were towed by rowboats—a slow and arduous process revealed in historic paintings as men toiling at oars while they towed ponderous sailing ships. The first towboats appeared as steam power was developing in the early nineteenth century and appeared on the Gulf by the 1830s. An 1838 illustration on the payment receipt of the Phenix Tow Boat Company of New Orleans dated December 5, 1838, shows a sidewheeled steamer pulling a sailing ship (Fig. 5-7). Though this may be a somewhat conjectural drawing, the towboat in this illustration appears to have been converted from an oceangoing vessel, and it is possible that similar converted vessels were employed in the larger harbors such as Galveston at the time. As we have seen in the case of the nimble *Laura*, paddle-wheelers could also be used to carefully push or prod other ships into position, that is, serve as "tugboats." Towboats and tugboats thus served as "auxiliary propulsion" to solve a problem that had become quite apparent by the early nineteenth century, for then as now "large ships require the assistance of tugs for docking operations, maneuvering in confined waters and narrow channels, and escorting to clearwater."[39]

Sidewheelers were well suited to towing and tugboat service, and they revolutionized the movement of maritime traffic in ports. Tugboats and towboats ensured the safe passage of ships that might otherwise have gone off course if relying solely on sail. Because sidewheel paddles could be controlled independently at this time, sidewheelers were quite maneuverable,

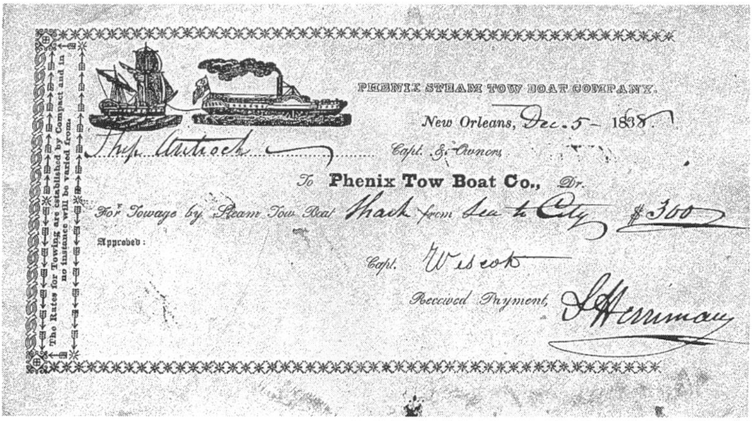

FIGURE 5-7

An 1838 payment receipt for the services of the Phenix Tow Boat Company of
New Orleans features what appears to be a former oceangoing vessel that has been
converted or downgraded into tugboat or towboat service. It is possible that early
towboats in Texas ports may have been similar. From the author's collection.

being able to do something virtually no other large vessel could do until
that time, namely, be quickly turned or brought around in a space not much
longer than their own length. Despite concern about their stability on the
high seas, sidewheeler paddle craft did rather well in the fairly calm waters
of ports and on rivers deep enough to accommodate their paddles; about a
fathom would be safe in most cases. Although the illustration of the towboat
in the Phenix Tow Boat Company illustration is conjectural, one assumes
that similar craft seen in lithographs and engravings of Texas ports in the
1840s served much the same purpose.

SAILING VESSELS IN MERCANTILE TRADE

Steam towboats and tugboats thus further helped open Texas harbors to
trade. During the Republic, this trade flourished, most of the tonnage being
shipped by sailing rather than steam-powered vessels. Despite the fact that
steam power captured the imagination of the public, and swelled the pride
of owners, it should be noted that the less spectacular schooner was certainly *the* ship of trade in the Republic of Texas, perfectly suited to hauling
cargo and passengers on relatively loose or flexible schedules. There is much
to be learned about the cargoes and operations of the more mundane, but
far more common, smaller sailing vessels that plied the Texas coast during

the period of the Republic of Texas. Although it is tempting to think that these vessels sailed with little official notice, it should be remembered that trade always generates revenue for the government that encourages and supports it. The Republic of Texas was no exception.

Consider, for example, the coasting license granted for the open sloop *Davie Crockett* (named after the Texian hero martyred at the Alamo in 1836) to operate for the period of twelve months from March 15, 1838. License No. Ten, District and Port of Matagorda, was issued to Alvin C. White and signed on that date by George W. Collingsworth, Colonel.[40] Thus, although we may never know much more about the *Davie Crockett*, this important fragment of information enables us to have a better idea of the vessel itself; in fact, the designation "open sloop" reveals something of its relatively small size and vulnerability to heavy seas. Vessels of this type often "coasted," that is, stayed close to the coast; and most took to the "inside," that is, stayed on the lagoons behind the barrier islands whenever possible. The Special Collections at the University of Texas at Arlington Library contains several of these rare coasting licenses, including the schooner *Black Jack* (license 11, attached to which is a full description of the ship from a temporary registration in New Orleans) and an "open boat" with the evocative name *Try It Again* (license 15), both of which were issued at Matagorda in 1838.

In the nineteenth century, when epidemic diseases were a constant concern, it was common for travelers of the period to record the ravages of diseases, such as "the fearful malady" yellow fever, and cholera. Vessels sailing would often require certificates of health that could yield important information about ships and their cargoes. A certificate of health provided clearance for the U.S. schooner *Independance* [sic] to leave Mobile, Alabama, on April 10, 1838, bound for Matagorda, Texas, "with an assorted cargo of which Isiah K. Pitman under God, is master . . . with fourteen persons included the Master of the said Schooner, and eight passengers," noting that the port of Mobile is free of "Plague, or dangerous contagious disease," as certified by Tho. Stringer, Ds. Collector.[41]

The Port of Mobile also figures in the operations of another Texas-bound schooner, the *Tiger*, which was "bound for Galveston with a cargo of lumber and ship stores" on May 14, 1838.[42] These merchandise and consignment forms were printed specially for the purpose, an indication of the briskness of maritime trade (Fig. 5-8). Because the vessel left U.S. waters, the form's text usually notes the "Act regulating passenger ships and vessels" that had been signed by [President] Monroe on May 2, 1819. A customs bond issued for the Sabine District and dated May 1, 1839, binds Thomas

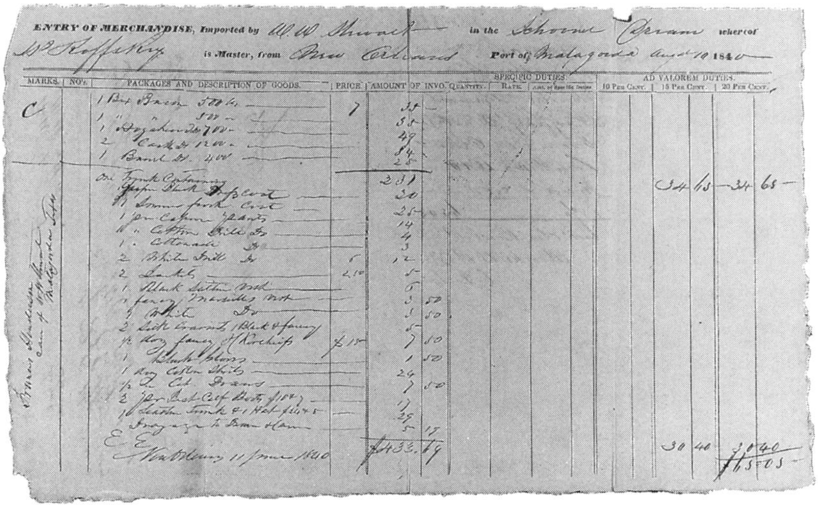
ENTRY OF MERCHANDISE, Imported by ... in the Schooner Dream whereof ... is Master, from New Orleans Port of Matagorda Aug 10 1840

MARKS.	NO's.	PACKAGES AND DESCRIPTION OF GOODS.	PRICE.	AMOUNT OF INVO.	SPECIFIC DUTIES Quantity.	Rate.	Amt. of Specific Duties	AD VALOREM DUTIES. 10 Per Cent.	15 Per Cent.	20 Per Cent.

FIGURE 5-8

Entry of merchandise form at Matagorda from August 1840 for the schooner Dream *reveals a diverse cargo from New Orleans. Such cargoes of finished products typified an imbalance of trade, with the Republic importing far more of value than products exported. Courtesy Special Collections Division, The University of Texas at Arlington Libraries, Arlington.*

W. Read (or Reid), John G. Bingham (?), and Thomas J. Allen for $508.28 1/4 against duties on goods arriving on the steamship *Cuba*, which had arrived from New Orleans. By 1839, it had become common for vessels in the coasting trade to post bonds; thus, the open boat *Tyron* posted a two-hundred-dollar "bond to be forfeited if the open boat *Tyron* when licensed as a coaster violates the customs laws during the one year following the issue of license," and Thomas Hanson swore on this document that he was owner of the boat, and a citizen of the Republic.[43]

Ports of the Republic

Despite this booming trade and considerable euphoria about the Republic's maritime prospects, most perceptive travelers to Texas expressed concern about the Republic's marginal port facilities. An anonymous narrative from 1837 notes of Velasco that "the want of accommodations on shore made it necessary for all to remain for the night in the vessel, a sad disappointment to many who, tired of confinement and the smell of bilge water, were anxious to be once more on land and to make their first acquaintance with the soil which was to be the theater of their future toil and enterprise."[44] This traveler also noted that, to reach the port of Velasco,

> the vessel had anchored some distance from shore owing to the shallows which put out from the land, and the long boat was launched. Notwithstanding the light draft of our boat, we were compelled to wade thirty or forty yards before we reached the dry part of the island. These shallows put out into the bay from the land at nearly every point in the harbor and present great obstacles to commerce, which can only be surmounted by the construction of docks at an immense expense.[45]

This description of Velasco characterized many Texas ports, for although the Republic of Texas encouraged the development of maritime commerce in the late 1830s, most Texas ports were still relatively small and rather primitive. In 1839–1840, Francis Sheridan corroborated the traveler's lament about Velasco, mentioned immediately above, when he described it as follows in his most interesting book subtitled *A Few Months Off the Coast of Texas*:

> Velasco is by no means a gigantic town, as it numbers no more than between 20 & 30 irregularly built huts & houses. Nor does it afford much gratification to the lover of the Picturesque situated as it is on a low sandy beach w[hic]h soon merges into a flat shrubless, prairie extending as far as the eye can reach.[46]

Sheridan's accounts also reveal the endemic problem with many early Texas ports: their shallow water. He commented that "it is a very great pity that the embouchure of the Brazos is not deeper, as it is navigable for 500 miles inland" but added that "two small flat bottomed steamers already furrow its waves & ply with produce to Galveston (where again we find no harbour & the cargo is discharged from the vessel into the merchantman destined to receive it)."[47] In order to reach Galveston Island, Sheridan's brig HMS *Pilot* anchored a considerable distance from land on February 3, 1840, waiting for the heavy seas to calm somewhat:

> We lay patiently off Velasco till this day, when the enterprising Ramsay & myself armed with Carpet bags essayed to land. On approaching the Bar however we found breakers w[hic]h were anything but inviting & in consequence returned crest fallen to the vessel but succeeded on a second attempt in the afternoon.[48]

To be able to reach land safely, Sheridan boarded a flat-bottomed steamer, the *Constitution*. The steamer that Sheridan describes had been wrecked on the coast near Galveston and "redeemed" from her former status as "an old, battered broken rig [?] pressured boat" by Thomas F. McKinney, who had put her into the cotton trade on the lower Brazos River—a reminder that the distinction between river steamboat and coastal trade steamer was often blurred in the period of the Texas Republic. Sheridan further described the primitive facilities for unloading a cargo of horses, wherein "two planks extended from the deck of the Steamer [*Constitution*] to the shore—the animal has his legs tied—a cord is passed under his shoulders & having been thrown down he is dragged on board across the planks."[49]

The difficulty of entering even the best of Texas harbors, Galveston, in the 1840s is made clear by Mrs. Houstoun. From her vantage point on the schooner yacht *Dolphin* off Galveston in 1843, Mrs. Houstoun set the scene by noting that "a large steamer, the New York, which we had observed some time previously occupied in getting up her steam, was seen coming towards us; her high-pressure engine was puffing and blowing, like some huge elephant out of breath, and her deck covered with curious passengers."[50] Mrs. Houstoun went on to explain that the captain of the 100-foot, 219-ton yacht *Dolphin* was apprehensive because she drew twelve feet of water—making the trip across the bar an event of real concern. Mrs. Houstoun then noted that "in a true Yankee spirit of 'making an operation,'" the captain of the steamer *New York* pulled the *Dolphin* over the bar and into Galveston harbor without incident. Mrs. Houstoun's writings confirm what all mariners on the Texas coast knew: Larger vessels often needed guidance in getting through the tricky narrows or passes, for the consequences of sailing through without knowledge could be disastrous. Pilot boats manned by knowledgeable pilots were commonplace in the ports of Texas by the late 1830s. It was reported on August 8, 1838, that "Capt. Simptons [pilotage] tariff and charge ranged from $2.50 per foot of vessels of 6 feet draft, to $4.50 per foot [for] vessels drawing 12 feet."[51] The difference in rates, of course, related to the increased difficulty in piloting or guiding vessels of greater draft across the treacherous bars at the entrances to the harbors.

Once vessels were in the primitive Texas harbors, other problems presented themselves. Getting cargo from seagoing vessels of considerable draft—say ten to fourteen feet of water—proved impossible in many Texas ports because of the shallow waters. Before any long piers were built, lighters were needed. A lighter is any boat, often a small open craft, that is rowed or sailed to a larger vessel in order to transship the cargo to land, or

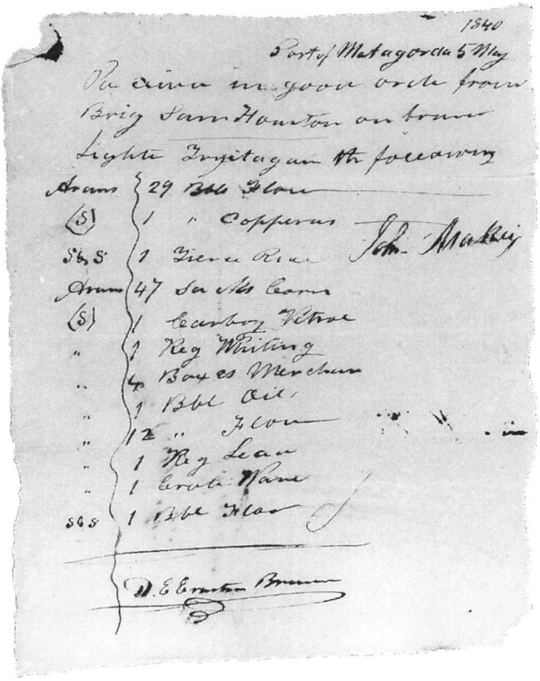

FIGURE 5-9
Handwritten receipt for goods off-loaded from the brig Sam Houston
and transferred to the lighter Try It Again *at Matagorda, May 5, 1840,
reveals a diverse cargo. Courtesy Special Collections Division,
The University of Texas at Arlington Libraries, Arlington.*

vice versa should the process need to be reversed. In this regard, we again find the small open boat *Try It Again* mentioned in the records: A receipt prepared at Matagorda on May 3, 1840, shows the *Try It Again* receiving from the brig *Sam Houston* a list of items, including goods and four flour [*sic*] pots,[52] while a similar handwritten receipt two days later reveals a diverse cargo of products ranging from Copperas to boxes of merchandise continuing to be off-loaded (Fig. 5-9).

We are given a better understanding of the diversity of cargo carried by vessels, such as the schooner *Maria*, from a manifest pertaining to its voyage from New Orleans for Matagorda and Linns Landing, Texas: Seven columns number and mark the cargo, designating the contents, place of consignee's residence, and port(s) of destination.[53] A review of cargoes of the *Maria* and other vessels at Matagorda reveals corn, flour, sperm candles, tobacco, starch, hardwood, sewing notions, spices and medicines, cowbells, molasses, hardware, fancy goods, crockery, shoes, hats, and dry goods. These records confirm that Texas maritime trade helped bring both necessities and amenities to the Republic, and they serve as testimony to how primitive—probably virtually impossible—life on the frontier would have been without shipping to render it more endurable, if not pleasant.

The earliest available printed record of commerce for the port of Galveston appeared in the *Civilian & Galveston Gazette* for 1839. In that year, 228 vessels were recorded, and their breakdown by type of vessel is quite revealing of the changes taking place in Texas maritime trade with foreign ports:[54]

Schooners	144
Steamers	44
Brigs	32
Sloops	5
Ships	3
Total	228

The total value of imports during that year was $1,108,238, while exports were valued at $120,548, a situation that reflected a balance of trade "greatly against the young Republic."[55] This severe imbalance of trade meant that the Republic of Texas was, economically speaking, hemorrhaging to the outside world at a rate of nearly ten to one through the very ports it hoped to develop. Interestingly, images of the vessels of the Texas Navy appeared on the paper currency of the Republic and on the official documents of the Consulate of the Republic of Texas (Figs. 5-10 and 5-11). The official documents and currency of the period depict three major types of vessels—sidewheel paddle riverboats, sidewheel paddle ocean vessels, and sailing vessels—common in the period of the Texas Republic. The frequent appearance of sailing and steam vessels on the Republic's currency underscores the importance of maritime trade and protection to Texas, but this currency was not universally accepted outside of Texas, or accepted only at reduced rates—a condition that caused further economic distress to those in the Republic.

Fragmentary records for all Texas ports permit us to construct a picture of active trade that began to boom as word of the Texas Revolution's success spread and Texans began producing crops, especially cotton, for sale while demanding goods produced elsewhere to ease the harshness of life on the frontier. Although all ports benefited from the influx of trade-bearing and

FIGURE 5-10

Featuring a conspicuously maritime theme, an engraved form of the Consulate of the Republic of Texas ratified on June 20, 1840, illustrated steam and sailing vessels of the Texas Navy, including what appears to be the Zavala (lower left), Invincible (upper left), and other unnamed vessels. Courtesy Special Collections Division, The University of Texas at Arlington Libraries, Arlington.

FIGURE 5-11

Texas currency in the late 1830s employed maritime images in addition to other symbols. Examples include ten-dollar notes featuring a sidewheel, oceangoing steamship (top) and a harbor scene containing a schooner (bottom). Courtesy Special Collections Division, The University of Texas at Arlington Libraries, Arlington.

passenger-carrying vessels, some benefited more than others. Without question, Galveston was the most promising and rapidly growing port in the Republic of Texas. Galveston's growth can be attributed to its geographic location, which included a harbor behind a fairly open pass, proximity to the communities developing inland in the vicinity of Houston, and proximity to New Orleans. The *Guide to the Republic of Texas* in 1839 noted that

> Galveston is on the Eastern Extremity of the island of that name and is at present the principal port of Entry in Texas. Two years ago the Town was not in existence, it now numbers three thousand inhabitants.[56]

Galveston continued to grow rapidly during the Republic, so much so that the preparers of the *Guide* cited above could claim in their 1845 edition that, "with a population of 5,000," Galveston was "the most thriving town upon the [Texas] sea coast."[57]

And yet, many perceptive travelers expressed concern about the site of Galveston, which, despite its port and its healthful and invigorating breezes in summer, seemed ominous. In 1837 an anonymous traveler noted that "the surface of Galveston Island is low, so much so that there have been times when it has been nearly covered with water through its whole extent by the violence of the winds and tide."[58] This prompted the traveler to discuss the site of the future city in detail, identifying its advantages and disadvantages with prophetic candor:

> Should the future city of Galveston realize the hopes of its founders, either genuine or pretended, it will be the first instance upon record where the spirit of speculation has not overrated the advantages and prospects of a particular situation. The spot which has been selected as the site of the city is doubtless the most eligible that could be found upon the island, on account of its elevation over all other positions and the great superiority of the harbor at this point over every other part of the bay. But unfortunately, almost the whole site is liable to inundation.[59]

The observant Mrs. Houstoun was even more prophetic in her observations about Galveston when she noted, in 1845: "The tremendous hurricane that occurred last September, as it was described to us, is calculated to give one the impression that on some future day the flourishing city of Galveston may be swept away by the overwhelming incursions of the sea."[60]

Despite the hazards of coastal storms, the Texas ports continued their lively growth during the period of the Texas Republic. Of the many travelers to Texas, Francis Sheridan attempted to describe the ports most carefully, noting that Texas in 1839–1840

> has four sea-ports that may be fairly called her best & principal ports, viz.
> The Sabine   Galveston   Matagorda   Aransaso.[61]

Sheridan added that "The Sabine will admit vessels drawing 8 feet of water. Galveston 12 or 13 feet, Matagorda [and] Aransaso 9 or 10 feet" and further noted that "they are all safe and secure harbours and no doubt the entrances can be much improved."[62] The names of these ports are indeed somewhat confusing, for Aransaso may refer to Copano, inside Aransas Pass, and The Sabine was also called Sabine City, though the large and proximate Sabine Lake offered other potentially good port sites. Regarding Aransas, Mrs. Houstoun noted that even the schooner yacht *Dolphin* was unable to enter that harbor, for the vessel drew twelve feet of water. This, despite Mrs. Houstoun's wish to see south Texas, ensured that the *Dolphin* would only enter Galveston. It can thus be seen that Galveston's major advantage was its naturally deeper pass, which nevertheless continued to alarm and challenge mariners entering that harbor.

In the spirit of the times, Texas ports were often developed by individuals who were well entrenched in politics, a good example being Sabine City (called The Sabine and, later, Sabine Pass), which had been laid out in 1836 by Philip A. Sublett and Sam Houston. To these fledgling ports Sheridan could have added Velasco, which, though shallow, experienced brisk trade at the mouth of the Brazos. Other Texas ports were what might be called paper towns in that they were platted but little or nothing occurred there. Typical in this regard was Port Preston, in Refugio County. Backed by New York capitalists, Stuart Perry had the townsite platted and several lots were deeded, but apparently only a few buildings were ever constructed, despite the town's being incorporated in 1839.[63]

Of the numerous ports visited by travelers in the early 1840s, one—Linnville—is often conspicuously absent from their reports. Located about twenty miles from Victoria, the ill-fated Linnville's story is worth retelling briefly. Originally called New Port upon its establishment by John J. Linn in 1831, Linnville quickly became the largest of four ports on Lavaca Bay (the others being Texana, Dimmit's Landing, and Cox's Point). Throughout the late 1830s, the port of Linnville prospered. It reportedly became one of the early Republic's most important ports of entry, and it was frequently mentioned in immigrant guides as a destination. By early 1840, Linnville seemed destined for greatness and prosperity: It possessed the custom house for the district of La Baca, a hotel, numerous warehouses, and a population of several hundred souls, including about a dozen slaves. But Linnville was to be short-lived despite the many schooners and other sailing vessels that called upon it: Attacked and virtually destroyed by Comanche Indians in August of 1840, the once thriving port community never recovered. Some entrepreneurs attempted to rebuild Linnville, but its fate had been sealed by both the Indian raid and the establishment of a new community, Labacca (or Port Lavaca), which was located a few miles away at the mouth of Linn Bayou. Testimony to the hardships of the Texas coastal frontier, the ghost town port of Linnville remains completely abandoned and partially sub-merged today, several historical markers commemorating the site.[64]

Of all the ports of the Texas Republic, Galveston naturally received the most comment in the late 1830s and 1840s and lived up to the enthusiastic expectations of its promoters (Fig. 5-12). The early port city was thriving at the time of Francis Sheridan's 1839–1840 visit. Sheridan commented that "the best entrance and harbour on the Coast of Texas is Galveston," where the "harbour is safe and good with 20 to 30 ft water [and] I am of the opinion that an expenditure of £25 to 30,000 wood [sic] so improve the entrance to that Harbour as to secure 17 to 18 ft water."[65] It was into Galveston that service by the Texas and New York Line of Packets, of which William and J. J. Hendley were local agents, was established earlier in the 1840s; by 1844 the firm's fleet was composed of four fine sailing vessels: the ship *Star Republic* (built by Sylvester Gildersteer at Portland, Maine, and said to be the first full-rigged vessel to fly the Texas flag as her private signal), and the brigs *Empire*, *M. B. Lamar*, and *May*. The Galveston historian Ben C. Stuart further noted that the port city was very cosmopolitan in 1843, with vessels from the United States, Britain, France, and Belgium in port; vessels plied routes from the distant port cities of Liverpool, London, Havre, Bremen, Hamburg, and Antwerp. These destinations revealed that the Texas immigrant guides that flourished during the 1840s were indeed working. Immigrants hailed from the United States, Ireland, Poland, Britain, and what are today Germany and the Czech Republic.

Many of these immigrants were lured to Texas by promotional materials, and maps were among the most effective tools depicting the Republic as a land of opportunity. Based in part on the cartography of Stephen F. Austin, these maps appeared either in atlases (such as Arrowsmith's 1842 world atlas, produced in London), or as sheet maps prepared in eastern U.S. cities such

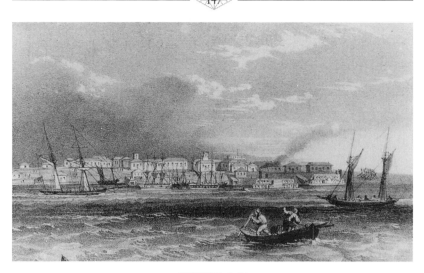

FIGURE 5-12

View of the Galveston harbor in the early 1840s showing the port city behind several vessels, including schooners, brigs, and two steam-powered riverboats (right, center), while in the foreground two men handle a lighter or long boat. From Mrs. Houstoun's Texas and the Gulf of Mexico; *courtesy Special Collections Division, The University of Texas at Arlington, Arlington.*

as Philadelphia and New York. Typical of these promotional maps was David Burr's map of the Republic of Texas, done in 1845–1846 (Fig. 5-13), which was printed in several colors and represented the state-of-the-art information about the waters of the Republic. Significantly, this map reveals the importance of Texas waters in several ways. First, fully 90% of the boundaries of the Republic are waters, including the coast and the larger rivers, such as the Rio Grande, Red, and Arkansas rivers. Secondly, the coast proper is delineated in considerable detail, and includes fairly accurate depictions of the barrier islands and estuaries. Thirdly, and quite significantly, the port of Galveston is so important that it rates its own inset, at a larger scale and in considerably more detail than other parts of the coast. This is natural, for Galveston became and would remain Texas' most important port during this period. It was at Galveston that many new arrivals first glimpsed Texas, though many continued by boat to the fledgling communities along Buffalo Bayou in what would later become Houston.

As European immigrants came in contact with the Texas coast, it was inevitable that they would compare the waters and topography of the Republic with those of home. The historical geographer Robin Doughty has

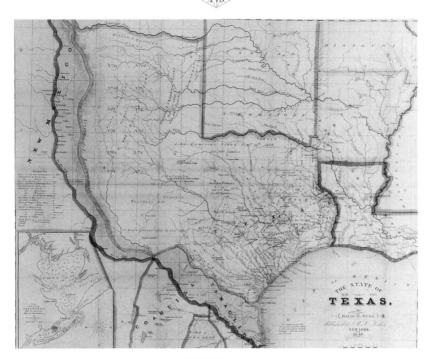

FIGURE 5-13

*David Burr's map of Texas from 1845–1846 featured the waters of Texas in
considerable detail and included a separate inset for Galveston at a larger, more
detailed scale. Burr's maps contained information from many sources, including
Stephen F. Austin and the Mexican Navy. Courtesy Special Collections Division,
The University of Texas at Arlington Libraries, Arlington.*

shown that an Irishman, James Power, "discovered landscapes from today's
Eire in coastal Texas," noting that "Wexford in southeast Ireland sat on a
bay just like Copano," and that "Live Oak Peninsula, north of present-day
Rockport, supposedly resembled the separation of Wexford Bay from St.
Georges Channel."[66] Doughty further noted that the German visitor/natu-
ralist Ferdinand von Roemer had remarked that a plantation near Industry,
on the Mill Creek tributary of the Brazos River, looked like "a certain region of the Rhine."[67] As Texas's climate and topography became somewhat
idealized by mid-century, many compared it favorably to the Mediterranean; as a vestige of this flattery, Corpus Christi bore the fanciful sobriquet
"Naples of the Gulf" in the nineteenth century.

Texans and visitors alike in the 1840s recognized that the sea was the
most realistic entryway to the Republic, for trails and roads were still pretty

much in their infancy, and construction of railroads, which were of much interest, would forever elude the officials of the impoverished Republic.[68] Despite much hoopla surrounding Texas's prospects, however, the Republic's revenues were small. This impoverishment in the face of such potential was attributable to several factors, not the least of which was a populace defiant about paying taxes or tariffs. Although the coast was recognized as the Republic's lifeline and the need for major focused improvements was obvious, maritime improvements under the Republic were uncoordinated at best, despite the fact that the Republic had a navy department.

To some outsiders, the Republic's lack of leadership and organization to improve its maritime transportation infrastructure reflected poorly on the body politic. The Republic's poor record with regard to maritime (and other) improvements led the observant and critical Francis Sheridan to comment in 1839–1840 that "to hear a Texian talk of his country you would suppose that he lived in as civilized a place as there is on the face of the globe" and to conclude caustically that that same Texian will "enlarge on the advantages of contemplated rail-roads & imaginary canals—when he knows all the time, that . . . the Govt have [sic] not the power of means to enforce them and that the republic of Texas is in fact at this time nothing more than a self-adopted name on the part of a collection of squatters without character or credit."[69] In all fairness, it may be said that Texas had relatively little time to mature into recognizing *how* to improve ports and maritime navigation despite knowing *what* was needed.

Navigational Hazards

The issue of lighthouses provides a good example of the Republic's inability to improve navigation. As maritime shipping traffic increased along the Texas coast in the early 1800s, so did accidents. Shipwrecks were all too common and their causes many, but groundings were among the most common. As noted, the Texas coast has many shoals and treacherous passes, and these needed to be both better indicated on nautical charts (which increased in sophistication in the nineteenth century) and properly marked by navigational warnings so that mariners could avoid them. Because shipping occurred at night, lights were employed to warn sailors of hazardous areas. By the time of the Texas Republic, mariners and port developers began to agitate for the construction of lighthouses,[70] or "lights" as they were sometimes called. That lighthouses could facilitate the passage of vessels into Texas harbor entrances is noted in the 1844 publication *A History of Texas, or the*

Emigrant's Guide to the Republic, which predicted of Galveston harbor that "the passage is of considerable width, and when the lighthouse, authorized by Congress, shall be completed, will be navigated with little if any difficulty."[71] Given the rather impoverished state of the Texas Republic's economy and the seemingly endless disagreements as to how, and where, to spend public funds, lighthouses (like railroads and many other improvements) would have to await annexation of Texas by the United States before becoming a reality.

What can explain Texas's reluctance to build lighthouses? Surely not technology, for lighthouses had in fact become commonplace on the eastern seaboard since the first one was erected in Boston in 1680; in fact, by 1817 fifty-five lighthouses dotted the U.S. coast, and their bright beams were widely credited with improving maritime safety and enhancing trade. The Republic of Texas's inability to build even one lighthouse during its ten years of existence is indeed perplexing, especially given the fact that "by 1838, two hundred lighthouses warned the ocean sailor that he approached the U.S. coast."[72] The construction of coordinated improvements such as lighthouses indicated that the U.S. public in the early nineteenth century was beginning to overcome their congenital fear of centralized government. Although funding was an issue, one may interpret Texas's failure to erect lighthouses as emblematic of a deep mistrust of centralized government. If, as the historian John R. Stilgoe has observed, the development of the lighthouse in the United States marked "the first time the old notion of local community control no longer applied to a structure" or, more to the point, that it symbolized "the new strength of nationalism over localism, the new power of new government,"[73] then it is not surprising that Texans, ever wary of surrendering power, never built one. Whatever the reason for the absence of lighthouses on the coast of the Republic of Texas, the result was that another hazard could be added to the list of conditions that jeopardized vessels, sailors, passengers, and cargoes.

A slowness in implementing safer and more effective navigation technologies also characterized Texas rivers during this period. As the Republic developed, steamboats reached ever higher into the riverine recesses of the interior. By 1840, a "new and light-draft steamboat" called the *Vesta* had been purchased for travel far into the interior of Texas; in April of that year, the *Galveston Weekly News* reported that the steamboat *Trinity* was now running from Alabama on the Trinity to Galveston . . . a distance of about 500 miles, and found the navigation uninterrupted, and could have gone much farther if it had been desired."[74] Such reports led many to believe that

FIGURE 5-14
A fanciful, romanticized view of Houston shows a sidewheeled steam-powered riverboat tied up at a dock in what appears to be more like a Mediterranean than a Texas port. From Mrs. Houstoun's Texas and the Gulf of Mexico; *courtesy Special Collections Division, The University of Texas at Arlington Libraries, Arlington.*

virtually unlimited access by steamboat to the interior was possible. Some even suggested that Santa Fe, New Mexico (which was claimed by Texas at this time), could be easily reached by riverboats on the Rio Grande.

Such speculation led to fanciful development schemes and equally fanciful illustrations that might tempt investors. Guidebooks of the times abound in misconceptions which resulted, in part, from a lack of knowledge of the complex geography of the Republic. For example, a romantic illustration of Houston in 1844 (Fig. 5-14) shows a steamboat docked at what appears to be a community nestled in steep hills—more in appearance like either a Mediterranean port or a community far inland like Austin—but decidedly not a Texas port on the coastal plain. Yet it was the rivers reaching up into Texas from ports like Houston that excited much interest. Never letting much of maritime interest escape her notice, Mrs. Houstoun commented in the 1840s that "the intention is to run iron steamers, with a very light draught, up and down the Trinity; the steamers having flat-bottomed rafts attached to them."[75] She went on to note that "a steamer, by name the *Ellen Frankland*, had returned in safety to the harbour, after having made a successful voyage up the Trinity River, to a distance of between four and five hundred miles from its mouth."[76] Her claims were based on newspaper stories of the time, and, if true, indicated exceptionally fortunate conditions for navigation. In most years, the Trinity River would prove impossible to navigate that far because of its shallows and snags. For Victorians, however, nothing seemed impossible, and Mrs. Houstoun even concluded that "it is now ascertained that a canal, connecting the Trinity with the Red River, would not be by any means an expensive undertaking, the distance being about sixty miles, and the country perfectly level."[77] But alas, Texas's poor economic condition militated against such internal improvements despite many bold schemes for their promotion. These, too, would have to await the arrival of statehood.

CHANGING PERCEPTIONS OF THE TEXAS COAST

By the 1840s, two very different cultural perceptions of the Texas coast become apparent. The first was functional, a result of people's being involved in the everyday business of getting from one place to another and/or making a living. The other was aesthetic, that is, recreation- or pleasure-oriented, which in turn found people pausing to appreciate the coast. The latter perception could be developed only when enough leisure time had become available—time that resulted from the accumulation of wealth as larger agricultural and industrial enterprises developed. Thus, as early as the early 1840s, Mrs. Houstoun introduced a rather new term, "yachting," into the Texas vocabulary less than ten years after its 1836 introduction into the U.S. lexicon as a popular term for pleasure boating. Although the term *yacht* had been used for hunting boats since the 1600s, and British royalty had used the term for their pleasure boating by the late 1700s, it now came to have a new meaning. Yachting, or sailing for recreation, pleasure, and enrichment, became a popular pastime of the wealthy in the United States as yacht clubs developed on the eastern seaboard in the early 1800s. Whereas to most people concerned with eking out a living the Texas coast remained simply another challenge, now, with leisure time, one could pursue the aesthetics of both sea and shore. Wealthy early Victorians in Texas left a record of the Gulf and its shore at its most serene, as their letters recording the beauties of nature—the pink fleecy clouds in turquoise skies over the Gulf and the magnificent beauty of seashells—attest. Bolstered by a sense of adventure and whimsy, a few wealthy Texans took to yachting (especially in sloops and schooners) as a way of exploring the coast for pleasure. This activity, it should be noted, was something the early Spanish and French explorers would have found very odd if not perfectly incomprehensible.

*I*MPROVEMENTS AT *M*IDCENTURY
1845–1860

Contrary to the commonly held opinion,
the majority of the first settlers came to Texas by way of the sea.
JIM DAN HILL, 1936

The year 1845 brought with it the annexation of Texas into the Union, followed a year later by the beginning of the Mexican-American War (1846–1848)—the seemingly inevitable conflict with Mexico over possession of much of the area that became the U.S. Southwest. Both conflicts were results of the European Americans' seemingly insatiable desire for land and their unstoppable movement westward. As in the Texas Revolution a decade earlier, sea power proved decisive in helping the European Americans in the Mexican-American War. Rumors that Mexico had declared war on the United States resulted in a blockading of the Mexican coast during late summer 1845. Military records reveal the quick naval deployment of troops and materiel to two points near the front: Corpus Christi, on the Nueces, and Brownsville, on the lower Rio Grande. Engravings and lithographs of the Mexican-American War depict the flotilla of vessels, both steam- and sail-powered, that conveyed U.S. troops to the anticipated battlefronts of South Texas, where, both symbolically and strategically, the Mexican-American War began.

It seems fitting that the first war the United States fought on foreign soil began in South Texas. The war lasted from 1846 to 1848 and effectively began with the arrival of U.S. troops at Saint Joseph's Island, about twenty-five miles from Corpus Christi. Lying just north of the contested area between the Rio Grande and Rio Nueces claimed by both Mexico and the United States, St. Joseph's Island served as a mustering point for troops that would launch an offensive deep into Mexico. These troops had arrived in late summer of 1845 by the most effective means of travel from New Orleans: ships. General Zachary Taylor wrote from aboard the steamship

FIGURE 6-1

A contemporary view of Taylor's army of occupation south of Corpus Christi in October 1845, by C. Parsons from a drawing by Captain D. P. Whiting, shows the orderly rows of white tents lining the beach, and several vessels, including a steamer, lying off the coast. Courtesy Special Collections Division, The University of Texas at Arlington Libraries, Arlington.

Alabama that the health of the troops in his command, which consisted of eight companies, was "greatly improved by the voyage."[1]

A contemporary view of Taylor's army of occupation in October 1845 (Fig. 6-1) shows the orderly rows of white tents lining the beach, and several vessels, including a steamer, lying off the coast. About fifteen hundred troops were stationed there by late summer of 1845. A newspaper report in the New Orleans *Weekly Picayune* described the encampment's location as "one of extreme beauty . . . along the shelly margin of the shore of Corpus Christi Bay," while Captain W. S. Henry praised the cooling effect of what he called the "never-ceasing trade-winds"[2]—no doubt a reference to the sustained southeasterly on-shore breezes during summer. During the next few months, however, the euphoria of the troops would turn to despair as the "most shocking weather imaginable" descended on the coast in the form of freezing northers alternating with warm spells. According to Ulysses S. Grant, "some of the old Texans say they have scarsely [*sic*] ever seen as disagreeable a winter as this one has been."[3] To rectify the erratic mail delivery that was beginning to demoralize the troops, General Zachary Taylor urged his superiors to authorize a "good seagoing steamer" as a dispatch vessel; in December the General's wish was granted as the steamer *Harney* was placed under his command.[4] The encampment at Corpus Christi gave the troops a foretaste of the debilitating diseases that plagued troops throughout the entire Mexican-American War or, as it is still called in Mexico—the Yankee invasion (*invasión Yanqui*).

The net effect of the troop buildup, which more than doubled to 3,860 in January 1846, was a phenomenal boom in the population of Corpus Christi. From its original population of about one hundred at the beginning of the buildup, Corpus Christi's population reached about two thousand; the newcomers, which consisted of Mexican and U.S. traders, entrepreneurs, and camp followers, gave Corpus Christi a decidedly boomtown look as half the structures were of canvas.[5] In this regard, events at Corpus Christi in 1845–1846 portended the defense-related spending that would stimulate port communities on the Texas coast in the twentieth century.

By May of 1846, war seemed inevitable, and a declaration of war was signed on May 13 after Congress was urged by President James K. Polk. The war underscored the importance of logistics in relation to the Gulf environment. Whereas General Taylor had originally prepared to pursue the enemy, the high seas off the mouth of the Rio Grande and rough water on the bar made it impossible for naval vessels to enter the river. By the time conditions improved on May 18, the army had crossed several miles upstream using small boats. The scarcity of water in the area also plagued the navy, and three ships (the *Cumberland, Potomac,* and *John Adams*) had to go to Pensacola to refill their water tanks. Using his remaining vessels, however, Commodore Conner was able to continue to blockade the coast, while reminding his superiors of the need for vessels drawing less than eight feet of water.[6]

Thus the U.S. Navy found itself in something of a dilemma. Although it possessed a large fleet, naval warfare in this area called for special vessels. Because a portion of the war was fought in the shallow coastal waters of the Gulf, small shallow-draft steamers, schooners, brigs, and storeships were required in some battles.[7] As it turned out, the U.S. Navy was easily able to invade Mexico despite concern about two British-built Mexican steamers (*Montezuma* and *Guadaloupe*) that had actually been repossessed at the outset of the war. On this Gulf front of the war, the schooners, brigs, and small steamers of the United States Navy enabled an active invasion of Mexico via Veracruz, while U.S. troops were able to push southward across the Rio Grande on pontoon bridges erected for the purpose.

Interestingly, the newness of steam power in military use meant that some commanders were more familiar with the steam-powered vessels than others. The fact that Commodore Matthew Perry was very knowledgeable about steam and the Senior Commodore Conner was less so led to a rumor that was perpetuated by Perry's biographer, William E. Griffis—namely, that "practically, though not officially, the Gulf or home squadron was divided. Conner had charge of the sail and Perry of the steam vessels." Lieutenant John A. Winslow had put it even more strongly in a letter on October 8, 1846: "Today Commodore Perry took command of the steamers of the squadron." However, the maritime historian Karl Jack Bauer has shown that Perry simply relieved the ailing Conner, who had, in fact, commanded operations that involved steamers.[8]

Lithographs, engravings, and paintings of the maritime aspects of the war reveal the extensive use of well-armed sailing vessels and steamships, but steamboats also figured in a number of troop and supply movements. Notable among these images is a view of Matamoros from Fort Brown by the peripatetic officer Sam Chamberlain, whose watercolor painting features the steamboat *Col. Taylor* (Fig. 6-2). This primitively styled but rather

FIGURE 6-2

"*Matamoros from Fort Brown,*" *a watercolor by the United States military officer Sam Chamberlain, shows the steamboat* Col. Taylor *on the Rio Grande, which was an important supply route for U.S. troops and materiel. Courtesy San Jacinto Museum, La Porte, Texas.*

FIGURE 6-3

As seen in this rare naval portfolio lithograph of U.S. sail and steam-powered vessels at Brazos Santiago in May, 1846, naval forces gave the United States a decisive strategic advantage over Mexico. Courtesy Special Collections Division, The University of Texas at Arlington Libraries, Arlington.

credible painting reveals the steamboat to be mostly white with red-capped smokestacks and red and blue trim on the ornately arcaded deck railings. According to the historian William Goetzmann, the presence of the large riverboat recorded by Chamberlain signified the strategic importance of Matamoros.[9] Chamberlain's painting also beautifully reveals a small, open ferryboat that conveyed passengers and goods across the river. This type of conveyance was common in frontier Texas before bridges were constructed—an activity greatly accelerated by the Mexican-American War, which witnessed the erection of pontoon bridges across the Rio Grande.

The Mexican-American War stimulated trade while expanding geographic knowledge of the coast as the military mapped it in advance of troop movements. Although the Mexican-American War is largely remembered for its land military battles and victories, it was maritime shipping of troops and materiel that enabled the United States to have such a decisive advantage over Mexico, as evidenced by the numerous sail and steamships that landed troops and materiel at Brazos Santiago and the Rio Grande in May of 1846 (Fig. 6-3).[10] In addition to being the first war fought on foreign soil, the Mexican-American War marked the U.S. Navy's first decisive use of steam power in war. The war also underscored the strategic importance of improving Texas ports as part of a broadening interpretation, some said abuse, of the Monroe Doctrine, which ensured U.S. hegemony over naval trade in the Gulf. With the defeat of Mexico and the ratification of the Treaty of Guadalupe Hidalgo in 1848, the southern boundary of Texas was permanently fixed at the Rio Grande. The Texas coast now became indisputably part of the U.S. coast and by midcentury it benefited from improvements aimed at stimulating hemispheric trade. The war also resulted in far more detailed reconnaissance and mapping of the lower Texas coast and the Rio Grande Valley.

INTERLUDE: THE ADVENTURES OF THE *Major Brown*

The war provided Bryant P. Tilden Jr., under the orders of Major General Patterson, U.S. Army, the opportunity to explore the upper Rio Grande. Tilden's goal was to better understand the river's strategic and military potential. In October of 1846, Tilden used the U.S. Steamer *Major Brown*, commanded by Captain Mark Sterling, for this reconnaissance. Tilden began his report with an oblique reference to Austin's *Ariel* by stating that "steamboats drawing five feet of water, it is well-known, have plied between the mouth of the Rio Grande and the town of Camargo, in Mexico, on the mouth of the San Juan, at a distance by water of four hundred and fifty miles from the Gulf," adding, however, that "the Rio Grande above the San Juan, has long been pronounced impracticable."[11] Tilden noted that with only one "forgotten or misbelieved" exception, all who have attempted to go further up river "have speedily returned, making adverse reports." Tilden then added that his expedition was "unwilling to rely implicitly on such reports," and he proceeded to relate a remarkable trip to Guerrera (or Reveilla) on the Salado, where the expedition investigated reports of, and found, bituminous coal deposits.

Leaving Guerrera, Tilden then described a harrowing accident on the Rio Grande "which threatened to dash the boat to pieces." After venturing farther upriver to where the waters narrowed, the *Major Brown* had been swung by the current onto two rocks that threatened to either roll the vessel over, or break it in two. According to Tilden, however, Captain Sterling, who commanded the vessel, and Captain McGowan, a well-known pilot, managed to steer the *Major Brown* from her predicament. Continuing upriver, Tilden reported only a few snags as far up as Laredo, the major difficulty being "in the narrowness of the passages through the reefs, all of

A
SKETCH OF THE
UPPER RIO GRANDE

Explored in the months of October and November 1846
on Board the U.S. Steamer Major Brown commanded by Capt. M. Sterling
of Pittsburgh
Under the direction of Lieut. Bryant P. Tilden, jr. 2d Regt. U.S. Infantry
by order of
MAJOR GENERAL PATTERSON U.S.A.
commanding the 2d division
of the army of occupation in Mexico.

LITH. OF T. SINCLAIR.

FIGURE 6-4

*A portion of the map prepared as an outcome of the reconnaissance expedition of
the steamer* Major Brown *in 1847 shows the lower Rio Grande in considerable
detail. Courtesy Special Collections Division, The University of Texas at Arlington
Libraries, Arlington.*

which may be easily widened at a comparatively slight expense."[12] There
Tilden noted that "the *Major Brown* astonished the people of Laredo by her
arrival at that port, destined beyond dispute to become the head of navigation on the Rio Grande."[13] Tilden concluded that it was "deemed inexpedi-
ent" to proceed farther because of the falling of the river, necessitating travel
by land to the town of Presidio, which Tilden described as, "without exception, the prettiest one on our southwestern frontier."[14] Beyond Presidio,
Tilden traveled by dugout boat, reporting a succession of reefs and falls of
two to three feet for twenty miles; these obstacles necessitated portaging.
Even the optimistic Tilden recognized that the country beyond was so rugged and dry that "no man can honestly invite the U.S. emigrant hither."[15]
Given the conditions under which Tilden made the trip—in the midst of a
temporary truce in the Mexican War—his observations about the river's
conditions and geology are remarkable. His report, and a map of the portions of the river navigated, are a lasting record of this expedition (Fig. 6-4).
The report and map also beautifully reveal that Texas rivers are navigable,
but only to a point, as confirmed by steamboats plying the Rio Grande.
According to Andrew W. Hall, an authority on Texas steamboats, the role of

the U.S. Quartermaster's Department in establishing steam navigation on the Rio Grande cannot be overemphasized, for by his count they brought at least forty boats to the river during this turbulent period in Texas and Mexican history.[16]

STEAMBOATS AND OTHER CRAFT ON THE RIVERS OF TEXAS

The outcome of the Mexican-American War ensured that the territory between the Nueces and Rio Grande (Rio Bravo) would belong to Texas, and those rivers and ports began to develop rapidly after about 1850. By the time William Emory and his surveyors traversed the border in 1853, there was a lively maritime trade on the Rio Grande in the vicinity of Brownsville. An illustration from Emory's report shows a schooner and a steam-powered riverboat on the river while the survey team sets up camp (Fig. 6-5).[17] The fascinating story of the development of active steamboating on the lower

FIGURE 6-5
This view of Brownsville, Texas, in William Emory's Report on the United States and Mexican Boundary Survey, *shows a sidewheel steamer and schooner on the Rio Grande. Courtesy Special Collections Division, The University of Texas at Arlington Libraries, Arlington.*

Rio Grande has been told elsewhere,[18] but victory in the Mexican-American War meant that aggressive, enterprising European American entrepreneurs like the former steamboat captain Richard King and Mifflin Kenedy would help further develop a pattern that had begun during the period of Mexican rule. King went on to found the legendary King Ranch and the Kenedy family controlled the fortunes of Corpus Christi, a port that would develop rapidly later in the nineteenth century. That not all Texas boat captains were as illustrious as King, however, is revealed in a personal letter to Henry Hubbell, owner of the steamboat *Wm. Penn*, concerning a captain formerly in his employ. The letter to Hubbell from his associate J. P. Delispine notes that "Capt S_____ is a damned scoundrel and a young man here says he can prove him so if you desire it."[19] A week later, Delispine wrote a letter in reference to the trial that was to be held regarding the *Wm. Penn*, noting that "Capt. Slapkin [?] is in town but I have very little to say to him—you know my opinion of him."[20]

Many Texas communities grew up along rivers that featured steamboat landings where vessels loaded and unloaded and took on firewood that was often sold by local farmers. As the Texas trade increased, the steam-powered riverboats continued to develop and their size increased. It has been noted that the typical steamer on the western rivers (a term commonly used for all rivers west of the Appalachian mountains, including those to the east of Texas, such as the Ohio and Mississippi) had two, and often three, decks by the 1840s, but by 1860 four-decked vessels were seen on the larger rivers (Fig. 6-6). Most Texas riverboats were relatively small, those with two decks being common. In contrast to the steamboats on the larger western rivers, most Texas steamboats of the period were about one hundred feet in length. On these vessels the large main deck extended to include a support for the side paddlewheels, the extension beyond the hull serving as a guard for the paddlewheels. By about the early 1840s, steamboats propelled by one large paddlewheel at the rear of the vessel enter the scene and they become common after midcentury (Fig. 6-7). At the same time, 1855, the word "sternwheeler" (called *rueda trasera* in Spanish) enters the vocabulary for such a vessel. The sternwheel steamboat was especially favored on the western rivers. These sternwheelers were well suited to the shallow and often swift waters of Texas rivers, for they provided a large surface area of blade or paddle that could propel the boat against the strong river currents while at the same time drawing little water. The sternwheel's position also better protected the paddles from snags and obstructions, such as floating logs that

FIGURE 6-6

An artistic rendition of Matagorda, 1860, shows a steamboat (left) and other small sailing vessels of the period. Like other sketches of the period, its depiction of the vessels may be somewhat conjectural rather than accurate. Photo courtesy Smithsonian Institution, Washington, D.C. and the Texas Historical Commission, Austin.

were often found in rivers, the reasoning being that the stout bow of the boat, rather than the more fragile paddlewheel, would strike these first. Although some sternwheelers, especially those seen on the Rio Grande, featured wooden curving guards over their paddlewheels, most of the paddlewheels were uncovered, leaving the thrashing motion of the wheel to entrance those passengers who frequented the stern of the vessel.

Riverboats of both the sidewheel and sternwheel variety usually had high-pressure (150 to 170 pounds per square inch) engines, the steam being generated by cylindrical return flue boilers. Their tall metal smokestacks, or "chimneys" as they were often called, were sometimes capped by ornate metal trim resembling acanthus leaves. Whereas the early steamers had only one engine, two engines had become common by the 1830s. Although at first fairly simple in architectural detailing, riverboats became increasingly ornate by midcentury. One maritime historian noted that "the western steamboat looked like a cheaply constructed, ornate, white wooden castle floating on a raft."[21] However, the East Texas historian Thad Sitton has observed that "Texas steamboats seem to have been a far cry from the floating palaces that plied the mighty Mississippi,"[22] and illustrations of the period reveal that to be the case. And yet, the typical Texas steamboat was probably the most impressive, even awesome, creation that most people had experienced, with its tall smokestacks, multiple decks, elaborate architectural trim, and loud whistle echoing along the river valleys of the Lone Star State.

As these steamboats became larger by midcentury, they often featured metal truss rods or hog chains to keep the ends of the vessel from drooping (a condition called "hogging"). In contrast to seagoing vessels, riverboats featured rather little sheer (that is, their hulls curved little between stem and stern) and they sat very low in the water. The typical riverboat could

FIGURE 6-7
*A small, sternwheeled steamboat is seen traversing the Red River in this
nineteenth century drawing. Sternwheelers became common after about 1850,
and were well suited to the shallow, narrow waterways of the state.
From* Amerika in Wort und Bild, *n.d.*

carry immense loads of cotton bales on its wide deck, each bale weighing between four hundred and five hundred pounds, its deck often only a foot or two above the waterline. The quest for speed on the water that was witnessed during the earlier period of the Texas Republic only increased by midcentury. Riverboat races became commonplace by this time, the crews of competing steamboats urged on by passengers who were excited by the prospect of traveling on the winner. As noted earlier, crews sometimes tied down safety valves in order to generate as much steam as possible. The exhilaration of such a race could not be denied as thick, spark-laden smoke trailed behind the vessels and their paddlewheels furiously churned the water to the cheers of passengers. That such races could have deadly consequences was apparent from newspaper headlines that described spectacular and tragic boiler explosions. Perhaps the most disastrous steamboat explosion in Texas occurred on March 26, 1853, when the steamboat *Farmer* exploded while racing the *Neptune* from Houston to Galveston. The explosion of the *Farmer's* boilers killed at least thirty-six people, including Captain Webb, and injured many others, including Sidney Sherman,[23] Massachusetts-born hero of the battle of San Jacinto and pioneer Texas railroad builder for whom the first locomotive in Texas was named in 1852. Less seriously injured than many, Sherman was thrown from his berth and clung to the wreckage of the *Farmer's* wheelhouse. A biographer of Sherman concluded that, despite his minor injuries, "an accident of this type in which many men all around Sherman were killed and wounded and in which he also could have been killed, was bound to be a disturbing mental factor for some time."[24] Accidents notwithstanding, the Texas riverboat trade continued to grow during this period.

STEAMSHIPS AT MIDCENTURY

Meanwhile, developments in steam-powered vessels continued to affect the vessels that plied the Gulf in the coastal maritime trade. The sidewheel steamers (often called "sidewheelers") now commanded the coastal waters of the Texas Gulf at midcentury, and a closer look at them is appropriate. The centerpiece of the sidewheel steamer was a huge, heavy walking-beam mechanism (Fig. 6-8), usually positioned amidship, whose purpose was to transmit the horizontal back-and-forth motion of the steam engine's pistons/rods to the revolving paddlewheels. This is the mechanism that so fascinated Charles Dickens a decade earlier, and it continued to be used well

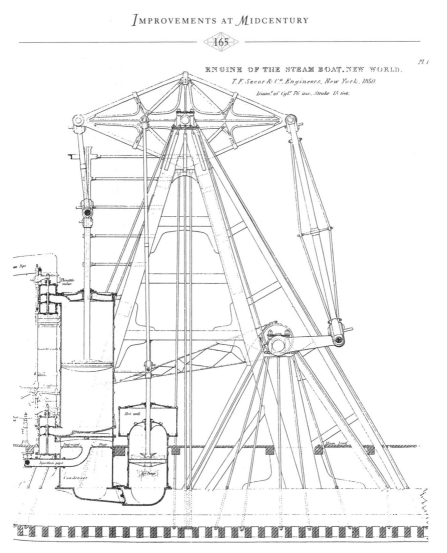

ENGINE OF THE STEAM BOAT, NEW WORLD.

T. F. Secor & Cᵒ. Engineers, New York, 1850.

Diamʳ. of Cylʳ. 76 ins., Stroke 15 feet.

FIGURE 6-8

The centerpiece of the sidewheel steamer was a huge, heavy walking-beam mechanism that was usually positioned amidships, and whose purpose was to transmit the horizontal back-and-forth motion of the steam engines' pistons/rods to the revolving paddlewheels. This walking-beam engine was illustrated in The Steam Engine, *by Thomas Tredgold (London, 1852). Author's collection.*

into the later nineteenth century. Walking-beam mechanisms were often 35 to 45 feet tall and some measured almost 60 feet.[25] The walking-beam mechanism was so large that it usually rose from deep inside the ship's hull at the keelson and extended above the superstructure, visible as a trapezoid-shaped metal arm that rocked up and down when the paddlewheels were rotating. The paddlewheels themselves created a peculiar pattern as they agitated the water on both sides of the vessel. In addition to the walking-beam mechanisms, some wooden steamers of the era featured large, wooden truss frames that looked much like bridges, and in fact served much the same purpose as truss rods on railroad cars of the era: They were used to keep the entire vessel rigid, to prevent the hull from hogging. These structural strengthening devices confirmed what naval architects knew quite well: Vessels of the era were reaching sizes too large for their wood components alone to be counted on to keep them intact—another reason why metal hulls became more and more desirable. These paddlewheel steamers had a tall stack, often two, from which black smoke drifted when steam was required. Located fore of the stacks, an ornate pilot house provided a fine vantage point from which to command the vessel.

As if to symbolize the versatility and dependability of the steamship, the sidewheeler *Globe* of the Morgan lines rescued the faltering schooner *Lucy Ann* off Galveston in 1848. The Galveston admiralty records on January 30, 1849, show the *Globe*'s owners successfully claiming "full satisfaction for their salvage one fifth part of the gross amount of said schooner and cargo," the *Lucy Ann* being valued at $2,600 and her cargo $21,325.73.[26] This seemingly altruistic action yielded Henry Place and owners of the steamship *Globe* the handy sum of $4,785.14, as judged by John Watrous at the urging of the *Globe*'s attorneys.[27]

ℒɪɢʜᴛʜᴏᴜsᴇs ᴀɴᴅ Oᴛʜᴇʀ ℐᴍᴘʀᴏᴠᴇᴍᴇɴᴛs

Incidents like the near loss of the schooner *Lucy Ann* underscored the dangers of navigation on the Texas coast—dangers that would have to be eased if a prosperous maritime trade were to develop as ships became larger, their drafts deeper, and their cargoes even more expensive. Statehood brought many improvements in ports and navigation. Lighthouses, which had been proposed under the Texas Republic, now became a reality. According to T. Lindsay Baker, a light vessel (that is, a securely anchored vessel equipped with a warning light) was placed at the entrance of Galveston Bay in 1849, and Texas's first lighthouse was constructed at Matagorda in 1852. Baker further noted that "after 1852 lighthouses began to blink on all along the coast of Texas, from Brazos Santiago at the southern end of Padre Island to Galveston Bay."[28] Most resemble the Port Isabel lighthouse (Fig. 6-9) on Laguna Madre, presenting the traditional appearance brought to mind by the word *lighthouse*. It features a tall, tapering cylindrical tower topped by a housing containing a warning beacon. Constructed in 1853, this lighthouse provides a splendid view of Padre Island and the coastal plain that stretches to the horizon. As designed, its light was visible for a dozen miles and served to guide vessels into the protected harbor.

Given the great distances from land to shoal waters in Texas, however, some lighthouses would be erected not on terra firma but rather on pilings in relatively shallow water some distance from land. The Halfmoon Reef Light Station is representative of this "screw pile" lighthouse; it originally consisted of a wooden superstructure erected atop wrought iron pilings that had been driven down into the bottom of Matagorda Bay. In 1859 the Lighthouse Board approved the change of its white light to ruby red in order to ensure that it would not continue to be confused with the light of the Matagorda Lighthouse.[29] Like all lighthouses of this type, the Half Moon Light required a lighthouse tender who reached the lighthouse by boat.

As scientific and meteorological observations improved in the mid-nineteenth century, knowledge of weather patterns began to emerge. In 1858 the Beaufort Scale of measuring winds enabled observers to gauge the severity of storms. Named after Sir Francis Beaufort, the scale provided quantitative intensity categories: Winds over 32 miles per hour were called gales, those over 64 miles per hour storms, and those over 73 miles per hour hurricanes; such storms were rated 7–10, 11, and 12, respectively, on a scale of severity. By the late 1850s and 1860s, the tracks of severe storms and hurricanes were becoming better understood as weather stations along the Gulf began to record weather in more detail. Nevertheless, there was no way of warning vessels once they put out to sea, and thus they were still at the mercy of the elements—and would remain so until well into the twentieth century. In the nineteenth century, vessels were warned by lights and signal flags, and thus the distances over which warnings could be communicated remained under a dozen miles.

Rapid development of the Texas coast depended on improvements in navigation, which helped mariners better determine the actual position of their ships and also permitted more effective mapping of the coastline itself.

FIGURE 6-9
The Port Isabel lighthouse on Laguna Madre was constructed in 1853. Its light, which was visible for more than a dozen miles, guided and warned navigators. Photo by author, 1996.

One navigational development coincided with the short life of the Texas Republic: In 1837, a U.S. captain, Thomas H. Sumner, discovered the concept of the astronomical position line by which a navigator is able to determine from an altitude observation, a line somewhere on which the ship is located, whether or not the latitude is known. When projected on a chart, the line is commonly called a position line, and the plotting of two such intersecting lines enables the ship's position to be determined accurately. Upon its being published in 1843, Sumner's discovery revolutionized astronomical navigation. Naturally, it took time to be adopted by mariners, but position line navigation and better mapping were to help make the Texas coast more accessible by the middle of the nineteenth century.

*T*HE *C*ONSEQUENCES OF *I*MPROVED *M*ARITIME *T*RADE

Given its larger population, abundant maritime traffic, general prosperity, and profusion of trees, it is not surprising that the East Texas coast near Galveston and Orange would become important shipbuilding centers. Whereas we tend to think of Orange, Texas, as a major shipbuilding community in the twentieth century, the foundation for this activity was laid in the mid-nineteenth century. Historians in Orange note that as early as 1846 Charles Baxter and John Fielding were engaged in building and repairing schooners at Green's Bluff, as Orange was then known. After Baxter moved away, Fielding became owner of the firm, selling it to Samuel H. Levingston and his brothers David and John, who were listed in the 1850 census as ship's carpenters.[30] Thus, shipbuilding at midcentury developed and sawmills and commerce proliferated in this part of coastal Texas, as large cypress and oak trees were transformed into sailing vessels. Most vessels serving Texas, however, were built elsewhere and entered into the brisk trade to the new state.

One consequence of Texas's booming maritime trade was the increase in the state's ethnic diversity. Earlier, Irish and German immigration had proven the viability of Texas ports before the mid-nineteenth century, but after 1850 numerous immigrant groups, for example Italians and Sicilians, arrived in Galveston from, respectively, the ports of Genoa and Palermo.[31] They were joined by many other Europeans, such as the Czechs and Poles, many of whom arrived in Texas through Galveston. Typical in this regard was the chartering of the sailing ship *Ben Nevis* by a group of five hundred Wendish (Slavic-German) settlers who arrived from Lusatia through the port of Galveston in 1854; their voyage is commemorated by a painting of the *Ben Nevis* that hangs in the Wendish Lutheran Church in Serbin, Texas. Texas's population, always somewhat surprisingly cosmopolitan, thus became even more so as its ports were improved, and a diverse population either settled directly in urbanizing ports like Galveston, moved inland by steamboat to newly developing port communities such as Harrisburg and Houston, took the numerous wagon roads to growing places such as Austin, or settled in the more interior rural portions of the new state. These immigrants were added to a large black population, largely held as slaves, near the coast or on plantations along the rivers of east Texas, further diversifying the population.

Along the South Texas coast, the ethnic makeup was dramatically different. There, immigrant groups encountered larger numbers of Mexican Americans whose roots could be traced back to the Mexican era. With the end of the Mexican-American War, trade began to boom on this part of the coast in South Texas and northern Mexico. After 1850 a lively commerce developed in northern Mexico near Matamoros, as Mexican entrepreneurs such as José Román and Francisco Armendaiz prospered at the mouth of the Rio Bravo (Rio Grande).[32] Large numbers of Irish immigrants settled in southern Texas, too, in the 1840s and 1850s, most of whom arrived by sea.

IMPROVEMENTS IN RIVER NAVIGATION

By the mid-nineteenth century, Texans began to understand the challenges that faced them in opening the state's ports and rivers to navigation. During the period from about 1850 to 1860, river traffic developed rapidly in Texas as steamboats plied the more navigable (lower) reaches of the state's rivers. As the frontier expanded into northern and western Texas, entrepreneurs' dreams of opening the upper reaches of the rivers assumed added urgency. The fledgling community of Dallas, far up the Trinity River from the Gulf, harbored dreams of steamboat access to the Gulf. Newspaper reports mention a Welsh navigator, Captain R. D. ApRice of Magnolia, who launched a new steamboat expressly for the Trinity River trade, and he was surely not alone in such endeavors. The Trinity proved troublesome for all types of river craft. In 1852 a flatboat named the *Dallas* set off from its namesake community down river with a load of twenty-two bales of cotton and several bundles of cowhides. However, this vessel got only about a third of the way, that is, as far as Porter's Bluff (or Taos as it was then called) after four months of poling and prodding, only to find the water too low to continue. The

cotton bales had to be loaded unceremoniously onto a wagon for the remainder of the trip to Houston.[33] This ill-fated trip occurred during the
same year that the U.S. Congress authorized a survey of the river, which
characterized it, somewhat optimistically, as the "deepest and least obstructed
river in the State of Texas," and found that "for purposes of navigation, this
stream is practicable during the time of high water for about 600 miles;
during low water, at present, for 100."[34]

The U.S. Congress did not act on this report, but the state did, approving
$315,000 for river improvements throughout Texas. Much of this funding
was used to remove snags and clear bars that enabled steamboats to navigate
well into the settled areas — on the Trinity, for example, as far north as
Trinidad in Kaufman County and Porter's Bluff in Navarro County, which
had become an important ferry location and shipping point for water-borne
commerce. The dreams of developers, however, remained elusive on the
upper reaches of the rivers, for despite herculean efforts that found some
small steamboats reaching far into the interior, most of these efforts turned
out to be one-time ventures.

That Texas rivers could prove as unpredictable as the coast, or even more
so, was made apparent in 1854, when the steamboat *Nick Hill* was wrecked
at the mouth of the Trinity during what the Texas riverboat historian W. T.
Block described as "a freak winter storm so severe that it drove the eighteen-
hundred-bale *J. H. Bell* (anchored at Lynchburg), the largest of the Trinity
steamboats, three hundred yards into the adjacent prairie."[35] This same storm
left the packet *Star State* "in a very critical condition," according to the
Nacogdoches Chronicle of January 10, 1854, but the *J. H. Bell* was refloated
after workers dug a canal to the stranded vessel.[36] As related in an 1893 interview by W. A. Bowen, an old steamboat man, the *J. H. Bell* had first made
the new channel going out of the Trinity into Galveston Bay at Anáhuac, for
the sternwheeler reportedly had a metal hull and was able to "plow as far as
her momentum would take her, and then back out and try it again."[37] The
fact that she drew slightly more water than other steamers ensured easier
going for those that followed.

Schooners and Sloops

As the interior communities and agricultural areas of Texas began to develop rapidly by the mid-nineteenth century, there is ample evidence of
small sloops and schooners sailing, poling, or even being pulled by rope
miles up Texas rivers; these sailing vessels coexisted with the steam-powered

riverboats. The waters of the Texas coast also teemed with a wide variety of vessels under sail and steam: the coastwise trade required the use of nimble sailing craft that had relatively shallow drafts to accommodate the shallow waters, yet were seaworthy enough to make the passage along the Gulf side of the barrier islands when required. Although oceangoing vessels continued to increase in size, small schooners and sloops were still perfectly suited for the tasks of carrying cargo and passengers from substantial ports like Galveston and Indianola to smaller ports like Velasco and Rockport that proliferated first under Texas, and then U.S., rule.

Although they are sometimes confused, sloops and schooners are usually defined, and differentiated, by the number of masts they carry. The term *sloop* is today used for a boat with only *one* mast, the sails of which are rigged fore and aft on this mast. Schooners, on the other hand, have similar fore and aft rigging, but have *two or more* masts. This makes spotting sloops and schooners quite easy. Schooners are usually larger than sloops and their bigger sail area requires a deeper hull and, consequently, deeper draft. Thus, schooners were often used for longer hauls on open seas than sloops, for the sheer size of a schooner was a factor in making the ship more seaworthy.

What is called the "Texas scow sloop" (Fig. 6-10) evolved to meet the unique conditions along the lagoons of the Texas coast. Its single mast and fore/aft rigging made the Texas scow sloop very maneuverable in the variable winds of the lagoons, as did its centerboard (a skeg that could be raised into the hull of the boat). Its especially shallow draft enabled the Texas scow sloop to glide into the shallow waters in the vicinity of shoals and oyster beds, for it could draw less than two feet of water—water shallower than knee-deep. Its "butt-headed" scow hull, which is essentially flat at the bow, helped the craft gain in stability and payload what it lost in speed. Built by small-boat builders on the Texas coast over a long period from the mid-1850s until as late as 1952, the Texas scow sloop seemed indigenous to the shallow waters of the region, though some speculate that its origin can be traced to a similar habitat: the Chesapeake Bay. The Texas scow sloop earned a place in maritime historian Howard Chapelle's classic *American Sailing Craft*, it being called by other names including the "Port Isabel Scow."

The nimble schooners that plied the Texas coast were also products of an evolution and development on the eastern seaboard. They perfectly characterized their early owners: enterprising merchantmen who carried cargoes to small, out-of-the-way places like those developing on the Texas coast during the period. Schooners, too, were built over a long period. They could be

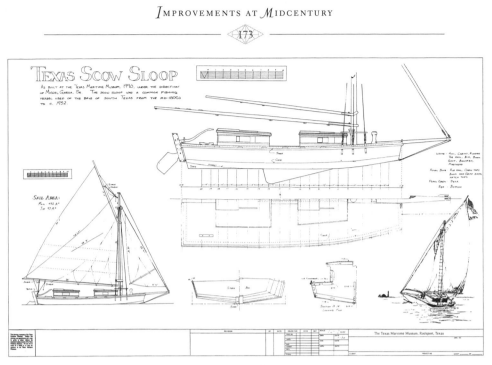

FIGURE 6-10

The "Texas Scow Sloop" was adapted to the unique conditions along the lagoons of the Texas coast: A single mast and fore/aft rigging made it very maneuverable in the variable winds of the lagoons, while its especially shallow draft enabled it to glide into the shallow waters in the vicinity of shoals and oyster beds.
Courtesy Texas Maritime Museum, Rockport.

equipped with a centerboard that ensured their ability to navigate the shallow lagoons of the Texas coast, yet they were often seaworthy and large enough to ply the coasts off the barrier islands as they carried their passengers and cargoes on the coastwise and interport trade routes to Texas ports from Gulf locations, such as New Orleans, Mobile, and even from the distant eastern seaboard ports such as Savannah, Newport News, Philadelphia, New York, and Boston. Schooners commonly sailed far into the rivers when conditions permitted, and the records at midcentury reveal a flourishing trade between rivers and ports. One such schooner was the *Uncle Bill*, employed by the enterprising Henry Hubbell, who owned several other vessels, including the steamers *Wm. Penn* and *Buffalo*, the schooner *Charles Wilcox*, and the sloop *Eliza*. The papers of Henry Hubbell reveal an interesting transaction regarding the schooner *Uncle Bill*: On September 3, 1853, witness E. P. Hunt verified the "two notes drawn by Nathan Smith, one for the sum of nine hundred dollars due payable forty days after date . . . the other for the sum of three hundred dollars and payable four months after . . . for the schooner *Uncle Bill*."[38] Even in the mid-nineteenth century, enterprising individuals purchased durable goods like this schooner on credit, as it were, in hopes of employing them in the potentially profitable business of maritime shipping.

Small sailing vessels, most of them privately owned, were the vessels of choice and necessity by the smaller shippers in the mid-nineteenth century. Engravings and early photographs—a new medium for recording harbor/port scenes at midcentury—reveal the distinctive masts of sloops and schooners dominating Texas ports. They also reveal the presence of what were coming to be called clipper ships, that is, long, square-rigged ships built expressly for speed and substantial cargoes. The midcentury witnessed the virtual perfection of the square-rigged merchant ship. Often three- and sometimes four-masted, the square riggers were employed in the transoceanic trade. They were more economical than steamships for the longest runs, and improvements in rigging lowered labor costs by reducing the size of crews required.[39] The typical oceangoing sailing merchant ship of the mid-1850s was about 350 tons, and its hull was of wooden construction, though iron was recognized as superior, and began to be used at that time.

Steamships at Midcentury

However, it was the steamship that continued to draw attention and portend changes in the shipping industry. By midcentury the steamship attained its familiar profile: It usually featured a fairly low, long, and narrow hull astride which two large paddlewheels churned. These, and the smudge of coal or wood smoke that drifted from the tall stack(s) or funnel(s), made the steamship immediately recognizable. Although they were not dependent on the wind for propulsion, steamships of the period still carried an impressive canvas on two, or sometimes three, masts, enabling them to capture the wind to reduce consumption of expensive fuel whenever possible, or to limp to port in the event of a mechanical breakdown. Although it freed owners and skippers from the vagaries of the wind, the steamship brought with it the requirement of skilled labor to tend its sometimes temperamental, recalcitrant machinery.

The public was very cognizant of the merits of sail and steam in the mid-1850s, as newspapers often ran stories about maritime developments. Joseph

Hutchins Colton's popular and beautiful 1854 map of the United States contains two illustrations of the ships of the era in the Gulf of Mexico (Fig. 6-11). One sail, the other a paddlewheel steamer, these vessels symbolize the changes taking place at midcentury. As oceangoing steamships continued their ascendancy, the relative merits of paddle-wheelers versus propellers were debated throughout the 1840s. However, the transition of steam power vessels from sidewheel to propeller was assured when it was conclusively determined that propellers were *both* faster and more powerful, as revealed in an impressive tug-of-war contest in England between two steam frigates that were otherwise equally matched (the screw-driven *Rattler* and side-wheeler *Alecto*).[40] It has been suggested that the screw-driven vessel is best constructed with a metal hull because the vibrations of the propeller at the stern post could cause the planking at the rear of the ship to open up,[41] but it was certainly recognized that metal hulls also offered greater strength overall. Thus, while the sidewheeler is seen to be compatible with its wooden sailing ship roots, the propeller ship is rather different: Propeller-powered vessels depended, as it were, on advances in new metal hull technology. The coming of the screw-driven ship, then, signaled the beginning of the end of the sail and wood era, and heralded the supremacy of iron and steam. The iron-hulled steamship was seen more frequently by the late 1850s and early 1860s, and although some iron-hulled vessels were powered by paddle wheels, screw-driven vessels were recognized as superior for both military and merchant shipping.

As events in the Atlantic Ocean would remind the nation and the world, paddlewheel steamers were also vulnerable to heavy seas. The loss of the SS *Central America* in a hurricane off the coast of South Carolina shocked the world as the steamer went to the bottom in 1855 with a load of gold bars and a number of California's most influential citizens—an accident that was attributable, at least in part, to the weakness of the hull and the vulnerability of the paddles to wave action.[42] A significant maritime tragedy of the era occurred off the Texas coast on August 8, 1856, when the steamship *Nautilus*, bound from Galveston to New Orleans carrying thirty thousand dollars in specie, thirty passengers, one hundred horses, and forty head of cattle, was pounded mercilessly by a hurricane. The *Nautilus* was wrecked, and its wreckage was scattered along the coast from Sabine Pass to Point Bolivar; reports at the time noted all hands were lost except a lone black man who clung to a cotton bale.[43] If sidewheelers presented a problem in high seas, Texans were well aware of these hazards when the *Nautilus* sank. Four years

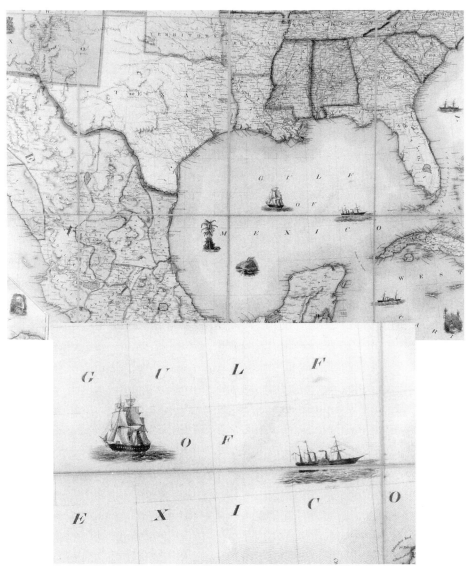

FIGURE 6-11
Joseph Hutchins Colton's popular and beautiful 1854 map of the United States
contains two illustrations of the vessels of the era in the Gulf of Mexico, one sail,
the other a paddlewheel steamer. Courtesy Special Collections Division,
The University of Texas at Arlington Libraries, Arlington.

earlier, in 1852 alone, their vulnerability had been underscored by the fact that two sidewheel steamers, the *Independence*[44] and the *Meteor*, were lost, respectively, at Matagorda Bay and Paso Caballo.

That not all steamship accidents were due to destruction by high seas was underscored by the tragic loss of the *Louisiana* on May 31, 1857. While en route from Indianola to Galveston, this Harris & Morgan Line steamer burned to the waterline and sank with a loss of thirty-five lives. The fact that the fire had consumed two of the *Louisiana's* three lifeboats added to the irony of this disaster five miles from Galveston.[45] Maritime travel of the era was always fraught with an element of danger, especially on the Texas coast, where nature and negligence conspired with calamitous results. If Texas gained a popular if colorful and sexist reputation in the nineteenth century as being "hell on horses and women," that was also proving to be true of vessels that traversed the waters of the new state. Newspapers of the time reported numerous wrecks and disasters on the state's coast and rivers with distressing frequency.

The steamships of the Morgan interests exemplify the hazards of maritime traffic at the time. In the early 1850s, Charles Morgan lost *four* steamships valued at $250,000 — all self-insured — within a sixteen-month period. One of these was the *Meteor*, mentioned above, the loss of which was the result of the negligence of the pilots at Paso de Caballo, an event that prompted Morgan to employ his own pilots to navigate the treacherous approaches to Texas ports after 1852.[46] Entrepreneurs/capitalists like Morgan helped bring technological changes to maritime Texas, and Morgan, in fact, is one of the rather unsung visionaries in Texas history, an omission that seems to accompany the general neglect of our state's maritime history. His steamships were a familiar sight on the waters of Texas for more than forty years (Fig. 6-12).

Morgan's steamships helped ensure the development of Indianola,[47] which began to thrive as a port after being chosen as a landing place for ships of the Morgan Lines in 1849 because of what Morgan perceived as excessive port charges by Port Lavaca on Matagorda Bay.[48] Morgan used Indianola as a shipping point for cattle bound to New Orleans and points east, and it was indeed a perfect location for tapping the growing Texas cattle industry, for the port city's hinterland was the vast open plains of southern Texas.[49] Throughout the 1850s, Indianola thrived, as its exports included hides, tallow, processed beef, and turtle meats, and one historian reports that cattle so shipped were called "sea lions."[50]

FIGURE 6-12

This 1861 view of Galveston's harbor shows what is probably a Morgan Line sidewheel steamer (left) at the Morgan wharf, while another similar vessel is partially obscured by the wharf building (right). Courtesy Rosenberg Library, Galveston, Texas.

The 1853 diary of Henry H. Field, an enterprising Alabama sawmill owner–merchant–planter who traveled through eastern and central Texas "looking for a better country than we left behind," contains some interesting observations about Texas travel, especially in the vicinity of south-central Texas near Indianola and Victoria. Traveling from New Orleans on the steamship *Perseverance*, Field arrived at Galveston, which he described as "a beautiful and flourishing town of about 7,000 inhabitants situated on Galveston Island which is about 30 miles in length by an average of 2 in breadth, streets at right angles and some beautiful houses." Field then noted that about half of the two hundred passengers left the steamship at this point, while he and the others continued their journey on it to Indianola. Owing to "good weather and a smooth sea the entire trip from New Orleans" to Indianola was made in "just three days" at a cost of $50.88. Field also noted that an associate, Mr. Beauchamp, had left Indianola for Lavaca, or Port Lavaca, in a "sail vessel" in order to visit a Mr. Allen Fitzpatrick's place. However, because of rain-swollen streams he had failed to get to his destination and instead arrived at Victoria on the lower Guadalupe River on another, undescribed vessel. Field's detailed expense ledger is quite interesting, for it shows the steamship fare from New Orleans to Indianola to be $20.00, and at least ten ferry crossings of Texas rivers cost him from 10 cents to 50 cents each. Field's Texas travel diary is typical in that it weaves maritime experiences into the drama of getting to the interior of Texas in the 1850s. Interestingly, although Field found some very promising country in Texas, he also commented on some poorer areas "with but few settlements and I think they would be materially benefited by moving to Alabama." Nevertheless, Field found Texas promising enough to move there two years later.[51]

As documented by Brownson Malsch in *Indianola: The Mother of Western Texas*, the port of Indianola was a major entrepôt of the era, second only in importance to Galveston. Indianola is known historically as having been an important port of arrival for many of the German immigrants who settled Texas communities, including New Braunfels and Fredericksburg, in the 1850s. The port at Indianola had also thrived in the 1850s, as a U.S. Army depot was erected there to supply the developing forts of the Texas interior. The legendary camels (ships of the desert) imported into Texas by the ingenious Jefferson Davis arrived through Indianola and were used in establishing the forts and expanding the military frontier of Central and West Texas. At this time, South Texas continued to generate increased cattle-related traffic, including hides and tallow, which were shipped via coasters; this activity helped open an area that would boom later in the century: Aransas Bay.

*I*MPROVEMENTS ON THE *C*OAST

Capitalists such as Charles Morgan worked closely with government officials who sought to improve the new state's transportation, including coastal shipping. From the earliest years of the development of the Texas coast, many astute observers (including Stephen Austin and Thomas J. Green) speculated that, with a few modifications, one might sail from one end of the Texas coast to the other on the lagoons and embayments—that is, on protected waters—rather than along the more dangerous Gulf coast side. With the arrival of enterprising merchants and speculators, that vision now seemed closer to reality. Perhaps the most imaginative of plans was the development of what we would later call the Intracoastal Waterway.

As early as 1846, a bill was introduced in the U.S. Congress in support of a project to dredge a channel to enable maritime transport to run nearly the length of the coast on the inside, that is, along the lagoons. In the legislative deliberations it was observed that "Texas, prior to her annexation to the United States, had not, of course, like the other States and Territories of the Union, the benefit of the topographical and hydrological surveys of the general government, . . . [and that] there is no port on the whole coast of Texas that is accessible to ships of war of the first class."[52] A proposal supported by Sam Houston, then a Texas senator, was made for a major excavation "through the bays and lagoons that stretch along the whole coast," in which the following details were noted:

> An excavation of thirty-three miles in extent will open such a communication, it is believed, from the Sabine to the Rio Grande, a distance of 364 miles, navigable for steamboats and coasting vessels of light draught, entirely landlocked, and protected alike from the swell of the ocean and the assaults of the enemy. Such a result is of incalculable importance, not only for commercial purposes at all times, but for military communications in time of war, which could be maintained through this inland channel even if the whole coast were blockaded. The Sabine may thus be connected with the Rio Grande by cutting only about thirty-three miles through the intervening lands lying between the Sabine bay and the bay of Galveston, and between the West bay at San Luis and Matagorda bay, which are low, level, and interlocked with creeks and bayous of navigable capacity; thus opening a water communication from the Sabine river to Corpus Christi bay, and thence to the Brazos Santiago, near the Rio Grande.[53]

According to Houston, the project would cost $21,050 for survey and a minimum of $250,000 for the principal dredging work in the vicinity of Galveston. Houston added:

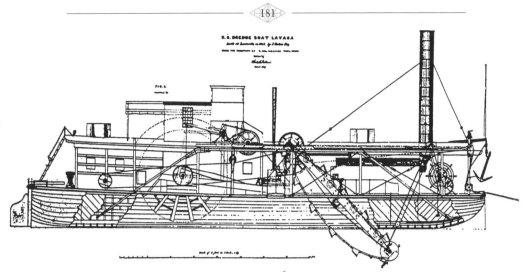

FIGURE 6-13

Construction of the steam-powered, ladder bucket dredge Lavaca *as authorized
by the federal government in 1846 helped ensure that channels would be deepened
and ports expanded after Texas statehood. Reproduced from David F. Bastian,
"The Development of Dredging Through the 1850s," Figure 3.*

It is impossible to contemplate the advantages of such an extended inland communication—attainable at such comparatively trifling cost, and
important alike for public purposes and private enterprises, for public
security and general prosperity—without insuring prompt and efficient
measures to accomplish the object. That such a result, if attainable, is of
the highest consequence, not only to Texas, but to the nation at large, will
not be disputed. That it is feasible at trifling cost, is believed by all intelli-
gent persons best acquainted with the subject; and it is evidently so regarded by the able board of engineers whose report is hereto appended.[54]

Houston and others argued that this dredging would result in improved
defense of the coast and stimulate its commerce—a fairly prophetic projection, given the military development on the South Texas coast in the Mexican-American War and the maritime trade that would flourish under statehood. Houston's plan was advocated at a time when Texans were proving
the viability of channelization to stimulate trade. Among the earliest of these
canal or channel-digging schemes was the Brazos Canal Company's plan to
construct a canal between the Brazos River and Bastrop Bayou and San
Luis Bay. Historians report that some work *may* have occurred as early as

1843, but the late 1840s saw these visions closer to becoming reality. By 1850 a channel was begun westward from Galveston Bay under the auspices of the Galveston and Brazos Navigation Company, and by January 31, 1854, the completed canal was opened to steamboats. It has been noted, however, that this canal was not an unqualified success, and that "problems with tidal currents and inshore breezes led company directors to limit traffic to sailing vessels, barges, and sternwheelers."[55] Nevertheless, this canal did provide a direct link between Brazoria County plantations and Galveston that helped stimulate commerce.

Viewed historically, it is noteworthy that significant dredging began only *after* Texas had attained statehood, no doubt one of the many benefits of a closer relationship to the United States government, which was becoming a major naval power and actively supported maritime improvements that would enhance commerce.[56] Although a true intracoastal waterway would have to await the next century, documented dredging did begin in Texas shortly after Houston's bill was proposed. The Mexican-American War proved to be the catalyst for the construction of a steam-powered, ladder bucket dredge, *Lavaca*, as authorized by the federal government in 1846 (Fig. 6-13). The *Lavaca* was built in Louisville, Kentucky, by J. Hulme under the direction of Lt. Colonel Stephan H. Long of the Army Topographical Engineers[57] and was intended to make the contested entryway of the lower Rio Grande more accessible to military vessels. According to a congressional report, the *Lavaca* could dredge "at least 150 cubic yards of mud and sand per hour," and she could move under her own power at approximately eight miles per hour.[58] Fitted with two dredge ladders, and furnished with four mud scows, the *Lavaca* proceeded slowly while dredging the bottom of mud and sand that obstructed navigation. The scows were loaded with the dredged material and were dumped elsewhere. In this way the Texas coast was slowly but surely reworked into a more navigable environment for shipping.

Ports and Railroads at Midcentury

Texas ports prospered after annexation. As a rapidly developing port by the late 1850s, Indianola presented an interesting sight to travelers arriving there in search of a new life in Texas. As revealed in a print in the Library of Congress (Fig. 6-14), Indianola had erected several piers into the harbor; these could be reached by vessels of relatively deep draft, including ocean-going brigs and schooners, and sidewheel steamers. Despite the fact that

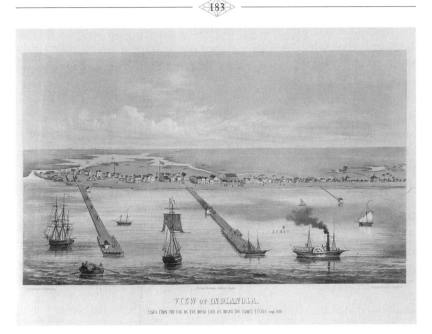

FIGURE 6-14

This view of Indianola from the vessel Texana, September 1860, represents an
interesting sight that greeted travelers arriving there in search of a new life in Texas.
Indianola had erected several piers into the harbor; these could be reached by vessels
of relatively deep draft, including oceangoing barques and schooners, and sidewheel
steamers. Lithograph by Helmuth Holtz, courtesy Library of Congress.

Indianola would not be served by a steam railroad for another ten years, the
enterprising merchants had laid rails onto the pier to expedite the handling
of cargo on the piers. These rails were traversed by handcars, though mules
or horses pulled similar cars in some ports. Typical of most ports of the time,
Indianola developed a "waterfront" of buildings that faced the harbor. In
response to, and further encouraging, trade were merchants selling wares
and individuals providing services. The illustration also reveals the precari-
ousness of Indianola's site, for much of the community was barely above the
level of high tide. As history would prove, the site was vulnerable to the tides
and waves that could accompany the nemesis of shipping and port life on
the Texas coast, the hurricane.

Galveston also boomed in the 1840s and 1850s, becoming the premier
port of Texas. However, Houston's position closer to the developing hinterland of East Texas in combination with its access to the Gulf, albeit by

relatively small vessels with fairly shallow draft, ensured its subsequent growth. Both ports stimulated the growth of the railroads, and a brief accounting of the railroads' development in relation to the ports is in order here. Significantly, Texas's first locomotive, the General Sherman (referred to earlier), was shipped in by *steamship* for service on the state's first railroad—the Buffalo Bayou, Brazos and Colorado. This pioneer railroad, which would later become an important link in the Southern Pacific's Sunset Route to the Pacific coast, reached westward from a point just west of Houston in 1852. This momentous development gave the area around Houston a tremendous boost, as it also possessed good water access to the Gulf via the Buffalo Bayou. A map of Texas railroads in 1860 reveals the significance of coastal connections: Aside from two fledgling railroad lines reaching westward from the Sabine, the bulk of Texas railroad mileage is concentrated on the Gulf coast. The names of these early railroads declare their connection to the coast: Galveston and Red River (1854), Galveston, Houston and Henderson (1857), San Antonio & Mexican Gulf (1858). Records show that Stafford's Point, in the vicinity of Houston, was the first Texas port (using the term broadly) reached by rail (1853), but that Cypress on the Sabine (1857), Port Lavaca (1858), Galveston (1860), and Sabine Pass (1861) had been reached by the eve of the Civil War.[59] The construction of these railroads indicates that the coast was flourishing during this period as speculators sought to develop ports, a number of which sprang into existence. The railroads, too, helped stimulate coastal and oceangoing shipping as they further helped to open up Texas's vast hinterland to development and trade.

Baughman has noted that, in the period from the 1830s to the 1850s, the pattern of Texas port development in relation to hinterlands emerged in three areas or zones: (1) Galveston dominated the region north and east of the Colorado; (2) Matagorda, Port Lavaca, and Indianola served the country between the Nueces and Colorado Rivers; and (3) Brazos St. Iago served the Rio Grande Valley.[60] Because roads were not well developed, a lively coasting trade developed between these ports. Charles Morgan capitalized on "the short-haul superiority of steam over sail in terms of speed, draught, and maneuverability,"[61] which enabled him to charge—and receive—higher rates than sailing vessels in the same trade. Steamers had found an important niche in a burgeoning market, and they began to arrive from increasingly distant ports. German immigrant brochures from the period indicate the "Dampfboot" steamship lines that could bring prospective settlers to the state.

*T*HE *S*AGA OF *S*TEAMBOAT *Mary Summers*

During the period in question (1845–1860), Texas grew rapidly in population—from about 141,000 to more than 604,000—but it was still somewhat peripheral to the most developed portions of the country. Its shipbuilding industry was in a primitive state. Although the steamboat *Kate Ward* had been built in Texas as early as the 1840s,[62] it is likely that most of the metal components were produced elsewhere and the remainder of the ship built on site—a situation indicative of the relatively primitive industrial conditions in the early years of the Lone Star State. A shipwreck recently investigated on the lower Navidad River in Jackson County (Fig. 6-15) appears, after much research, to be the *Mary Summers*.[63] This steamboat's long career spanned the period in question, from before the mid-nineteenth century to the Civil War. According to the marine archaeologist Charles E. Pearson, this iron-hulled steamboat was assembled in the United States in 1838–1839 from prefabricated parts produced in England by the famous shipbuilder John Laird. The production of metal components for fabrication elsewhere was typical of the early Victorian era, when locomotives and other railroad components were often shipped great distances. Proper assembly

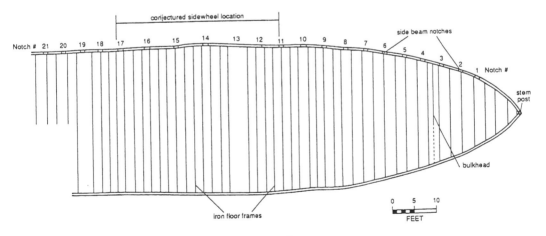

FIGURE 6-15
Schematic representation of a shipwreck recently investigated on the lower Navidad River in Jackson County proved to be the Mary Summers, *a sidewheel steamer constructed in 1838–1839 and scuttled during the Civil War. Courtesy Charles Pearson.*

often required elaborate instructions and, usually, a knowledgeable person provided by the company to ensure that the components went together correctly.

Operating at first on the Savannah River for several years before being purchased by the United States government for service in the Mexican-American War, the *Mary Summers* then stayed on the Texas and Louisiana coast under a number of owners until it sank on the lower Navidad during the Civil War. The *Mary Summers* appears to be the oldest iron-hulled steamboat found in the United States.[64] The wreck, including the major portion of the iron hull, yielded dimensions typical of a steamer of the period: length 114 feet; beam 27 feet, 8 inches; depth of hold 6 feet, 5 inches; these dimensions indicated a sidewheeler steamer with a draft of approximately 3 feet.[65] In addition to numerous iron components, wood samples indicate U.S. northeastern or eastern construction, including portions of the ship's bow (bald cypress), bow deck stanchions (southern yellow pine and white oak), midship stanchion and starboard engine and sister keelsons (white pine), and a hanging knee (of either spruce or larch). Spanning the years 1839 to 1863, the lengthy career of the *Mary Summers* typified the workhorse role of many steamboats of the period: commercial, military, cargo, and passenger service. Like many a vessel, the *Mary Summers* was scuttled by confederate sympathizers rather than letting her fall into union hands.

MIDCENTURY: TIME OF CHANGE ON TEXAS WATERS

Despite the frequent reference to steamboats during this era, it should be recalled that many smaller hand- or sail-powered vessels still conveyed much of the water-borne trade in Texas. Throughout the 1840s and 1850s, keelboats and flatboats were a common sight on Texas rivers. A flatboat is usually a rectangular vessel constructed much like a box, its sides straight and its bottom consisting of flat planks. The typical flatboat had no deck, that is, was open. Many flatboats had no cabins, but sometimes makeshift shelters were added to protect the crew. Keelboats, on the other hand, were constructed more like sailing vessels rather than rafts, having a longitudinal beam, or keel, running from bow to stern. In his fascinating book *Texas Riverman* William Seale notes that "a keelboat was more expertly designed than a flatboat and required a great deal more work to build." Its hold was roomy and its cabin sometimes cramped. Seale described Captain Andrew Smyth's experience with the keelboat *Jasper*, which he operated along with a flat-boat, noting that "to man the flatboat were three Negroes, while Andrews, Holland and the fourth Negro operated the *Jasper*."[66]

At midcentury, a substantial amount of cargo in the new state of Texas, like that during the period of the Republic about a decade earlier, was handled by these slower, more prosaic but still important vessels. The historian Thad Sitton further describes the *Jasper*, which was used on the Neches River in 1846, as a long, narrow oval (that is, both the bow and stern were curved) with a large decked cargo box filling most of the hull and rising above the gunwales, on top of which was mounted a small cabin. Keelboats like the *Jasper* were powered by the river's current, or oars, and sometimes by sails. These keelboats were easily moved downstream despite their heavy loads of cotton and other cargoes. Getting them back upstream, however, was usually back-breaking work, with men straining and otherwise leaning hard against oars or poles.[67]

Thus, although the steamboat's advantages on the rivers were well understood, many enterprising flatboat and keelboat operators competed for the freight business at this time, using craft that were cheaper to construct or purchase than steamboats. Interestingly, Seale speculates that the *Jasper* may have been dismantled after she disappeared from the account books, and used in the construction of the Smyth's house, "which would explain the peculiar pieces of lumber incorporated into the building—a bowed joist here, a timber which had mortises unfilled there."[68] Captain Andrew Smyth made the transition to steam thereafter, purchasing several steamboats for operation on the rivers of East Texas later in the century.

Because this period witnessed incredible changes in transportation technology, it is no surprise that some travelers romanticized the older forms of transportation, such as sailing vessels, while others embraced the new technology. Washington Irving, the famous New York writer and traveler, in the 1850s left a revealing comment when he wrote with nostalgia about the "good old times before steamboats and railroads had driven all poetry and romance out of travel."[69] Other travelers, especially those in a hurry, were less nostalgic, as evidenced by the recollections of George W. Baylor in regard to his traveling from Texas to the California gold fields in 1854. Baylor wrote that "I determined to try the sea, and went to Port Lavaca and took the steamer to New Orleans, . . . being delayed by bad weather and sailing qualities of the old tubs that used to run between Texas and Louisiana."[70] Whether one approved of the transportation technology of the era or not, it was apparent that railroads and steamboats were revolutionizing travel and the places they served. The Texas coast thus found itself linked to the rest of the country by a broadening network of rail and steamboat/steamship lines in the 1850s—lines that were becoming increasingly "Southern" in character as sectional identities intensified. As the 1850s wound to a close and the 1860s began, these sectional rivalries reached the breaking point; Texas would soon find itself in the midst of a civil war that started swiftly on the East coast and soon enveloped the entire country.

BLOCKADES AND
BLOCKADE RUNNERS
1861–1865

*Our disaster at Galveston has thrown us back and
done more injury to the Navy than all the events of the war.*
ADMIRAL DAVID G. FARRAGUT, USN, 1863

During the spring and summer of 1995, a special exhibit entitled "The Civil
War and the Texas Coast" at the Texas Maritime Museum in Rockport drew
thousands of curious and interested Texans. The exhibit portrayed a fascinating and neglected aspect of the state's history. Most Texans knew that
their state was Southern in its allegiance during the Civil War, Texas having
joined the Confederate States of America (CSA), but few knew about Texas's
military significance during this great conflict—especially in relationship
to maritime history.[1] This chapter is based in part on the exhibit mentioned
above, and on numerous books and articles on Texas and the Civil War,
including two recently published books in the "Civil War Campaigns and
Commanders" Series, *Cottonclads! The Battle of Galveston and the Defense
of the Texas Coast*, by the Civil War era historian Donald Frazier,[2] and
Raphael Semmes and the Alabama, by Spencer Tucker.[3]

Occupying the relatively short time period of only about four and a half
years, the Civil War on the Texas coast is nevertheless deserving of its own
chapter for several reasons. First, it reveals much about Texas's relationship
to sectional stresses that confronted the United States in the middle to late
nineteenth century. Although Texas was somewhat peripheral to the main
centers of military action during the Civil War, naval actions on the Texas
coast had ramifications that reached back to Washington and Virginia, the
headquarters, respectively, of the Union and the Confederacy. Second, the
war severely affected the population and economy of the coast by stifling
trade, in effect shifting the efforts of Texas authorities away from improving
the coast to simply defending it. Finally, Texans fought several ferocious sea

battles that humbled the United States Navy, and these battles should be placed in the context of maritime technology generally and Texan naval ingenuity in particular.

A COAST BLOCKADED

In the early spring of 1861, sectional tensions culminated in several Southern states, Texas among them, which seceded from the United States over irreconcilable differences in political and social philosophy. The historian Ralph A. Wooster has noted that "secession in Texas was part of the central conflict of the nineteenth century, a conflict between forces that encouraged the splintering of the United States into smaller social, political, and economic units and forces that bound the nation more tightly together."[4] In February of 1861, some months before the actual start of the Civil War, Col. John S. Ford was directed by the Secession Convention in Texas to capture Brazos Santiago and Fort Brown on the Rio Grande, which were vestiges of the federal military presence in Texas during the Mexican-American War. Ford was successful, seizing numerous cannons and other arms in the process, some of which would later be used in the defense of Texas harbors by the Confederates.[5]

Civil War soon followed similar bold secessionist activities, the actual war itself precipitated by the firing by secessionists on the federally occupied Fort Sumter, South Carolina, on April 12, 1861. This attack on federal authority brought a swift military response from Union forces. Naval vessels like the steam-powered revenue cutter *Harriet Lane* (Fig. 7-1) were immediately ordered into action along the Atlantic coast of the Southern states. On April 19, less than a week after the war began, Abraham Lincoln ordered a naval blockade of the South. Blockading, the process of intercepting and seizing maritime trade in order to cripple an enemy, was decided upon as a major strategy by the North, its main goal being to isolate the Confederacy. This naval blockade had two purposes: to debilitate the South's commercial trade by depriving the Confederacy of a market for its cotton and other crops produced with slave labor, and to keep armaments and other military supplies out of the hands of Confederate troops. Although some military leaders like Winfield Scott believed that a blockade would, like an anaconda, strangle the South into submission economically and hence politically, full-scale war soon erupted on land and sea and throughout the entire nation.

The Union's naval blockade went into effect immediately, but it was difficult to enforce because 189 Southern ports from Virginia to the Rio

FIGURE 7-1

Originally built as a revenue cutter in 1857, the 619-ton, copper-sheathed steamer
Harriet Lane *was sent to reinforce the Union garrison at Fort Sumter, South
Carolina, in 1861 and fell into Confederate hands during the Battle of Galveston on
January 1, 1863. Converted into a blockade runner early in 1864, the* Harriet Lane
carried a cargo of cotton to Havana under her new Confederate name, the Lavinia,
*in April of that year. Courtesy Naval Historical Center and Texas Maritime
Museum, Rockport.*

Grande were involved. Civil War historians have noted that two classes of
Texas ports were eyed for blockading as the Union developed a strategy to
halt Confederate maritime commerce in this distant part of the Gulf of
Mexico. Of primary importance were either the thriving ports closer to the
centers of Texas population and Confederate military power (such as Sabine
Pass and Galveston), or those close to the Rio Grande centers of international commerce, such as Brazos Santiago. Secondary targets for blockading included Velasco, at the mouth of the Brazos, and Indianola and Port
Lavaca, on Matagorda Bay.[6] Given Galveston's strategic importance and
proximity to the prosperous hinterland of slave-holding East Texas and beyond, it is no surprise that this entrepôt was singled out for blockading by
the federal forces soon after the war began. Considerable blockading activity occurred in the vicinity of Galveston, whose population numbered about
7,500, early in the war.[7] The historian David McComb noted that at least
half of the city's population soon moved inland, fearing Union occupation.[8]

Stretching from the Sabine to the Rio Grande, the Texas coast was designated the "West Gulf" by the Union Navy and proved somewhat difficult to blockade for several reasons. The fact that the Union lacked a sufficient number of warships to completely blockade the coast ensured that some Confederate vessels would be able to penetrate the blockade. The environment of the coast also made a complete blockade difficult, for its numerous embayments enabled Confederate vessels to hide from view behind the barrier islands. Logistically, the great distance of the Texas coast from the critical mass of the Union supply points also made blockading difficult, for a Navy always needs supplies, including fresh water, food, and a supply of coal for steam-powered vessels. Exacerbating the situation was Mexico's proximity: On the Texas side of the lower Rio Grande, Brownsville served a lively trade of entrepreneurs who could circumvent the naval blockade entirely by ostensibly shipping to Mexico, just across the river in Matamoros, and having the cargo be considered land-delivered rather than marine-delivered, a technicality that served and protected the interests of the South but had to be honored by the Union to avoid international discord with Mexico.

To these conditions one might add the long European American tradition of defiance of centralized authority that had characterized Texans, especially along the coast, for nearly half a century. Texans were likely to resist a blockade by its very nature, for it represented an imposition by an outside power. To some older Texans who could remember the Texas Revolution twenty-five years earlier, the Union blockade and threat of Union military action orchestrated from a distant city (Washington) seemed reminiscent of Mexico's strategy in the mid-1830s. Although Texans were not completely unified in their opposition to the North, and considerable Union sympathy was evident in many locations, notably North Texas and the Hill Country near Austin, Texans living along the coast generally considered the Union blockade a manifestation of a foreign power stifling their natural right to conduct maritime trade. That trade was based in large measure on the slave labor that produced large cotton and sugar cane crops in southeastern Texas, not far from the coastal ports. Ironically, the slavery issue had also been an important issue thirty years earlier, with the centralized power (Mexico) disapproving of Texans' holding of African slaves as chattel.

The Civil War virtually tore Texas apart politically. Governor Sam Houston, a Unionist at heart, had been deposed in March of 1861 when he refused allegiance to the Confederacy. A famous speech made by Houston in Galveston, which anticipated the ultimate defeat of the Confederacy and the difficulties of reconstruction, also helped lead to his ouster. It was during the war that Sam Houston and his family returned to Huntsville, which is located on a relatively high point of land between the Trinity and the San Jacinto rivers. Here, according to the Houston biographer John Hoyt Williams, "the Houstons rented the eccentrically designed 'Steamboat House,' named for its appearance from the street" before Sam Houston's death in Huntsville in 1863.[9] Built in 1858 by Rufus Bailey,[10] the Steamboat House was described as narrow and two stories tall with a four-foot-wide gallery on each side—a design that was indeed reminiscent of the ornate steamboats then so common on Texas rivers (steamboats that Houston had often traveled on as he conducted business in the state). The appellation "Steamboat House" was appropriate, given that the steamboat had become one of the more widely used forms of transportation on Texas rivers leading from the coast to the interior, and the term *steamboat* had become a household word in Texas by the 1860s.

The Civil War had a profound effect on all commercial development in Texas. In general, it brought to a virtual halt the internal improvements along the rivers, such as the dredging of sandbars and the removal of snags, that had enabled Texas agriculture and commerce to thrive. On the coast, it has been noted that Texas lighthouses suffered at the hands of the Confederates, who damaged them because it was felt that lighthouses were of greater benefit to ships of the Union than to blockade runners.[11] Oceangoing maritime trade suffered both as a result of the Union naval blockade and from the aggressive seizing of Union vessels by Confederate vessels.

Many owners of vessels at first refused to acknowledge the effects of blockades, tending to business as usual: for example, even after the lower Southern states had seceded in early 1861, Charles Morgan maintained regular routes, augmented civilian service with income derived from increased military activity in the Gulf, and reportedly even made his vessels available to *both* secessionist and Union forces![12] Morgan's attempt to play both sides in the conflict is revealed by his chartering his Southern Steamship Company's *General Rusk* to Confederate Colonel John S. Ford for the successful capture of Union troops at Brazos Santiago for $14,750, then immediately chartering the ship to the defeated federal commander for $12,500 to permit the evacuation of Union troops to Key West despite Morgan's professing Southern loyalties.[13] Morgan's vessels operated through the spring of 1861, but tensions increased in May, when Confederate General Sidney Sherman seized the *General Rusk* and the *Orizaba*. Although the *Orizaba* was returned, it was later prevented from returning to New York from Texas by

Southern loyalists. With little economic incentive remaining as the blockade was declared, Morgan's vessels were idled at New Orleans until his
remaining Gulf fleet of twelve was seized by the Confederacy on January 16,
1862. Under Confederate command, most of these vessels became privateers and blockade runners. According to Morgan's biographer, James Baughman, the Civil War prompted the ever tenacious Morgan to play both ends
against the middle by further developing his interests in the more profitable
North (including the Morgan Iron Works and his order for five new vessels),
while also aiding the South by using the *Frances* as a blockade runner later
in the war.[14] However, according to Wise, in *Lifeline of the Confederacy*,[15]
Morgan had actually *sold* the *Frances* to blockade-running interests. Thus,
Morgan himself did not employ the vessel as a blockade runner, but apparently was aware of its involvement in this service.

Although enterprising merchants soon engineered methods by which
the blockade could be circumvented, its consequences were serious, even
debilitating for many Texans who depended on external markets. As noted
earlier, the blockade's effect became obvious within months of its initiation,
and by late spring and early summer of 1861, Galveston had begun to feel
the squeeze of the blockade as numerous vessels were seized and trade slowed
considerably. In July of that year, the U.S.S. *South Carolina*—a 1,150-ton
steam propeller blockader—had captured or destroyed eleven enemy sailing vessels near Galveston as its commander, James Alden, endeavored to
"close up every hole and corner" of the Texas Coast.[16] And yet, given the
convoluted nature of the Texas coastline, this was more easily said than
done. The paucity of blockading vessels also made a complete blockade
impossible, and the historian Alwyn Barr has noted that "blockaders off the
Texas coast in early 1862 numbered only five, thinly spread in an attempt to
cover its numerous harbors while the main Gulf Squadron under Admiral
David G. Farragut attacked New Orleans."[17]

Quite aside from suppressing commercial trade, the Union had another
even more important reason for enforcing the blockade as aggressively as
possible. Military supplies were finding their way to Texas and other Southern states by sea, a situation made all the more frustrating to the Union as
President Benito Juárez granted Confederate vessels anchoring in Mexican
waters the same guarantees as those of other countries.[18] This ensured that
some military supplies would arrive despite the blockades of Texas ports.

Naturally, Texans feared the presence of Union war vessels for more than
their simple power to blockade maritime trade. The Union vessels represented a threat of invasion. It has been noted that "Texans in 1861 found

themselves utterly helpless before a sea assault and could breathe only an uneasy sigh of relief because the original Federal fleet numbered but forty-two ships for the entire southern blockade."[19] That sigh of relief was short-lived indeed, for several small naval battles were fought off the Texas coast during the summer and fall of 1861, including skirmishes between land batteries and Union vessels at Galveston. The Union attack on the Confederate schooner *Royal Yacht*, which resulted in that vessel's partial burning on November 12, 1861, confirmed the superior naval power of the Union and strengthened the Texans' resolve to fortify the coast. By the spring of 1862, conditions worsened as Union blockade vessels increased in number and several Texas harbors were entered by Union forces. Corpus Christi, which was small and easily penetrated, presented a tempting target. In August of 1862, a flotilla consisting of three Union schooners (USS *Sachem*, USS *Corypheus*, and USS *Reindeer*), a sloop (USS *Belle Italia*), and the bark-rigged USS *Arthur* under the command of Lt. John W. Kittredge destroyed five commercial vessels and drove Confederates inland (Fig. 7-2). This victory was only temporary and inconclusive, however, because Kittredge was unable to take the fort and occupy the port. Other battles followed, the Union vessels pounding the shore batteries in widely separated locations from Sabine Pass to San Luis Pass, Matagorda, and Velasco, but it soon became obvious that the Union had no way to sustain ground forces despite its naval superiority. The Texans were fortifying and otherwise digging in for what would prove to be a long fight.

PRELUDE TO THE BATTLE OF GALVESTON

Galveston was the largest community in the state on the eve of the Civil War, and it served and guarded, as it were, the most prosperous part of Texas. By late summer 1862, "having struck at both ends of Texas' coastal defenses, the Federal blockading fleet in early October aimed its main blow at Galveston, the commercial, military and diplomatic center of Texas affairs."[20] The Unionists resolved to capture Galveston, whose harbor approaches at Point Bolivar, Fort Point, Pelican Spit, and San Luis Pass were guarded by batteries of Confederate troops and cannons. Commander Farragut ordered the capture of Galveston to begin on September 24, 1862. Two Union vessels (the schooner USS *Rachel Seaman* and mortar boat USS *Henry Janes*) sailed into Galveston and engaged the cannon and gunfire of the Confederate forces stationed at the fort there. This engagement, though not decisive, revealed that the Union vessels could stay out of the reach of Confederate

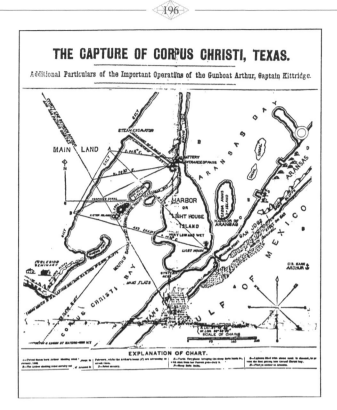

FIGURE 7-2

The capture of Corpus Christi by Union forces using the gunboat
Arthur *was illustrated in the November 16, 1862, issue of the*
New York Herald. *Author's collection.*

cannons and still inflict damage on Galveston's fortifications. Sizing up the situation, the Confederates abandoned the fort and evacuated the garrison.

The taking of Galveston in early October of 1862 increased the confidence of the Union forces. Sensing the ease with which the coast could be penetrated, several Union vessels, including the *Rachel Seaman* and USS *Kensington*, conducted a number of raids in the fall of 1862. These two Union vessels were typical of the armed schooners that served side by side with steam-powered warships, the latter of which were propelled by sidewheels or propellers and, usually being larger, were even more heavily armed. The diverse vessels of the Union conducted raids into the rivers and embayments of east Texas, including Sabine Lake near Beaumont, destroying much of the port town of Sabine Pass (and its vital railroad bridge) in the process.

However, Texan resistance soon intensified, and Texans placed obstructions at the mouths of the Neches and Sabine rivers, forcing the Union vessels to draw out into the Gulf. A stalemate of sorts persisted because the Union forces could not spare enough men to make a land invasion, and the Southerners lacked sufficient sea power to stop the Union forces from raiding the coast. As the historian Donald Frazier colorfully put it in his book *Cottonclads! The Battle of Galveston and the Defense of the Texas Coast*, "The Union Navy needed to grow legs, while the Confederates needed to grow fins."[21] The Union now recognized the significance of Sabine Pass, through which munitions of war had entered Texas and cotton was exported. The commander of the USS *Kensington* informed Admiral Farragut that at least eight steamers and six schooners, as well as large quantities of cotton and "quite a force of troops," were lying in wait in the upper reaches of the river. As we shall soon see, those vessels, forces, and even the baled cotton would soon play a role in one of the most humiliating defeats ever suffered by the U.S. Navy.

In the fall of 1862, the Union now nominally held part of the Texas coast in the vicinity of Galveston and Sabine Pass, but it became increasingly difficult to maintain as Texans ambushed Union sailors who went ashore for supplies. The Confederates also marshaled numerous vessels (including six steamboats, a mortar boat, and several schooners) in support of their cause. In response to the Texans' growing military capabilities through both the enhancement of fortifications and the acquisition of armed vessels, Captain William Renshaw arrived to strengthen the Union's hold on the coast. Renshaw was evidently frustrated by the navigational hazards here, for his flagship, the USS *Westfield*, grounded half a dozen times on the bar at Port Lavaca, each time having to be pulled off the bar by the *Clifton*. This prompted one officer to sarcastically comment that the *Clifton* was serving as "little more than Renshaw's personal tugboat."[22]

THE BATTLE OF GALVESTON

Although the Union held Galveston during the fall of 1862, things were about to change as Texans began assembling a flotilla of vessels jury-rigged into warships. Among the most peculiar of these were the "cottonclads," whose name was derived as a variation of the formidable ironclads that were making headlines on the East coast off Virginia and the Carolinas. In contrast to ironclads, which featured metal plating or sheathing to protect vessels from enemy cannon, cottonclads used stout bales of cotton for much the same purpose. Said to be the invention of the Confederate Commander John B. Magruder, who realized that Texas lacked the iron mills to produce impressive and potent vessels like the CSS *Virginia*, cottonclads were steamboats of various kinds retrofitted into warships at Buffalo Bayou near Houston. By removal of her upper texas deck, for example, the *Bayou City* developed "the rakish look of an ironclad ram, if not the potency."[23] Five-hundred-pound cotton bales were placed on their sides three tiers high and were backed by another row of bales lying flat; these served as platforms for sharpshooters, while a refurbished thirty-two-pound cannon was mounted to the bow. It may be noted that the arrangement of bales on cottonclads was little different than the way these same boats were loaded when carrying large cargoes of cotton. Other vessels, such as the former mail packet *Neptune*, and two smaller vessels, *John F. Carr* and *Lucy Gwinn*, were similarly converted into cottonclads.

Having been converted into these makeshift battleships, the cottonclads were now ready to enter the fray. Their destination: Galveston; their mission: to retake the city from the Union forces, which now had several warships, including the USS *Harriet Lane*, USS *Owasco*, USS *Corypheus*, USS *Sachem*, and the flagship, USS *Westfield*, stationed at Galveston Harbor. What has come to be called the "Battle of Galveston" is nearly legendary in the short annals of Texas maritime history. Magruder's Confederate cottonclads quietly steamed into the harbor in the early hours of New Year's Day, 1863, hoping to surprise the Union forces with a combined sea offensive and land offensive (Rangers of the Sea, and Rangers of the Prairie). They were detected, however, and fierce fighting broke out as Union vessels began firing at both the advancing ground troops and the flotilla of cottonclads.

As documented in detail by Donald Frazier,[24] several key aspects of the Battle of Galveston bear retelling here. At about 4 A.M. the battle began in earnest, as the gunboats had maneuvered in the bay and land forces prepared for heavy battle. When the sky was illuminated with the intense fire and the concussions of the cannon fire reverberated through the harbor, Major Leon Smith ordered his steamships to advance, reportedly yelling down the tube to the engine room "give me all the steam you can crack on."[25] The shelling of advancing Texans by the federal warships, including the USS *Harriet Lane*, was intense. In the course of the naval battle, the makeshift cottonclad *Bayou City* and the other Confederate paddle-wheelers appeared through the chilling early morning haze and battle smoke that hung over the harbor, "puffing and snorting from their high-pressure

FIGURE 7-3

The surprise and capture of the United States steamer Harriett Lane *by the Confederates under General Magruder "shows the Texans from the Bayou City storming aboard the stricken Union steamer." Reproduced from* The Soldier in Our Civil War: A Pictorial History of the Conflict, 1861–1865, *New York: J. H. Brown, 1884–1885; courtesy U.S. Naval Historical Center and the Texas Maritime Museum, Rockport.*

steam."[26] The *Bayou City* made for its target, the *Harriet Lane*, as Captain Lubbock had hoped to come close enough either to board her or ram her if necessary. However, in the process, the *Bayou City*'s port paddlewheel housing was smashed by the bow of the *Harriet Lane*, and the boarding plank missed, further damaging and temporarily crippling the cottonclad.

Meanwhile, Captain Sangster ordered his cottonclad, *Neptune*, of the Confederacy's Texas Marine Department, to join the attack on the *Harriet Lane*. The *Neptune* slammed into the Union vessel about ten feet aft of the starboard paddlewheel. This maneuver badly damaged the bow of the *Neptune*, which was taking heavy fire from nearby Union vessels and, leaking badly, backed away from the fracas and headed for shallower water. The *Harriet Lane* survived the impact of this collision nearly unscathed. The battle might have ended here, but the crew of the *Bayou City* had cleared its damaged paddlewheel of debris and turned her about. Distracted and seeking protection from the Confederate sharpshooters on the slowly sinking *Neptune*, the crew of the *Harriet Lane* was greeted by a deafening splintering crashing sound as the *Bayou City* rammed her port paddlewheel

FIGURE 7-4

*A panoramic view of the Battle of Galveston drawn by eyewitness James E. Bourke
as it appeared at 6:30 A.M. on January 1, 1863, shows the disabled* Harriett Lane
rammed by cottonclad steamboat Bayou City *(far right).*
Courtesy Rosenberg Library, Galveston.

housing, heeling the Union warship over to starboard. In the process of this
violent ramming, the *Bayou City* had become stuck fast into the wreckage.
Both vessels were immobilized, but the Confederates stormed onto the
Harriet Lane (Fig. 7-3). Major Smith fatally shot Union Commander J. M.
Wainwright, and the vessel's executive officer, Lt. Albert Lea, was mortally
wounded, as were several other Union sailors. Attempts by the USS *Owasco*
to recover the captured *Harriet Lane* proved futile, and the would-be res-
cuer was forced to flee as she came under withering fire from the Confederates. Now in possession of the *Harriet Lane*, the Confederates attempted to
separate her from the *Bayou City*, but to no avail; both vessels were towed
away and it was realized that skilled carpenters and mechanics would be
needed to extricate them from their deadly embrace.[27]

As seen in a panorama or bird's-eye view, the Battle of Galveston (Fig.
7-4) represented a serious loss for the Union. Without naval support, the
Union ground forces were forced to surrender. Their surrender, and the
sight of the survivors of the *Harriet Lane* being marched up Galveston's

27th Street, was sobering for the Unionists but was met with glee by the Texans. Viewed from the USS *Westfield*, which was stuck aground off the harbor, the situation could not be more bleak. According to Frazier, an amazing rumor had circulated through the Union fleet for days, namely, that the *Bayou City* was actually a casemated ironclad ramming vessel[28] — patently untrue but seemingly credible in light of its ferocious encounter with the *Harriet Lane*. Taking no chances, Renshaw ordered the Union vessels to sea despite the Federals' having agreed to a truce. Rather than leave the grounded *Westfield* to the Confederates, Renshaw ordered the flagship destroyed; the crew complied by spilling turpentine and gunpowder below decks and setting a slow fuse. As fate would have it, however, the fuse was deceptively slow, and appeared to have extinguished itself. Furious at such seeming incompetence, Renshaw ordered to be rowed back to the *Westfield* by the longboat crew; this was a fatal miscalculation, for as soon as the impatient Renshaw got back aboard the *Westfield*, the ship's magazines ignited, obliterating the *Westfield*, Renshaw, and the longboat's crew in a fiery explosion that rained flaming debris down on the harbor and left little of the *Westfield* in its aftermath except twisted machinery and a shattered, smoking hull. While the stunned Union forces watched this horrifying spectacle in disbelief, the Confederates turned their attention to other matters, capturing several intact vessels that the Federals had abandoned in their haste, including the schooner *Le Compte*, and the supply boats *Cavallo* (which was still loaded with coal and supplies) and *Elias Pike*.

Despite the fact that it occurred in what was considered a military backwater,[29] the Battle of Galveston was covered widely in the popular press, for it represented a humiliating loss for the Union and a moment of glory for the Confederates. A contemporary illustration of the "Attack of the Rebels Upon Our Gun-boat Flotilla . . ." by a special artist in *Harper's Weekly* reached the U.S. public within the month; it featured a dramatic and somewhat stylized view of the fierce action of that New Year's Day (Fig. 7-5). In this view, the steamer *Westfield* is shown exploding in characteristic Victorian fashion — a bright flash and parts of the vessel and humanity thrust skyward — while the steamship's stack and walking-beam mechanism yield to the force of the explosion, and hapless Union sailors in ships' boats brace for its impact. To the left, the artist depicts the *Harriet Lane* engaging the cottonclads while other vessels steam into the battle and shells explode overhead. This illustration's action gains some credibility from the words of Henry Martyn Trueheart, from whom a letter to his sister Mary, now in Galveston's Rosenberg Library, told of a cry that arose at the beginning of the battle:

FIGURE 7-5

Harper's Weekly *on January 31, 1863, featured this graphic depiction of the "attack of the Rebels upon our gun boat flotilla at Galveston, Texas, January 1, 1863."*
It shows the Westfield *exploding (right) while the* Harriett Lane *and* Bayou City *(left) remain wedged together after a battle earlier that morning.*
Courtesy Texas Maritime Museum, Rockport.

"'Here come the Gunboats under full headway making right for the Lane' — and then such deep & meaning thunder as followed — it fairly shook the earth."[30]

In the Aftermath of Galveston

The Union navy nearly suffered another major loss the morning after the Battle of Galveston. The federal steamer *Cambria* appeared on the Gulf with more than one thousand Texan Unionists (wryly referred to as "First Texas Traitors" by Confederates) aboard. In another of his eccentric and brilliant moves, Magruder attempted to lure the *Cambria* into port by re-hoisting the Union flag aboard the *Harriet Lane* and the customs houses, creating the appearance that Galveston was still safely in Union hands. Those on board the *Cambria* discovered the real identity of a bogus pilot boat sent out to meet the *Cambria*, however, and she steamed safely back to sea before the ruse turned to disaster.

The USS *Hatteras*[31] was not so discerning, or so lucky, however. On January 11, 1863, less than two weeks after the disastrous battle of Galveston, Captain Blake of the *Hatteras* was ordered by Commodore Bell to intercept an unidentified bark-rigged vessel cruising well off the Texas coast. That unidentified vessel feigned being a badly handled blockade runner that had become incapacitated at sea. When within hailing distance, the commander of the *Hatteras* demanded that the seemingly stricken vessel identify herself, which prompted the *Alabama*'s commander, Raphael Semmes, to falsely claim identity as one of Her Britannic Majesty's steamers (either the *Petrel* or *Ariel*).[32] Pulling alongside, the *Hatteras*'s Captain Blake and his crew were surprised when a voice soon announced, "This is the Confederate States Steamer Alabama," followed shortly thereafter by a series of heavy cannon rounds roaring simultaneously, tearing apart the walking-beam mechanism and badly damaging the hull of the *Hatteras*. Within minutes, the *Hatteras* was burning and sinking, many of its crew killed by the *Alabama*'s deadly fusillade. Captain Blake surrendered, and the *Alabama* rescued about 118 survivors. Known to have captured or destroyed sixty-six Union vessels, the exploits of the *Alabama* (Fig. 7-6) exemplified the

FIGURE 7-6
The steam-powered sloop-of-war C.S.S. Alabama, *scourge of Union military and commercial shipping during the war, is known to have captured or destroyed sixty-six vessels, including the* Hatteras *off the Texas coast. Courtesy Naval Historical Center and Texas Maritime Museum, Rockport.*

dangers of blockading to those charged with enforcing such policies until she was sunk by the USS *Kearsarge* off the coast of France in June 1864.

The historian Spencer Tucker has characterized the CSS *Alabama* as "a sleek, three-masted, bark-rigged, sloop built of oak with a copper hull," and her commander, Raphael Semmes, described her as "a very perfect ship of her class."[33] The CSS *Alabama* was perfectly suited for her missions as a Confederate raider. About 900 tons burden, 230 feet in length, and drawing 15 feet of water when fully provisioned and coaled, the *Alabama* was further described by Semmes as "barkentine rigged, with long lower masts, which enabled her to carry large fore-and-aft sails, as jibs and try sails, which are of so much importance to the steamer, in so many emergencies." Semmes added that "her sticks were of the best yellow pine that would bend in a gale, like a willow wand, without breaking, and her rigging was of the best Swedish iron wire." This vessel "was so constructed that in fifteen minutes, her propeller could be detached from the shaft and lifted in a well contrived for the purpose, sufficiently high out of the water, not to be an impediment to her speed," a situation that made the *Alabama* "to all intents and purposes, a sailing ship." Semmes continued his fascinating description, noting that "on the other hand, when I desired to use her as a steamer, I had only to start the fires, lower the propeller, and if the wind was adverse, brace her yards to the wind, and the conversion was complete."[34] The CSS *Alabama* could cruise at just over thirteen knots, although her speed was often overestimated by the Union. She carried six 32-pound guns and other armaments, and was justifiably considered by her builder, John Laird, to be "the finest cruiser of her class in the world."[35] Reprovisioned by the spoils taken from the vessels she captured or sank, the *Alabama* was able to remain at sea for long periods—exactly the goal of Commander Semmes.

The *Alabama* prowled the waters off Texas for a short part of her career in early 1863, but many other, more mundane vessels also assisted the Confederacy. Using a wide variety of vessels as part of the Confederacy Texas Marine Department, Texans continued to be a source of consternation for the Union navy. The ability of the cottonclads having been proven at Galveston, Magruder used the technique again at Sabine Pass. The sidewheel steamer *Josiah H. Bell* was fitted with a 64-pound rifle at the bow and stacked cotton bales as a parapet for riflemen; it was accompanied by the *Uncle Ben*, which was smaller and armed with two 12-pound guns at the bow. Magruder set these cottonclads out to capture two Union sailing vessels, the USS *Morning Light* (a former clippership armed with eight guns) and the schooner *Velocity*, which were becalmed off Sabine Pass on January 21, 1863.

Although they tried to outrun the approaching cottonclads, the situation was hopeless for the Union vessels. After considerable firing, they surrendered and were captured along with more than one hundred Union sailors. The Confederates towed both vessels back toward Sabine Pass, but the *Morning Light* stuck on a sandbar and was set afire to avoid its possible recapture by the Union.[36]

BATTLE OF SABINE PASS

As the war dragged on, the Texas coast remained in a state of anxiety, its economy suffering severely and its residents on edge from nearly constant harassment of maritime trade by blockading Union vessels, the outright capture of some ports, and the incessant rumors of possible invasion by Union troops from the sea. Their fears were not unfounded and it should be remembered that Confederate forces continued protecting the coast, using any number of ingenious techniques, including blocking entry to the waters of the coast. As noted earlier, Union vessels had pounded and nominally silenced the Confederate Fort Griffin at Sabine Pass in September of 1862. To do so, they had used a combination of sail and steam-powered vessels, including the schooner USS *Rachel Seaman* and the mortar boat USS *Henry Janes*. This action had caused the temporary abandonment of the fort, but it also caused the Confederates to redouble their efforts—and become more vigilant about the coast's vulnerability to attack by Union forces. In efforts to fortify the coast from further Union inroads, the Confederate engineer Major Julius Kellerburg had ordered eighty-foot-long barges filled with clamshell to be sunk in order to deter the Union forces from occupying Sabine Lake in October 1862.[37]

Not quite a year later, the scene was set for the second significant Civil War naval battle—the Battle of Sabine Pass. This battle took place in September of 1863 as the Union attempted to take the coast, once again using the Sabine Pass as a point of entry. As described by Donald Frazier,[38] and by military reports and the popular press at the time, it was as much a debacle as a battle. Twenty Union vessels carrying five thousand troops sailed from New Orleans on September 5, 1863, with the objective of capturing Sabine Pass. Arriving at the Sabine Bar on September 7, the Federals planned to attack the fort using three gunboats, the *Arizona, Clifton,* and *Sachem.* This time, however, the Confederate Texans were better prepared to resist. On the afternoon of the next day, both the *Clifton* and the *Sachem* advanced toward the fort, but Confederate cannon fire quickly put the *Sachem* out

FIGURE 7-7
*During the Battle of Sabine Pass, on September 8, 1863, the small Confederate
fort there accomplished the seemingly impossible task of disabling and capturing
two Union vessels, the* Clifton *(a former ferryboat) and the* Sachem *(right).*
Leslie's Illustrated Newspaper, *October 10, 1863; courtesy Texas Maritime
Museum, Rockport.*

of action. Next the Confederates fixed on the *Clifton*, which, becoming
grounded, surrendered (Fig. 7-7). Major General William B. Franklin, in
charge of the Union advance, was disgraced in this engagement with the
recalcitrant Texans, who once again proved a formidable adversary. This
battle, which lasted only forty-five minutes, proved to be nearly as humiliating to the Federals as had the Battle of Galveston, for Franklin reportedly
became the first U.S. general to lose a fleet in a contest with land batteries
alone.[39]

Newspapers across the divided nation reported the Battle of Sabine Pass
in detail, some featuring engravings of the vessels being pounded by Confederate cannon fire, the action framed by the opening of the pass with the
Sabine Pass lighthouse prominent (Fig. 7-8). A very different view of this
battle from a completely different perspective—that is, from the Confederate stronghold—is displayed in the Museum of the Gulf Coast in Port Arthur
(Fig. 7-9). Here, in a dramatic mural-style painting that occupies a portion
of the museum's interior wall depicting the history of the coast, the Battle of
Sabine Pass is represented as if one were looking *outward* from the fort to
the hapless Union vessels, including the *Clifton*, being bombarded. In this
early 1990s mural by Travis Keese and Melinda Dixon, dense columns of

FIGURE 7-8
The Battle of Sabine Pass on September 8, 1863, as depicted in the October 10 issue of
Harper's Weekly, *shows the rebel battery (left), the* Clifton *(below and to the right of
the battery), the transport vessel* General Banks, *the* Sachem, *and the* Arizona, *as well
as the prominent Sabine Pass lighthouse. Courtesy Texas Maritime Museum, Rockport.*

FIGURE 7-9
*The Battle of Sabine Pass, as depicted in a modern mural in the Museum of the Gulf
Coast, shows the* Clifton *(center) under fire by the Confederate forces. Note the shell
craters (foreground), smoke from Union vessels (distance), and Sabine Pass Lighthouse.
Photo by the author, 1995; courtesy Museum of the Gulf Coast, Port Arthur, Texas.*

coal smoke from the funnels of the Union vessels rise on a southeast breeze and cannon fire from the fort takes its toll on the *Clifton* and other Union vessels. The Sabine Pass lighthouse, which remains an area landmark, stands like a sentinel in the distance.

As reported at the time, and recorded in the annals of naval warfare, the result of the Battle of Sabine Pass was totally humiliating for the Union, for two steamers and nineteen men (some sources claim forty-two) were lost and 315 Union sailors were taken prisoner in a battle that resulted in absolutely no losses for the forty-two Texans. The historian Andrew Forest Muir attributed the Confederate victory to both the brilliance and the tenacity of Confederate Lt. Richard W. (Dick) Dowling and the ineptness of Union Major General William B. Franklin.[40] Regardless of the individual personalities, however, the Battle of Sabine Pass proved once again that although the Union could keep the coastal waters blockaded to some degree, it could not effectively capture and occupy the most important parts of that coastline.

One vessel associated with the battle of Sabine Pass—the *Clifton*—continues to excite the interest of Texas maritime historians. This 892-ton sidewheel steamer's hull measured 210 feet by 40 feet by 13 1/2 feet, and records confirm that she was built by Jeremiah Simonson, of Brooklyn, New York, in 1861.[41] Reported as having served briefly as a New York ferryboat in 1861, the *Clifton* was typical of vessels that were built for passenger service but were pressed into military service when the demand for gunboats increased. After serving the Union during the attack on Vicksburg, Mississippi, where she received a shot to her boiler that killed seven of her crew, the *Clifton* was soon repaired and then assisted in the taking of Galveston in October of 1862. Following her capture in the Battle of Sabine Pass in 1863, the *Clifton* next served as a Confederate blockade runner until her luck ran out: She was wrecked near Sabine Pass while unsuccessfully trying to run a Union blockade on March 21, 1864. After being burned by the Confederates to prevent her falling into Union hands, the *Clifton*'s wreckage[42] was visible for years, appearing in numerous photographs taken before the turn of the century as a superstructure and mast looming out of the water. Leads such as these photographs and historic descriptions of the *Clifton*'s last days have prompted Danny Sessums, director of the Museum of the Gulf Coast in Port Arthur, to encourage J. Barto Arnold and his team of Texas marine archaeologists to relocate the wreck for possible study of her illustrious and varied career as a blockade runner.[43] Interestingly, the wreckage of the *Clifton* yielded its walking beam to salvors many years ago, and this distinctive mari-

FIGURE 7-10
*A portion of the walking-beam mechanism from the USS Clifton
was salvaged and is now on exhibit in Riverfront Park in the city of
Beaumont. Photo by the author, 1995.*

time artifact is currently on exhibit at the Riverfront Park in Beaumont, where a historical plaque briefly relates the story of the Battle of Sabine Pass (Fig. 7-10).

THE WAR GRINDS ON

Meanwhile, the war was affecting South Texas. To the consternation of the Union, this strategic area continued to provide the Texas Confederates a market for their cotton and a source of military materiel. Although Port Isabel had been a haven for blockade runners for the first half of the Civil War, its status changed when a Union attack on May 30, 1863, resulted in the sinking or capture of all vessels in the harbor there. This gave the Union a strong presence in South Texas. To further enhance this position, a major expedition into South Texas was mounted under the command of Major General N. P. Banks in the fall of 1863. Still stinging from the recent losses of vessels at the Battle of Sabine Pass (not to mention the disastrous losses at Galveston very early in the year), Union vessels moved toward South Texas with some trepidation. Major Banks was aware of the many hazards to navigation in the vicinity of Texas, and soon experienced the fury of the Gulf, losing several vessels as he proceeded with Union plans to occupy South Texas. The roster of lost vessels from this mission was indeed sobering: While in the Gulf off the Texas coast en route to the battlefront, the steamer *Union* was lost, and two schooners foundered on October 31, 1863. Less than three weeks later, on November 5, the steamer *Nassau* was lost at Aransas Pass along with the schooners *Partidge* and *Kate*. To make matters even worse, less than two weeks later (on November 18) the steamer *Bagby* was lost at Aransas Pass. The year 1863 would go on record as a year of tremendous losses for the United States Navy, a good deal of these losses occurring in Texas. Despite these setbacks, however, the Union naval forces persevered and by January 1, 1864, could claim possession of the Texas coast from the Rio Grande to Matagorda,[44] including the strategic port of Corpus Christi.

By early 1864, then, the Union forces were able to occupy portions of the central and southern Texas Gulf coast—at least temporarily—and thus keep the Confederate forces on constant alert. Indianola had been captured along with Corpus Christi in November of 1863, giving Union forces a base of operations on the central coast. Because the Confederates anticipated a strong Union effort to take this important seaport, their frantic actions there before the city was attacked reveal the sometimes ironic aspects of the war. Indianola's possible capture by Federals had led John B. Magruder to destroy the lighthouses at Saluria and Pass Cavallo and to burn the bridges to Indianola lest they fall into the hands of the Union. These actions, however, caused the resentment of Indianolans, because they effectively ruined the port's economy and infrastructure in the process,[45] and yet did not prevent the Federals from capturing and occupying it. Thus it was that this important port was in Union hands until the troops were secretly withdrawn from this part of the Texas coast for what has been called the "Red River Campaign" in 1864.[46] That disastrous campaign found Major General Banks, flushed with his victory in Central and South Texas, attempting to invade northeastern Texas via the Red River, using a fleet of gunboats. In a significant setback, Banks was defeated in northwestern Louisiana in a battle that involved many Texas Confederate troops. Meanwhile, in South Texas, the Union failed in an attempt to take Laredo, which was considered a strategic point on the Rio Grande. In July of 1864 Colonel John S. Ford had recaptured Brownsville; by late summer the Union troops had evacuated the lower Rio Grande Valley and the South Texas coast except for Brazos Santiago and the Matagorda Peninsula.

By late 1864 the beleaguered Confederates still were able to defend portions of the Texas coast, especially that crucial area in the vicinity of Galveston and Sabine Pass. The historian Martha Doty Freeman has noted that the Galveston and Brazos Navigation Company canal connecting the Brazos River with the west end of Galveston Bay at this time proved to be of strategic importance to Confederate Texas, which relied on the cotton and other supplies being transported through this canal by blockade runners.[47] Through a selective process of improving or maintaining certain protected waterways, and obstructing other more accessible waterways, the Confederate Texans kept the Union vessels at bay in many areas.

As the war entered its last year, the Confederate forces continued to actively fortify the coast to resist penetration by Union forces. Their successful efforts appear to be an outcome of their recognizing the ineffectiveness of brick forts and their extensive use of earthwork fortifications that better withstood bombardment by the enemy. The strategic Virginia Point, near Galveston, was in fact so well protected by fortifications, and so inaccessible to Union naval vessels, that it was *never* bombarded.[48] Confederate forts protecting the eastern portion of the Texas coast included Fort Sabine, Fort Green (Bolivar Peninsula), Fort Herbert (Virginia Point), the Fort on Mud Island, Fort Velasco at the mouth of the Brazos, Fort Debray (Saluria, on Matagorda Island), and Fort Jackson (on Pelican Spit). In addition to Fort Jackson, Galveston itself was protected by several forts, including the South Battery, Fort Scurry, Fort Bankhead, Fort Point, and Fort Moore.

It should be remembered that very few of these forts existed before the war. Their construction was a testimony to the tenacity of the Texans, who sought to defend themselves from the constant likelihood of Union invasion by sea. All of these Confederate forts faced the water in anticipation of attacks by sea-borne Union troops, and they ensured that Galveston and nearby portions of the Texas coast would remain in the hands of Confederate Texans. Thus it was that the Union periodically invaded Texas by sea, only to be either repelled by Texans or recalled to other fronts of military activity. This stalemate dragged on until the end of the war on April 9, 1865. Although rumors of surrender had reached Texas, it is interesting to note that the last land battle of the Civil War was actually fought more than a month *after* the war officially ended, when Rio Grande-based Confederate troops attacked surprised Union troops at Palmito Ranch, near Brownsville, on May 13, 1865.[49]

THE BLOCKADE IN RETROSPECT

During the entire Civil War, the blockading of the Texas coast was a vital part of the Union's strategy, but how effectively had it worked? What effect did blockading have on shipping and the vessels that were engaged in it? The answer is that blockading was successful—to a point. History has shown

FIGURE 7-11
*During the Civil War, the lower Rio Grande boomed as Matamoros became a
shipping center for Texas cotton that was bound for the mills of England, because
international law prohibited its blockading by Union vessels. From John Phillips,*
Mexico Illustrated *(London: E. H. Atchley, 1848). Courtesy Special Collections
Division, The University of Texas at Arlington Libraries, Arlington.*

that blockades bring about ingenious responses. One popular solution to
prevent vessels from being harassed or confiscated by either side involved
their sale in order to transfer their identity from Confederate or Union to,
say, British. Thus, Charles Adams sold his bark *Aaron L. Reid* to William
Barnes, an Englishman clerking in Adams, Jordan & Company in
Galveston.[50] This enabled the vessel to sail relatively unmolested. Similarly, Adams's partner, Charles Jordan, sold the brig *William M. Rice* to
Barnes, and the vessel was promptly renamed *Delta* and placed under British colors.[51]

The war had the effect of rapidly internationalizing what was, in reality,
Texas trade. Given its proximity to Mexico, the lower Rio Grande boomed
as Matamoros received Southern cotton, much of it from Texas, that was
bound for the mills of England on vessels of many flags (Fig. 7-11). As noted
earlier, this condition existed because Union warships could not molest vessels entering or leaving the lower Rio Grande at Matamoros without risking
an international incident. Tampico, in northern Mexico, also boomed as
Southern cotton was shipped on vessels of many nationalities, some bogus
in that their owners were still U.S. citizens but had made surreptitious ar-
rangements for vessels to fly foreign flags. As the merchant Charles Stillman

brazenly put it, "We must all turn Turks or Japanese, and carry some of their rags at the mast head," sarcastically noting that his New York–based brig *John Jewett* would sail to Brownsville, where "I will sell her to some Mexican friend, and will adopt the Turkey Buzzard now that the Eagle has her wings clipt [*sic*]."[52] The historian L. Tuffly Ellis has noted that hundreds of vessels changed registration by simply allowing a ship owner to register his vessel with a British consular agent.[53] It should be further noted that the British had a special interest in facilitating cotton trade to England, as the blockade had idled thousands of cotton mill workers there, precipitating an economic crisis and social unrest.

Although blockade runners kept some trade moving between the Confederacy and the outside world, the blockade exacted a terrible toll on the South, including Texas. When cotton and other goods could leave, they often did so on erratic schedules and under trying conditions. The voyage of the tinsmith and merchant Seba Bogart Brush from Bagdad-Boca del Rio, a small port on the South Texas/Mexican border, to Havana, with a cargo of cotton in January 1864 took fourteen days. Brush's trip was illustrative of the sometimes harrowing voyages experienced by vessels during the war. His diary documents a grueling trip on the English barque *Jane Cockerell*. The winter of 1863–1864 was especially severe, and the *Jane Cockerell* was pounded by several northers while a broken rudderhead and a rebellious crew threatened to scuttle the voyage from the outset. So touchy had the situation between captain and crew become that on January 14, "all hands refused to work until they received their pay and advanced wages."[54] The captain actually had refused to pay the crew, realizing that they would leave as soon as they received their pay; however, after receiving assistance from the crew of a man-of-war, which partially defused the situation, the captain paid his men and they went back to work. Seasick most of the voyage, Brush arrived in Havana after additional terrifying experiences on the Gulf, including breakers that were "strikeing [*sic*] so hard that the chances was [*sic*] that we would go to pieces."[55]

Out-and-out blockade running, the riskiest of maritime trading, could be highly profitable. Naturally, it has also become the most romanticized. Only the fastest or most agile vessels could enter and stay in the blockade-running business. At first sloops and schooners were employed, respectively, for intracoastal and interport blockade running. By about 1863, however, the lucrative blockading trade employed fast, steam-powered vessels. Following her seizure in the Battle of Galveston by the Confederates, the swift sidewheeler *Harriet Lane*, it will be remembered, became, after repair (and

FIGURE 7-12

The blockade runner is among the most romanticized of vessels. Two steam-powered
vessels named Banshee *served as blockade runners. The Clyde-built* Banshee (II)
was a 627-ton vessel known to have made eight successful attempts at running the
Union blockade, including the run from Galveston to Havana and back in 1864.
Courtesy Naval Historical Center and Texas Maritime Museum, Rockport.

a name change), the blockade runner *Lavinia*. In their service as blockade
runners, some steamships reportedly were painted dirty white or dark colors
as camouflage of sorts. This is the picture that most often comes to mind
when the words "blockade runner" are mentioned, an image immortalized
in Charles Boynton's classic book, *The History of the Navy During the Re-*
bellion (Fig. 7-12). Blockade running also required careful attention to the
types of fuel burned. The historian Stephen R. Wise noted that the steam-
powered blockade runners stocked two types of coal, hard and soft (probably anthracite and bituminous, respectively). He states that "the hard coal,
being more efficient and smokeless, was used during the actual running of
the blockade when low visibility and quick bursts of speed were required,"
adding that the smokier-burning, poorer-quality "soft coal was used on the
open sea, since most blockade runners could usually outrun warships even
when using the soft coal."[56]

As the war progressed, with the blockade enforced aggressively along the
eastern seaboard and the Confederacy losing more seaports, Texas ports
became more important to the Confederacy. By 1864, Galveston remained
firmly in Confederate hands and the remaining blockade runners shifted

their attention from the South's Atlantic seaboard to the Gulf of Mexico. Large, fast, steam-powered blockade runners made many daring dashes through the blockade in the vicinity of Galveston. As noted by Stephen Wise, a historian of the Union blockade from March to the end of May in 1865, at least thirteen runs were made to Galveston, some by vessels well known in the blockade-running trade, such as the *Banshee* (II) and the *Fox*.[57] Two of the most famous blockade runners of all, *Denbigh* and *Will of the Wisp*, were wrecked at Galveston while trying to get past a federal blockading squadron.

Blockade running resulted in some nearly legendary pursuits. Early in the war the *Royal Yacht*, a forty-ton schooner carrying a cargo of ninety-seven bales of cotton, was chased for six and a half hours by the U.S. bark *William G. Anderson* and finally captured just before nightfall. Other blockade runners were more successful, as Admiral David Farragut had to concede when the *Mobile* (a Confederate ironclad that had been captured earlier in the war) lost the *Susanna* in a squall after dark, but not before the captain of the fleeing blockade runner threw virtually everything overboard—including four hundred bales of cotton, furniture, and even the vessel's anchor—in what proved to be a successful effort to make the *Susanna* sail faster than her would-be captor.

In general, blockade running was harrowing but lucrative. L. Tuffly Ellis estimated that between 1,480 and 2,220 blockade runs were made off the coast of Texas during the Civil War; of these, only 175 (about 10 to 15 percent) were intercepted.[58] This translates to a success rate of 85 percent to 90 percent for the blockade runners. Whether the risks were worth the rewards is difficult to determine; in one case, however, H. Bidwell of Houston purchased a cargo for about $2,000 off the Rio Grande and brought it up the Texas coast on the schooner *John Douglas*, disposing of that same cargo for $21,500 upon reaching his destination.[59] To risk takers, a tenfold profit such as this might indeed be good odds and well worth the risk. Odds such as these guaranteed that at least some mariners would run, or attempt to run, the blockade gantlet thrown up by the Union.

Considered economically, the blockade effectively increased the costs of producing cotton. The maritime historian Ben C. Stuart estimated that an average of only about thirty-five thousand bales of cotton were exported during any one year of the Civil War—a striking contrast to the 142,972 bales exported in 1861.[60] If these figures are correct, the blockade served to reduce trade of this type to a quarter of what would normally have been expected.

How long might a blockade runner last in such hazardous service? In a chapter entitled "The Final Ledger," Stephen Wise states that the average lifetime of a blockade runner was just over four runs, or two round-trips. He further notes that cotton was a relatively small part of the cargoes of blockade runners, which supplied countless essential items such as food, clothing, chemicals, and medicine. A British visitor to Texas during the war noted that the blockade so deprived Texans of one important product—coffee—that they were forced to produce coffee substitutes from a number of alternatives such as okra, peanuts, sweet potatoes, and corn, usually without much success.[61]

Because blockade runners supplied military necessities, including rifles, saltpeter (for gunpowder), and other arms,[62] it can be concluded that blockade runners helped prolong the war. For this reason alone, it appears that the blockade itself was a viable strategy in helping to cripple the Confederacy, for it did stop some of that traffic. The blockade thus generally achieved its purpose of keeping the South economically hamstrung and, to some extent, reducing the Confederacy's military strength. As seen in a beautiful sketch by George W. Grover (1824–1901), the federal blockading vessels that were stationed in Galveston during the later part of the war (1864–1865) were steam-powered (Fig. 7-13). Blockading and blockade running generally proved the effectiveness—and superiority—of propeller-driven steamships. They were fast and, if properly maintained, less prone to breakdown in military service. Experience gained in the Civil War would forever change the form of both military and civilian vessels. The presence of these steamships, some of the sidewheel configuration but a growing number of "propellers," marked a peculiar situation. These vessels kept up the crippling blockade and implied a strong federal presence, while much of Texas itself, especially its premier port Galveston, retained its Southern allegiance and demeanor to the end.

The Civil War in Texas: A Maritime Perspective

It is worth noting that only about half of the Texas troops employed to defend the Confederacy fought outside Texas; at least half of the remainder pressed into service helped to defend the Texas coast from invasion. Despite Texans' efforts to keep the Unionists out, however, the federal presence was indeed palpable. Although there was considerable Union sentiment in parts of Texas, with as much as a third of the population supporting the federal cause, the coast—particularly the southeast coast—was strongly Southern

FIGURE 7-13
The beautiful "sketches of vessels in blockading service [at Galveston] October 1864"
by George Grover illustrates and identifies thirteen steamers, some of which are
sidewheelers (Numbers 4 and 6), while most appear to be propeller-driven;
the key identifying the ships by number has been lost.
Courtesy Rosenberg Library, Galveston, Texas.

FIGURE 7-14
Port Isabel, as depicted in Leslie's Illustrated Newspaper *on February 13, 1864,
shows several steam-powered riverboats (left), a sidewheel steamer (center), and
numerous sailing vessels farther out in the harbor, while troops occupy and fortify
positions in the foreground. Courtesy Texas Maritime Museum, Rockport.*

in its allegiance. As part of the Southern economy, the Texas hinterland had
continued to produce cotton, but the hostilities had wrought havoc with the
labor force, as so many Texans were either engaged in the battles raging in
the East or busy defending the coast. It is known that many slaves were
pressed into service by the Confederacy, especially in building fortifications
on the Texas coast, sometimes within sight of Union vessels lying offshore,
intent on ending the institution of slavery.

Although the Union kept up its blockade of the Texas ports, which had
a debilitating effect on the economy of Texas, it is worth restating that
the Union navy could never gain—and maintain—an effective hold on the
entire Texas coast. In reporting on the war, the Northern newspapers depicted Texas scenes in areas where Union troops managed to gain control,
especially in the vicinity of Matagorda Bay near Pass Caballo and southern
Texas near Port Isabel. These illustrations are important to maritime historians, for they often feature the three types of vessels that typified Texas in
the later half of the nineteenth century; they consistently show steamboats,
small sailing vessels, and oceangoing steamers (Fig. 7-14). They illustrate

vessels of all kinds, from the smallest sloops to steamships and steam-powered riverboats, that had been appropriated by both the Union and the Confederacy.

The Civil War affected the daily lives of every Texan, especially those who lived along the coast, which seemed constantly open to Union invasion by seaborne troops. In this regard, the saga of the Port Aransas lighthouse is instructive. Of the dozen major lighthouses dotting the coast from the Sabine to the Rio Grande, the venerable Port Aransas light is the longest-lived. Constructed on Harbor Island in 1854, it protected the coast until its temporary closing in 1956, only to be reactivated as a private aid to navigation on July 4, 1988. Like other lighthouses, the Port Aransas light featured a beehive-like cut-glass Fresnel lens, an ingenious European invention that consisted of many beveled angles that, in effect, boosted the power of a single light to an impressive several thousand candlepower. The bright white light at the top of its sixty-seven-foot red brick tower is visible for about nine miles and operates in inclement weather and darkness to keep ships from straying onto the bars. Folklore has enriched the history of this lighthouse, whose original lens is said to have been hidden in the sand somewhere on the island to protect it from an attack by Union soldiers during the Civil War. But, alas, the lens was never found after the war, and a new lens was installed in 1866.[63] As is the case of many restored historic properties, the Port Aransas lighthouse features parts salvaged from other historic sites; the lens in today's reopened lighthouse, for example, had been manufactured in France in the 1880s and was obtained from a Massachusetts antique collector in 1989. The lighthouse tender's buildings require constant maintenance because, as caretaker Rick Pratt described the situation, "Being surrounded by salt water, this whole place is constantly trying to return it to the soil."[64]

When viewed in context, the Civil War on the Texas coast, like most Civil War history in the Lone Star State, has been overshadowed by military events elsewhere. Although Texas was not the scene of the legendary ironclad battles, such as those between the Union's *Monitor* and the Confederacy's *Merrimac* off the Virginia coast, its cottonclads were ingenious and lethal weapons of war. It somehow seems fitting that two vessels that played such an important role in the Civil War era maritime history of Texas—the USS *Harriet Lane* and the CSS *Alabama*—have been manufactured as popular scale models, that is, fairly accurate detailed miniature kits that are constructed by model ship enthusiasts; this type of miniaturization represents yet another way that maritime history is perpetuated.[65]

In the Civil War, Texans had again proven themselves indomitable when it came to repelling central authority on the coast through the use of ingeniously adapted craft and unconventional, sometimes savage, military techniques. The Texas naval forces did so not as part of the Confederate States Navy, or CSN, but rather under the command of the Texas Marine Department, which was itself controlled by the Army of the Confederacy. Thus it was that officers like John Magruder were able to use the limited resources available so effectively in coordination with land forces. At the same time, however, it should also be noted that Texans had no real maritime strategy, and that most of the vessels spent the war years in valuable (but decidedly unromantic) service, that is, in mundane logistical roles, such as shuttling supplies and troops back and forth between isolated coastal garrisons.[66] Through these efforts, the Texans managed to keep the U.S. naval forces at bay along parts of the coast for much of the war.

By the end of the Civil War in 1865, Texans had remained defiant, if not unbeaten, though their cause—the Confederacy—was ultimately crushed in the grueling battles in the distant states of Mississippi, Tennessee, Virginia, and Pennsylvania. With the surrender of the Confederacy at Appomattox, the state of Texas once again joined the Union, though it took several years to make the transition back to official statehood. Following the Civil War, the fate of Texas and the fate of its ports and maritime trade were once again bound to the United States of America, which was positioning itself to become a major international commercial and military maritime power by century's end.

THE END OF AN ERA
1865–1900

My introduction to steam was not appealing. . . .
My God, I thought, give me back my old sailing ship—any old time.
CAPTAIN L. R. W. BEAVIS, *Passage from Sail to Steam*

In the last third of the nineteenth century, Texas became a major player in the reconstructed South and a gateway to the rapidly developing Southwest. Immigration records reveal Galveston to be a major port at that time; some claim it to have been the second port in importance after New York, at least in terms of new arrivals during the latter part of the 1800s. That claim, however, has been questioned, and a closer look at the records reveals Galveston more likely was the second most important point of embarkation and debarkation on the Gulf of Mexico.[1] Nevertheless, Galveston must be considered to have been a significant port by any standards. As the railroads during the period reached toward the coast, in effect ensuring markets through improving ports, the economy of the coast boomed. During the period, Galveston's population grew from ten thousand to nearly forty-five thousand; other ports such as Rockport and Port Aransas on the southern coast also expanded as increased trade and entrepreneurial efforts brought prosperity.

Direct steamship service from New York to Texas began in the years immediately following the Civil War. For a short time, Williams and Guion provided sporadic service, but in 1866 and 1867 Spofford and Tileston began regular "permanent" operations, using a small fleet of propeller-driven steamships (the *Tybee*, *Perit*, and *Tradewind*), which ranged in length from 150 to 180 feet and drew 10 to 12 feet of water when loaded. By 1871, direct service between the booming port of Indianola and New York was initiated by the steamship *Bolivar*, of the Connecticut-based Mallory Line, which would prove to be stiff competition to the steamers of Morgan Lines.[2] Although upset by the exorbitant rates charged by the Galveston Wharf Company, the shipping magnate Charles Morgan also considered the approaches to Galveston harbor unsafe. The early 1870s witnessed improvements, including the construction of a jetty and dredging intended to help Galveston retain its position as Texas's premier port in the face of increasing competition from Houston[3] and the rapidly developing ports of Indianola and Rockport.

The private sector stimulated trade to Texas ports, but government was then, as it is now, a major factor in encouraging maritime shipping. In the study of Texas maritime history, government emerges as a two-edged sword, a point that became more apparent in the period following the Civil War. It would be both unfair and impossible not to credit the United States in assisting Texas maritime development. Several agencies, specifically the U.S. Coast and Geodedic Survey, the U.S. Coast Guard, and the U.S. Army Engineers, respectively, mapped, protected, and improved the Texas coast. Immediately following the Civil War, reconstruction imposed new taxes on transportation enterprises, including quarantine taxes in Texas. However, the taxes in turn were often used to improve transportation facilities, including the dredging of channels and the creation of jetties. Mail contracts helped subsidize vessels. For example, the run from New Orleans to Brazos St. Iago netted the Morgan Line $12,000 per year for twice-monthly service in 1870; Indianola and Galveston service was supported by mail subsidies throughout much of the 1870s, whereas Rockport service was unsubsidized.[4] An 1875 issue of *Bryant's Railroad Guide—the Tourist's and Emigrant's Hand-Book of Travel* features an illustration of a sailing ship (Fig. 8-1) for an advertisement of regular triweekly passenger packets (identified as "copper fastened schooners") carrying U.S. mails from Indianola to Rockport and Corpus Christi. The copper fastening referred to was the technique of using copper bolts or screws to join portions of the ship's frame together. Copper was also commonly used for sheathing that was applied to hulls below the waterline in the nineteenth century as a way of preventing damage to the hull by borer worms and other marine organisms; because barnacles could not cling to copper-sheathed hulls, such sheathing also helped reduce their drag on the hull. Copper thus helped make sailing ships more durable, more efficient, and safer.

The Rise and Fall of Texas Ports

The late nineteenth century was particularly good for some Texas ports, and disastrous for others. The Texas coast is littered with the remains of many nineteenth-century ghost ports that, at first blush, would seem to have been

Regular Tri-Weekly Passenger Packets !

COPPER FASTENED SCHOONERS,

Carrying

U.S. Mails.

From Indianola to Rockport and Corpus Christi.

CHAS. BURBANK, Agent, Indianola, Texas.

FIGURE 8-1

The 1875 issue of Bryant's Railroad Guide—the Tourist's and Emigrant's Hand-Book of Travel *features an illustration of a sailing vessel for an advertisement of regular triweekly passenger packets identified as "copper fastened schooners" carrying U.S. mails from Indianola to Rockport and Corpus Christi. Courtesy Special Collections Division, The University of Texas at Arlington Libraries, Arlington.*

the victims of storms but were more often done in by changing economics. St. Mary's is typical: A recent newspaper article noted that "the town thrived from its inception in 1857 until the storm of 1886 all but did her in,"[5] but the story is somewhat more complicated—and tied to the rise of a competing port, called Rockport, on Aransas Bay. In *El Copano*, the author Hobart Huson made note of the fact that St. Mary's was a major shipper of cattle and lumber but had suffered greatly during the Civil War. The 1862 blockade, and the evacuation of population from the coastal islands in anticipation of the arrival of a federal gunboat fleet, had caused problems in St. Mary's, but they were less significant than the site's inherent problems as a port, namely, the fact that the channels into St. Mary's were tortuous and perilous because of submerged reefs, including "Long Reef."

Comparisons of population figures and business records reveal that Rockport began to grow much faster than St. Mary's by the early 1870s. The John and Nancy Clark Wood family helped Rockport thrive. John H. Wood, formerly of New York, is listed as an incorporator of the Rockport, Fulton, Laredo & Mexican Pacific Railroad Co., and was active in port improve-

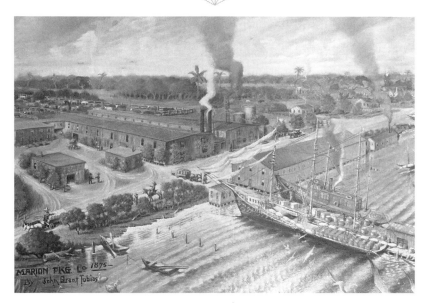

FIGURE 8-2
*An evocative, but somewhat romanticized, painting by John Grant Tobias depicting
the Fulton waterfront at the "Marion Packing Company in 1875" shows the site
where cattle were processed into tallow and hides, which were then shipped to
their destinations by both sailing and steam-powered vessels.
Courtesy Texas Maritime Museum, Rockport.*

ments. Although the enterprising Wood also invested in St. Mary's, his
Rockport investment was better founded, as it was a more promising location. Thus, the scene was set when the first hurricane of 1875 badly damaged St. Mary's. Although the townsfolk regrouped and rebuilt, the days of
St. Mary's were numbered. In 1886 a second storm spelled doom for the
town, which exists as a shadow of its former self in the town of Bayport,
while Rockport continued to grow and attract the attention of the transportation magnate Charles Morgan. Fulton, too, benefited from the stimulus
of entrepreneurial efforts by Morgan and others. An evocative, if somewhat
romanticized painting depicting the waterfront at the "Marion Packing
Company in 1875," shows the site where cattle were processed into tallow
and hides, which were then shipped to their destinations by sail and steam-
powered vessels (Fig. 8-2). However, this painting, done by John Grant Tobias,
perhaps as early as the 1920s, is somewhat conjectural. As the former curator
of the Texas Maritime Museum has noted, the painting may contain several minor technical errors, including the presence of palm trees, which

only appeared after about 1900 as they were introduced by settlers.[6] Nevertheless, it conveys the atmosphere of a small Texas port facility in a long-vanished era.

LIFE AND TIMES OF THE STEAMSHIP *Mary*

The comings and goings of vessels in a rather typical Texas port in the third quarter of the nineteenth century is revealed in the fascinating journal of George W. Fulton Jr., whose father was a businessman and ranch owner. Fulton's large Victorian-era Italianate Villa style mansion built between 1874 and 1877 still stands at Rockport as a reminder of a vanished age on the Texas coast, and is today a state park. When George Fulton junior was a young man of twenty years, he wrote a most interesting diary in order, as he put it, to "divert my mind" from the dullness of life in Rockport and Fulton, which, incidentally, were still about a decade away from having rail service and relied almost exclusively on the Gulf for a connection to the outside world. From the Fulton diary of the summer of 1873 we are provided a remarkably detailed account of a trip to Cincinnati, part of which (Rockport to Brashears, Louisiana) consisted of a voyage on the SS *Mary* (Fig. 8-3), an iron-hulled 234-foot sidewheel steamer built in 1866 for the Morgan Line, which would sink off Aransas Pass three years later (on November 30, 1876). Recent excavations of the wreck of the *Mary* reveal many important facts about her design and construction. For most of her career, she served Rockport and other Texas ports, including Brazos, from Morgan's port at Brashears, Louisiana.

Fulton's diary entries beginning in July convey a sense of anticipation as he awaits the arrival of the seven-year-old SS *Mary* from Brazos: "Tomorrow night the steamer will be in and the next day we say goodbye to home, dear friends, and old Texas."[7]

Fulton mentions that "the steamer has arrived at Rockport and will be up in an hour . . . [and] the horses and buggy are waiting at the gate to convey us with our baggage to Hall's Wharf." He then notes with apparent resignation that "the steamer is aground in the bay and we will not be likely to get off today," adding that "she will leave very early in the morning if not tonight."[8] Given the shoal waters in many relatively primitive Texas ports, the temporary inconvenience of a grounding was to be taken in stride. Fulton wrote his next entries on July 25 from "Stateroom R.12-On board SS Mary-Rockport Texas," which he noted was "the most pleasant room on the whole ship."[9] Once under way, Fulton relates, "Rockport appears like a panorama

FIGURE 8-3

The steamship Mary *of the Morgan Lines called frequently at the Texas ports of Rockport and Galveston. There is no confirmed painting or photo of the SS* Mary; *this painting of the* Mary *may or may not be the* Mary *that served Texas as a Morgan liner. The artist has apparently omitted her two masts, whereas the records reveal she retained them until the end. Enrollment documents list Morgan's* Mary *as having one deck, whereas this vessel appears to have two. Courtesy the Museum of Mobile, Mobile, Alabama.*

in the distance," but adds sarcastically, "Confound the ship—shakes so that it is almost impossible to write."[10] That mention of shaking reveals one reason why paddle wheel steamers were being replaced by propeller-driven ships toward the end of the nineteenth century. As noted earlier, screw steamers involved a more efficient design that propelled the ship smoothly rather than thrashing through the water.

The next day Fulton noted that he felt "a little qualmish but have not yet been sea sick," adding that "it is very pleasant on deck though rather rough."[11] Fulton's voyage occurring in the summer, he noted a typical condition of the Texas Gulf coast at that time of year: "The wind has been in the southeast ever since we crossed Aransas Bay—the ship sails have been set all the time without the necessity of changing them as the wind is so steady and nearly a-beam."[12] It was typical for steamships of the period, which were often fully rigged, to take advantage of the wind as a way of saving fuel; in some situations, sails enabled the vessel to make better time than steam paddlewheels alone. Fulton continued his account of the *Mary* as it sailed into the waters off Louisiana: "We have changed our course somewhat and consequently are not so much in the trough of the sea," and he added, with a characteristic Victorian combination of prose and drama: "They have squared the sails a little and we are sailing most directly before the wind and it is perfectly delightful up here on the main deck in the shade of the jib with just enough of the balmy sea breeze to remind us of the dear old home which every moment sinks deeper and deeper into the shadowy past."[13] At Brashear Fulton met the train of the Morgan Line that would take him to New Orleans. His adding that it had been five years since he had heard the sound of a locomotive further underscores the relative isolation of his home life back in Rockport and Fulton. His observations also help us view the SS *Mary* as an important link in an evolving transportation system.

We know much about the SS *Mary* from corporate records of the Morgan Line, but this vessel has a special place in the annals of Texas, for she was sunk off the Texas coast on November 30, 1876.[14] As reported by Mrs. S. G. Miller, a passenger on that fateful last trip from Morgan City to Rockport, the weather was bad the entire trip, and the sea rough: "We were travelling over a choppy sea with the wind shifting from one quarter to another and causing the waves to run back and forth," which "made hard going for the ship."[15] Hard going indeed! Paddle wheel steamers were notorious for their inability to deal with such laterally moving high seas, which would cause the ship to naturally roll, and raise one paddle wheel out of the water briefly while the other "dug" too deeply into the high water on the other side. Conditions worsened and Mrs. Miller recalled that "the night we reached the bar [off Aransas Pass] a terrific freezing norther swept out from the land and struck the vessel." By morning "water . . . was pouring through the ship like a mighty river."[16] The SS *Mary* was evidently slowly sinking; but still in the hope that she would be able to get through despite waves that "dashed over the sides of the ship as though they were great monsters," a pilot boat was awaited, for what seemed an eternity. When the pilot boat did not arrive, Captain Benson decided to cross the bar, hitting a buoy that gashed the hull. When the pilot boat finally arrived, it was too late for any action but rescue. The SS *Mary* was totally wrecked, but all hands, including the crew of thirty and its eight passengers, were saved. Most heart-rending of the losses were Mrs. Miller's prized horses, which were trapped in the wreckage and drowned.

When she sank, the *Mary* was ten years old, "so old," according to the bitter Mrs. Miller, "that it was not fit to run any longer." However, it should be remembered that travelers of the era were becoming accustomed to advances in ship design, and thus even an older but distinctly seaworthy vessel might be so criticized as unfit for service. Mrs. Miller's claim could be added to many leveled at the Morgan Lines, and often at Charles Morgan himself, who soon ordered several new propeller-driven steamships for the Texas trade despite having so much confidence in his vessels that he refused to insure them.

As described and interpreted by Steven Hoyt and the staff of Espey, Huston & Associates, and a more recent archaeological report by Charles E. Pearson of Coastal Environments, Inc., the wreck of the SS *Mary* was still visible in the 1880s, but subsequent storms and jetty construction, as well as possible intentional dynamiting of the wreck removed it from sight. Hoyt reported in 1990 that the SS *Mary* now rests "quietly on [the] edge of the channel slowly falling victim to corrosion, erosion and dredging."[17] This condition is confirmed by the 1995 Coastal Environments report that the *Mary*'s proximity to turbulence of vessels in the channel makes her wreck somewhat perilous to explore.

A search of historic records led Espey, Huston & Associates to reconstruct the ten-year career of the ill-fated SS *Mary*. Like most steamships of the time, the SS *Mary* was built on the East coast. Her builder, Harlan and Hollingsworth Company of Wilmington, Delaware, built the SS *Mary* for Charles Morgan of New York in 1866, but she had been "rebuilt and readmeasured" prior to 1872 and registered in New Orleans that year. Records describe the vessel as having a plain head (simple pointed bow), rounded stern, one deck, and two masts. In this regard, the SS *Mary* was rather typical of the steamships serving the Texas coast. Despite her 234-foot length, she drew only 9.3 feet of water, a decided advantage in the shoal waters off the Texas coast. Divers have found that the wreckage is slowly sliding down the slope of the channel side, that the stern of the vessel is demolished, and that the exposed wreckage of the SS *Mary* is in very poor condition. Nevertheless, because approximately 170 feet of the hull remains, and more wreckage may be present under the clay at the bottom of the wreck site, the SS *Mary* site has been listed on the National Register of Historic Places.[18] The wreck of the SS *Mary* has now been interpreted by two professional

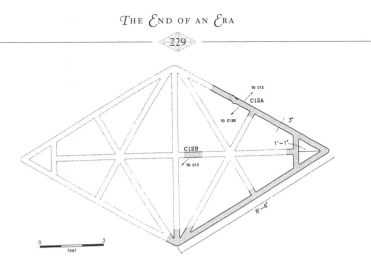

FIGURE 8-4
Underwater archaeologists located a portion of the walking-beam of the
SS Mary *and completed this drawing of a reconstruction of that important part of*
the vessel's steam mechanism. Reproduced from Charles E. Pearson and Joe J.
Simmons, Underwater Archaeology of the Wreck of the Steamship Mary, *p. 121;*
courtesy Coastal Environments, Inc., Baton Rouge, Louisiana.

marine archaeology firms, and it has yielded a tremendous amount of information about vessels of the era. The recovery of portions of the walking-beam mechanism of the SS *Mary* enabled archaeologists to reconstruct its appearance (Fig. 8-4).

PROPELLERS AND SQUARE RIGGERS

By the time the *Mary* sank, propeller ships were recognized as superior. In 1871, C. H. Mallory & Company began operating larger vessels, including the *Ariadne*, the *City of Galveston*, and, later, the *City of Houston*. By November 1, 1873, the steamer *City of Waco* was added to Mallory's New York and Galveston line. The *Nautical Gazette* notes that she was an iron screw steamer of about 1,700 tons, and was 245 feet in length, with a depth of 20 feet, the hull being covered with "Tibbal's Indestructible Composition." According to contemporary reports, "the main salon presents a bright and cheerful appearance. The joiner work, finished in French polish, is composed of maple stiles and rails, mahogany moulding, and panels of California redwood, burl, and French walnut."[19] But it was the thirteen-foot bronze propellers of the *City of Waco* that excited much interest and wonder. The term "screw ship" is often heard in the late nineteenth century as a way of differentiating a propeller-driven steamship from a sidewheeler. The term *screw* is indeed appropriate, for the propeller is based on the principle of the screw and the thrust with which its spiral motion forces the screw forward. One of the first vessels to effectively use a propeller in service was the British steamer *Archimedes*, launched in 1838 and aptly named for the ancient Greek scientist who first recognized the utility of the rotating screw. When attached to the drive shaft of a vessel, and modified to consist of two or more blades (usually three or four) that reproduce a part of the efficient screw design, the propeller is highly efficient. The propeller is also much stronger than a paddle wheel (for it can be cast in one piece) and much lighter. Because the propeller is mounted entirely *below* the water, and because it is placed toward the rear of the ship, it is much less prone to damage.

The arrival of new propeller-driven steamships on the Texas coast was a reflection of the state's growing economic power and coincided with the development of the state's interior. In 1867 Charles Morgan contracted with a major South Texas packer, W. S. Hall, and the stockmen Johns M. Thomas and Henry Mathis, to carry a thousand dollars worth of hides and tallow every ten days from the newly founded town of Rockport, in which Morgan constructed warehouses and cattle pens.[20] Rockport thus found itself directly connected to New Orleans by the steamships of the Morgan Lines, two of which each week connected the two port cities.

It was these numerous, flourishing ports that attracted sailing vessels and steamships from various ports of the world. Although steamships were being improved, one might also call the late nineteenth century the golden age of sail. A diversity of sailing craft plied the waters of the Texas coast, but few have attracted more attention than the square riggers, such as the *Elissa* (Figs. 8-5 and 8-6), which is anchored at Galveston. The *Elissa* was launched on October 27, 1877, from the shipyard of Alexander Hall in Aberdeen, Scotland, and sailed for twenty years as a British merchant ship. She is a typical example of a barque—a three-masted sailing vessel square-rigged on fore and main masts, and fore- and aft-rigged on the mizzen. The *Elissa* is 202 feet in overall length, her deck being 149.5 feet. Her beam is 28 feet and she draws 16 feet of water. Although her metal hull and more modest sail area remove the *Elissa* from the category of the true wooden clipper developed somewhat earlier in the nineteenth century, she represents a number of the technological improvements of the late nineteenth century that were sweeping the maritime trade and, indeed, all transportation. Iron hulls like *Elissa*'s were safer and stronger, and hence able to haul larger and heavier cargoes. The *Elissa*'s gross tonnage is listed as 430 tons, which represented a typical displacement for a ship of moderate size during this period.

FIGURE 8-5

A diversity of sailing craft plied the waters of the Texas coast, but few have attracted more attention than the square rigger Elissa, an 1877 iron-hulled barque. Saved from near destruction by scrappers and restored, Elissa now calls Galveston home port. Courtesy Galveston Historical Foundation and Texas Seaport Museum, Galveston.

FIGURE 8-6

Plans of the Elissa show more clearly the vessel's barque (or bark) rigging. Courtesy Galveston Historical Foundation and Texas Seaport Museum, Galveston.

ELISSA

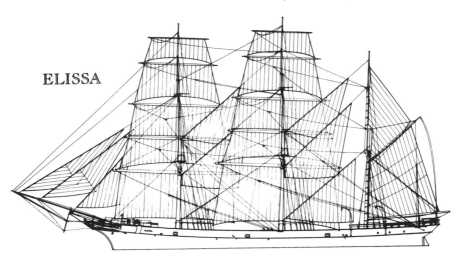

In about 1880, the barque rigging became common on medium-sized sailing ships. Probably evolved from the schooner rig, the barque produced "a combination of the advantages of the three- or four-masted schooner and the square rigger."[21] In some ways, the *Elissa's* barque configuration epitomizes the nearly constant search for speed and stability on the high seas, and it is a compromise between square and triangular sail shaping (and positioning) that began with the *caravela redonda* rigging configurations at the dawn of the age of exploration. Rather than thinking of the *Elissa* as a thoroughbred packet, we might properly place her in the category of workhorse; beautiful she is, but, like most vessels, her ultimate purpose is to carry cargo from one port to another as efficiently as possible. By the time *Elissa* was built, the days of sail were nearing an end.

A study of the index of vessels licensed at Galveston from 1868 to 1883 shows the improvement in technology as steel hulls began to replace iron. An otherwise unremarkable entry for July 2, 1882, shows the registry of the steamer *Aransas*, which had originally been registered at New Orleans but was now registered in Texas. At 1,156 tons, the *Aransas* dwarfed most other vessels in the harbor and epitomized the modern steamship, whose profile thereafter changed little for more than a half century. The maritime historian James Baughman notes that the *Aransas* was "a shallow draft ship designed for the shallow approaches to Rockport and Corpus Christi,"[22] and in this regard we can consider her a remarkable adaptation to the environment of the Texas coast.

In addition to her iron hull, the *Aransas* featured a number of mid-nineteenth-century developments, or rather improvements, that made her faster, safer, more efficient, and more dependable than her sidewheel predecessors. Propeller-driven steamships were easily recognized from any angle by their lack of paddle wheels, which gave their profiles a sleeker look and considerably reduced the width of the ship with the elimination of the bulging paddle wheel housings amidships. A painting of the propeller-driven *Aransas* (Fig. 8-7) reveals a glimpse of the future; the vessel's smooth, streamlined hull, simplified superstructure, and raked or tilted smokestack portend the "ocean liners" that later dominated international travel until the development of dependable airliners in the late 1940s and early 1950s. The *Aransas* was built in 1878 by Harlan & Hollingsworth for the Morgan Line; she was 240 feet in length, 35.6 feet wide, and had a hull 18.6 feet deep. The *Aransas* displaced 1,157 tons. Only the vestigial masts on the *Aransas* tell us she is a nineteenth-century ship, for otherwise she fits the picture of an early twentieth-century liner. Down in the hulls of the more advanced steam-

FIGURE 8-7
Painting of the propeller-driven Aransas *by William L. Challoner revealing a glimpse of the future. The ship's smooth streamlined hull, simplified superstructure, and raked or tilted smokestack portend the "ocean liners" that would dominate international travel for another sixty years. Courtesy Mariners' Museum, Newport News, Virginia.*

ships of the era, triple expansion boilers made more efficient use of the steam produced, effectively increasing the speed and the range of ships between fueling.

The *Aransas* is similar in overall appearance to a vessel built ten years later, the Mallory Lines' *Nueces* (Fig. 8-8), although the later vessel is much larger. Records show the *Nueces* to be an iron-hulled screw-driven steamship built in 1887 by the Delaware River Iron Shipbuilding & Engine Works for C. H. Mallory. However, the *Nueces* was 328 feet long and 44 feet wide, and her hull was 21.2 feet. At 2,465 net tons, the *Nueces* was fully one-third larger than the *Aransas* of a decade earlier. As was typical during this time period, the builders of these vessels hired model-makers who constructed beautiful wooden half-hull models that both enabled prospective ship

FIGURE 8-8
The Mallory Lines Nueces, *as shown in an 1887 photograph.*
Courtesy Peabody Essex Museum, Salem, Massachusetts.

buyers to better envision the form of the vessel and served as guidance to those who fabricated the full-scale vessel.

Improvements in ship design were often advertised, for the public was growing increasingly concerned about speed and safety. Words such as "indestructible" and "fireproof" were intended to reassure the public, but they usually were more fancy than fact. For example, the *City of Waco*, which was claimed on October 27, 1875, to be "as good and seaworthy as the day she was launched," met with disaster less than two weeks later (November 8, 1875) outside the bar at Galveston. Despite her being outfitted with "Gardener's Fire Extinguishers . . . placed throughout the ship, in addition to steam pumps and hoses," the steamship burned furiously, with the loss of all seventeen passengers and thirty-two crew members.[23] Advances in technology could go only so far in protecting passengers from the hazards of maritime travel.

Although this era also is associated with ever sleeker steamships, it marked a high point for the tall, square-rigged sailing vessels, as represented by the magnificent bark *Elissa*—which sailed into Galveston on at least two occasions, in 1883 and 1886. It also witnessed sustained technological improvements to maritime shipping, among them refrigerated steamships, originally pioneered in the early 1870s by Charles Morgan. His refrigerated steamship *Agnes* proved that Texas meats and food products could be shipped effectively but lasted only two years in such service before falling victim to financial difficulties and competition. Within the next two decades the railroad refrigerator car would prove too much competition, for the railroads were able to guarantee that Texas products could reach eastern markets in considerably less time than aboard ships—ideally three days versus about ten.

While the virtual explosion of railroad development in relation to the Texas ports during the late nineteenth century is outside the scope of this work, it requires summarizing here. The 1875 issue of Bryant's *Texas Railroad Guide* shows much of the Texas coast connected to the cities of the interior (Fig. 8-9). The records of railroad construction from 1865 to century's end reveal a litany of no fewer than sixteen railroads having Texas ports in their corporate titles, including: the Galveston & Houston Junction (1865);

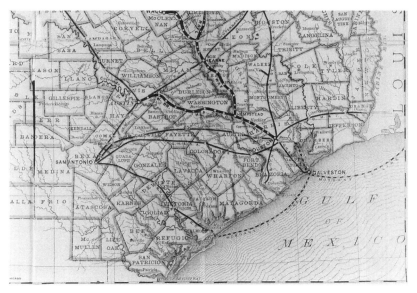

FIGURE 8-9

A map from Bryant's Texas Railroad Guide (1875) shows an elaborate network of rail lines reaching into the interior from the coast; the steamship lines of the Morgan interests also are shown connecting Indianola and Galveston with New Orleans. Courtesy Special Collections Division, The University of Texas at Arlington Libraries, Arlington, Texas.

FIGURE 8-10
*The Mallory Line advertisement from the 1878–1879 Texas Business Directory
claims rapid delivery for freight, but it ironically used what was rapidly becoming
an obsolete type of vessel, the sidewheel steamship, to do so. Courtesy Special
Collections Division, The University of Texas at Arlington Libraries.*

Indianola Railroad (1870); Gulf, Western Texas & Pacific (1873); Galveston, Harrisburg & San Antonio (1874); Galveston, Brazos & Colorado Narrow Gauge (1876); Gulf, Colorado & Santa Fe (1877); Corpus Christi, San Diego & Rio Grande (1878); Brownsville & Gulf (1883); San Antonio & Aransas Pass (1885); North Galveston, Houston & Kansas City (1893); South Galveston & Gulf Shore (1893); Gulf, Beaumont & Kansas City (1894); Gulf & Interstate of Texas (1895); Aransas Harbor Terminal (1896); Sabine Pass, Alexandria & Northwestern (1896); Beaumont Wharf & Terminal (1900), and Gulf & Brazos Valley (1900).[24] By acquisition, major systems such as the Southern Pacific (through its Texas subsidiary the Texas & New Orleans) and the Santa Fe reached the Texas ports during this period.

In the late nineteenth century, passenger ship schedules and railroad passenger service were coordinated, but freight shipments dominated the revenues; railroads usually reached the ships via piers or wharves. Despite their making connections, however, railroads and the steamship lines were often in direct competition on the longer routes; thus, an advertisement by the Mallory Line in the *Texas Business Directory for 1878–1879* touted the line's ability in the Galveston-to-New York trade, optimistically stating that "freight reaches New York as quickly as if carried by rail."[25] Interestingly, in this advertisement (Fig. 8-10) an increasingly obsolete sidewheel steamship is shown moving swiftly on the high seas, with the reassuring words that "the benefits arising from a sea voyage, particularly to those long resident in the interior, are too well known to be stated here."[26] In point of fact, improved railroad transportation was becoming increasingly attractive to all residents, whether from the interior or not, and the ports of Texas felt its impact.

TEXAS PORTS: GROWTH AND NAVIGATION

Yet Texas ports continued to boom during this period. Even in the smaller ports, infrastructural developments began to keep pace with changes in maritime technology. The Morgan steamship *Gussie* was the first steamship to enter Corpus Christi, on May 31, 1874, by way of the newly dredged Morris and Cummings eight-foot channel between Aransas and Corpus Christi—an event, according to one local historian, that the city had awaited for nearly twenty years.[27] Records in the Mariners' Museum show the *Gussie* to have been an iron-hulled sidewheeler built by Harlan & Hollingsworth in 1872; she was 222 feet in length, 33 feet wide, had a 19-foot hull depth, and displaced 998 tons.[28] With the dredging of the channel and subsequent arrival of such large vessels, Corpus Christi's future as a major port was secure, yet several more years would elapse before the largest ships could safely enter the harbor.

A bird's-eye view of Corpus Christi in 1887 (Fig. 8-11) provides a glimpse into the bustling activity of a small Texas port in the latter part of the nineteenth century and also underscores the relationship between maritime and railroad shipping. Done on commission, these bird's-eye views are executed as if the artist were on a very high vantage point, or perhaps flying, above the harbor. Note that this view shows the piers erected into the harbor, and most of these wooden piers are served by railroad tracks. The ships and boats are especially representative of the period: The artist has been careful to identify the Morgan Line's steamer *Aransas*, which is docked at the pier, while numerous schooners and sloops, unnamed by the artist, glide along or rest at anchor in the harbor. Despite the commentary about the big steam-powered vessels which were introduced during the period, most of the smaller vessels depicted could easily have been in service twenty years earlier. Note that sailing vessels and boats greatly outnumber steam—by nearly 15 to 1—in this view, a condition that indicates Corpus Christi was not yet as important a port as Galveston.

As maritime traffic along the Texas coast increased in the late nineteenth century, so, too, did the potential for collisions with other vessels, especially at night and in foggy weather. As part of a developing set of maritime standards that ensured better, safer navigation, ships of the period now featured standard running lights that warned other sailors of a vessel's position and direction, the latter indicated by a red light at the port (left) side and a green light at starboard (right).[29] Mariners could now tell whether another vessel was headed toward them or across their path by a simple determination of the position of running lights. This system became essential as port and coastal traffic increased and as steam power brought with it faster and larger vessels capable of inflicting tremendous damage in collisions.

Increases in maritime traffic also demanded that better navigational aids be used to mark channels through which ships of deeper draft could pass—channels that, if strayed from, would result in disaster or at least major inconvenience. Buoys were used from the beginning of regular navigation in Texas earlier in the nineteenth century, but by the late nineteenth century their design became standardized and they were used to mark the channels at entrances to all Texas ports. Anchored to the bottom by cables, buoys are, in effect, stationary floating signs that guide mariners through hazardous areas by indicating which side of the buoy should be passed. Mariners in

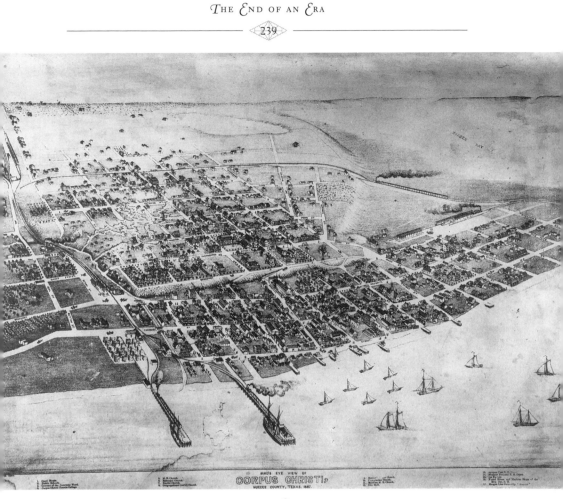

FIGURE 8-11

A bird's-eye view of Corpus Christi, Nueces County, in 1887 provides a glimpse into the bustling activity of a small Texas port in the latter nineteenth century and also underscores the relationship between maritime and railroad shipping. The Morgan Line's steamship Aransas *is docked at the pier. Courtesy Special Collections & Archives Department, Texas A&M University–Corpus Christi, Bell Library.*

the late nineteenth century used the buoy's painted sign pattern by day, and illuminated lenses at night, to steer into safe passages and avoid hazards—a system that persists to this day.

By the 1880s and 1890s, all major Texas harbors were actively engaged in dredging, which deepened harbors and in effect opened them up to larger vessels. A close reading of the March 17, 1892, issue of the *Aransas Harbor Herald* is instructive, for it documents a dredge in operation. The steamer

FIGURE 8-12
A drawing in the special "Texas" issue of Frank Leslie's Illustrated Newspaper *in October of 1890 shows the plan of the contemplated terminal facilities of the New City of Aransas Harbor. Courtesy Special Collections Division, The University of Texas at Arlington Libraries, Arlington.*

Horatio was able to make "the first voyage ever undertaken by a heavy draught vessel through the new ship channel to the point where the dredge boat is working."[30] A considerable crowd had gathered to welcome the vessel. The dredges that they watched clear the way for deeper-draft vessels like the *Horatio* were most interesting: At the interface between nautical and mining technology, a dredge is a floating device that scrapes mud and sand from the depths, piling these waste materials elsewhere as it digs a deeper channel.

The 1890s were times of large-scale developments, some of which never got off the drawing board. In addition to harbor deepening, some visionaries revisited the old idea of developing an intracoastal waterway to, in effect, make possible coastwise maritime trade without ships having to enter the Gulf. Overcoming natural obstacles and local resistance, the railroad and port developer Arthur Stilwell (who had created Port Arthur in 1895) constructed a canal connecting Sabine Lake to the deep-water Gulf. Opened in 1899, this canal involved, like all major projects of the time, appropriated federal funding and assistance from the U.S. Army Corps of Engineers.

Engineering works of this type were harbingers of the Intracoastal Waterway of the twentieth century. Like most improvements of Texas waterways,
they were first envisioned by the enterprising transportation developers, who,
working in concert with land owners, constantly sought to "improve" the
maritime environment to stimulate the coastal and regional economy.

Emblematic of the aspirations of developers, the City of Aransas envisioned itself as a major harbor in the late nineteenth century. A drawing in
the special "Texas" issue of *Frank Leslie's Illustrated Newspaper* in October
of 1890 shows the plan of the contemplated terminal facilities of the New
City of Aransas Harbor (Fig. 8-12). Of special interest is the plan of the city:
a series of six rectangles, the center of each being the meeting point of
radiating streets, and a commodious harbor served by the trains of the San
Antonio & Aransas Pass Railroad, as well as numerous ship lines. The drawing is especially interesting to maritime historians, for it shows numerous
tugboats (or towboats) steaming around the harbor but what appear to be
only sailing vessels—mostly schooners—engaged in commerce. This illustration is a classic "bird's-eye view" that provides a perspective that implies a
sense of order and control, a common technique of Victorian-era illustrators and promoters, who were attempting to generate a sense of confidence
that would, hopefully, be followed by investment.

By this time (1890) steamships were common along the Texas coast, and
the same issue of *Frank Leslie's Illustrated Newspaper* noted that "the Mallory
Line of to-day is comprised of ten iron steamships, all of modern build and
furnishing, and has a new steamer of about 3,000 tons burden in course of
construction." The article also noted that "the principal business of the line
is its Texas service, which during the winter months is made tri-weekly from
each port, and is immense in volume."[31] The reference to winter may puzzle
some readers, but during the nineteenth century ship service to Texas was
generally somewhat restricted in the summer months, and some reports
and publications note a virtual suspension of service in summer—a result,
perhaps, of both the stifling heat and the potential for dangerous tropical
storms and hurricanes.

This era of optimism witnessed the creation of several new ports with
grand ambitions, such as Portland, across the bay from Corpus Christi. As
to aspirations farther north along the Texas coast, a characteristically visionary bird's-eye illustration prepared in 1891 and entitled "Deep Water at Mouth
of Brazos River a Fact Not a Promise" reveals the significance of channel
modifications to promote deep-water traffic in hopes of creating a major
port. In this illustration, the old port city of Velasco, so important in the days

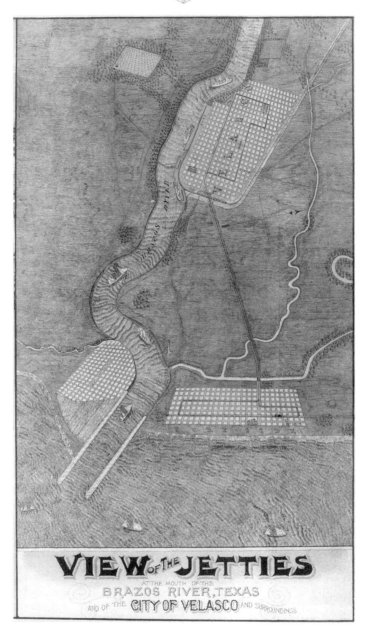

VIEW OF THE JETTIES
AT THE MOUTH OF THE
BRAZOS RIVER, TEXAS
AND OF THE CITY OF VELASCO AND SURROUNDINGS

FIGURE 8-13
*A bird's-eye illustration prepared in 1892 reveals the deepwater traffic aspirations
of Velasco developers at the time. Courtesy Special Collections Division,
The University of Texas at Arlington Libraries, Arlington.*

FIGURE 8-14

Photographs taken in Galveston during the last decade of the nineteenth century and in the early twentieth century reveal a busy port where rail cars lined sidings on the docks and large oceangoing steamers like the Teutonia *(carrying a Texas flag on her mast) loaded cargoes for distant ports. Photo courtesy Rosenberg Library, Galveston.*

of the Republic, is eclipsed by new developments, including two platted communities straddling a narrow but presumably deeply dredged channel. Lined by jetties and marked by lights or lighthouses, the channel connecting the Brazos River and the Gulf teems with maritime trade. In a similar vein, a lavishly illustrated brochure from 1892 (Fig. 8-13) unfolds to reveal spectacular drawings and maps of "Velasco. The First and Only Deepwater Port on the Coast of Texas. The Commercial Hope of the Trans-Mississippi."[32] This handsome brochure also features an optimistic view of the future harbor, complete with a small tugboat, the *Aruna*. Velasco became the dream of promoters who saw it usurping Galveston's place and, possibly, rising to replace the vanquished Indianola.

In reality, despite improvements to Velasco and other ports, Galveston was preeminent and would remain so until the century's end. Maritime

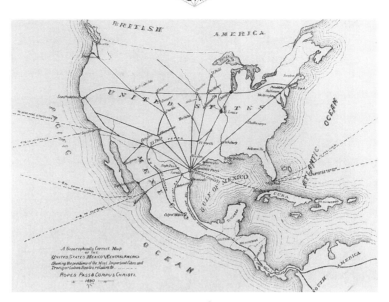

FIGURE 8-15

Map from Frank Leslie's Illustrated Newspaper *in 1890 showing Corpus Christi as*
the *most centrally located point on the North American continent. Courtesy Special
Collections Division, The University of Texas at Arlington Libraries, Arlington.*

traffic records, especially bills of lading for cargoes and passenger rosters of
liners, reveal Galveston to be the busiest port in Texas by century's end.
Historical photographs show rail sidings at the docks full of railroad cars,
and large, oceangoing steamers of many flags become common during this
period (Fig. 8-14). However, Galveston's supremacy did not stop other communities from vying aggressively for the position of premier Texas seaport
and may have even increased their ardor, for the prize—a booming regional
wheat, grain, and cotton-producing hinterland reaching as far inland as
Denver—was irresistible.[33] Instructive in this regard is a map from *Frank
Leslie's Illustrated Newspaper* in 1890 (Fig. 8-15) that shows Corpus Christi
as *the* most centrally located point on the North American continent!

Although one is tempted to dismiss such maps as the efforts of overzealous
boosters, they reveal the spirit of the era on the Texas coast. Competition
between Texas ports was so intense during this period that port developers
used any and all methods to promote their facilities. During the late nineteenth century, Texas ports lobbied for federal subsidies or private capital, and
sometimes both, to implement their dreams. While Velasco boasted that most
of its improvements were privately funded, three areas in particular—Gal-

veston, Aransas, and the mouth of the Brazos—sought inclusion in major congressional bills aimed at improving harbors. Through tactful arguments and effective lobbying, Galveston garnered the lion's share of this funding.

COASTWISE SHIPPING

Trade throughout the Gulf increased in the last third of the nineteenth century. In addition to the major ports of New Orleans, Mobile, and Pensacola to the east of Texas, the Mexican ports of Tampico, Tuxpan, and Veracruz also figure prominently in Texas maritime history. Like their U.S. counterparts, each of these Mexican ports served a hinterland, Veracruz being the largest and most important, as it has historically served as Mexico City's Gulf port since the 1500s. Tampico and Tuxpan have had a lively trade with various Texas ports, especially during the nineteenth century, as revealed in the ships registers. In 1883, the *Galveston Daily Record* noted: "Bananas for Sale; the British bark *Elissa* having just arrived from Tampico with a small cargo of choice bananas, the same will be sold at Labadie Wharf this day."[34]

Throughout the late nineteenth century, Texas ports continued to be engaged in active coastwise shipping trade, that is, shipping that connected the various ports along the coast with each other. For example, the smaller ports of Velasco and Lavaca often received cargo that had been off-loaded from larger, oceangoing vessels that called only at the major ports, such as Galveston. The maritime historian Eric Steinfeldt, of San Antonio, is currently compiling detailed records of the many sail-powered vessels involved in the coastwise trade. Typical of these was the schooner *Mary Lorena*, which was built at Cedar Bayou, Texas, in 1883, and spent much of her career transporting assorted cargoes, including lumber, in the coastwise trade. Interestingly, as steamships continued their ascendancy, schooners were placed in coastwise trade to haul coal to the fueling facilities where the steamers stopped.[35] Although some of this coal for steamers may have originated from the developing mines in Texas, much of it originated from as far away as Virginia. Steinfeldt has noted that large schooners handled much of this coal traffic (Fig. 8-16). There also existed a flourishing trade in cattle horns and bone that were shipped east for use as fertilizer.

THE RISE OF COMMERCIAL FISHING

By the late nineteenth century, the railroad lines that linked many larger Texas Gulf port communities with the rest of the nation helped ensure that products arriving from elsewhere through the Gulf coast ports could be shipped inland to cities such as St. Louis and Kansas City. Although oysters had been shipped to distant cities by rail from the Chesapeake Bay as early as the 1860s, their quality suffered after the long trips despite refrigeration. Concerned that East coast oysters were often dead — and thus less tasty — by the time they arrived at distant cities, the enterprising railroad builder Arthur E. Stilwell of the Kansas City, Pittsburgh & Gulf Railroad[36] saw an opportunity for Texas to enter the oyster-shipping trade. In 1897 the Pullman Company of Chicago built a special "Stilwell Oyster Car" for Stilwell's Port Arthur route. The railroad historian John White Jr. describes the process by which the oysters were shipped to meet the sophisticated tastes of Kansas Citians:

> Gulf oysters and salt water from Port Arthur, Texas, were loaded into round hatches on top of the rectangular tank. They were unloaded through side hatches upon arrival in Kansas City. Ice was added during hot weather to hold temperature levels agreeable to the mollusks as they rattled through midwestern communities whose corn- and beef-eating inhabitants could not be expected to understand the taste for so strange a dish as raw oysters.[37]

FIGURE 8-16
Toward the end of the nineteenth century, increasingly large schooners like the Eleanor F. Bartram, *some with as many as five masts, handled much of the coal traffic from the Chesapeake Bay ports to Texas. Photo, ca. 1900, by Paul Verkin, courtesy of and copyright by Eric Steinfeldt.*

But public tastes were indeed changing, for with refrigeration and rapid transportation fresh seafood products could now reach markets, and these developments would ultimately transform the Texas coast into a major producer of ocean fish and shellfish, including oysters and shrimp. Whereas the commercial fishing fleets prospered in the twentieth century, that prosperity had thus begun in the period after the Civil War.

The most definitive information on the subject is found in the *Report of the Commissioner* of the United States Commission of Fish and Fisheries for 1889 to 1891.[38] The investigation of the U.S. Fish Commission in 1880 had revealed that 601 men were employed in the fisheries of Texas; by 1890 the figure had doubled to 1,277. Likewise the volume and value of fish had essentially doubled during that decade, from 3,858,875 pounds and $128,300 in 1880, to 7,961,400 pounds and $313,912 in 1890.[39] Nevertheless, the report concluded that "on account of the incomplete transportation facilities, the difficulty of preserving fish in a warm climate for a considerable length of time, and the generally undeveloped condition of affairs on the coast, the fisheries of this State have not heretofore attracted great attention."[40] During the late nineteenth century, Texas fishing was dominated by bay seining (that is, net fishing) in either the sheltered waters of lagoons and bays or out on the Gulf. Second in importance was the oyster industry, which, observers prophetically noted, "will doubtless rank first within a few years."[41] Additionally, each locality had its own minor fisheries, such as turtle, crab, and shrimp, and in some locations surf-seining and hook-and-line fishing were practiced.

Who, one might ask, were these fishermen who worked the Texas coast in the 1890s? The U.S. Commissioner's report cited above noted that "only a small portion of the Texas fishermen were born in America; they are chiefly natives of Italy, Sicily, Greece, Austria, and Mexico" who, "as a class . . . are independent in their manners and habits, but are nearly always poor and unthrifty."[42] The report also noted that "the negroes along the coast do not engage in fishing, except in a small way from the wharves with cast nets, lines, etc."[43] This implies the same social stratification on the Texas coast that prevailed elsewhere. Fishermen were likely close-knit, clannish, relatively poor, traditional in their views, and defensive about their territories.

This report contains an interesting reference to fishing craft, noting that "along the Texas coast the expression 'boat' is applied to all sail craft, while the word 'skiff' is used to designate something propelled by oars."[44] It further states that "the construction and the rig of the sailboats do not materially differ from the styles in general use along the coasts of the middle and

New England States," and that "in order to easily pass through the shoal waters of these bays, these boats are built very shallow, having either a flat or round knuckle (one-half flat) bottom," the boats being "usually from 22 to 34 feet long, from 8 to 12 feet wide, and from 1 1/2 to 3 feet deep."[45] These sailboats were built without elaborate finish and were decked over fore and aft, frequently for their entire length; all had a cabin that served as a sleeping room. These fishing sailboats did not have "wells" in which live fish were kept; rather what were called "cars" (small craft roughly constructed of slats and about the size of a skiff) were hauled aboard the boats to the fishing locations, and towed behind the fishing boats when full. The Texas scow sloops discussed in Chapter 6 became very common by the late nineteenth century, and were a mainstay of the fishing industry in the lagoons.

Life on a fishing trip was described as "rough" for the crew, which usually consisted of two to four men who slept on the hard floor of the cabin, with a blanket over it serving as a bed. The cabin floor also served as a table from which provisions of salt meat, bread, hard tack, onions and garlic, potatoes, and coffee were served. Cooking was done on a small open stove or by an open fire in a pot.[46] Fishermen of the Texas coast usually went out for several days at a time. Their main catch consisted of redfish, sea trout, and sheepshead; redfish was preferred for shipping owing to its better ability to travel and its popularity, even though sea trout was considered the finest of these fish. Interestingly, it was noted that only at Galveston did the demand for fish sometimes outstrip the supply, while in Matagorda, Aransas, and Corpus Christi bays, and at Point Isabel many of the crews were idle for several days "on account of an oversupplied market."[47]

The outfit used for "grubbing oysters," a local expression then in use for oyster fishing, usually consisted of one sailboat, one or two skiffs, and appropriate equipment, such as tongs, baskets, and small hammers to separate the clusters of oysters. By 1890, a total of 189 sailboats and 268 skiffs were used to grub oysters in the waters off Texas.[48] The boats and skiffs in oyster fishing differed little from those used for regular fishing. As oyster reefs were aggressively exploited in the 1870s, laws were passed in 1879 prohibiting them from being collected or caught "from the 1st of May to the 1st of September in any year."[49] Texas's first oyster law was passed on March 8, 1879, when "An Act for the Preservation of oysters and oyster beds . . ." provided for both public and private oyster grounds, but made all natural oyster beds in navigable waters public, and all grounds in waters not navigable the exclusive property of the owners of the adjoining shores.[50] Nevertheless, with technological improvements, including the employment of experimental

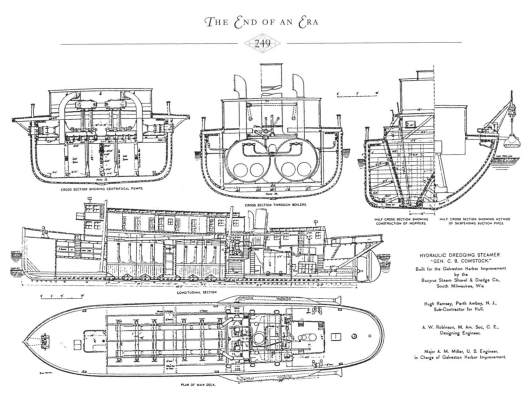

FIGURE 8-17

Plans of this dredge Gen. C. B. Comstock *reveal that it had hoppers into which
the dredged material, such as mud and sand, was placed until it could be
dumped elsewhere by the opening of the hopper hatches or doors.
Reproduced from* Engineering News, *1895.*

dredging of oyster beds by the schooner *Highland* off Corpus Christi in
1890–1891, the oyster catch continued to increase.

Regardless of its impact on oyster beds in areas close to navigation, dredging continued at a furious pace in the latter part of the nineteenth century.
In 1895 the *Gen. C. B. Comstock* was built for the U.S. Corps of Engineers
under a contract let to Bucyrus Steam Shovel and Dredge Company of
Milwaukee, Wisconsin; the copper-sheathed wooden hull of the dredge was
built by Hugh Ramsay of Perth Amboy, New Jersey. The *Gen. C. B. Comstock*
was delivered at Galveston on August 31, 1895, where she began a ten-day
trial period.[51] She was 177 feet in length, had a beam of 35 1/2 feet, drew
12 feet of water, and displaced 1,650 tons. A steam engine located toward the
stern propelled the dredge, and its pumping engines, located farther forward, powered the dredging equipment. Plans of this dredge (Fig. 8-17) reveal that it had hoppers into which the dredged material was placed until it
could be dumped elsewhere by the opening of the hopper hatches. The

Gen. C. B. Comstock operated much as bottom fish, by churning and suck-
ing up sediments as it slowly moved along the harbors and channels, dredging up sediment for the completion of the jetties. Thanks largely to the work
of "mudhens" like the dredge *Gen. C. B. Comstock*, Captain Ahm could
report in 1897 that "wrecks were [once] very frequent," but "have been reduced," so that "unless there is mismanagement a vessel can now come
safely into the river."[52] Records show that the dredge continued to work on
many Texas coast projects until well into the twentieth century, but ironically the *Gen. C. B. Comstock* herself came to grief in 1913, burning to the
waterline while working to improve conditions in the vicinity of Freeport.

𝒯EXAS 𝒭IVERBOATS IN THE 𝓛ATE 𝒩INETEENTH 𝒞ENTURY

Meanwhile, transportation developments were taking place on the rivers of
Texas. The steamboats that had proven their worth on Texas rivers throughout much of the nineteenth century had opened the lower reaches to nautical navigation, and in so doing enabled the crops of farmers to reach wider
markets. By the 1880s, however, the developing network of railroads helped
precipitate the decline of the riverboat, which lasted until around the turn
of the century in some places, including the lower Brazos and Sabine rivers.
And yet, despite the arrival of the railroad, some entrepreneurs persisted in
advocating river trade. As early as 1867, a scant five years before railroad
development in northeast Texas, citizens of Dallas and Kaufman Counties
offered a vessel named *Job Boat No. 1* a $15,000 bonus if it could reach the
then-aspiring community of Dallas. The sixty-foot-long sternwheeler had a
capacity of twenty-six tons but drew only three feet of water—a perfect can-
didate for the challenge of navigating what amounted to a virtually unnavi-
gable river. After seven grueling months, from October 1867 to May 1868,
Job Boat No. 1 finally reached Dallas.

And yet, as if this venture did not cast enough doubt on such enterprises,
a similar event was reenacted nearly thirty years later as the newly created
and optimistically named Trinity River Navigation and Improvement Company slowly cleared the river, using the appropriately named 64-foot
sternwheeler *Snagboat Dallas* (Fig. 8-18). Its way cleared, the 113-foot steamboat *H. A. Harvey* (Fig. 8-19) steamed from Galveston to Dallas on a trip
that took nearly two months and witnessed a continuous battle clearing logs
and, on one occasion, even bodily lifting a railroad bridge to enable the
vessel to pass beneath it![53] Despite, or perhaps because of, its arduous and
time-consuming journey, the *H. A. Harvey* drew a huge crowd when she

FIGURE 8-18
The appropriately named Snagboat Dallas *was photographed in the 1890s
while clearing snags from the Trinity River. Courtesy Dallas Historical Society,
Potter Collection.*

arrived in Dallas (Fig. 8-20). Although the *H. A. Harvey's* performance on
the Trinity River would seem to permanently doom navigation so far inland, it should be remembered that the disillusionment was only temporary, for the early twentieth century would witness a resurrection of plans to
open the Trinity to oceangoing vessels. The lure of developing certain Texas
rivers, like the Trinity, would outlast the nineteenth century, for in Texas
dreams of empire die hard. And yet, a crucial development occurred in
1890 that was a harbinger of future river development: the construction of
Texas's first major dam at Austin on the Colorado River. Texans would soon
value their rivers more for water and recreational resources than transportation corridors. This, and the potential for reducing floods by damming, ensured the demise of river traffic by the early to middle twentieth century.
Thus, many factors in addition to the railroads rendered the steam-powered
riverboat obsolete by about century's end.

FIGURE 8-19

The H. A. Harvey *poses beneath a Trinity River bridge ca. mid-1890s while a small group of onlookers gather on the bridge. Photo courtesy Dallas Historical Society, Potter Collection.*

FIGURE 8-20

The arrival of the steamboat H. A. Harvey *at Dallas on May 24, 1893, draws a huge crowd to witness the memorable event. Photographer's vantage point provides an excellent view of the sternwheel. Photo courtesy Dallas Historical Society.*

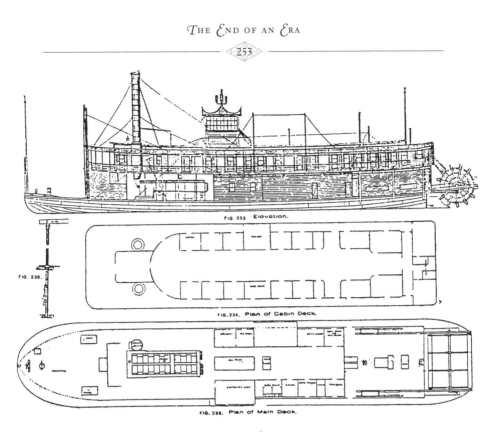

FIG. 233 Elevation.

FIG. 236.

FIG. 234. Plan of Cabin Deck.

FIG. 235. Plan of Main Deck.

FIGURE 8-21

*Plans of a small sternwheel steamer similar to the types of vessels seen on
Texas rivers in the latter nineteenth century. Reproduced from John Fehrenbatch,
A Library of Steam Engineering.*

Despite their obsolescence, the steam-powered riverboats of the late nineteenth century have earned a place in the state's maritime history. Of these rivergoing steamboats, the sternwheeler *Alice Blair* is typical. Built in 1891, she was about 110 feet in length and drew only about three feet of water, carrying an immense load of baled cotton in the process.[54] Steamboats like the *Alice Blair* often featured what appear to be large locomotive-style oil-fired headlamps, which made night travel easier and safer. By 1893 the *Neches Belle* steamboat sported an electric headlight,[55] but the steamboats by that time represented a vanishing form of technology and their crews a vanishing breed. The Texas riverboat historian W. T. Block noted that the lower Sabine River appears to have been the last Texas stronghold of the steamboat.[56] With their numerous decks and often ornate trim, they were symbols of late Victorian-era travel on the rivers of Texas that would soon come to an end (Fig. 8-21).

To many casual observers, steamboats seemed like floating hotels or palaces and, as noted earlier, some people thought ornate houses with galleries were reminiscent of steamboats. In an intriguing article entitled "Architecture's Debt to Transportation," the cultural geographer Fred Kniffen speculated nearly fifty years ago that the steamboat's ornate decks may have served as inspiration for the beautiful galleried porches and verandas on southern homes of the middle to late 1800s such as the steamboat house in Huntsville. In at least one case, riverboat architecture certainly did indeed inspire at least one ornate Texas building, albeit far from any navigable river. Constructed in the mid-1870s, in a style reminiscent of the multidecked ornate steamboats, the huge Nimitz "Steamboat Hotel" on Main Street in Fredericksburg is an important—if somewhat eccentric—landmark that has a double connection with the state's maritime history; Chester Nimitz, who became Fleet Admiral in World War II, was born in Fredericksburg shortly after his uncle constructed this unique riverboat-themed hotel (Fig. 8-22).

FIGURE 8-22

The ornate Victorian-era "Steamboat Hotel" on Main Street of Fredericksburg, became a prominent landmark in the 1870s when Chester Nimitz's uncle remodeled an earlier hotel using this riverboat theme. The Steamboat Hotel now houses the Admiral Nimitz State Historic Site and Museum. Photo courtesy Admiral Nimitz Museum, Fredericksburg, Texas, 1996.

FIGURE 8-23

A remarkable photograph taken ca. 1885–1887 in the harbor at the port of Orange reveals six small vessels — a sloop, two steam-powered launches, and three tugboats posed for the photographer. Note the locomotive-style headlights on the two tugboats, the diminutive size of the two steam launches, and the docking facilities behind these vessels. Courtesy Howard C. Williams, Orange, Texas.

CORNUCOPIA: VESSELS AND PORTS AT CENTURY'S END

In the late nineteenth century, the port of Orange on the Sabine began its rise as a shipbuilding center. Samuel H. Levingston continued building paddle wheel steamboats until 1893, when his son George took over the management of the enterprise. By the end of the 1890s, George Levingston acquired an interest in Joseph Weaver and Son shipbuilders and built barges for the Galveston Navigation District; thus, Orange in the nineteenth century was the site of shipbuilders who constructed river steamboats (probably all sternwheelers) and small sailing craft, but these activities would set the scene for Orange to become a major shipbuilding community in the twentieth century.[57] A remarkable photograph of six small vessels tied up abreast at the pier in front of the Ocheltree House in the port of Orange reveals something of the diversity of vessels (Fig. 8-23). Similarly, an 1895–1896 photo of the wharf at Houston shows several sloops and barges lining the wharf

FIGURE 8-24

*Wharf scene at Houston in the winter of 1895–1896 shows several sloops and barges—
mundane and unsung vessels that were extremely important in Texas maritime trade
at the century's end. Henry Stark photo, courtesy Dallas Historical Society.*

FIGURE 8-25

*Toward the end of the century, a photographer in Galveston recorded this scene
of a two-masted schooner loaded with barrels and other cargo. Other small sailing
vessels cram the docks, and a sternwheel steamboat is seen in the background.
Courtesy Rosenberg Library, Galveston, Texas.*

FIGURE 8-26

The Stella, *a tugboat photographed at Sabine Pass in May 1898, was typical of the larger tugs seen in Texas harbors at century's end. Note the cannons (on railroad cars at right) destined for service in the Spanish-American War. Courtesy Museum of the Gulf, Port Arthur, Texas.*

(Fig. 8-24). In Galveston, a photograph recorded a schooner and other small sailing vessels moored near a sternwheeler riverboat (Fig. 8-25).

In the latter years of the nineteenth century, tugboats and towboats abounded in Texas harbors, where they served many important tasks, including hauling barges and scows. As immortalized in a painting by the noted Texas maritime artist Julius Stockfleth, the *Charlotte M. Allen* was representative of the medium-sized towboats. Built at Clear Creek, Texas, in 1894, she measured 85 feet 7 inches in length, had a beam of 14 feet and a draft of 4 feet. The *Charlotte M. Allen's* career was played out in Galveston Harbor, where she embarked passengers from the Beaumont-Galveston train at Point Bolivar. She is reported to have side-towed a train barge from Bolivar into Galveston.[58] Another towboat (the *J. W. Terry*) later did that work in the Galveston Bay and bore the markings of the Santa Fe Railroad[59]—a testimony to the intricate relationship between maritime and railroad operations on the Texas coast. Tugboats and towboats were designed to be the workhorses of the harbor, often serving the same purpose that switch engines served in railroad yards. For much the same reason, tugboats and towboats were rarely photographed, although a typical tugboat, *Stella*, was photographed at Sabine Pass at century's end with her crew aboard (Fig. 8-26),

FIGURE 8-27

In this P. H. Rose stereopticon photograph, ca. 1890, a tugboat stands moored at the Galveston docks while the masts of schooners and other sailing vessels loom in the background. Courtesy Rosenberg Library, Galveston.

and a rare stereopticon image of a tugboat photographed more or less by accident next to other vessels in the harbor at Galveston has preserved a typical harbor vignette for posterity (Fig. 8-27).

The late nineteenth century brought with it many changes. Whereas about twenty-five years earlier (ca. 1875) one could realistically expect only about one in ten vessels in any particular Texas harbor to be steam-powered, by century's end the steamers now dominated. Their supremacy was assured by a steady supply of high-quality coal that arrived on the coal-carrying vessels mentioned earlier. By the 1890s a new form of power for vessels, the gasoline engine (variously called "vapor" or "naphtha" engines), appeared. Vapor engines powered smaller vessels such as launches and small riverboats, but after the turn of the century internal combustion would further revolutionize maritime transportation. Late-nineteenth-century photographs show the larger Texas ports, such as Galveston, Port Arthur, and Rockport, to be cluttered with a diversity of vessels with registry from many of the world's ports. To this one could add an ever growing number of small pleasure craft, including a few sleek, steam-powered yachts. As leisure time and excess capital became available, pleasure boats could be found in most Texas ports. A rare photograph of the Texas State Cup Sailboat Race in Aransas Bay in 1893 conveys the sense of exhilaration provided by fast pleasure craft (Fig. 8-28)—harbingers of the sail-powered pleasure craft that abound in Texas harbors today. At the same time, fishing boats and a wide range of shrimping/shellfishing craft also appeared as the commercial fishing economy began to grow rapidly and further differentiate itself into two separate cultures and economies: one based on the resources of the lagoons and embayments, the other on the open waters of the Gulf.[60]

FIGURE 8-28
A rare photo of the Texas State Cup Sailboat Race on Aransas Bay shows Jed Bludworth taking in the outer jib as the racing sloop Novice *crosses the finish line in July of 1893. Built at the Bludworth boatyard, the* Novice *featured an exaggerated sail plan and sharp lines, and was well known as the fastest vessel on the bay. Courtesy Texas Maritime Museum, Rockport.*

The vessels that one saw in the Texas harbors in 1900 were the result of incredible changes that transformed maritime commerce. The historian Michael Marshall noted that "the nineteenth century saw the greatest, most rapid shipping revolution the world has seen," adding that "by the end of the century sails were replaced by steam engines, wind energy by coal, and wooden planks for timber frames by steel plates and girders."[61] This is something of a dramatic oversimplification, but it does convey the changes that were occurring. By the end of the century, the wooden schooners and square-rigged barks were still common, but passengers usually opted for the more dependable, and ultimately faster, propeller-driven, iron-hulled steamships, called "liners," operated by firms such as Morgan Line and Mallory Company. It was these large passenger and cargo-carrying steamships that shared space in Texas ports with a wide variety of sailing craft in the late nineteenth century. With the creation of Mallory's New York and Texas Steamship Lines in 1886, the Morgan Line steamers now faced a severe competition that culminated in shipping rate wars during that decade. These rate wars ensured that Texas ports, especially Galveston, would experience a thriving trade in goods and passengers in the later years of the century.

The vitality of Galveston's port is beautifully captured in early photographs and paintings and in the ships registers of the era. A study of the certificates of registry of vessels in Galveston toward the end of the nineteenth century tells the story of a busy seaport, with tugboats, barges, ships, schooners, barks, and screw-driven steamships listed. In just a few years, from 1897 to 1900, however, the certificates of registry reveal the continued decline of sail and the rise of steam. Whereas sailing vessels were still the majority of registries in 1897, the year 1900 witnessed about half and half sail to steam power. After 1900, steam power dominates (and barges proliferate), as seen in the table below:

TABLE 1
SHIP REGISTRIES IN GALVESTON, 1897–1910*

Type of Vessel	1897–1900	1900–1910
Steam	14	24
Sail	25	14
Other (barge)	1	16

* *Source*: Certificates of Registry Collector's Office, Galveston, Texas, 1897–1913. Prov. G-12, Fort Worth Records Center, The National Archives.

FIGURE 8-29

Docked bow to bow in Galveston in this dramatic ca. 1895 photograph, the steam-powered, iron-hulled John Bright *and the sail-powered barque* Bonita *provide a vivid contrast. Another sailing vessel and the huge grain elevator are seen in the background, and bales of cotton crowd the dock in the foreground.*
Courtesy Rosenberg Library, Galveston.

The vessel registries in Galveston, being most complete, simply confirm what one could see along the entire Texas coast. Here, as elsewhere, the industrial revolution had effected a revolution in maritime technology. The iron-hulled, propeller-driven steamships in the Galveston harbor dwarfed the smaller, but still effective, traditional craft, such as schooners, sloops, and barques, most of which would have not been out of place earlier in the century, but whose days were now certainly numbered. Photographs taken in the 1890s in Galveston's harbor show the contrast between steam and sail vessels that had taken place by century's end (Fig. 8-29).

THE CENTURY'S END IN GALVESTON

During the nineteenth century, Galveston's position as a major port was indisputable but constantly challenged by other ports, such as Rockport and the new Port Arthur. However, one city in particular—Houston—posed a serious threat. The inadequacies of Galveston's railroad connections were underscored by the incompatibility of the gauge of the Galveston, Houston & Henderson with other railroads serving Houston.[62] As early as 1869, Galveston's inability to connect with Houston had so irritated Charles Morgan that he formed the Ship Channel Company, which was chartered specifically to dredge an eight-foot-deep channel from Galveston to Houston via Buffalo Bayou. Texas transportation historians, including S. G. Reed, have noted that Charles Morgan was not the first to attempt the dredging of a channel connecting Houston with the head of navigation on Buffalo Bayou: The Direct Navigation Company and the Texas Transportation Company were organized for that purpose in 1866 by local entrepreneurs, giving rise to the first use of the term *ship channel*. And yet, the virtual failure of these efforts by 1873 found Morgan ready to pick up where they had left off: It was Morgan who would be credited with making the ship channel a reality. Stalled by the depression of 1874 and lack of public support, Morgan redoubled his efforts and contracted to construct a nine-foot channel at least 120 feet wide from Galveston Bay to Houston. By mid-1875 eight dredges, six tugs, and twelve derricks and barges were working around the clock, and on April 21, 1876, this engineering feat was completed. This, according to Charles Morgan's biographer, James Baughman, enabled the magnate to avoid "Galveston, its quarantines, its wharf company, and its railroad [and to proclaim that] 'Houston, not Galveston, is our terminus.' "[63]

Morgan's control of the Houston and Texas Central and the completion of the Southern Pacific through Houston from New Orleans to California further ensured Houston's rise as *the* major city of Southeast Texas, and the relative decline of Galveston, a process that was well under way at century's end. The Mallory Line and the Morgan Line worked closely with the Texas railroads—the former affiliated with the Missouri Pacific, Katy and Santa Fe, and the latter staunchly allied with the Southern Pacific's Texas and New Orleans Railroad. Thus, by the late 1890s, the Mallory Line and the Morgan Line maintained complete control of the Galveston–New York trade and rail connections in Texas. The Morgan Line's familiar blue burgee featured a white star in which a red letter *M* was positioned, a subliminal association of this steamship line with the Lone Star State. The smokestacks or funnels of the Morgan Lines Steamers also featured this familiar white star.

The control that the Morgan Line and Mallory Line exerted on trade to Texas was challenged only once between 1879 and 1902—by the Miami Steamship Company's so-called Lone Star Line, in 1897. This threat caused Mallory and Morgan to tighten their control by slashing rates; their affiliated railroad companies declined to honor through bills of lading and refused to form through rates. Infuriated, the Lone Star Line took the situation to the federal courts, which found in favor of the Mallory Line, an action that caused the fledgling competitor to withdraw its four steamships from the route in 1899.[64]

The steamship companies were an important force economically and socially in the Texas ports. Because Texas maritime history (like all maritime history) developed along the lines of the prevailing economy and society, it has been socially and ethnically stratified. Those in control of ships and shipping, that is captains and ship owners, were overwhelmingly white. However, as noted in the case of fishermen, peoples of many ethnic backgrounds played an important role in maritime commerce. African Americans, for example, worked in many roles, notably as cooks and sometimes as sailors, but they were especially visible in the backbreaking role of stevedores and longshoremen. Social change slowly crept into the Texas ports; in the second half of the nineteenth century, it was tied to the rise and development of organized labor: These changes are best seen in Galveston, where as early as the 1860s black longshoremen had joined with those in other trades to demand better pay and working conditions. The labor strikes of 1877 in Galveston further unified the black wharf workers, who toiled in ninety-nine-degree heat and the high humidity of the Gulf Coast summer.[65] By 1885 black and white union competition on the wharf of the Mallory Lines led to arbitration, which resulted in greater participation by blacks in organized labor[66]—a harbinger of the twentieth century. While the late 1890s witnessed the Mallory Line breaking strikes by hiring scab labor to replace black union members on barges from Houston to Galveston—an action that resulted in considerable violence—the labor organizations of the late nineteenth century on the Texas coast nevertheless helped set the scene for later developments. Although blacks had an important role on the Texas coast, as did Mexicans and Southern Europeans, their accomplishments, like those of all minorities, were often overshadowed by those of people in more glamorous or powerful positions. They left few written records, and their roles would be lost to history if only the writings of the wealthy elite were consulted in a maritime history. Recent scholarship suggests that African American crewmen may have been more common than popularly thought, their presence revealed by careful scrutiny of ships' lists—including New Orleans-bound vessels in the early to late nineteenth century.[67]

By the century's end, Galveston was the largest city on the coast, with almost 40,000 people, but Houston's population was growing about as rapidly because it had became a major rail center and had its own port facilities. Although Galveston served as Texas's major port, considerable trade moved inland towards Houston on barges and vessels of all types. And yet, in 1900, the year before the fabulous Spindletop would make oil a household word in Texas, Galveston sat like a pearl in an oyster shell; its harbor prospered, and its fresh sea breezes brought huge throngs of people by train to "the sea" to experience moderate temperatures and escape the otherwise daunting Texas summers.

Trade figures verified Galveston's growth and importance. From 1890 to 1895 shipments of cotton rose—in large part because of improved transportation connections—from about 1,000,000 bales to more than 1,500,000 per season despite the financial panic of 1893. The city had successfully lobbied for support of its inclusion into the Rivers and Harbors bill for the completion of jetties and dredging in 1890. Through the last decade of the nineteenth century, harbor improvements there seemed to assure that Galveston would remain preeminent in its access to the sea, as vessels drawing twenty-four feet of water could now enter the harbor. So, too, did the fact that Galveston had obtained better railroad connections by the late 1890s. Somewhat ominously and prophetically, however, the president of Southern Pacific Railroad, Collis P. Huntington, was reported in the *Galveston Daily News* to have opined that "the cities of the Gulf Coast have paid entirely too much attention to the water," adding that manufacturing rather than shipping should be their focus.[68]

The spring of 1900 witnessed a most remarkable maritime event that created quite a sensation locally and underscored Galveston's problems as a port. On March 26, the Mallory Line's Steamship *Lampasas* was driven aground near Grain Elevator A in Galveston harbor when a high wind called the "elevator puff" caught the crew unawares. The local press noted that the wind caught the *Lampasas*, which stood "well out of the water, and as her houses [were] above the spar deck she presented plenty of surface for the wind." So stuck did the *Lampasas* become that days of effort by four tugboats (Fig. 8-30) failed to budge her. The Galveston newspaper reported quite a crowd gathering and added that "the record of the event will be handed down to posterity in the shape of photographs from views taken by the Kodak Club yesterday afternoon."[69] Among the photographers present was the noted Paul Verkin, whose classic photo of the four tugs (*Seminole, Nimrod, Charles York*, and *Cynthia*) attempting to pull the *Lampasas* (whose propellers are seen churning the water in vain) did indeed immortalize the struggle. The liner's distress caused such concern that Charles Mallory him-

FIGURE 8-30

A spectacular action photograph, taken in Galveston's harbor in 1900, shows four tugboats (left to right, the Seminole, Nimrod, Charles York, *and* Cynthia) *attempting to free the stranded Mallory Line's* Lampasas *(right), whose propellers furiously churn the water in a futile effort to remove the big liner from a muddy shoal. Photograph by Paul Verkin, 1900; copyright Eric Steinfeldt, courtesy Eric Steinfeldt Collection.*

self arrived by April 1 to oversee the operation, which soon involved the Mallory liner *San Marcos* in attempting to pull the mired *Lampasas* out of her predicament, to no avail. Finally, on April 3, it was reported that the steamer *Nueces* "did the act" of smoothly extricating the *Lampasas* with no damage to either vessel. This embarrassing and costly event, estimated at $1,000 per day to the Mallory's New York & Texas Steamship Co. prompted the *Galveston Daily News* to opine that "the grounding of the Lampasas may be the occasion for especial pressure to be brought on congress for the deepening of the channel."[70] Had he been alive, Charles Morgan might have had the last laugh, for he had long advocated Houston as a better port for the larger ocean-going vessels that were forced to move about Galveston's harbor with such caution.

Despite these ongoing navigational difficulties, Galveston remained the major port in Texas at century's end. Few could have suspected, however, that Galveston's reign was about to end, for nature would soon deal a major blow—the now legendary Galveston Hurricane. That September 1900 hurricane ravaged the city, and made apparent Galveston's vulnerable position, which, as we have seen, perceptive travelers had commented on—even fore-warned Galvestonians about—since the community's inception. In the course of several hours on September 8 and 9, the powerful hurricane wreaked havoc on Galveston; the Gulf side of the island bore the brunt of winds and high seas that reduced houses to kindling and piled their re-mains many blocks from the coastal shore. Though located on the inland side of the island, Galveston's harbor, too, was wrecked; virtually every boat and ship was either damaged or destroyed. The death toll from the 1900 Galveston hurricane still staggers the imagination. A death toll of 6,000 being the commonly accepted figure, the Galveston hurricane remains the most deadly disaster in United States history. Although the story of Galveston's hurricane has been told and retold in considerable detail, it should be noted that this storm also ravaged other ports along this part of the coast. Velasco, which had only a decade before improved its harbor and welcomed ocean-going vessels, suffered major damage.

While the world read with near disbelief the stories of death and destruc-tion on the Texas coast in the vicinity of Galveston in 1900, events were under way that further shifted the balance of power to Houston. The ship channels that had been constructed in the late nineteenth century by Charles Morgan ensured that the queen city of Galveston would be eclipsed as a port and that Houston would become Texas's preeminent port in the twen-tieth century. Houston aggressively lobbied for major improvements that would find it becoming Texas's major port after about 1920. Also in Houston's favor was that city's closer proximity to the Spindletop oil fields, which would boom after 1901. That oil boom, interestingly, increased the value of vessels that could haul oil as cargo—a situation that led to the development or conversion of large, multimasted schooners in the oil trade and ultimately to the use of oil for fuel in steamships in the twentieth century. Until well into the 1910s, large wooden vessels, including schooners and barques, were built at Orange as a result of the booming regional oil-based economy of Southeast Texas. These developments further shifted the focus of maritime activity away from Galveston.

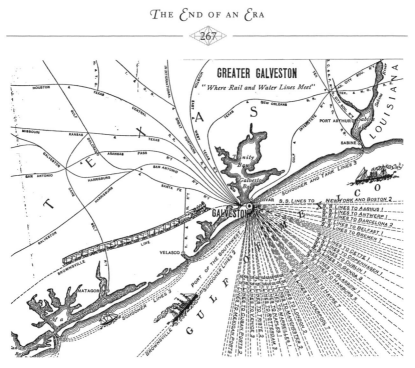

FIGURE 8-31

In the early twentieth century, the Galveston Chamber of Commerce used this map on the verso of their stationery, as evidenced on a letter, dated February 13, 1908, sent to B. B. Paddock of Fort Worth. In reality Houston, which is not even shown on this map, could more accurately claim to be situated "Where Rail and Water Lines Meet." Courtesy Center for American History, The University of Texas at Austin; Paddock Papers Collection.

Thus, although Galveston rebuilt behind a sea wall that offered considerably more protection from hurricanes, the city never recovered its former position as the most populous city on the Texas Gulf coast following the hurricane of 1900. With the site of Galveston now regarded with apprehension, other port cities aggressively and successfully vied for trade: Houston began a rapid ascendancy in the early twentieth century based in part on its strategic location and the improvement of its port facilities. Galveston's valiant efforts to maintain its premier spot in Texas maritime affairs after the great hurricane is seen in a striking map that was used on the verso of Galveston Chamber of Commerce stationery during the difficult period of recovery (Fig. 8-31). The map at first seems to confirm Galveston's indisputable place in all transportation affairs, for *all* of the railroads on it converge on the port, fully fifty-nine steamship lines to distant ports radiate from it, and eight schooner lines and steamship lines link it with other Texas ports.

But the map is seen, on closer inspection, to be wishful thinking. Entirely missing from this booster's graphic hyperbole is Houston, into which most of those railroads actually ran and into which an increasingly larger share of Texas maritime trade was now being funneled.

While developments now ensured that Houston would eclipse Galveston to become the major city of the Texas Gulf area, even Corpus Christi would supersede Galveston later in the twentieth century. By the late twentieth century, Houston's population of 1,655,900 and Corpus Christi's population of 260,200 confirms their phenomenal growth, while Galveston, which grew very slowly and now possesses only about 60,000, basks in its former glory as the Queen City of the Texas coast. This slow growth, however, has ensured that Galveston's historic character remained intact enough to encourage a tourist industry based on its rich maritime heritage. Other places along the coast were not as fortunate, historically speaking, as major developments in the twentieth century—including the creation of new port facilities for oil shipping, new shipyards to meet the demands of two world wars, and housing for recreation on the coast—would all but obliterate traces of the past in many parts of the Texas coast.

CONCLUSION:
TEXAS MARITIME HISTORY
IN RETROSPECT

Sailors think of a ship as a living creature, a symbolic body on a metaphorical journey. They say she is born on the day of her launch and dies on the day of her destruction, and during the time between is on a voyage through a genuine, vital, breathing life.
PETER H. SPECTRE AND DAVID LARKIN, *Wooden Ship*

By the end of the nineteenth century, or more properly the dawn of the twentieth century, the waters of Texas had served an important role. The coast had served as the first point of arrival for hundreds of thousands of new citizens, whose vessels entered Galveston and other ports. Texas rivers, too, served as corridors along which flowed the commerce of the Republic and early Lone Star State. The nineteenth century also witnessed the rise of a vigorous coastwise shipping network that would last until the development of a road and highway system in the twentieth century, an improvement that would all but obliterate the small, enterprising schooners. Before the virtual completion of the railroad network in Texas, coastal ports had shipped the majority of Texas products, such as cotton and beef, to markets around the world on a wide variety of sail and steam-powered vessels.

These vessels had a powerful effect on the popular mind in the nineteenth century, for they symbolized freedom and wealth in an age that offered the hope of both social and geographic mobility. The toys of the era reflect these dreams and aspirations. Although it is likely that miniature ship models or replicas were appreciated in the early to middle years of the nineteenth century, they became very popular in the latter 1800s, when mass production techniques, a thriving economy, and a growing middle class made replicas of vessels available to an increasing number of people. Of the cast-iron toys that proliferated after about 1870,[1] steamships were among the most popular. Typical of the maritime-oriented cast-iron toys is a beautifully proportioned, if not perfectly detailed, replica of a sidewheeler steamship (Fig. C-1). Purchased by the author at an antique shop in Arlington, Texas, this small (7.5 inches) miniature steamer was intended to be pulled or pushed by a child—or very likely his or her parents! Probably produced in New York or Philadelphia in about 1880, this delightful miniature is very similar to the Morgan Line steamers, such as the *City of Norfolk*, that served the booming Texas ports of Indianola, Galveston, and Rockport in the 1870s. It features a prominent funnel or stack, simulated walking-beam mechanism, and two covered decks. As a testimony to the creativity of the toy designers of the era, this vessel's [paddle] wheels are mounted slightly eccentrically on their axles, so that the miniature steamship actually gently rocks from side to side as it is pulled, much like the motion of a real vessel on a cross swell; while this motion probably delighted those who played with this toy, one can be sure that it was disconcerting to many of those who rode real steamships and experienced seasickness or apprehension. Through miniaturization as well as everyday experience, the steamship became part of U.S. popular culture in the later nineteenth century.

The sailing vessel, too, was miniaturized and romanticized during this era. In about 1895, the African American folk artist Henry Morris of San Antonio captured the drama of a bustling port in a remarkable shadow box (Fig. C-2). Constructed of wood, string, and canvas, this diorama conveys a sense of the importance and aesthetics of vessels of the late nineteenth century. Prominent in the diorama is an impressionistically proportioned, but properly rigged, sailing vessel in a harbor crowded with smaller craft, including a steam launch and a longboat. Morris has been described as an imaginative man who had a knowledge of the sea.[2] Noteworthy in Morris's otherwise primitive scene are the navigation aids such as a detailed buoy in the foreground and a lighthouse painted on the background of the shadow-box. Although his work survived and is part of the Witte Museum's Collection, little is known about Henry Morris, who served as a porter in the store of A. G. Castañola & Sons in San Antonio. It is not known whether Morris based the diorama on a scene he had actually viewed or on a photograph or painting. However, this scene and a model of the famed steamboat *Robert E. Lee* earned Morris the epithet of "Captain"; these marine models have earned Captain Morris a rightful place in the annals of nineteenth century folk artists. Many other people built (or attempted to build) models of the ships that had captured the collective imagination at the time. Morris's selection of a fully rigged sailing vessel (as well as a steamboat) for his major works is symbolic, for these vessels were soon to be superseded by larger, less ornate vessels. By the late 1890s, changes were sweeping the industry,

FIGURE C-1

Although only 7.5 inches in length and meant to serve as a child's toy, this cast iron steamship is accurately proportioned, and its sidewheels actually turn as it is pulled or pushed along by hand. It possesses the prominent features that made steamships of the era so recognizable: side paddlewheels in ornate housings, smokestack, walking-beam mechanism, and ornate decks. Author's collection.

FIGURE C-2

In about 1895, the San Antonio folk artist Henry Morris captured the drama of a bustling port in a remarkable shadow box. Constructed of wood, string, and canvas, this diorama depicts an impressionistically proportioned, but properly rigged, sailing ship in a harbor crowded with smaller vessels, such as a steam launch and longboat. Courtesy Witte Museum, San Antonio.

and these changes would lead toward more efficient and safer maritime trade. Within a generation, the scenes and vessels recorded by Morris would become history.

Painters also helped preserve Texas maritime history, and few better captured the drama of the Texas maritime trade in the late nineteenth century than Julius Stockfleth (1857–1935). Active in Galveston from 1885 to 1907, the German-born marine and landscape painter Stockfleth witnessed sweeping changes in the industry as he painted a wide variety of vessels, from lowly sloops and tugs to the grandest square-rigged barks and the fastest steam-powered liners. Although photography was recognized as the most technically accurate way to record vessels during Stockfleth's day, his marine paintings were popular and many were sold locally; these paintings captured conditions, like the color and mood of the sea, the intensity of the sky, and the overall character of the vessels in ways that photographs could not. It is touching to realize that several of Stockfleth's closest relatives were lost in the Galveston Hurricane, and that the storm probably also claimed many of his maritime paintings; Stockfleth painted many tragic scenes of the storm's aftermath but several years later he moved back to his native village of Wyk on the island of Föhr in the North Sea. There Stockfleth could be seen strolling restlessly along the sandwall dike that protected the beach whenever storm waves threatened, a lasting result of the trauma he had suffered on the Texas coast in 1900.[3] Julius Stockfleth and Captain Morris captured a fleeting moment at the end of one era of maritime history, and the beginning of another.

The legacy of the vessels and people who opened the Texas coast during the first four centuries (1500–1900) also remains in the form of place names, shipwrecks, and historic lighthouses, and, more recently, in the artifacts and historic photographs that are featured as museum exhibits in several fine maritime history museums, including the Texas Seaport Museum in Galveston, the Museum of the Gulf Coast in Port Arthur, the Texas Maritime Museum in Rockport, and the Corpus Christi Museum of Science and History. Additionally, the archival collections in the Rosenberg Library in Galveston, the Texas Maritime Museum in Rockport, the Libraries at the University of Texas (Austin and Arlington), and Texas A&M University– Corpus Christi, are important destinations for the maritime historian.

Although the Texas coast is rich in history, it remains important today. In fact, the twentieth century has brought the Texas Gulf coast to prominence as the deepwater channel developments of the 1910s and 1920s ensured the dominance of Houston—which is recognized as one of the world's great seaports. Similarly, the rapid growth of the formerly sleepy port of Corpus Christi[4]—which boomed as a major naval facility opened there during World War II—is a reminder of the importance of the Texas coast in the twentieth century. The rise of Texas as a major shipbuilding center in the early to middle twentieth century should also serve as a reminder that many seemingly recent developments got their start in the nineteenth century.

Perceptions of the Texas coast and rivers have changed through time, but have always been related to how the coast is experienced first-hand. As noted earlier, peoples' perceptions of any body of water depend, in part, on whether they are experiencing it for work or for pleasure. Those whose occupations *demand* that they be at sea rarely love it in the same way as those who choose to experience it in their leisure time. Of seamen and fishermen, Robert Lee Maril noted that "the sea tires a man, [and] . . . etches lines of fatigue and stress permanently into his skin" but "most of all, though, it threatens his life." Therefore, Maril concludes, "I think the sea is rarely ever loved, [nor is] its beauty appreciated for its own sake, because it does what no shrimpers, other commercial fishermen, or merchant mariners, or sailors can ever forgive it for—it totally isolates them from those they love and from the society to which they belong."[5] That statement was probably as true in the 1500s or 1600s as it was when Maril wrote about Texas shrimp boat crews in the 1980s. Life on the waters of Texas was often monotonous and hazardous, although, to be sure, it had its brief moments of beauty and serenity.

The twentieth century further accelerated trends in personal wealth and leisure—trends that began in the nineteenth century and, by the middle to the late twentieth century, had found the Texas coast teeming with an activity that most early travelers never would have envisioned: recreational boating. Pleasure craft now fill many marinas, and pleasure boating has become a major industry in itself on the Texas coast. These pleasure craft are descendants of either the long tradition of sail or the cantankerous naphtha engines pioneered in the late nineteenth century, and they give new generations of mariners—the pleasure boaters—an intimate look at the waters of Texas. But appreciating the waters and vessels of Texas aesthetically is, as noted earlier, something of a fairly recent phenomenon. To travelers in much of the first four centuries, the Texas coast was by turn hostile and beautiful; moreover, experiencing it was usually a temporary phenomenon, that is, only a prelude to the penetration of the interior, where other parts of the drama of Texas history would be played out.

One hundred years later, the vessels that were commonplace in Captain Morris's and Julius Stockfleth's day continue to inspire the thousands of people who visit the maritime museums and ship model galleries in Texas. Large sailing vessels of the square-rigged variety—the "Tall Ships"—continue to enchant people who experience them first-hand today. *Texas Highways* magazine editor Ann Gallaway described her enchantment by the *Elissa* after several days at sea in the spring of 1996 as the famous bark sailed on one of her occasional ventures into the open water. In describing the impact of this brief voyage from New Orleans to Galveston, Gallaway intimated that "I wake sometimes in the middle of the night and find myself reliving those 58 hours at sea," where "once again she rides the waves, reveling in fog, brilliant sunlight, chilly mists, and changing winds." Gallaway characterized the *Elissa* as "old and wise, young and lighthearted, a free spirit," whose "siren song . . . calls my name."[6] To a generation of travelers jaded by the efficiency of modern air travel, the sound of the wind rising in the sails of a square-rigged vessel, its spars and rigging groaning and singing in the wind, creates a feeling of awe. The *Elissa's* enduring power to capture the imagination is made all the more poignant by the realization that her iron hull came very close to being cut up at a Greek scrapyard in 1974. In a dramatic scenario, the *Elissa* was rescued just before time ran out, and within several years she was restored as a "seaworthy exhibit" by the Galveston Historical Foundation.[7]

That the steamboat also continues to have a powerful, romantic appeal is apparent in the many recreational "steamboats" (many of them diesel-powered) that ply the ports and rivers of Texas and the United States. Typical of such modern but historically styled steamboats are the *Colonel*, a Galveston-based, harbor-touring triple-deck vessel that emulates the more ornate sternwheeler steamboats of the mid-nineteenth century,[8] and the smaller, somewhat more stylized paddle-wheeler *Flagship*, used for Corpus Christi harbor tours. The powerful lure of the steamboat is realized in the words of the popular 1990 song "Mandolin Rain," by Bruce Hornsby, in which a steamboat's spinning sidewheels are described, and reference is made to the steamboat's whistle bringing back memories of a lost love. According to the songwriter John Hornsby, who with his brother Bruce grew up in the South, the romance of the riverboat endures.[9]

Today, of course, the sight of a restored, fully rigged barque like the *Elissa*, or even a glimpse of a portion of the engine of a sunken steamship like the *Clifton*, can evoke a sense of history or stir a sense of nostalgia, but at the end of their technological heyday these vessels were often simply considered former state-of-the-art technology whose time for replacement had come. And yet, their obsolescence only increases their beauty and drama. Because we associate the vessels of yore with romance and adventure, it is understandable that we have preserved at least some of the more colorful aspects of them in art, song, and themed attractions, as well as the more serious, educational museum exhibits.

Sporadic news of major shipwreck discoveries likewise continue to fuel the imagination as diligent archaeologists comb the coast and interested Texans read about their finds in newspapers. Private and public agencies, such as the Austin-based NUMA (National Underwater and Marine Agency) and the Texas Historical Commission, have worked diligently to identify and excavate Texas shipwrecks. Their 1986 discovery of the wreck of the *Zavala* in Galveston proved the value of their efforts. However, of an estimated 1,935 shipwrecks off the Texas coast, only about 200 have so far been discovered and investigated. Some, such as the 1554 shipwrecks or the remains of La Salle's vessels from the ill-fated attempts to colonize Texas in the 1680s, are discoveries of global importance. Of the many remaining shipwrecks that await discovery, those like the *Invincible* and *Clifton* will help historians either rewrite Texas history or confirm the written records. Even the most mundane of wrecks promises to yield important information about everyday life along the coast. In retrospect, the aggressive establishment of marine archaeology programs in Texas that some skeptics questioned in the 1970s has paid untold dividends as the coastal waters and lower reaches of the rivers of the Lone Star State have yielded, and continue to yield, remarkable discoveries like the *Belle* and *Zavala*.

Finally, Texas's maritime salvage laws have also had a positive impact on maritime history. Called the most restrictive in the country by some, they nevertheless ensure that nineteenth-century and earlier wrecks *in state waters* are protected. Texas maritime salvage laws prohibit the private exploitation of many historic shipwrecks in state waters, and this will in turn ensure that future generations will be the beneficiaries of underwater archaeology.[10] In closing, it should be noted that Texas is rather unusual, perhaps even visionary, in that the state's jurisdiction extends ten, rather than three, miles from shore—the result of traditions in Texas statehood that are a lasting legacy of the Republic of Texas. Thus it is that Texans are ensured that future discoveries in both the archaeological and written record will permit a better understanding of their state's maritime history. Hopefully, *From Sail to Steam* will help place these discoveries in context for future generations of Texans.

Notes

INTRODUCTION

1. Shuler, "Shore Line," p. 31.

CHAPTER 1
FOUR HUNDRED MILES OF DESOLATION AND BEAUTY

1. Tveten, *Coastal Texas*, p. 18.
2. Morton, *Shoreline Changes*, p. 357.
3. Nuñez Cabeza de Vaca, *Account*, p. 22.
4. Ibid., p. 56.
5. Paine and Morton, *Shoreline and Vegetation-Line Movement*, pp. 5–6.
6. Ibid.
7. *A Visit to Texas: Being the Journal of a Traveller Through Those Parts Most Interesting to American Settlers* (New York: Goodrich & Wiley, 1834), p. 14.
8. Ibid., p. 153.
9. Pratt, *Galveston Island*, pp. 31–32.
10. Muir, *Texas in 1837*, pp. 4–5.
11. Spearing, *Roadside Geology*, pp. 48–49.
12. Carroll, *Béranger's Discovery of Aransas Pass*, p. 23.
13. Ibid., p. 22.
14. It should be noted that the Gulf of Mexico, unlike other seas, technically has two high and two low tides daily.
15. Nuñez Cabeza de Vaca, *Account*, p. 69.
16. Gilliam, *Travels*, p. 29.
17. Ibid.
18. Ibid., p. 31.
19. Muir, *Texas in 1837*, pp. 8–9.
20. Bowen et al., *Effects of Hurricane Celia*, p. 9.
21. St. John, *South Padre*, p. 41.
22. Muir, ed. *Texas in 1837*, p. 7.
23. Pratt, *Galveston Island*, p. 22.
24. Maril, *Texas Shrimpers*, p. 45.
25. See, for example, Nick Fotheringham and Susan Brunenmeister, *Beach-*

comber's Guide to Gulf Coast Marine Life: Florida, Alabama, Mississippi, Louisiana & Texas (Houston: Gulf Publishing Co., 1989), and Mary Michael Cannatella, *Plants of the Texas Shore: A Beachcomber's Guide* (College Station, Texas: Texas A&M University Press, 1985).

26. Pratt, *Galveston Island*, p. 53.

27. Ibid.

28. Carroll, *Béranger's Discovery of Aransas Pass*, p. 23.

29. See Martin and Martin, *Contours of Discovery*.

30. It should be noted that this is a recent development, a consequence of dredging. In the nineteenth century, Matagorda Bay was clear, or open, from one end to the other.

31. Martin Duralde, 1802 (in Swanton, 1907, as cited in Aten, *Indians of the Upper Texas Coast*).

32. Aten, *Indians of the Upper Texas Coast*, p. 77.

33. Aten, p. 149.

34. Carroll, *Béranger's Discovery of Aransas Pass*, p. 22.

35. Newcomb, *Indians of Texas*, p. 67.

36. Charles A. Hammond, "The Carancahua Tribe of Texas," in Gatschet, *Karankawa Indians*, p. 10.

37. Alice W. Oliver, "Notes on the Carancahua Indians," in Gatschet, *The Karankawa Indians*, p. 80.

38. Albert S. Gatschet, *The Karankawa Indians*, 1891, p. 60.

CHAPTER 2
THE POWER OF THE WIND, 1500–1685

1. The Vikings are known to have reached northeastern North America by ca. A.D. 1100, and it is possible that other mariners found their way to the Americas from either Asia or Africa before Columbus, although these encounters left little evidence and, apparently, had rather little impact.

2. Technically, to "tack" is to turn ship's bow across the eye of the wind; making successive tacks to move upwind is "beating."

3. Kemp, *History of Ships*, p. 64.

4. Ibid., p. 67.

5. Roger Smith, *Vanguard of Empire*, p. 206.

6. Ibid., p. 31.

7. Demetrio Charalambous, "Reconstruction of a Pre-Columbian American Map" (paper presented at the Cantino Map Roundtable, annual meeting of the Society for the History of Discoveries, Arlington, Texas, November 3, 1995).

8. Personal communication, Louis DeVorsey to the author, Arlington, Texas, November 4, 1995.

9. Dennis Reinhartz, personal communication, Arlington, Texas, November 4, 1995.

10. Arne Molander, presentation at the Cantino Map Roundtable, annual meeting of the Society for the History of Discoveries, Arlington, Texas, November 4, 1995.

11. Gregory McIntosh, presentation at the Cantino Map Roundtable, annual meeting of the Society for the History of Discoveries, Arlington, Texas, November 4, 1995.

12. Buisseret, *Sea Charts to Satellite Images*.

13. Garcia, *Alvarez de Piñeda*.

14. Chipman, "Cabeza de Vaca's Route."

15. It should be noted, however, that this critically acclaimed feature film depicted Cabeza de Vaca being cast ashore on a rocky beach among Amazonian Indians who lived in stilt houses in a river!

16. Kemp, *History of Ships*, pp. 93–95.

17. Davis, *Treasure*, p. 24.

18. See also de Ledesma, "Seven Salvage Techniques."

19. Ibid.

20. Arnold and Weddle, *Nautical Archaeology*.

21. Ibid., p. 79.

22. Ibid., pp. 79–80.

23. Ibid., p. 81 and Haring, *Trade and Navigation*, 1918, p. 266.

24. Buisseret, *Tools of Empire*, introduction page.

25. Roger Smith, *Vanguard of Empire*, p. 190.

26. Arnold, "Flota Disaster," p. 27.

27. Phillips, *Six Galleons*.

28. Buisseret, "Mapping of the Gulf," pp. 3–17.

CHAPTER 3
TROUBLE ON THE SPANISH SEA, 1685–1821

1. Joseph David Cooper, "17th Century Cannon Found in Texas Bay," *Fort Worth Star-Telegram*, Friday, July 14, 1995, pp. 23A–24A, Arlington metro section.

2. "Artifact Pulled from Bay May Be Old Cannon," *Dallas Morning News*, Friday, July 14, 1995, p. 11A.

3. J. Barto Arnold III, personal communication with author, April 24, 1996.

4. Cooper, "17th Century Cannon," p. 23A.

5. J. Barto Arnold III, "Matagorda Bay Underwater Archaeology Project: La Salle's Shipwreck *La Belle*" (paper presented at the Society for Historical Archaeology Conference on Historical and Underwater Archaeology, Cincinnati, Ohio, January 3–7, 1996, p. 4).

6. Weddle, *French Thorn*, pp. 32–33.

7. Arnold, "Matagorda Bay Project," p. 29.

8. Personal communication, J. Barto Arnold to author, July 29, 1996.

9. Arnold, "Matagorda Bay Project," p. 27.

10. J. F. Jameson, in Hackett, *Historical Documents*, p. 471.

11. Ibid., p. 475.

12. Boudriot, *Historique de la Corvette*, p. 15.

13. Arnold, "Matagorda Bay Magnetometer Survey," p. 15.

14. Buisseret, *Tools of Empire*, map 16, plate 22.

15. Hackett, vol. 1, p. 480.

16. Ibid.

17. Casis, "Discovery of Bay of Espíritu Santo," pp. 293–295.

18. Refer to the *Diccionario de la lengua Española*. Madrid: Real Academia Española, 1992.

19. Anderson and Anderson, *The Sailing Ship*, p. 170.

20. *American Heritage Dictionary of the English Language*, 1978.

21. Anderson and Anderson, *The Sailing Ship*, p. 164.

22. Ibid., p. 171.

23. Raymond Ashley, "From the Helm," *Mains'l Haul, A Journal of Maritime History*, 31, no. 4(Fall 1995): p. 5.

24. Ibid.

25. For an informative discussion of remote sensing techniques, see Pearson et al., *Underwater Archaeology*, pp. 55–74.

26. Arnold, "Matagorda Bay Project," p. 17.

27. James P. Delgado et al., *National Register Bulletin 20 — Nominating Historic Vessels and Shipwrecks to the National Register of Historic Places* (Washington: U.S. Department of the Interior, National Park Service, nd.), p. 12.

28. "Cofferdam Launches La Salle Shipwreck Recovery," *The Medallion* (Texas Historical Commission; Preservation News in Texas), May/June, 1996, p. 3.

29. Sobel, *Longitude*.

30. Weddle, *Changing Tides*, p. 20.

31. Sheire, *Padre Island Study*, pp. 20–21.

32. Weddle, *Changing Tides*, pp. 26–27.

33. Personal communication, letter by Charles Pearson to author, October 13, 1995; for a detailed study of *El Nuevo Constante*, refer to Pearson and Hoffman, *The Last Voyage of El Nuevo Constante*.

34. Phone interview with Danny Sessums, Director, Museum of the Gulf Coast, Port Arthur, Texas, December 6, 1995.

35. See Brasseaux and Chandler, "The *Britain* Incident," pp. 357–369.

36. Weddle, *Changing Tides*, p. 79.

37. Ibid., p. 80.

38. It should be noted, however, that by the eighteenth century, a "frigate" was a specific type of warship.

39. Ibid.

40. Weddle, *French Thorn*, pp. 213, 244–245.

41. Gournay, *Texas Boundaries*, p. 7.

42. Cutter, *Defenses of Northern New Spain*, p. 91.

43. Ibid., p. 93.

44. Ibid.

45. Ibid.

46. McDermott, *Frenchmen and French*, p. 244.

47. Weddle, *Changing Tides*, pp. 192–193.

48. Chapelle, *American Sailing Ships*, p. 130.

49. Walter Prescott Webb and H. Bailey Carroll, eds., *Handbook of Texas*, vol. 2 (Austin: Texas State Historical Association), p. 5. Hereafter cited as *Handbook*.

50. Pratt, *Galveston Island*, p. 56.

51. Ibid.

52. The letters of Louis Michel Aury are found in the manuscript box of the Harvey Alexander Adams Collection, Center for American History, the University of Texas at Austin.

53. Warren, "Aury, Louis Michel," pp. 289–290.

CHAPTER 4
SMOKE ON THE HORIZON, 1821–1836

1. Elmer W. Flaccus, "Commodore David Porter and the Mexican Navy," *Hispanic American Historical Review*, 34, no. 3(August 1954): p. 366.

2. Arturo Lopez de Nava, "Mexico y la Independencia de Cuba," *Revista de Ejercito y de la Marina*, 14, no. 7(July 1933): p. 71.

3. Eugene C. Barker, ed., *Annual Report of the American Historical Association for the Year 1919*, 2 vols., "The Austin Papers" (Washington, D.C.: Government Printing Office, 1924), part 1, p. 417.

4. Christopher Long, "Lively" entry in *The New Handbook of Texas*, ed. Ron Tyler (Austin: Texas State Historical Association, 1996), vol. 4, p. 240. Hereafter cited as *New Handbook*.

5. Gregg Cantrell, "The Partnership of Stephen F. Austin and Joseph H. Hawkins," *Southwestern Historical Quarterly*, 99, no. 1(July 1995): pp. 6–7.

6. See W. S. Lewis, "The Adventures of the '*Lively*' Immigrants," part 1, *Quarterly of the Texas State Historical Association*, vol. 3, no. 1(July 1899): 1–32; part 2, vol. 3, no. 2(October 1899): pp. 81–107.

7. Lewis, "Adventures of the '*Lively*' Immigrants," part 1, p. 12.

8. Ibid., p. 14.

9. Ibid., p. 16.

10. Ibid.

11. Bugbee, "What Became of the *Lively?*" pp. 145–147.

12. Cantrell, "Partnership of Austin and Hawkins," p. 7.

13. Chapelle, *American Sailing Ships*, pp. 31–32.

14. Kenneth E. Hendrickson Jr., *The Waters of the Brazos: A History of the Brazos River Authority* (Waco: Texian Press, 1981), p. 2.

15. Barker, "Austin Papers," part 1, pp. 472–483.

16. Ibid., p. 778.

17. Ibid., p. 880.

18. Ibid., pp. 943–956.

19. Ibid., pp. 963–985.

20. Ibid., vol. 2, Part 2, p. 1086.

21. Malcolm D. McClean, ed., *Papers Concerning the Robertson Colony in Texas, Vol. 2, 1823 through September 1826, Leftwich's Grant* (Fort Worth: Texas Christian University Press, 1975), p. 461.

22. Ibid., pp. 461–462.

23. Ibid., p. 462.

24. Barker, "Austin Papers," part 1, pp. 1145, 1152.

25. Ibid., p. 1155.

26. Ibid., p. 1201.

27. Ibid., p. 1281.

28. Ibid., p. 1150.

29. Ibid., p. 1444.

30. Ibid., p. 1472.

31. Easley, *Ships Passenger Lists*.

32. J. D. Hill, *Texas Navy*, p. 6.

33. "J. C. Clopper's Journal and Book of Memoranda for 1828. Province of Texas," *Quarterly of the Texas State Historical Association*, 13(1910): 52.

34. Ibid., p. 53.

35. Ibid., p. 58.

36. Barker, "Austin Papers," vol. 2, 1924, pp. 105, 109, 152.

37. Ibid., p. 555.

38. S. A. Townsend, "Steamboating on the Rio Grande."

39. *Texas Gazette*, October 24, 1829, vol. 1, p. 15.

40. Ibid.

41. Although popularly called the *Clermont*, Fulton's history-making boat was initially simply named *The Steamboat*, and later *The North River Steamboat of Clermont*.

42. Paul Forsythe Johnston, *Steam and the Sea* (Salem, Massachusetts: Peabody Museum of Salem, 1983), pp. 21, 35.

43. William R. Hogan, "The Life and Letters of Henry Austin, 1782–1852," master's thesis, University of Texas at Austin, June 1932, p. 34.

44. Ibid., pp. 39, 43.

45. Ibid., p. 44.

46. Paul Horgan, *Great River: The Rio Grande in North American History* (New York: Holt, Rinehart and Winston, 1954), p. 482.

47. Ibid., p. 484.

48. S. A. Townsend, "Steamboating on the Rio Grande," p. 11.

49. Personal telephone communication, author with Tom Fort, Hidalgo County Historical Museum, Edinburg, Texas, November 30, 1995.

50. *Texas Gazette*, Saturday, October 24, 1829, vol. 1, no. 4, p. 16.

51. *Texas Gazette*, Saturday, February 13, 1830, vol. 1, no. 10, p. 3.

52. Although cartographers tended perhaps to be more aware of vessels than the general public, they, too, might include vessels that were more stylized or generic rather than perfectly accurate representations of particular vessels.

53. David G. Burnet to Martin Van Buren, Cincinnati, April 10, 1829, Burnet Papers, Eugene C. Barker History Center, The University of Texas at Austin, as quoted by David Narrett in "A Choice of Destiny: Immigration, Slavery, and Social Progress as Defining Issues in Early Texas History," paper presented at "The Chal-

lenge of Statehood: A Sesquicentennial Symposium on Texas Annexation," University of Texas at Arlington, October 20, 1995.

54. Luke Gournay, *Texas Boundaries: Evolution of the State's Counties* (College Station: Texas A&M University Press, 1995), pp. 15–16.

55. Barker, "Austin Papers," p. 711.

56. Ibid., p. 625.

57. Ibid., p. 696.

58. Ibid., p. 8.

59. Ibid., p. 101.

60. Ibid., p. 18.

61. J. D. Hill, *Texas Navy*, p. 21.

62. Ibid.

63. Ibid., pp. 22–23.

64. Ibid., p. 31.

65. Ibid., p. 48.

66. Ben C. Stuart, "The Slave Ships and Their Story," *Galveston News*, Sunday, September 11, 1910, p. 17.

67. In point of fact, the headwaters of the Rio Grande are farther south, more in the latitude of Virginia than New York.

68. *Handbook of Texas*, vol. 2, p. 835.

CHAPTER 5
ON THE WATERS OF THE LONE STAR REPUBLIC, 1836–1845

1. "Wreckage of Texas Navy Ship That Aided Sam Houston Believed Found," Associated Press story, *Dallas Morning News*, Wednesday, August 23, 1995, p. 23A.

2. Hobart Huson, "Horse Marines," in *New Handbook*, vol. 3, p. 704.

3. See J. D. Hill, *Texas Navy*, and Alexander Dienst, "The Navy of the Republic of Texas," *Quarterly of the Texas State Historical Association*, vols. 12–13, 1908–1910.

4. M. B. Lamar, "Third Address to the Senate, April 10, 1838," in Charles A. Gulick Jr., ed., *Papers of Mirabeau Buonaparte Lamar* (Austin: Texas State Library, 1921–1927), vol. 2, p. 227.

5. *Handbook*, vol. 2, p. 750.

6. A beautiful model of the *Zavala* by Fred Tournier can be seen at the Texas Seaport Museum in Galveston; the model is based on the wreck of the *Zavala*, which was discovered off Galveston in 1986 by Clive Cussler and Robert Esbenson. For more information on the wreck site of the *Zavala*, see J. Barto Arnold III, Clive Cussler, and Wayne Gronquist, "The Survey for the *Zavala*, a Steam Warship of the Republic of Texas," Proceedings of the Conference on Historical and Underwater Archaeology, Tucson, Arizona, 1990, pp. 105–109.

7. Elizabeth R. Baldwin, "*T.S.S. Zavala*: The Texas Navy's Steamship-of-War," *INA Quarterly* (Institute of Nautical Archaeology), 22, no. 3(Fall 1995): 10–15.

8. Ibid., p. 12.

9. Wells, *Commodore Moore*, p. 8.

10. Ibid., pp. 11–20.

11. E. Baldwin, "T.S.S. Zavala," pp. 12-15.

12. Wells, *Commodore Moore*, p. 28.

13. Ibid., pp. 21–23.

14. Arnold, Cussler, and Gronquist, "Survey for the *Zavala*."

15. Mrs. Houstoun, *Texas and the Gulf of Mexico or, Yachting in the New World* (Philadelphia, G. B. Zieber & Co., 1845), pp. 73–74.

16. Anonymous, *Daily Bulletin* (Austin), January 7, 1842.

17. Sam Haynes, ed., *Journal of the Texian Expedition Against Mier* (Austin: W. Thomas Taylor, 1993), p. ix.

18. Ibid., p. xii.

19. Francis Moore Jr., *Map and Description of Texas, Containing Sketches of Its History, Geology, Geography, and Statistics* (Philadelphia: H. Tanner, Junr., 1840), pp. 53–54.

20. Ibid., p. 70.

21. Muir, *Texas in 1837*, pp. 64–65.

22. Rupert Richardson, Ernest Wallace, and Adrian Anderson, *Texas: The Lone Star State* (Englewood Cliffs, N.J.: Prentice Hall, 1988), p. 138.

23. Terry G. Jordan, *Environment and Environmental Perception in Texas* (Boston: American Press, 1980), p. 26.

24. James Baughman, *Charles Morgan and the Development of Southern Transportation* (Nashville: Vanderbilt University Press, 1968), p. 21.

25. Ibid., p. 27.

26. William R. Hogan, "A Social and Economic History of the Republic of Texas," Ph.D. dissertation, University of Texas, 1942, p. 6.

27. Ibid., pp. 6–7.

28. Baughman, *Charles Morgan*, p. 34.

29. Rev. A. B. Lawrence, *A History of Texas or the Emigrant's Guide to the New Republic by a Resident Emigrant, Late from the United States* (New York: Nafis & Cornish, 1844), p. 25.

30. Charles Dickens, quoted in F. E. Dayton, *Steamboat Days* (New York: Tudor Publishing Co., 1939), pp. 109–110.

31. Ibid.

32. Charles Adams Gulick Jr. and Winnie Allen, eds., *Papers of Lamar*, vol. 4, part 1 (Austin: Von Boeckmann-Jones Co., 1924), pp. 217–218.

33. Stuart, "Texas Steamboat Days."

34. Puryear and Winfield, *Sandbars and Sternwheelers*.

35. Texas Maritime Museum Research Photograph Collection Sheet, nd.

36. Ibid. The final fate of the *Yellow Stone* is unclear. In *Voyages of the Steamboat Yellow Stone*, Donald Jackson discusses the possibility that she was wrecked in Texas, but also offers evidence that the boat left Texas in 1837 and returned to the Ohio River, where her name was likely changed.

37. It should be noted that a boat with only two decks would not have a "texas" deck—which was present only on the largest boats.

38. "The Life and Adventures of Henry Woodland, A Texas Veteran and Mier

Prisoner," typed manuscript copied from the original in the possession of L. W. Kemp, Houston, Texas, by the Barker Texas History Center Archives, 1957 (Box Number 2R311, pp. 33–34).

39. Edward M. Brade, *Tugs, Towboats and Towing* (Centreville, Md.: Cornell Maritime Press, 1967), p. 1.

40. Coasting license for the Open Sloop *Davie Crockett*, 10-11, 1838, in the Shipping in the [Texas] Republic Collection, Jenkins Garrett Library, the University of Texas at Arlington.

41. Certificate of Health, District of Mobile. Clearance for the American schooner *Independence*, 10-11-2 (1838), Shipping in the [Texas] Republic Collection, Jenkins Garrett Library, Special Collections, the University of Texas at Arlington.

42. Customs House of Clearance, District and Port of Mobile. Clearance for the schooner *Tiger*, 10-11-3, Shipping in the [Texas] Republic Collection, Jenkins Garrett Library, Special Collections, the University of Texas at Arlington.

43. Document concerning the open boat *Tyron*, 10-12-3, in the Shipping in the [Texas] Republic Collection, Jenkins Garrett Collection, the University of Texas at Arlington.

44. Muir, *Texas in 1837*, p. 4.

45. Ibid.

46. Pratt, *Galveston Island*, pp. 18–19.

47. Ibid., pp. 20–21.

48. Ibid.

49. Ibid., p. 29.

50. Houstoun, *Yachting*, p. 93.

51. Stuart, "Texas and Its Sea Trade."

52. This receipt makes reference to lost luggage, a record of the casualties of travel on the Texas coast. Two days later (May 5, 1840) it notes another load of cargo off-loaded from the *Sam Houston* to the lighter *Try It Again*. Source: Shipping in the [Texas] Republic Collection, Jenkins Garrett Library, Special Collections, the University of Texas at Arlington.

53. "Report and manifest for a ship or vessel of the United States, from a foreign port," item #10-14-5, in the Shipping in the [Texas] Republic Collection, Jenkins Garrett Library, Special Collections, the University of Texas at Arlington.

54. Stuart, "Texas and Its Sea Trade," p. 40.

55. Ibid.

56. Hunt and Randel, *Guide to the Republic of Texas*, p. 45.

57. Hunt and Randel, *New Guide to the Republic of Texas*, pp. 54–55.

58. Muir, *Texas in 1837*, p. 5.

59. Ibid., p. 8.

60. Houstoun, *Yachting*, vol. 2, p. 147.

61. Pratt, *Galveston Island*, p. 129.

62. Ibid., p. 128.

63. *Handbook*, vol. 2, p. 395.

64. T. Lindsay Baker, *Ghost Towns of Texas* (Norman: University of Oklahoma

Press, 1986); and Craig H. Roell, "Linnville, Texas," in *New Handbook*, p. 209.

65. Ibid., p. 142.

66. Robin Doughty, *At Home in Texas: Early Views of the Land* (College Station: Texas A&M University Press, 1987), pp. 53–54.

67. Ibid., p. 52.

68. Reed, *Texas Railroads.*

69. Pratt, *Galveston Island*, p. 98.

70. See Baker, *Lighthouses of Texas.*

71. Lawrence, *Emigrant's Guide*, p. 86.

72. John Stilgoe, *Common Landscape of America* (New Haven: Yale University Press, 1982), p. 116.

73. Ibid., p. 111.

74. W. T. Block, *Cotton Bales, Keelboats, and Sternwheelers: A History of the Sabine River and Trinity River Cotton Trades, 1837–1900*, p. 181.

75. Houstoun, *Yachting*, vol. 2, p. 92.

76. Ibid., p. 90.

77. Ibid., p. 93.

CHAPTER 6
IMPROVEMENTS AT MIDCENTURY, 1845–1860

1. U.S. Congress, House, *Mexican War Correspondence*, House Executive Documents, 30th Cong., 1st sess., H. Doc. 60, serial no. 520, p. 98.

2. Darwin Payne, "Camp Life in the Army of Occupation: Corpus Christi, July 1845 to March 1846," *Southwestern Historical Quarterly*, 73, No. 3(January 1970): pp. 328, 331.

3. Ibid., p. 334.

4. Ibid., p. 340.

5. Ibid., p. 335.

6. Karl Jack Bauer, *Surfboats and Horse Marines: U.S. Naval Operations in the Mexican War, 1846–48* (Annapolis, Md.: United States Naval Institute, 1969), pp. 17–18.

7. Ibid., p. 18.

8. Karl Jack Bauer, "U.S. Naval Operations During the Mexican War," (Ph.D. Dissertation, Indiana University, 1953), Part 1, pp. 103–104.

9. William Goetzmann, *Sam Chamberlain's Mexican War—The San Jacinto Museum of History Paintings* (Austin: Texas State Historical Association, 1993), p. 48.

10. For more information on this location, see "Brazos Island Harbor Navigation Project, Cameron County, Texas," report by Espey, Huston, & Associates, January 1992.

11. Tilden, *Notes on the Rio Grande*, pp. 7–8.

12. Ibid., p. 21.

13. Ibid., p. 22.

14. Ibid., p. 25.

15. Ibid., p. 31.

16. Andrew W. Hall, personal communication, response to original manuscript, May 23, 1996.

17. Emory, *Boundary Survey*, facing p. 60.

18. Kelley, *River of Lost Dreams*.

19. Letter from J. P. Delispine to H. Hubbell, August 8, 1853, Henry Hubbell papers, 70-0151, the Rosenberg Library, Galveston, Texas.

20. Letter from J. P. Delispine to H. Hubbell, August 16, 1853, Henry Hubbell papers, 70-0153, the Rosenberg Library, Galveston, Texas.

21. Robert Gardiner, ed., "Steam Navigation in the United States," in *The Advent of Steam: The Merchant Steamship Before 1900* (London: Conway Maritime Press, 1993), p. 66.

22. Sitton, *Backwoodsmen*, p. 84.

23. See Hayes, *Galveston*, pp. 724–725; *Tri-weekly News*, March 29, 1853 and April 5, 1853, clipping file, Rosenberg Library Archives.

24. W. N. Bate, *General Sidney Sherman: Texas Soldier, Statesman, and Builder* (Waco: Texian Press, 1974), p. 215.

25. Whittier, *Paddle Wheel Steamers*, pp. 11–17.

26. Galveston Admiralty Minute Book, December 7, 1846–February 8, 1851, p. 18. National Archives–Fort Worth Records Center, 48-5-030.

27. Admiralty records, Galveston, 1849.

28. Baker, *Lighthouses of Texas*.

29. Ibid., pp. 35–36.

30. Williams, *Gateway to Texas*, pp. 150–151.

31. Valentine J. Belfiglio, *The Italian Experience in Texas* (Austin: Eakin Press, 1983), p. 14.

32. Mario Cerutti, "Espanoles, gran comercio y brute fabril en el norte de Mexico (1850–1910)," *Siglo 19, Cuadernos de Historia*, Año 1, Numero 2, Febrero de 1992, p. 55.

33. Jackie McElhaney, "Navigating the Trinity," *Legacies, A History Journal for Dallas and North Central Texas*, 3, no. 1(Spring 1991): p. 5.

34. U.S. Congress, House Executive Documents, 33rd Cong., 1st sess., December 1, 1853, pp. 573–576, as cited in McElhaney, "Navigating the Trinity," p. 13.

35. Block, *Cotton Bales*, p. 32.

36. Ibid.

37. Ibid., p. 34.

38. Henry Hubbell Collection, Statements, Receipts, etc., #70-0100 (70-0157), record September 3, 1853, recorded by A. D. Labadie. Rosenberg Library, Galveston.

39. David R. MacGregor, *Merchant Sailing Ships, 1850–1875—Heyday of Sail* (Annapolis, Md.: Naval Institute Press, 1988).

40. Kemp, *History of Ships*, p. 158.

41. Ibid.

42. Normand E. Klare, *The Final Voyage of the Central America, 1857: The Saga of a Gold Rush Steamship, the Tragedy of Her Loss in a Hurricane, and the Treasure Which Is Now Recovered* (Spokane, Wash.: Arthur H. Clark Company, 1992).

43. Stuart, "Texas and Its Sea Trade," manuscript #29-0028, p. 1.7, Rosenberg Library, Galveston, Texas.

44. The *Independence* was located in 1978 by archaeologists of the Texas Historical Commission, as noted in Arnold, *Matagorda Bay Magnetometer Survey.*

45. Malsch, *Indianola*, p. 109.

46. Baughman, *Charles Morgan*, p. 88.

47. A detailed account of Indianola's rise and fall is found in Malsch, *Indianola.*

48. *Handbook*, vol. 2, p. 883.

49. Baughman, p. 128.

50. Ibid.

51. Terry G. Jordan and Alyson L. Greiner, "The Texas Travel Diary of Henry H. Field, 1853" (Notes and Documents Section), *The Southwestern Historical Quarterly*, 99, no. 3(January 1996): pp. 351–368.

52. U.S. Congress, Senate, Mr. Houston made the following Report, 29th Cong., 1st Sess., July 22, 1846, [443], pp. 2–3.

53. Ibid., p. 2.

54. Ibid.

55. Martha Doty Freeman, *A History of Civil War Military Activities at Velasco & Quintana, Brazoria County, & Virginia Point, Galveston County, Texas*, Reports of Investigations, no. 103 (Austin: Prewitt and Associates, April 1995), pp. 6–7.

56. Lynn M. Alperin, *Custodians of the Coast: History of the United States Army Engineers at Galveston* (Galveston: Galveston District, U.S. Army Corps of Engineers, 1977).

57. Stephen R. James Jr., Charles E. Pearson, Kay Hudson, and Jack Hudson, *Archaeological and Historical Investigations of the Wreck of the Gen. C. B. Comstock, Brazoria County, Texas* (Baton Rouge, La.: Coastal Environments, Inc., April, 1991).

58. Bastian, "Development of Dredging."

59. Charles P. Zlatkovich, *Texas Railroads: A Record of Construction and Abandonment* (Austin: Bureau of Business Research, The University of Texas, and Texas State Historical Association, 1981), p. 216.

60. Baughman, *Charles Morgan*, p. 136.

61. Ibid., p. 135.

62. Uncertainty exists as to the actual date of the *Kate Ward's* construction. J. Barto Arnold, III mentions a possible date as early as the 1830s (personal communication with author, April 24, 1996).

63. Pearson et al., *Underwater Archaeology*, pp. 80–110 and 115–120; and personal communication, Charles Pearson to author, October 13, 1995.

64. Ibid.

65. Ibid., p. 81.

66. Seale, *Texas Riverman*, pp. 70–71.

67. Sitton, *Backwoodsmen*, pp. 85–86.

68. Seale, *Texas Riverman*, p. 100.

69. Washington Irving, *The Home Book of the Picturesque or American Scenery, Art, and Literature* (New York: G. P. Putnam, 1852), p. 73.

70. Jerry D. Thompson, ed., *Into the Far, Wild Country: True Tales of the Old Southwest* [by George Wythe Baylor] (El Paso: Texas Western Press, The University of Texas at El Paso, 1996), p. 92.

CHAPTER 7
BLOCKADES AND BLOCKADE RUNNERS, 1861–1865

1. Neyland, "The Naval War," pp. 115–122.

2. Donald Frazier, *Cottonclads! The Battle of Galveston and the Defense of the Texas Coast* (Fort Worth: Ryan Place Publishers, 1996), p. 18.

3. Spencer Tucker, *Raphael Semmes and the Alabama*, (Fort Worth: Ryan Place Publishers, 1996).

4. Wooster, *Lone Star Blue and Gray*, p. 7.

5. Alwyn Barr, "Texas Coastal Defense 1861–1865," in Wooster, *Lone Star Blue and Gray: Essays on Texas in the Civil War* (Austin: Texas State Historical Association, 1995), p. 153.

6. Frazier, *Cottonclads!*, p. 8.

7. According to the *Texas Almanac*, 1860, the censused population of Galveston County was only 8,229. McComb's history of Galveston gives the 1860 population of the city at about 7,500.

8. McComb, *Galveston*, p. 72.

9. John Hoyt Williams, *Sam Houston: The Life and Times of the Liberator of Texas, an Authentic American Hero* (New York: Simon & Schuster, 1993), p. 356.

10. John W. Payne Jr., "Steamboat House," in *New Handbook*, vol. 6, p. 78.

11. Baker, *Lighthouses*, p. xi.

12. Baughman, *Charles Morgan*, p. 116.

13. Ibid., p. 118.

14. Ibid., pp. 120–122.

15. Wise, *Lifeline of the Confederacy*, p. 328.

16. L. Tuffly Ellis, "Maritime Commerce on the Far Western Gulf, 1861-1865," *Southwestern Historical Quarterly*, 77, no. 2(October 1973): p. 167.

17. Barr, "Texas Coastal Defense," p. 158.

18. Ibid., p. 185.

19. Ibid., p. 152.

20. Ibid., p. 161.

21. Frazier, *Cottonclads*, p. 26.

22. Ibid., p. 32.

23. Ibid., pp. 48–49.

24. Ibid., p. 66.

25. Ibid., p. 66.

26. Ibid., p. 73.

27. Ibid., p. 80.

28. Ibid., p. 82.

29. "A 'Spirited Account' of the Battle of Galveston," in *Rebel Brothers: The Civil*

War Letters of the Trueharts, ed. Edward B. Williams (College Station: Texas A&M University Press, 1995), January 1, 1863, p. 205.

30. Ibid., p. 212.

31. For a detailed study of this vessel and its fate, see Arnold and Richard Anuskiewicz, "U.S.S. Hatteras," pp. 82–87.

32. Tucker, *Semmes and the Alabama*, p. 58.

33. Ibid., p. 39.

34. Ibid., p. 40.

35. Ibid., p. 41.

36. Frazier, *Cottonclads!*, pp. 102–103.

37. Block, *Cotton Bales*, p. 70.

38. Frazier, *Cottonclads!*, pp. 105–113.

39. *Handbook of Texas*, 1952, vol. 2, p. 525.

40. Andrew Forest Muir, "Dick Dowling and the Battle of Sabine Pass," in Ralph A. Wooster, *Lone Star Blue and Gray*, pp. 176–208; see Frank X. Tolbert, *Dick Dowling at Sabine Pass* (New York: McGraw-Hill, 1962) for a biography of the enterprising Dick Dowling.

41. Wise, *Lifeline of the Confederacy*, p. 294.

42. For more information on the Clifton shipwreck site, see Hoyt and Schmidt, *Assessment of the* Clifton.

43. Personal communication, author with Danny Sessums, December 16, 1995.

44. Henry Steele Commager, introduction to *The Official Atlas of the Civil War* (New York: Thomas Yoseloff, 1958), pp. 44–45.

45. Malsch Brownson, *Indianola: The Mother of Western Texas* (Austin: State House Press, 1988), pp. 170–171.

46. Ibid., p. 180.

47. Martha Doty Freeman, *Civil War Military Activities*, Number 103, pp. 7–8.

48. Ibid., p. 16.

49. Some historians claim that the Texans knew of the surrender at Appomattox but deliberately attacked the Union troops anyway; others dispute this interpretation.

50. Ellis "Maritime Commerce," p. 171.

51. Ibid.

52. Ibid., pp. 171, 175.

53. Ibid., pp. 177–179.

54. Peyton O. Abbott, "Business Travel Out of Texas During the Civil War: The Travel Diary of S.B. Brush, Pioneer Austin Merchant" (Notes and Documents), *Southwestern Historical Quarterly*, 96, no. 2(October 1992): 267.

55. Ibid., p. 269.

56. Wise, *Lifeline of the Confederacy*, p. 201.

57. Ibid., p. 217.

58. Ellis, "Maritime Commerce," p. 197.

59. Ibid., p. 189.

60. Stuart, "Texas and Its Sea Trade," p. 4.

61. Ralph A. Wooster, "Civil War" entry in *The New Handbook of Texas*, p. 125.

62. Wise, *Lifeline of the Confederacy*, pp. 221–226.

63. Carolyn Poirot, "On the Lookout: Rick Pratt Keeps Private Island, Lighthouse Looking Shipshape," *Fort Worth Star-Telegram*, Monday, September 4, 1995, Life and Arts Section, pp. B-1–B-2.

64. Ibid., p. B-2.

65. The *Alabama* was manufactured as a plastic model by Revell, and the *Harriet Lane* is represented by a more challenging wood and metal model by Model Shipways/Model Expo; both kits are approximately 1:100 scale. However, unless drawn from accurate plans, it should be noted that there is no guarantee that such replicas are near-perfect, in contrast to the more painstakingly researched museum-quality models.

66. Communication to author in manuscript review by Andrew Hall of Galveston, Texas, May 23, 1996.

CHAPTER 8
THE END OF AN ERA, 1865–1900

1. Personal communication with Curt Voss, Director, Galveston Seaport Museum, September 15, 1995.

2. Malsch, *Indianola*, p. 215.

3. Mallory Line file, Mariners' Museum, Newport News, Virginia.

4. Ibid., pp. 179–180.

5. Spencer Pearson, "Ghost Town Was Once a Thriving Port—Hurricane's Fury Killed St. Mary's," *Dallas Morning News*, November 13, 1988.

6. Bruce Taylor-Hille, personal communication, Rockport, Texas, July 23, 1995.

7. Fulton Diary—George W. Fulton Jr., courtesy of Mrs. Wilfreda Hooper Fors, Ingleside, Texas, provided by Kandy Taylor-Hille, Fulton Mansion, July 1995, p. 58.

8. Ibid., p. 63.

9. Ibid., p. 66.

10. Ibid.

11. Ibid., p. 68.

12. Ibid.

13. Ibid., p. 72.

14. See Pearson and Simmons, *Wreck of the Steamship Mary*, pp. 49–126.

15. *National Register Assessment of the SS Mary, Port Aransas, Nueces County, Texas*, Espey, Huston & Associates, Austin, Texas, Steven D. Hoyt, Principal investigator, October 1990, Appendix C, p. C-1.

16. Ibid., pp. C-1, C-2.

17. Ibid., p. 27.

18. Ibid., p. 53.

19. Mallory file, Eldredge Collection, Steamer *City of Waco*, The Mariners' Museum Library, Newport News, Virginia.

20. Baughman, *The Mallorys*, p. 129.

21. Chapelle, *American Sailing Ships*, p. 290.

22. Baughman, *Charles Morgan*, p. 226.

23. Eldredge Collections, Mallory Line Folder, Steamer *City of Waco*, Mariners' Museum, Newport News, Va.

24. Zlatkovich, *Texas Railroads*, pp. 27–36.

25. *Texas Business Directory for 1878–1879* (Galveston: Shaw & Blaylock, 1878), p. 108.

26. Ibid.

27. McCampbell, *Growth of Corpus Christi*, p. 51.

28. Southern Pacific Morgan Line file, #85214, Mariners' Museum, Newport News, Va.

29. Because each running light was mounted at the same position (usually on the ship's cabin) on each side of a vessel and shielded from behind (so that the light could be seen only from the side or front of the vessel and not from the opposite side), mariners could thus tell which side of another vessel was in view at any time, and would know that if two different-colored lights were seen, they were viewing either the vessel's bow (in which case a green light would show to the left, red to the right) or one side, in which case only one light would be visible (green light to the right or starboard, red to left or port).

30. "At Aransas Harbor Docks," *Aransas Harbor Herald*, March 17, 1892, p. 1.

31. "The Mallory Steamship Line: The Royal Route from New York — The Great City — To Texas — The Great State — The Finest American Fleet Afloat," *Frank Leslie's Illustrated Newspaper*, October 18, 1890, p. 16.

32. Aug. Gast Bank Note & Litho. Company, Map Publishers (St. Louis, ca. 1892,) Special Collections Division of the Libraries at the University of Texas at Arlington.

33. See Earle B. Young, *Galveston and the Great West* (College Station: Texas A&M University Press, forthcoming).

34. *Galveston Daily Record*, December 26, 1883.

35. For a description of schooners in the coal trade along the Texas coast, see Stephen R. James Jr., Jack C. Hudson, and Kay Hudson, *The 303 Hang: Archaeological Investigations of a Two Masted Schooner Wrecked Offshore Freeport, Brazoria County, Texas*, August 1991, report submitted by Panamerican Consultants, Inc. to the U.S. Army Corps of Engineers–Galveston District.

36. See Keith L. Bryant Jr., "Arthur E. Stilwell and the Founding of Port Arthur, A Case of Entrepreneurial Error," *Southwestern Historical Quarterly*, 75, No. 1(July 1971): pp. 19–40.

37. J. H. White, *American Railroad Freight Car*, p. 302.

38. United States Commission of Fish and Fisheries, *Report of the Commissioner for 1889 to 1891* [from July 1, 1889 to June 30, 1891], part XVII (Washington: Government Printing Office, 1893).

39. Ibid., p. 374.

40. Ibid.

41. Ibid.

42. Ibid., p. 375.

43. Ibid. It is interesting that African Americans were involved in the Texas coast

from nearly the beginning of European exploration. Estevanico the Moor, one of those shipwrecked in the Narvaez expedition, possibly on or near western Galveston Island, appears to have been of African origin. No doubt many served as sailors, and some may have commanded vessels during the first four centuries of Texas maritime history; perhaps because Europeans and European Americans exercised strong control of the Texas maritime trade during the period covered by this book, records of the achievements of sailors of color are often wanting.

44. Ibid., p. 376.
45. Ibid.
46. Ibid.
47. Ibid., p. 380.
48. Ibid., p. 388.
49. Ibid., p. 390.
50. Ibid.
51. James et al., *Wreck of the Comstock*.
52. *Annual Report of the Chief of Engineers*, Office of the Chief of Engineers, U.S. Army Corps of Engineers, 1897, p. 1875.
53. See McElhaney, "Navigating the Trinity," pp. 7–8.
54. For studies of Texas riverboats, see Puryear and Winfield, *Sandbars and Sternwheelers*, and E. M. White, *East Texas Riverboat Era*; for a more general treatment of riverboats, see Hunter, *Steamboats on the Western Rivers*.
55. Block, *Cotton Bales*, p. 113.
56. Ibid.
57. Williams, *Gateway to Texas*, pp. 149–157.
58. McGuire, *Julius Stockfleth*, p. 52.
59. Ibid.
60. See Mullen, *I Heard the Old Fisherman Say*.
61. Marshall, *Ocean Traders*, p. 126.
62. The Galveston, Houston & Henderson was 5'6" compared to the 4' 8 1/2" of the standard-gauge lines.
63. Baughman, *Charles Morgan*, p. 201.
64. Baughman, *The Mallorys*, p. 184.
65. McComb, *Galveston*, pp. 111–112.
66. Ibid., p. 112.
67. See, for example, Martha S. Putney's *Black Sailors: Afro-American Merchant Seamen and Whalemen Prior to the Civil War*.
68. *Galveston Daily News*, March 16, 1900.
69. "Nueces Pulled at Her," *Galveston Daily News*, April 2, 1900.
70. "Lampasas Is Off Uninjured," *Galveston Daily News*, April 3, 1900.

CONCLUSION
TEXAS MARITIME HISTORY IN RETROSPECT

1. Some observers have speculated that the foundries that once produced Civil War materiel were now refocused on the architectural trades and leisure products.

2. Cecilia Steinfeldt, *Texas Folk Art: One Hundred Fifty Years of the Southwestern Tradition* (Austin: Texas Monthly Press, 1981), pp. 248–249.

3. McGuire, *Julius Stockfleth*, pp. 1–13.

4. For a historical overview of Corpus Christi's harbor, navigation, and shipwrecks, see Pearson and Wells, *Magnetometer Survey of the Gulf Intracoastal Waterway*.

5. Maril, *Texas Shrimpers*, pp. 6–7.

6. Ann Gallaway, "Homeward Bound—*Elissa's* Historic Voyage," *Texas Highways*, 43, no. 7(July 1996): p. 15.

7. R. H. Smith, *Guide to Maritime Museums*, p. 231.

8. Significantly, the *Colonel's* sternwheel is strictly cosmetic. It provides no propulsive power at all, whereas the *Natchez* at New Orleans and the boats of the Delta Queen Steamboat Company are true sternwheelers.

9. "Mandolin Rain," by Bruce Hornsby and the Range, from the album *The Way It Is*; personal telephone conversation by the author with the song writer John Hornsby, September 23, 1996.

10. Recent wrecks and those on private property, however, are open to salvage or looting.

Glossary of
Nautical Terms

astrolabe — an instrument used for determining latitude by measuring the altitude of the sun or stars; it consists of a circular vernier and a rotating alidade with two sight holes.

ballast — a load of stone or other dense, heavy material placed in a vessel's hold to offset the efforts of the wind on the masts and sails and provide stability.

bar — a submerged or partly submerged bank (as of sand) along a shore or in a river often obstructing navigation.

bark (or barque) — a three-masted sailing vessel with foremast and mainmast square-rigged and mizzenmast fore-and-aft-rigged.

beam — the width of a vessel's hull; one of the principal horizontal members of a vessel's frame.

boatswain — a petty officer on a merchant ship having charge of hull maintenance and related work.

brigantine — a two-masted vessel, square-rigged on foremast and fore- and aft-rigged on mainmast, differing from a brig in not carrying a square mainsail.

captain — a naval officer who is commander of a vessel.

caravel — a small fifteenth- and sixteenth-century vessel that has broad bows, a high and narrow poop, and usually three masts with lateen or both square and lateen sails.

careen — to cause (a boat) to lean over on one side; to clean, caulk, or repair (a boat) in this position.

centerboard — a retractable keel used especially in sailboats.

clipper — a fast-sailing ship, especially one with long, slender lines, an overhanging bow, tall raking masts, and a large sail area.

corvette — a warship ranking in the old sailing navies next below a frigate; a highly maneuverable armed escort ship that is smaller than a destroyer.

draft — the depth of water necessary to float a vessel; hence, a vessel is said to draw so many feet of water.

fathom — a unit of length equal to six feet, used especially for measuring the depth of water.

foremast — the mast nearest the bow of a sailing vessel.

galleon — a heavy, square-rigged sailing vessel of the fifteenth to early eighteenth centuries used for war or commerce, especially by the Spanish.

gunwale—the upper edge of a vessel's side, originally designed to support swivel guns.

hawser—a large rope used for mooring or anchoring.

hooker—a single-masted fishing or cargo-carrying boat; shoreship.

hulk—a heavy, clumsy vessel; the body of an old vessel unfit for service; an abandoned wreck or shell; a vessel used as a prison.

kedge—a small anchor used to keep a vessel steady in harbor or for moving a vessel from one location to another.

keel—the principal timber or backbone of a vessel.

keelson—a longitudinal structure running above, and fastened to, the keel of a vessel in order to stiffen and strengthen its framework.

knee—a crooked piece of timber, having two branching arms, used to connect the beams of a vessel with its sides; or a timber serving to strengthen the assembly. Knees are either lodging or hanging: The former are fixed horizontally, the latter vertically.

lateen—being or relating to a rig used especially on the north coast of Africa and characterized by a triangular sail extended by a long spar slung to a low mast.

league—any of various units of distance from about 2.4 to 4.6 statute miles.

log—a device for measuring a vessel's speed through the water, consisting of a reel and line to which is fixed a piece of wood that will float on the water.

longboat—one of the service boats belonging to a larger, seagoing vessel.

mainmast—a sailing vessel's principal mast, usually second from the bow.

midship frame—the timbers that make up the broadest part of the vessel's hull, usually around the middle of its length.

mizzenmast—the mast aft or next aft of the mainmast of a sailing vessel.

packet—a passenger boat carrying mail and cargo on a regular schedule.

poop deck—the highest and aftermost deck of a vessel.

privateer—an armed private ship commissioned to seize the commerce or warships of an enemy.

purser—an official on a vessel responsible for papers and accounts and, on a passenger vessel, also for the comfort and welfare of passengers.

rake—the projection of the upper parts of a vessel at the height of the stem and stern beyond the extremities of the keel. If a plumb bob is hung from the top of a vessel's sternpost down to the level of the keel, the distance between the after end of the keel and the plumb will be the length of the "rake aft," or the rake of the stern.

reef—a chain of rocks or ridge of sand at or near the surface of water; a hazardous obstruction.

rigging—the entire system of line, chain, and tackle used to support and control the mast, yards, and sails of a sailing vessel.

schooner—a typically two-masted fore-and-aft-rigged vessel with a foremast and a mainmast stepped nearly amidships.

scupper hole—one of a series of channels cut through the sides of a vessel at certain intervals to drain water from the deck into the sea.

shallop—a usually two-masted sailing vessel with lugsails; a small open boat propelled by oars or sails and used chiefly in shallow waters.

sheer—the longitudinal curve of a vessel's deck or hull.

sheer line—the sweep of the deck up to the stempost and sternpost.

ship—technically, a sailing vessel having a bowsprit and usually three masts each composed of a lower mast, a topmast, and a topgallant mast; popularly any large seagoing vessel.

ship's master—the person in charge of the overall operation of the vessel.

shoal—a sandbank or sandbar that makes the water shallow.

skipper—the master of a vessel; especially, the master of a fishing, small trading, or pleasure boat.

sloop—a fore- and aft-rigged sailboat with one mast and a single headsail jib.

sounding lead—a lead plummet on a rope that is let down to the seabed in order to gauge water depths.

square rigger—a square-rigged craft (a sailing vessel rig in which the principal sails are extended on yards fastened to the masts horizontally and at their center).

stem—the timber that unites the sides of a vessel at its forward end.

sterncastle—the aftermost superstructure, housing the binnacle, tiller, and living areas.

sternpost—a long piece of straight timber erected on the after end of the keel, and providing a place for the rudder to be mounted.

sternwheeler—a paddlewheel steamer having a sternwheel instead of sidewheels.

stevedore—one who works at or is responsible for loading and unloading vessels in port.

strake—a series of planks joined to one another and running from the stem to the stern.

tiller—the bar or lever attached to the head of the rudder to turn it.

transom—beams or timbers extended across the sternpost of a vessel to strengthen and cover the after part of the vessel.

urca—a ship of the hooker type, often sloop-rigged; a storeship.

windlass—a machine consisting of a horizontal cylinder mounted on deck and turned with handspikes to wind the hawser and lift the anchor from the bottom.

BIBLIOGRAPHY

Abbott, Peyton O. "Business Travel Out of Texas During the Civil War: The Travel Diary of S. B. Brush, Pioneer Austin Merchant" (Notes and Documents). *Southwestern Historical Quarterly* 96, no. 2(October 1992): pp. 259–271.

Abell, Sir Westcott S. *The Shipwright's Trade*. Cambridge: Cambridge University Press, 1948.

Albion, Robert G. *Square Riggers on Schedule: The New York Sailing Packets to England, France, and the Cotton Ports*. Princeton, N.J.: Princeton University Press, 1938.

———. "Early Nineteenth-Century Shipowning: A Chapter in Business Enterprise." *Journal of Economic History* 1 (May 1941): pp. 1–11.

———. *Naval and Maritime History: An Annotated Bibliography*. Mystic, Conn.: Marine Historical Association, 1972.

Alperin, Lynn M. *Custodians of the Coast: History of the United States Army Engineers at Galveston*. Galveston, Tex.: Galveston District, U.S. Army Corps of Engineers, 1977.

Ames, John W. "Leaving Texas." *Overland Monthly*, February 12, 1874, pp. 130–137.

Anderson, Romola, and R. C. Anderson. *The Sailing Ship*. New York: W. W. Norton & Co., 1963.

Arnold, J. Barto III. *An Underwater Archeological Magnetometer Survey and Site Test Excavation Project Off Padre Island, Texas*, Texas Antiquities Committee Publication no. 3. Austin: Texas Antiquities Committee, 1976.

———. "The Flota Disaster of 1554." In *Beneath the Waters of Time: The Proceedings of the Ninth Conference on Underwater Archaeology*. Texas Antiquities Committee Publication no. 6. Austin: Texas Antiquities Committee, 1978.

———. *1977 Underwater Site Test Excavations Off Padre Island, Texas*. Texas Antiquities Committee Publication no. 5. Austin: Texas Antiquities Committee, 1978.

———. "A Matagorda Bay Magnetometer Survey and Site Text Excavation Project." Texas Antiquities Committee Publication no. 9. Austin: Texas Antiquities Committee, 1982.

———. "The Mystery of Matagorda Bay: An Archaeological Discovery." In *The Philosophical Society of Texas Proceedings of the Annual Meeting at Corpus Christi*, vol. 59, pp. 68–76, 1996.

Arnold, J. Barto III, and Richard Anuskiewicz. "U.S.S. Hatteras: Site Monitoring and Mapping." In *Underwater Archaeology Proceedings from the Society for Historical Archaeology Conference*, edited by Paul F. Johnson. Society for Historical Archaeology, 1995, pp. 82–87.

Arnold, J. Barto III, Clive Cussler, and Wayne Gronquist. "The Survey for the *Zavala*, a Steam Warship of the Republic of Texas." In *Proceedings from the Conference on Historical and Underwater Archaeology*, edited by Toni L. Carrell. Tucson, Ariz., 1990, pp. 105–109.

Arnold, J. Barto III, George Roseberry, Laura Landry, Jim Hauser, and Toni Carrell. "Preliminary Mapping of the Caney Creek Wreck: A Model of Appropriate Private Sector Access to an Historic Shipwreck." Paper presented at the Society for Historical Archaeology meeting, Vancouver, January 5–9, 1994.

Arnold, J. Barto III, and Robert Weddle. *The Nautical Archaeology of Padre Island: The Spanish Shipwrecks of 1554*. New York: Academic Press, 1978.

Ashley, Raymond. "From the Helm." *Mains'l Haul, A Journal of Maritime History* 31, no. 4(Fall 1995).

Aten, Lawrence E. *Indians of the Upper Texas Coast*. New York: Academic Press, 1983.

Baker, T. Lindsay. *Lighthouses of Texas*. College Station: Texas A&M University Press, 1991.

Balder, A. P. *Mariner's Atlas of Texas, Upper Texas Coast*. Houston: Gulf Publishing Co., 1992.

Barksdale, E. C. *The Meat Packers Come to Texas*. Austin: University of Texas Press, 1959.

Barnes, Al. *The Texas Gulf Coast: Interpretations by Nine Artists*. College Station: Texas A&M Press, 1979.

Barr, Alwyn. "Texas Coastal Defense, 1861–1865." *Southwestern Historical Quarterly* 45 (July 1961): pp. 1–31.

Bastian, David F. "The Development of Dredging Through the 1850s." In *On the History and Evolution of U.S. Waterways and Ports*, National Waterways Round Table Papers, Proceedings. Norfolk, Va.: U.S. Army Engineer Water Resources Support Center, 1980 pp. 1–22.

Bates, A. L. *The Western Rivers Steamboat Cyclopedium*. Leonia, N.J.: Hustle Press, 1981.

Baughman, James P. *Charles Morgan and the Development of Southern Transportation*. Nashville: Vanderbilt University Press, 1968.

———. *The Mallorys of Mystic: Six Generations in American Maritime Enterprise*. Middletown, Conn.: Wesleyan University Press, 1972.

Beavis, L. R. W. *Passage From Sail to Steam*. Bellevue, Wash.: Documentary Book Publishers, 1986.

Bennett, Frank M. *The Steam Navy of the United States*. Pittsburgh: W. T. Nicholson, 1896.

Blake, Edith. "The Astrolabe." *Sail* 3, no. 7(July 1972): pp. 64–65.

Block, W. T. "Cotton Bales, Keelboats, and Sternwheelers: A History of the Trinity River Trade, 1838–1893," 61 p. 28 cm.

Block, W. T., *Cotton Bales, Keelboats, and Sternwheelers: A History of the Sabine River and Trinity River Cotton Trades, 1837–1900.* Woodville, Texas: Dogwood Press, 1995.

Boudriot, Jean. *Historique de la Corvette, 1650–1850.* Paris: Collection Archeologie Navale Francaise, 1990, p. 15.

Bowen, J. H., C. G. Groat, L. F. Brown Jr., W. L. Fisher, and A. J. Scott. *Effects of Hurricane Celia—A Focus on Environmental Geologic Problems of the Texas Coastal Zone.* Austin: Bureau of Economic Geology, University of Texas, August 1970.

Boynton, Charles. *The History of the Navy During the Rebellion.* 2 vols. New York: D. Appleton, 1868.

Brasseaux, Carl A., and Richard Chandler. "The *Britain* Incident, 1769–1770: Anglo-Hispanic Tensions in the Western Gulf." *Southwestern Historical Quarterly* 87, no. 4(April 1984): pp. 357–370.

Britt, John, and Muriel Tyssen. *Baytown Vignettes: One Hundred and Fifty Years in the History of a Texas Gulf Coast Community.* Baytown, Tex: Lee College, ca. 1992.

Buckley, Pamela. "Galveston When *Elissa* First Arrived." *Sea History,* Winter 1982–1983 (Commemorative Issue, reprinted from Fall 1979), pp. 16–17.

Bugbee, Lester G. "What Became of the Lively?" *Quarterly of the Texas State Historical Association* 3, no. 2(October 1899): pp. 141–148.

Buisseret, David. *Tools of Empire: Ships and Maps in the Process of Westward Expansion* ([Guide to] An Exhibit at the Newberry Library, Opening on 3 June 1986). Chicago: The Newberry Library, 1986.

———. "Spanish and French Mapping of the Gulf in the Sixteenth and Seventeenth Centuries." In *The Mapping of the American Southwest,* ed. Dennis Reinhartz and Charles Culley. College Station: Texas A&M Press, 1987.

———. *From Sea Charts to Satellite Images: Interpreting North American History Through Maps.* Chicago: University of Chicago Press, 1990.

Carroll, William M. *Béranger's Discovery of Aransas Pass—A Translation of Jean Béranger's French Manuscript.* Corpus Christi: Friends of the Corpus Christi Museum, 1983.

Carter, Robert Foster. "The Texan Navy." *U.S. Naval Institute Proceedings* 59, no. 365(1935): pp. 1032–1038.

Casis, Lilia M. "Discovery of Bay of Espíritu Santo" [translation of the Carta de Don Damian Manzanet a Don Carlos de Siguenza Sobre el Descubrimiento de la Bahía del Espíritu Santo]. *Quarterly of the Texas State Historical Association* 2, no. 4(April 1899): 253–312.

Chapelle, Howard I. *The History of American Sailing Ships.* New York: W. W. Norton, 1935.

———. *The History of the American Sailing Navy.* New York: W. W. Norton, 1949.

———. *The Search for Speed Under Sail, 1700–1855*. New York: Bonanza, 1967.

———. *American Sailing Craft*. Camden, Me: International Marine Publishing Co., 1975.

Chipman, Donald. "In Search of Cabeza de Vaca's Route Across Texas: An Historiographical Survey." *Southwestern Historical Quarterly* 91, no. 2(October 1987): pp. 127–148.

———. "Cabeza de Vaca, Alvar Nuñez de." *The New Handbook of Texas*, vol. 1. Austin: Texas State Historical Association, 1996, pp. 882–883.

Cipolla, Carlo M. *Guns, Sails, and Empires: Technological Innovation and the Early Phases of European Expansion, 1400–1700*. New York: Minerva Press, 1965.

City of Galveston Island, in Texas, with a History of the Title of the Proprietor and a Brief Account of All Its Advantages; Accompanied with a Plan of the City and Harbor, and a Map of Texas, Showing the Commercial Channels with the Interior Through Which the City Is to Derive Its Extensive Trade. New Orleans: Hotchkiss & Co., 1837.

Clark, Joseph Lynn. *The Texas Gulf Coast, Its History and Development*. New York: Lewis Historical Pub. Co., 1955.

Clay, John V. *Spain, Mexico and the Lower Trinity: An Early History of the Texas Gulf Coast*. Baltimore: Gateway Press, 1987.

Cole, E. W. "La Salle in Texas." *Southwestern Historical Quarterly* 49, no. 4(April 1946): pp. 473–500.

Culver, Henry B. *The Book of Old Ships and Something of Their Evolution and Romance*. New York: Garden City Publishing Co., 1924.

Cumberland, Charles C. "The Confederate Loss and Recapture of Galveston, 1862–1863." *Southwestern Historical Quarterly* 51 (October 1947): pp. 109–130.

Cutter, Donald. *The Defenses of Northern New Spain: Hugo O'Conor's Report to Teodoro de Croix, July 22, 1777*. Dallas: Southern Methodist University Press, 1994.

Daniel, James M. *The Ships of the Texas Navy: A List Compiled by James M. Daniels*. San Jacinto Museum of History Association, 1948.

Davenport, Harbert. "Notes on Early Steamboating on the Rio Grande." *Southwestern Historical Quarterly* 49, no. 2(October 1945): pp. 286–289.

Davis, John. *Treasure, People, Ships, and Dreams: A Spanish Shipwreck on the Texas Coast*. San Antonio: Texas Antiquities Committee, 1977.

Dawson, Frederick. "Petition of Frederick Dawson, James Schott, and Elisha Dana Whitney, Praying Payment for Certain Vessels, Etc., Furnished Texas and Given Up by Texas to the U.S. on the Annexation of Texas," 6 pp. Senate. 30th Cong., 1st sess., Misc. no. 27. Washington: Government Printing Office, 1848.

de Ledesma, Pedro. "The Description of Seven Salvage Techniques." Madrid: Museo Naval, MS 1035, Seccíon C, ca. 1623, as translated by J. Barto Arnold in *Documentary Sources for the Wreck of the Spain Fleet of 1554*, ed. David McDonald and J. Barto Arnold III. Austin: Texas Antiquities Committee, 1979.

Denham, James M. "Charles E. Hawkins: Sailor of Three Republics." *Gulf Coast Historical Review* 5, no. 2(Spring 1990): pp. 92–103.

Douglas, Claude Leroy. *Thunder on the Gulf; or, The Story of the Texas Navy*. Dallas: Turner Company, 1936.

Emory, William H. *Report on the United States and Mexican Boundary Survey*, vol. 1. *Made Under the Direction of the Secretary of the Interior*. Austin: Texas State Historical Association, 1987.

Favata, Martin A., and Jose B. Fernandez, eds. *The Account: Alvar Núñez Cabeza de Vaca's Relación*. Houston: Arte Público Press, University of Houston, 1993.

Fehrenbatch, John. *A Library of Steam Engineering*. Cincinnati: Ohio Valley Company, 1895.

Fisher, Ernest G. *Robert Potter: Founder of the Texas Navy*. Gretna, La.: Pelican Publishing Co., 1976.

Fisher, W. L., J. H. McGowen, L. F. Brown Jr., and C. G. Groat. *Environmental Geologic Atlas of the Texas Coastal Zone*. 6 vols. Austin: University of Texas at Austin, Bureau of Economic Geology, 1973–1980.

Fluth, Alice F. "Indianola, Early Gateway to Texas." M.A. thesis, St. Mary's University, 1939.

Fotheringham, Nick, and Susan Brunenmeister. *Beachcomber's Guide to Gulf Coast Marine Life: Florida, Alabama, Mississippi, Louisiana & Texas*. Houston: Gulf Publishing Co., 1989.

Freeman, Martha Doty. *A History of Civil War Military Activities at Velasco & Quintana, Brazoria County, & Virginia Point, Galveston County, Texas*. Reports of Investigation, no. 103. Austin: Prewitt and Associates, 1995.

Freeman, Martha Doty, and Sandra L. Hannum. *A History of Fortifications at Fort San Jacinto, Galveston Island, Texas*. Reports of Investigation, no. 80. Austin: Prewitt and Associates, 1991.

Freeman, Martha Doty, and Elton R. Prewitt. *Sargent Beach Project: A History of Confederate Defense at the Mouth of Caney Creek, Matagorda County, Texas*. Reports of Investigation, no. 98. Austin: Prewitt and Associates, 1994.

Galveston Genealogical Society. *Ships Passenger Lists, Port of Galveston, Texas, 1846–1871*. Easley, S.C.: Southern Historical Press, 1984.

Garcia, Clotilde. *Captain Alonso Alvarez de Piñeda and the Exploration of the Texas Coast and Gulf of Mexico*. Austin: San Felipe Press, 1982.

Garrett, Jenkins. *The Mexican-American War of 1846–1848: A Bibliography of the Holdings of the Libraries—The University of Texas at Arlington*, prepared and edited by Katherine R. Goodwin. Special Collections Publication no. 2. College Station: Texas A&M University Press, 1995.

Garza, Roberto. "An Island in Geographic Transition: A Study of the Changing Land Use Patterns of Padre Island, Texas." Ph.D. dissertation, University of Colorado, 1980.

Gatschet, Albert S. *The Karankawa Indians, the Coast People of Texas*. Cambridge, Mass.: Peabody Museum of American Archaeology and Ethnology, 1891. Reprint, New York: Kraus Reprint Corp., 1967.

Gilliam, Albert M. *Travels over the Table Lands and Cordilleras of Mexico During the Years 1843 and 1844*. Philadelphia: John W. Moore, 1846.

"Great Commercial Advantages of the Gulf of Mexico." *DeBow's Review* 7, (December 1849): 510–523.

Gournay, Luke. *Texas Boundaries: Evolution of the State's Counties.* College Station: Texas A&M University Press, 1995.

Guérin, Léon. *Histoire Maritime de France,* vol. 3. Paris: Dufour et Mulat, Editeurs, 1854.

Guevin, Bryan. "Archaeological Bibliography: Geographical Subject Index of Texas Shipwrecks by Waterway." U.S. Army Corps of Engineers–Galveston District, April 1996, 17 pp.

Guthrie, Keith. *Texas Forgotten Ports.* 2 vols. Austin: Eakin Press, 1988.

Hackett, Charles Wilson, ed. *Historical Documents Relating to New Mexico, Nueva Vizcaya, and Approaches Thereto, to 1773.* 2 vols. Washington, D.C.: Carnegie Institution, 1923, 1926.

Hamilton, Earl. "Wages and Subsistence on Spanish Treasure Ships, 1503–1660." *Journal of Political Economy* 37 (1929): pp. 430–450.

Hannemann, Max. *Die Seehäfen von Texas: Ihre geographischen Grundlagen, ihre Entwicklung und Bedeutung,* vol. 2, no. 1. Frankfurt: Frankfurter Geographische Hefte, 1928.

Haring, Clarence Henry. *Trade and Navigation Between Spain and the Indies in the Time of the Hapsburgs.* Cambridge: Harvard University Press, 1918. Reprinted, Gloucester, Mass.: Peter Smith, 1964.

Harland, J. *Seamanship in the Age of Sail.* Annapolis, Md.: U.S. Naval Institute Press, 1987.

Hayes, Charles W. *Galveston: History of the Island and the City.* 2 vols. Austin: Jenkins Garrett Press, 1974.

Hill, Jim Dan. *The Texas Navy in Forgotten Battles and Shirtsleeve Diplomacy.* Austin: State House Press, 1987.

Hill, Ralph N. *Sidewheeler Saga: A Chronicle of Steamboating.* New York: Rinehart, 1953.

Holdcamper, Forrest R., ed. *Merchant Steam Vessels of the United States, 1807–1868: The "Lytle List."* Mystic, Conn.: Marine Historical Association, 1952.

Horner, David. *The Treasure Galleons: Clues to Millions in Sunken Gold and Silver.* New York: Dodd, Mead & Co., 1971.

Houstoun, Mrs. Matilda Charlotte (Jesse) Fraser. *Texas and the Gulf of Mexico: or, Yachting in the New World.* 2 vols. London: J. Murray, 1844.

Howard, F. *Sailing Ships of War, 1400–1960* New York: Mayflower, 1979.

Hoyt, Steven D., *National Register Assessment of the SS Mary, Port Aransas, Nueces County, Texas.* Austin: Espey, Huston & Associates, October 1990.

Hoyt, Steven D., and Robert Gearhart. *Underwater Investigations: Brazos Island Harbor Navigation Project, Cameron County, Texas.* Austin: Espey, Huston & Associates, January 1992.

Hoyt, Steven D., and James S. Schmidt. *Magnetometer Survey of Sabine Pass Channel and Assessment of the Clifton, 41JF65, Jefferson County, Texas.* Austin: Espey, Huston & Associates, September 1994.

Hunt, Richard S., and Jesse F. Randel. *Guide to the Republic of Texas: Consisting of a Brief Outline of the History of Its Settlement.* New York: Hunt & Randel, 1839.

———. *A New Guide to the Republic of Texas.* New York: Hunt & Randel, 1845.

Hunter, Louis C. *Steamboats on the Western Rivers: An Economic and Technological History.* New York: Octagon Books, 1969.

Huson, Hobart. *El Copano, the Ancient Port of Béxar and La Bahía.* Refugio, Tex.: The Refugio Timely Remarks, 1939.

Hutchins, John Greenwood Brown. *The American Maritime Industries and Public Policy, 1789–1914: An Economic History.* Cambridge: Harvard University Press, 1914.

Jackson, Donald. *Voyages of the Steamboat Yellow Stone.* New York: Ticknor and Fields, 1985.

Jackson, Jack. *Mapping Texas and the Gulf Coast: The Contributions of St. Denis, Oliván, and Le Maire.* College Station: Texas A&M University Press, 1990.

———. *Flags Along the Coast: Charting the Gulf of Mexico, 1519–1759: A Reappraisal.* Austin: Book Club of Texas, 1995.

James, Stephen R. Jr., Jack C. Hudson, and Kay G. Hudson. *The 303 Hang: Archaeological Investigations of a Two Masted Schooner Wrecked Offshore Freeport, Brazoria County, Texas.* Report submitted by Panamerican Consultants, Inc., to the U.S. Army Corps of Engineers–Galveston District, August 1991.

James, Stephen R. Jr., and Charles E. Pearson. *Magnetometer Survey and Ground Truthing Anomalies—Corpus Christi Ship Channel, Aransas and Nueces Counties, Texas.* Report submitted by Coastal Environments, Inc., to the U.S. Army Corps of Engineers–Galveston District, December 1991.

James, Stephen R. Jr., Charles E. Pearson, Kay Hudson, and Jackson Hudson. *Archaeological and Historical Investigations of the Wreck of the Gen. C. B. Comstock, Brazoria County, Texas.* Report submitted by Coastal Environments, Inc., to the U.S. Army Corps of Engineers–Galveston District, April 1991.

Jordan, Terry. *Environment and Environmental Perceptions in Texas.* Boston: American Press, 1980.

Jordan, Terry, with John L. Bean Jr. and William M. Holmes. *Texas: A Geography.* Boulder, Colo.: Westview Press, 1984.

Kelley, Pat. *River of Lost Dreams: Navigation on the Rio Grande.* Lincoln: University of Nebraska Press, 1986.

Kemp, Peter. *The History of Ships.* London: Macdonald & Co., 1988.

———, ed. *The Oxford Companion to Ships and the Sea.* New York: Oxford University Press, 1976.

Kennedy, William. *Texas: The Rise, Progress, and Prospects of the Republic of Texas.* 2 vols. London: R. Hastings, 1841.

———. *Texas: Its Geography, Natural History and Topography.* New York: Benjamin and Young, 1844.

King, Irving H. *The Coast Guard Under Sail: The U.S. Revenue Cutter Service, 1789–1865.* Annapolis, Md.: U.S. Naval Institute Press, 1989.

Knox, Thomas W. *The Life of Robert Fulton.* 1886.

Landström, Björn. *The Ship*. Garden City, N.Y.: Doubleday; London: Allen & Unwin, 1961.

——. *Sailing Ships*. Garden City, N.Y.: Doubleday & Co., 1969.

Lane, Carl D. *American Paddle Steamboats*. New York: Coward-McCann, 1943.

Lang, Steven, and Peter Spectre. *On the Hawser: A Tugboat Album*. Camden, Me.: Down East Books, 1980.

Lewis, W. S. "The Adventures of the 'Lively' Immigrants, I." *Quarterly of the Texas State Historical Association* 3, no. 1(July 1899): pp. 1–32.

——. "The Adventures of the 'Lively' Immigrants, II." *Quarterly of the Texas State Historical Association* 3, no. 2(October 1899): pp. 89–107.

Lytle, William M., and Forrest R. Holdcamper. *Merchant Steam Vessels of the United States, 1790–1868*. Staten Island, N.Y.: Steamship Historical Society of America, 1975.

Mahan, William. *Padre Island: Treasure Kingdom of the World*. Waco: Texian Press, 1967.

Malsch, Brownson. *Indianola: The Mother of Western Texas*. Austin: State House Press, 1988.

Maril, Robert Lee. *Texas Shrimpers: Community, Capitalism and the Sea*. College Station: Texas A&M University Press, 1983.

——. *Cannibals and Condos: Texans and Texas Along the Gulf Coast*. College Station: Texas A&M University Press, 1986.

Marshall, Michael W. *Ocean Traders—From the Portuguese Discoveries to the Present Day*. New York: Facts on File, 1990.

Martin, Robert S., and James C. Martin. *Contours of Discovery: Printed Maps Delineating the Texas and Southwestern Chapters in the Cartographic History of North America, 1513–1930*. Austin: Texas Historical Association in cooperation with the University of Texas at Austin, 1981.

Martinez-Hidalgo, Jose Maria. *Columbus' Ships*. Barre, Mass.: Barre Publishers, 1966.

Marx, Robert F. *The Treasure Fleets of the Spanish Main*. Cleveland: World Publishing Co., 1968.

——. *Shipwrecks of the Western Hemisphere 1492–1825*. New York: World Publishing Co., 1971.

Mathewson, R. Duncan III. *Treasure of the Atocha*. New York: E. P. Dutton Pices Books, 1986.

McCampbell, Coleman. *Texas Seaport: The Story of the Growth of Corpus Christi and the Coastal Bend Area*. New York: Exposition Press, 1952.

McComb, David G. *Galveston: A History*. Austin: University of Texas Press, 1986.

McDermott, John Francis, ed. *Frenchmen and French Ways in the Mississippi Valley*. Urbana: University of Illinois Press, 1969.

McDonald, David, and J. Barto Arnold III. *Documentary Sources for the Wreck of the Spain Fleet of 1554*. Austin: Texas Antiquities Committee, 1979.

McGowen, J. H., C. G. Groat, L. F. Brown Jr., W. L. Fisher, and A. J. Scott. *Effects of Hurricane Celia—A Focus on Environmental Geologic Problems of the Texas*

Coastal Zone. Austin: Bureau of Economic Geology, University of Texas at Austin, 1970.

McGuire, James Patrick. *Julius Stockfleth: Gulf Coast Marine and Landscape Painter*. San Antonio: Trinity University Press; Galveston: Rosenberg Library, 1976.

McMurry, Gerda. *The Texas Coast: A Verbal and Artistic Portrait*. Corpus Christi: Texas News Syndicate Press, 1975.

"The Morgan Line and Its Founders: A Sketch of Mr. Charles Morgan." *Nautical Gazette*, November 3, 1875.

Morison, Samuel Eliot. *The European Discovery of America: The Southern Voyages, A.D. 1492–1616*. New York: Oxford University Press, 1974.

Morrison, John H. *History of American Steam Navigation*. New York: W. F. Sametz & Co., 1903.

Morton, Robert A. *Historical Shoreline Changes and Their Causes: Texas Gulf Coast*. Austin: Bureau of Economic Geology, University of Texas at Austin, 1977.

———. *Shoreline Changes on Mustang Island and North Padre Island*. Austin: Bureau of Economic Geology, University of Texas at Austin, 1977.

Morton, Robert A., and Joseph H. McGowen. *Shoreline Changes on Matagorda Peninsula*. Austin: Bureau of Economic Geology, University of Texas at Austin, 1976.

Morton, Robert A., and Mary J. Pieper. *Shoreline Changes in the Vicinity of the Brazos River Delta*. Austin: Bureau of Economic Geology, University of Texas at Austin, 1975.

———. *Shoreline Changes on Matagorda Island and San Jose Island*. Austin: Bureau of Economic Geology, University of Texas at Austin, 1976.

———. *Shoreline Changes on Central Padre Island*. Austin: Bureau of Economic Geology, University of Texas at Austin, 1977.

Mott, Lawrence V. *The Development of the Rudder: A Technological Tale*. College Station: Texas A&M University Press, 1996.

Muir, Andrew Forest, ed. *Texas in 1837: An Anonymous Contemporary Narrative*. Austin: University of Texas Press, 1958.

Mullen, Patrick B. *I Heard the Old Fishermen Say: Folklore of the Texas Gulf*. Logan: Utah State University Press, ca. 1988.

Naish, G. P. B. "Ships and Shipbuilding." In *A History of Technology*, 3d ed., vol. 3. Edited by Charles Joseph Singer et al. Oxford: Clarendon Press, 1969, pp. 471–500.

Neu, C. T. "The Case of the Brig *Pocket*." *Quarterly of the Texas State Historical Association* 12(April 1909): pp. 276–295.

Newcomb, W. W. *The Indians of Texas*. Austin: The University of Texas Press, 1961.

———. "Yo Ho Ho and . . ." *The Mustang* (newsletter of the Texas Memorial Museum, University of Texas at Austin) 11, no. 4(Aug.–Sept. 1969). Also issued as *Mimeographed Papers*, no. 13.

Neyland, Robert F. "The Naval War for the North Texas Coast." In *Proceedings from the Society for Historical and Underwater Archaeology Conference*. Edited by Shelli W. Smith. Kansas City, Mo., 1993, pp. 115–122.

North, D. J. "The Astrolabe." *Scientific American* 230, no. 1(January 1974): 96–106.

Nuñez Cabeza de Vaca, Alvar. *The Account: Alvar Nuñez Cabeza de Vaca's Relación*, edited by Martin A. Favata and José B. Fernandez. Houston: Arte Público Press, 1993.

Oertling, Thomas J. *Ships' Bilge Pumps: A History of Their Development, 1500–1900*. College Station: Texas A&M University Press, 1996.

Olds, Dorris L. *Texas Legacy from the Gulf: A Report on Sixteenth Century Shipwreck Materials Recovered from the Texas Tidelands*. Miscellaneous Papers Number 5, Texas Memorial Museum; Publication Number 2, Texas Antiquities Committee Austin: The Texas Memorial Museum, 1976.

Paine, Jeffrey G., and Robert A. Morton. *Historical Shoreline Changes in Corpus Christi, Oso, and Nueces Bays, Texas Gulf Coast*. Geological Circular 84-6. Austin: Bureau of Economic Geology, University of Texas at Austin, 1984.

———. *Shoreline and Vegetation-Line Movement, Texas Gulf Coast, 1974 to 1982*. Geological Circular 89-1. Austin: Bureau of Economic Geology, University of Texas at Austin, 1989.

———. *Historical Shoreline Changes in Copano, Aransas, and Redfish Bays, Texas Gulf Coast*. Austin: Bureau of Economic Geology, University of Texas at Austin, 1993.

Parry, J. H. *The Age of Reconnaissance: Discovery, Exploration and Settlement 1450–1650*. New York: World Publishing Co. and New American Library; London: J. H. Parry, 1963. Reprint, New York: Praeger Publishers, 1969.

Paul, Paula G. *Sarah, Sissy Weed, and the Ships of the Desert*. Austin: Eakin Press, 1985.

Pearson, Charles E. *Phase 2 of Emergency Investigation of Submerged Historic Property, Freeport Harbor 45-Foot Project, Brazoria County, Texas*. Report submitted by Coastal Environments, Inc., to the U.S. Army Corps of Engineers–Galveston District (contract no. DACW64-87-D-0004; delivery order no. 0009), 1989.

Pearson, Charles E., Jacques Bagur, and James Duff. *Identification and Analysis of Historic Watercraft in the Shreveport, Louisiana to Daingerfield, Texas, Navigation Project*. Report submitted by Coastal Environments, Inc., to the U.S. Army Corps of Engineers–Vicksburg District (contract no. DACW38-91-D-0014; delivery order no. 007), 1994.

Pearson, Charles E., and Paul E. Hoffman. *The Last Voyage of El Nuevo Constante: The Wreck and Recovery of an Eighteenth Century Spanish Ship Off the Louisiana Coast*. Baton Rouge: Louisiana State University Press, 1995.

Pearson, Charles E., Stephen R. James Jr., Kay G. Hudson, and James A. Duff. *Underwater Archaeology Along the Lower Navidad and Lavaca Rivers, Jackson County, Texas*. Report submitted by Coastal Environments, Inc., to the U.S. Army Corps of Engineers–Galveston District (contract no. DACW64-91-D-0009; delivery order nos. 3 and 5), May 1993.

Pearson, Charles E., and Joe J. Simmons III. *Magnetometer Survey of the Gulf Intracoastal Waterway (GIWW), Port Aransas to Live Oak Point, Aransas and Calhoun Counties, Texas*. Report submitted by Coastal Environments, Inc., to the U.S.

Army Corps of Engineers–Galveston District (contract no. DACW64-94-D-0004; delivery order no. 0001), 1994.

———. *Underwater Archaeology of the Wreck of the Steamship Mary 41NU252 and Assessment of Seven Anomalies, Corpus Christi Entrance Channel, Nueces County, Texas.* Report submitted by Coastal Environments, Inc., to the U.S. Army Corps of Engineers–Galveston District (Texas Antiquities Permit no. 1261), July 1995.

Pearson, Charles E., and Tom Wells. *Magnetometer Survey of the Gulf Intracoastal Waterway (GIWW), Corpus Christi Bay to Point Penascal, Nueces, Kleberg, and Kenedy Counties, Texas.* Report submitted by Coastal Environments, Inc., to the U.S. Army Corps of Engineers–Galveston District (contract no. DACW64-94-D-0004; delivery order no. 0003), 1995.

Peterson, Mendel L. "Ordnance Material Recovered from an Early Seventeenth Century Wreck Site." *Military Collector and Historian* (Journal of the Company of Military Collectors and Historians) 13, no. 3(Fall): pp. 69–82.

Phillips, Carla Rahn. *Six Galleons for the King of Spain: Imperial Defense in the Seventeenth Century.* Baltimore: Johns Hopkins University Press, 1986.

Power, Hugh Irvin. *Battleship Texas.* College Station: Texas A&M University Press, 1993.

Pratt, Willis W., ed. *Galveston Island or A Few Months Off the Coast of Texas: The Journal of Francis Sheridan, 1839–1840.* Austin: University of Texas Press, 1954.

Price, Marcus W. "Ships That Tested the Blockade of the Gulf Ports, 1861–1865." *American Neptune* 11(October 1951): pp. 262–290; 12(January–July 1952): pp. 52–59, 154–161, 229–256.

Puryear, Pamela Ashworth, and Nath Winfield Jr. *Sandbars and Sternwheelers: Steam Navigation on the Brazos River.* College Station: Texas A&M University Press, 1976.

Putney, Martha S. *Black Sailors: Afro-American Merchant Seamen and Whalemen Prior to the Civil War.* Contributions in Afro-American and African Studies, no. 103. Westport, Conn.: Greenwood Press, 1987.

Rafferty, Robert. *Texas Coast: Discover Delights Along the Gulf Coast of Texas.* Austin: Texas Monthly Press, 1986.

———. *Texas Coast and the Rio Grande Valley.* Houston: Gulf Publishing Co., ca. 1991.

Reed, S. G. *A History of the Texas Railroads and of Transportation Conditions Under Spain and Mexico and the Republic and the State.* Houston: St. Clair Publishing Co., 1941.

Revello, José Torres. "Merchandise Shipped by the Spaniards to America 1534–1586." *Hispanic-American Historical Review* 23 (1943): pp. 773–781.

Robinson, Samuel Murray. *A Brief History of the Texas Navy.* Houston: Sons of the Republic of Texas, 1961.

Robinson, William Morrison. "The Sea Dogs of Texas." *Military Engineer* 28 (November–December 1936): pp. 446–457.

Rybka, Walter P. "The Restoration." *Sea History,* Winter, 1982–1983, pp. 10–15 (Commemorative Issue, reprinted from Fall, 1979).

———. "Elissa." *Nautical Quarterly*, Spring, 1987, pp. 7–23.

Sadler, Jerry. *Treasure Tempest in Texas*. Austin: Texas General Land Office, 1967.

Salinas, Martín. *Indians of the Rio Grande Delta*. Austin: University of Texas Press, 1990.

Schubert, Paul. *Come On, Texas*. New York: J. Cape & H. Smith, 1930.

Seale, William. *Texas Riverman: The Life and Times of Captain Andrew Smyth*. Austin: University of Texas Press, 1966.

"Searching for History on the Bottom of Matagorda Bay," *The Medallion*, July–August 1995, pp. 1–2.

Sheire, James W. *Padre Island National Seashore Historic Resource Study*. Washington, D.C.: Office of History and Architecture, U.S. Department of the Interior, 1971.

Ships Passenger Lists, Port of Galveston 1846–1871. Easley, S.C.: Southern Historical Press, 1984.

Shuler, Ellis N. "The Influence of the Shoreline, Rivers, and Springs on the Settlements and Early Development of Texas." *Texas Geographic Magazine* 4, no. 1(Autumn 1940): pp. 26–31.

Sibley, Marily McAdams. *The Port of Houston: A History*. Austin: University of Texas Press, 1968.

Simmons, Joe J. III. *Those Vulgar Tubes: External Sanitary Accommodations Aboard European Ships of the Fifteenth Through Seventeenth Centuries*. College Station: Texas A&M University Press, 1996.

Sitton, Thad. *Backwoodsmen: Stockmen and Hunters Along a Big Thicket River Valley*. Norman: University of Oklahoma Press, 1995.

Smith, R. H. *The Naval Institute Guide to Maritime Museums of North America*. Annapolis, Md.: U.S. Naval Institute Press, 1990.

Smith, Roger C. *Vanguard of Empire: Ships of Exploration in the Age of Columbus*. New York: Oxford University Press, 1993.

Smylie, Vernon. *Taming of the Texas Coast*. Corpus Christi: News Syndicate Press, ca. 1963.

Sobel, Dava. *Longitude: The True Story of a Lone Genius Who Solved the Greatest Scientific Problem of His Time*. New York: Walker and Company, 1995.

Spearing, Darwin. *Roadside Geology of Texas*. Missoula, Mont.: Mountain Press Publishing Company, 1991.

Spectre, Peter, and David Larkin. *Wooden Ship: The Art, History, and Revival of Wooden Boatbuilding*. Boston: Houghton Mifflin Company, 1991.

Spell, Timothy Dale. *John Bankhead Magruder, Defender of the Texas Coast, 1863*. M.A. thesis, Lamar University, 1981.

St. John, Bob. *South Padre: The Island and Its People*. Dallas: Taylor Publishing Company, 1991.

Stanford, Peter. "Elissa: The Long Sea Career." *Sea History*. Winter, 1982–1983, pp. 3–5 (Commemorative Issue, reprinted from Fall, 1979).

Stuart, Ben C. "Texas and Its Sea Trade: A Retrospective of: The Beginning and Development of the Commerce of the Gulf Ports with Special Reference to that of Galveston—Together with Some Accounts of the Pioneer Steamships in the New Orleans and New York Trade—The First Steam Foreign Merchantman to Arrive at a Texas Port, Historic Marine Disasters, etc.," unpublished manuscript, Rosenberg Library, Galveston, Texas, 1914.

——. "Texas Steamboat Days: Annals of Steam Transportation on Inland Waters from the Colonial Period to the End of the Era, with a List of Boats and River Men." Unpublished manuscript, Rosenberg Library, Galveston, Texas.

[The] *Stuart Book—A Series of Articles of Historic Interest Relating to Galveston and Texas, Published in the Galveston News During the Years 1906 to 1911.* Rosenberg Library, Galveston, 1913.

Sutherland, William. *The Ship Builder's Assistant, or Marine Architecture.* London: W. and J. Mount, T. Page & Son, 1755.

Taggart, Robert. *Evolution of the Vessels Engaged in the Waterborne Commerce of the United States.* January 1983 Navigation History, NWS-83-3. National Waterways Study—U.S. Army Engineers Water Resources Center—Institute for Water Resources.

Taylor, E. G. R. "Cartography, Survey, and Navigation 1400–1750." *A History of Technology,* vol. 2. Edited by Charles Singer et al. Oxford: Clarendon Press, 1957, pp. 546–625.

Taylor, George Rogers. *The Transportation Revolution: 1815–1860.* Economic History of the United States, vol. 4. New York: Holt, Rinehart and Winston, 1951.

Tilden, Bryant Parrot. *Notes on the Upper Rio Grande: Explored in the months of October and November, 1846, on Board the U.S. Steamer Major Brown, Commanded by Capt. Mark Sterling, of Pittsburgh. By order of Major General Patterson, USA Commanding the Second Division, Army of Occupation, Mexico.* Philadelphia: Lindsay & Blakiston, 1847.

Townsend, Stephen Andrew. *Steamboating on the Lower Rio Grande River.* M.S. thesis, Texas A&I University, 1989.

Townsend, Tom. *Texas Treasure Coast.* Burnet, Tex.: Eakin Press, ca. 1979.

Tredgold, Thomas. *The Steam Engine: Its Invention and Progressive Improvement, an Investigation of Its Principles, and Its Application to Navigation, Manufactures, and Railways.* New ed. London: J. Weale, 1838.

Tryckare, Tre. *The Lore of Ships.* New York: Holt, Rinehart, & Winston, 1963.

Tveten, John L. *Coastal Texas: Water, Land, and Wildlife.* College Station: Texas A&M University Press, 1982.

Villiers, Alan. *Men, Ships and the Sea.* Washington, D.C.: National Geographic Society, 1962.

Warren, Harris Gaylord. "Aury, Louis Michel." In *The New Handbook of Texas,* vol. 1. Austin: Texas State Historical Association, 1996.

Weber, David J. *The Spanish Frontier in North America.* New Haven: Yale University Press, 1992.

Weddle, Robert S. *Wilderness Manhunt: The Spanish Search for La Salle.* Austin: The University of Texas Press, 1973.

———. *Spanish Sea: The Gulf of Mexico in North American Discovery 1500–1685*. College Station: Texas A&M University Press, 1985.

———. *The French Thorn: Rival Explorers in the Spanish Sea, 1682–1762*. College Station: Texas A&M University Press, 1991.

———. "Exploration of the Texas Coast: Alvarez de Pineda to La Salle." *Journal of Gulf History* 8, no. 1(Fall, 1992): pp. 30–41.

———. *Changing Tides: Twilight and Dawn in the Spanish Sea*. College Station: Texas A&M University Press, 1995.

———, ed. *La Salle, the Mississippi, and the Gulf: Three Primary Documents*. College Station: Texas A&M University Press, 1987.

Wells, Tom Henderson. *Commodore Moore and the Texas Navy*. Austin: University of Texas Press, 1960.

White, Edna McDaniel. *East Texas Riverboat Era and Its Decline*. Beaumont: LaBelle Printing & Engraving Co., 1965.

White, John H. Jr. *The American Railroad Freight Car—From the Wood-Car Era to the Coming of Steel*. Baltimore: Johns Hopkins University Press, 1993.

Whittier, Bob. *Paddle Wheel Steamers and Their Giant Engines*. Duxbury, Mass.: Seamaster, Inc., 1987.

Williams, Howard C. *Gateway to Texas: The History of Orange and Orange County*. Orange: Heritage House Museum of Orange, 1986.

Winston, James E. "New Orleans and the Texas Revolution." *Louisiana Historical Quarterly* 10 (July 1927): pp. 317–354.

———. "Notes on Commercial Relations Between New Orleans and Texas Ports, 1838–1839." *Southwestern Historical Quarterly* 34(October 1930): pp. 91–105.

Wise, Stephen R. *Lifeline of the Confederacy: Blockade Running During the Civil War*. Columbia: University of South Carolina Press, 1988, p. 328.

Wood, Virginia Steele. *Live Oaking: Southern Timber for Tall Ships*. Boston: Northeastern University Press, 1981.

Wooster, Ralph A. *Lone Star Blue and Gray: Essays on Texas in the Civil War*. Austin: Texas State Historical Association, 1995.

1836 Semi-Centennial Memoir of the Harlan & Hollingsworth Company. Wilmington, Del.: 1886.

*I*NDEX